Kremlin in Transition

Volume II

ALSO AVAILABLE FROM UNWIN HYMAN

Kremlin in Transition: Volume I
From Brezhnev to Chernenko, 1978 to 1985
by John W. Parker

Kremlin in Transition

Volume II

Gorbachev,
1985 to 1989

John W. Parker

The views expressed in this book are solely those
of the author and do not represent the positions
or policies of any agency or department of the
United States government.

Boston
UNWIN HYMAN
London   Sydney   Wellington

Unwin Hyman, Inc.
955 Massachusetts Avenue, Cambridge, Mass. 02139, USA

Published by the Academic Division of
Unwin Hyman Ltd
15/17 Broadwick Street, London W1V 1FP, UK

Allen & Unwin (Australia) Ltd
8 Napier Street, North Sydney, NSW 2060, Australia

Allen & Unwin (New Zealand) Ltd, in association with the
Port Nicholson Press Ltd
Compusales Building, 75 Ghuznee Street, Wellington 1, New Zealand

First published in 1991

Library of Congress Cataloging in Publication Data

Parker, John W., 1945–
  Kremlin in transition / John W. Parker.
        p.   cm.
  Contents: v. 1. From Brezhnev to Chernenko, 1976–1985 —
v. 2. Gorbachev, 1985 to 1989.
  Includes bibliographical references and index.
  ISBN 0–04–445889–4 (v. 1) : $75.00.
  ISBN 0–04–445890–8 (v. 2)
  1. Soviet Union—Politics and government—1953–1985. 2. Soviet
Union—Politics and government—1985–   . 3. Brezhnev, Leonid
Il'ich, 1906–   . 4. Andropov, UI. V. (UIrii Vladimirovich),
1914–   . 5. Chernenko, K. U. (Konstantin Ustinovich), 1911–
6. Gorbachev, Mikhail Sergeevich, 1931–   . I. Title.
DK274.P32   1990
320.947—dc20   90–12810
                                                              CIP

British Library Cataloguing in Publication Data

Parker, John W.
  Kremlin in transition.
1. Soviet Union. Politics, history
I. Title
320.947

ISBN 0–04–445889–4 v.1
ISBN 0–04–445890–8 v.2

Typeset in 10 on 12 point Palatino
Printed in Great Britain by the University Press, Cambridge

Contents

To Susan, Maggie and Clare:
for their patience
—and their impatience

Preface

*T*his is a history, but it is also a story. It is based on facts, but it is an analytical construct: an effort to fit the pieces together without glaring mismatches but without precluding other analytical solutions. The resulting narrative mosaic is by no means faultless; numerous events are open to alternative interpretations. And as lengthy as it is, the account is also unfinished. Many of the events and trends in this story are still unfolding and at too close range for the study to be exhaustive. With the passage of time, furthermore, new facts will surely come to light which will at least shade if not fundamentally alter my own interpretations of the events covered. New nuances and connections still suggest themselves with every review of the evidence. My own view of Gorbachev evolved considerably over the several years I spent writing these two volumes and continues to evolve.

All that said, however, this is an attempt at a systematic representation and interpretation of a crucial transitional decade in recent Soviet political history: from the death of Fedor Kulakov in July 1978, which reopened the Brezhnev succession struggle and made possible Mikhail Gorbachev's promotion to Moscow, to Gorbachev's seeming mastery of the Kremlin by 1989; from the Soviet-provoked war of nerves against NATO's dual-track intermediate-range nuclear missile (INF) decision beginning in the late 1970s, to the unilateral force and defense budget reductions Gorbachev announced in December 1988 and early 1989; and from a Kremlin of mostly secretive elite politicking to a new order of "democratization" and expanding mass politics.

After years of anticipating Brezhnev's passing and speculating on the consequences, it finally happened. And although the process of change began much later than most would have thought, once it started to unfold it occurred more quickly and far more thoroughly than most would have guessed, and is still continuing. It was a fascinating and remarkably illuminating period in Soviet politics. Brezhnev's loosening grip, the inability of his aging contenders and ailing successors to impose their policy views on their rivals, and then the age of *glasnost* and "socialist pluralism" rung in by Gorbachev gave outsiders fairly clearly stated alternative views on what Soviet priorities and policies should be.

The present narrative stops with the convening of the new Congress of Peoples Deputies on May 25, 1989. The explosion of electrifying political discourse that followed marked the beginning of a new era in Soviet politics—and the beginning of someone else's book. Moreover, the rush of events since that time makes it impossible to call the present work a contemporary history: the bloody repression of the student prodemocracy movement in Beijing's Tiananmen Square; the first sessions in Moscow of the Congress of Peoples Deputies and of the reformed Supreme Soviet; the Kuzbas and Donbas coal mine strikes; the push for independence in the Baltics; the rise of a Solidarity government in Poland; communal and antiregime violence in a number of Soviet republics and pressure for a new Treaty of the Union; the crumbling of communist regimes throughout Eastern Europe; the Soviet apology for the 1968 invasion of Czechoslovakia; the incarceration of Erich Honecker and Todor Zhivkov and the Christmas Day execution of Nicolae Ceausescu; the dismantling of the Berlin Wall and quick steps toward German reunification; the series of widely publicized revolts against local party bosses in the Soviet provinces, most notably in Volgograd; the massive demonstrations of proreform forces in downtown Moscow; the opening of the door to a multiparty system in the USSR at the February 1990 plenum of the Communist Party of the Soviet Union (CPSU) Central Committee; Gorbachev's creation of a new Soviet presidency; the raucous May Day demonstration on Red Square at which calls for Gorbachev and the Politburo to resign revealed to television viewers abroad the depth of the disenchantment with Gorbachev at home, now spreading and deepening among the liberal intelligentsia; the radical Boris Yeltsin's election as chairman of the Supreme Soviet of the Russian Republic (RSFSR) in May 1990; the explosion of republic "sovereighty" declarations led by that of the RSFSR; conservative Ivan Polozkov's victory as leader of the new RSFSR communist party in June 1990; Yegor Ligachev's dramatic defeat and retirement from the leadership by secret ballot at the 28th CPSU Congress in July; and, subsequently, the uneasy Gorbachev-Yeltsin center-left alliance and push toward a market-oriented economy, and the Supreme Soviet's granting of additional powers to Gorbachev to implement economic reform.

In effect, Gorbachev's pleas since July 1986 for the party rank and file and the Soviet public to pressure local bosses finally caught fire, spread almost uncontrollably and even more spectacularly to Eastern Europe, and then blazed back into the Soviet Union.

Ironically, however, after what the Soviet public perceived to be four years of unproductive political talk while the economy worsened, in late summer 1989 Gorbachev's popularity began to plummet at home even as it soared to new heights abroad. As a strategist, Gorbachev continued to embrace ever more radical goals; as a tactician, however, he remained a convinced centrist—even as the center lost ground to both extremes and in fact shifted to the left. A common thread seemed to connect Gorbachev's willingness to work within the confines of the Chernenko interregnum, patience in tolerating an increasingly outspoken and contradictory Ligachev, and opposition to those calling for Ryzhkov's summary dismissal. Gorbachev insisted on a bloodless revolution and resisted the urge to search out and destroy all opponents or doubters. If at all possible, he sought to convince them and bring them along. What struck many as Gorbachev's constant hesitation and lagging behind the radicalization of public opinion increasingly made him in 1989–90 the target of the very same public scorn for entrenched *apparatchiks* which he himself had done so much to unleash. Yet despite displays of impatience and closed-mindedness toward his critics, his optimism and capacity for change never seemed to leave him.

This book includes some factual revelations about events before mid-1989 which came to light after that time. Rather than try to update descriptions of the mood and the judgments I held as I finished the basic manuscript, I have left them intact if only as analytical benchmarks by which to measure the momentousness and unexpectedness of what happened so soon afterward. At the same time, what now reads in some respects as ancient history serves to underscore how far back and how deep are the roots of much of what we have seen develop under Gorbachev since the book's narrative leaves off. Certainly the revolutionary events of 1989–90 have in turn revolutionized our own understanding of the significance—whether fully intended or not—of the changes introduced by Gorbachev and his allies since the mid-1980s as they struggled to set the flywheel of change in motion in the USSR and the world. In this respect recent events give even greater import to the innovations in Soviet political discourse to which this book pays so much (but in retrospect probably not nearly enough) attention: democratization, pluralism, freedom of choice, common European home, and so on.

Nevertheless, while future Kremlin succesions will not be the same as the recent ones—in fact, qualitatively different if democratization continues rather than fails—it is important to look back and assess what happened in the serial transitions from Brezhnev to Gorbachev, and why. Knowing how things turned out helps, of course, but can impart a false and misleading sense of retrospective certitude. As events originally unfolded, analytical assurance was often either nowhere to be found or wrong. What follows is only one way of telling this story. Kremlinology—don't throw it away yet!—can never be straightforward documentary. In examining this period different analysts can look at the same set of facts and end up spinning vastly different and at times conflicting interpretations of them. They can disagree among themselves even on individual facts and on what set of facts the interpretation of a given event should be based.

The often flimsy nature of the evidence during the years treated in this book can drive still practicing Kremlinologists batty: if they're lucky, only rendering them indecisively sensitive to their colleagues' alternative explanations; more sadly, sometimes driving them out on one or another ridiculous limb in defense of their own reading of the facts. Whatever the psychiatric descriptions of these afflictions, they are an occupational hazard. But in the end they will surely lead to an intellectual treat for aficionados of Soviet politics: numerous plausible and often implausible reconstructions of what will go down in Soviet history as one of its most fascinating periods.

The reader can make up his or her mind on the extent to which the present author has fallen victim to such follies. To the extent possible, however, I have tried to avoid "on one hand, but on the other hand" explanations of events and have attempted to present definite interpretations of what happened. Although many puzzles still remain—which are underscored as the narrative proceeds—it is now increasingly possible to make sense of the personalities, issues, and trends at play during the decade covered in these two volumes, and to embed them firmly in the previous years of the Brezhnev era which set the stage.

In both senses, as history and story, this study took on an unintended and wholly unexpected shape in the telling—to say nothing of its unplanned length. Actors and events increasingly imposed a surprising and almost novelistic coming-full-circle story structure to many of the study's lines of analysis—a process that still has not ended. At home, for example, the Brezhnev clan rose and fell while associates of Kosygin and Kirilenko fell only to rise again as interest revived in economic reform. Abroad, the negotiations over INF evolved from talks apparently totally devoid of political solution to a precedent-shattering U.S.-Soviet treaty. It was the first major result of Gorbachev's stress on "civilized relations" and of former President Reagan's vision—at first taken lightly, later controversial—of a nuclear-free world.

At the beginning my intention was to do a case study of Moscow's response to the Western reaction to the Soviet SS-20 deployment decision. When I finished the book had become a much wider recounting of the Soviet leadership's coming to grips with the sustained rise of the "conservative wave" in the West and the "precrisis" symptoms at home: economic stagnation, demographic decline, and growing social despair. The elections and reelections of Margaret Thatcher, Ronald

Reagan, Helmut Kohl, François Mitterrand, and others beginning in 1979 accelerated the Kremlin's coming to grips with its own domestic failings and its widening technological lag behind the advanced industrial nations of the world. But this was probably inevitable. The very seriousness of the reforms under Gorbachev, their antecedents—however timid—in earlier decades of Soviet power and Gorbachev's own reported long-standing reformist inclinations increasingly confirm that the changes he instituted have been fundamentally a reaction to Soviet congenital "contradictions"—even though Reagan and his counterparts helped to precipitate the process in its last stages.

The study thus covers not only the foreign political and security scene but the domestic context as well. Overlying these two facets are the intricacies of the political transition from Brezhnev to Gorbachev and then the new leadership's unveiling of its programs and their increasing radicalization. Chronologically this is a straightforward recounting of the politics of the multiple successions in Moscow. Thematically the story focuses on those national security issues, both domestic and foreign, which seemed to be the subject of greatest dispute: the economy, in particular the debates over resource allocations and management reform; civil-military relations, especially the contretemps provoked by chief of the General Staff Nikolay Ogarkov, and then the "new stage" in Soviet national security affairs ushered in under Gorbachev and Ogarkov's successor, Sergey Akhromeyev; arms control, primarily how the Soviet leadership played the INF negotiations in Geneva and then worked its way toward major unilateral reductions; and relations with the United States, Europe, and China and their synergistic impact on Soviet politics at home.

The physical as well as political fragility of the leadership during the years prior to Gorbachev cannot be underestimated. The Politburo was narrowly and chronically divided, best exemplified by the infrequency of removals from the Politburo. No member was ousted between November 1982, when Kirilenko was forced out but did not disappear, to mid-1985, when Romanov was retired. Except for Ustinov's death in December 1984, no one entered or left the Politburo or Secretariat during the entire Chernenko period.

The role of the military during these serial successions was paradoxical. The assertive Ogarkov was able to take advantage of the narrowly divided civilian leadership to press his views vigorously on national security issues. More widely, institutional concerns expressed by military spokesmen—over economic stagnation, societal malaise, and the international environment—to an important extent helped shape the agenda of the succession period. Yet after Chernenko's death and the accession of Gorbachev, no other institution suffered such a drastic decline in external indicators of political status.

The study thus describes the political crucible that formed Gorbachev and which he then set out to change. A fairly sharp course correction took place in Soviet politics both at home and abroad already in August-September 1984. Although it was not clear at the time, this was the real beginning of the Gorbachev era, even though Konstantin Chernenko was still alive and general secretary: Ogarkov was removed from the General Staff, and the military's demands for scarce resources began to be dampened; Gromyko was made to accept an invitation to visit President Reagan at the White House, a prelude to Moscow's return to the Geneva negotiations; and Mongolian leader Tsedenbal was ousted in Ulan Bator, an indirect token of the seriousness of Moscow's intentions to repair relations with Beijing. Much of Soviet politics and policies before and after can be appreciated and understood only by examining this period, which marked the real threshold of the new Gorbachev era.

In charting disputes and currents of opinion and in pinpointing the issues at stake, my basic tool was the old-fashioned chronology. I had thought that I had already been over the ground covered in this book minutely as it happened. But taking the time to put together a retrospective chronology revealed numerous coincidences that had previously escaped me or had simply been impossible to detect because key events had been kept secret, and not just by the Soviet side. A good example was USA Institute Director Georgiy Arbatov's analysis of the stresses and strains within NATO which appeared in *Pravda* on July 16, 1982. Only six months later did the outside world find out that INF negotiators Paul Nitze and Yuliy Kvitsinskiy had engaged that very day in the famous "walk in the woods" outside Geneva. The Arbatov piece was thus invaluable in providing one highly placed assessment of the vulnerabilities within NATO from which Moscow could be expected to try to benefit. It helped to explain Moscow's quick rejection of the exploratory package put together by Nitze and Kvitsinskiy.

The problem, of course, is that analysts never have in hand—or are even aware of—all of the evidence pertaining to a given incident at the time it happens. Relevant bits of information and insight reach them with varying time lags. Only by going back and putting all the bits together in the proper time frame can analysts begin more faithfully to reconstruct a picture of what was important to what happened when it happened. The mere passage of time, in addition, makes students of politics more sensitive to themes and developments at first thought to be of little significance. On some key points Soviet spokesmen have in retrospect openly confirmed what had previously been only rumored, suspected, or less than authoritatively asserted. In nominating Gorbachev for general secretary, for example, Gromyko confirmed that Gorbachev had been chairing the Secretariat while Chernenko was alive, something widely presumed but not established until Gromyko's statement.

Despite all that was going on in Moscow from 1985 to 1989, I was at times completely absorbed in sorting out events that had taken place a decade or more before. Only when I stumbled on why Fedor Kulakov most likely committed suicide in 1978 and thus opened the way for Mikhail Gorbachev's move to Moscow did I know how this story should begin. Deductions and discoveries such as these made the researching of this book exhilarating; evidentiary flares suddenly exploded and illuminated dark landscapes from the past. But these flares were also excruciating, wrenching my attention from the dynamism of the present to the fascination of the still not well enough understood past.

My main sources for this chronology were the Soviet media. A careful reading of leadership speeches, party and government statements, newspaper editorials, television commentaries and similar materials was essential for analysis of power and policy in Soviet politics until well into the Gorbachev era. This approach was based on the premise that the distortions or nuances imposed on statements were not random but formed patterns according to their source, the intended audience, the source's control of the media, and other such key variables. All this was supplemented by investigation of career patterns and patronage links, attention to public appearances, and discriminating use of rumors, sometimes for their factual content but always in order to attempt to divine their inspiration and intent.

Soviet political discourse has been enriched and radically changed under Gorbachev, but this approach still constitutes the core and necessary beginning of any analysis of the period covered by this book. High-level politics within the Soviet communist party (CPSU) remained a closely guarded secret, not yet responsive to the demands for increased openess posed by democratization and its new or reformed institutions. Paradoxically, the growing cacophony of *glasnost* made textual analysis and the traditional approaches to understanding Soviet politics more important than ever. Amid the rumors flying around in 1987 concerning differences between Gorbachev and Ligachev, for example, only close attention to crucial differences on a key formula—what guarantees *perestroika*? democratization, or the leading role of the party?—could provide an understanding of the fundamental issue at stake.

In trying to anchor the bulk of the narrative on textual analysis, I have tried to find the first meaningful use of policy-relevant formulations, such as "democratization." Here the context and subsequent track record were crucial. Who ever paid attention to the 1977 "Brezhnev" constitution's assertions that "the principal direction in the development of the political system of Soviet society is the extension of socialist democracy, . . . greater *glasnost*, and constant responsiveness to public opinion" (Chap. 1, Art. 9)? But Gorbachev's remarks in December 1984 concerning democratization *were* of significance, though easy to dismiss. It would take years for outsiders to appreciate them.

As for conflict, my assumptions in this study are those of the middle-of-the-road school of Kremlinology, confirmed rather than rejected by the onset of "pluralism." There *is* conflict in the CPSU leadership, but it ebbs and wanes. The Politburo and Secretariat are not one big happy family, but neither are they continually rent by white-hot disputes. Members of the leadership both react to circumstances and seek to shape the environment they face to maximum political advantage—something increasingly important as democratization breaks down both their insularity and their singularity. Nevertheless a great deal of CPSU politics still takes place within a narrow oligarchy, though even before democratization members of the leadership sought to manipulate and engage wider circles of opinion in an effort to pressure one another and gain advantage.

Personality, group dynamics, and the accidental and unforeseen play as significant a role in Soviet politics as in the politics of any other country. Political decisions are not simply the mechanistic outcomes of bureaucratic pressures, and increasingly—given the advent of democratization—must pay heed to public opinion. In toting up the casualties, even I was surprised at the extent to which the politics of the transition from Brezhnev to Gorbachev turned out to be a matter of life and death—either unnatural or untimely—for a number of central figures through suicide, execution, or heart attack. There were plenty of arrests, ousters, and disgraces, as well as posthumous dishonorings. *Perestroika* was never a propaganda ploy designed to fool the West. From the beginning, its domestic antagonists took it seriously—and had serious reasons for doing so.

Moscow, July 1990

Acknowledgments

I wish to thank in particular those individuals not singled out for special appreciation in one or another note, yet who either got me started on this study, encouraged me to go on, and/or eventually read and constructively reviewed the resulting manuscript: Isabel Kulski, Martha Mautner, Wayne Limberg, Bob Baraz, Mort Abramowitz, Dale Herspring, Gerhard Wettig, Werner Hahn, Steve Hurst, Jeremy Azrael, Abe Becker, Paul Goble, Raymond Garthoff, Jack Matlock, Bill Courtney, Don Oberdorfer, Judy Deane, Don Kelley, Leona Schecter, Lisa Freeman, Lois Smith, and my parents, Darrell and Ellen Parker, and my wife's parents, Merritt and Mary Ludwig.

In addition, I wish to remember those sources, not all of them Soviet, who best remain anonymous but not at all forgotten.

Part I

Gorbachev: The First Year

Overview

In April 1985, the exiled liberal Czech politician Zdenek Mlynar suggested that Mikhail S. Gorbachev as general secretary would work against rule by bureaucratic-administrative orders from the center and toward a devolution of responsibility to lower-level leaders outside party and ministerial headquarters in Moscow. Mlynar had been a leading member of Alexander Dubcek's reformist "socialism with a human face" regime in Czechoslovakia in 1968, and based his assessment of Gorbachev on a friendship dating from days together at Moscow University in the early 1950s under Stalin. Mlynar had last visited Gorbachev in 1967 in Stavropol.[1]

Mlynar eventually was to prove remarkably accurate. In May 1985, however, when asked by Italian Premier Bettino Craxi about Mlynar's portrayal of him, Gorbachev reportedly answered with some amusement, "A 'Prague Spring' intellectual issuing a very positive verdict on me could cause some tongues to wag."[2] Nearly a year after replacing Chernenko, when asked by *L'Humanité* in early February 1986 whether his leadership was embarking on a "new revolution," Gorbachev answered categorically, "Of course not."[3]

Nevertheless, in March 1985 the Central Committee must have been well aware that it was getting a very different kind of leader in Gorbachev. The basic dividing lines on policy, after all, had been sharply drawn under Andropov, and during the Chernenko interregnum Gorbachev had done little to blur them. In December 1984, as we have seen, Gorbachev had used his speech on ideology to revive Andropov's "force of example" arguments and even to broach the need for democratization and glasnost. Not long after, he used his speech to the British parliament to pick up on foreign policy "new thinking" where Andropov had left off at the June 1983 plenum. After Chernenko, many must have longed for someone at least a little different. But even most of Gorbachev's supporters then could not have known the radical turn that the Gorbachev leadership would take in summer 1986—and perhaps neither did Gorbachev. But that was at least a year down the road.

For now, during his first year in power a great deal of Gorbachev's success in consolidating his power hinged on his tactical flexibility

3

and ability to compromise. Gorbachev's speech at Chernenko's funeral on March 13 sought unmistakably to evoke Andropov's aura of a law-and-order reformer intent on cleaning up the home front. Socialism would prove its advantages, said the new leader, "not by force of arms but by force of example in all fields of society's life—economic, political and moral."[4] But Gorbachev willingly moderated his policy preferences in the short term in order to expand his base of support for future, less orthodox initiatives.

Gorbachev masterfully posed as an imaginative and dynamic—but far from radical—politician. The slogan of the day was still only "acceleration," and the new general secretary's initial domestic program went no further than to combine Kirilenko's proinvestment platform, Kosygin's modest management reforms, and a vigorous cleaning out of corrupt or superannuated cadres. On Victory Day in May he openly played to conservative audiences with praise of Stalin. It would be at least another year before the "radical" Gorbachev would call for wide-ranging "restructuring" and "democratization."

Gorbachev bided his time, evidently reluctant to push further or faster than his political support would allow him. To this end, he forced some long-overdue, major personnel changes at the very top. Since October-November 1982, when Andrey Kirilenko had been forced out, attrition from the Politburo had come only as the result of death from natural causes, with no living members being expelled on political grounds. The Andropov-Gorbachev and Brezhnev-Chernenko factions had each been able on occasion to add supporters, but they had had to continue to live with long-time opponents in their midst. The deadlock became even more pronounced under Chernenko. During his tenure there had been absolutely no movement into or out of the Politburo or Secretariat, except for Ustinov. Under Gorbachev this quickly began to change. In April he moved spectacularly to obtain a working majority against what was left of the Chernenko faction. By July his group was strong enough not only to bring supporters into the party's highest echelons but to oust key opponents, beginning with Romanov.

In foreign policy, the first few months under the new Gorbachev leadership were an uneasy balance favoring Gromyko orthodoxy. This began to shift, however, following the April 1985 plenum and the first sight of flexibility. Then new flickers of experimentation became visible almost immediately after Gromyko's departure from the Foreign Ministry in July 1985, as Gorbachev all but rushed off to Paris and then to Geneva, where he met with Reagan for the first time. Compared with the fairly open battles over economic policy, the seeds of what would evolve into Gorbachev's new foreign policy line had been all but invisible in the highly charged international atmospherics of the first half of the 1980s. But after the 27th Party Congress in February-March 1986 it was in diplomacy and security affairs, rather than domestic policy, that Gorbachev would enjoy the greatest flexibility not only to call for but actually to institute dramatic departures from the past.

The more civil atmospherics and the initial attempts to make the INF negotiations more interesting were minor revolutions in and of themselves. At an even more fundamental level, however, in Paris and in the draft new Party Program released soon afterward in Moscow Gorbachev began to lay out and develop in public the new ideological orientations that would justify the spectacular policy reversals and adjustments of the next several years: reasonable sufficiency; deemphasis of class struggle; and a new appreciation for the United Nations. The new trends in Soviet foreign policy, however, remained for the most part confined to ideological formulations and rhetorical buzzwords until after the party congress, and so were still easy to dismiss as no more than "charm diplomacy": cosmetic and superficial, designed to infuse old lines of action with new energy and to make target audiences more receptive to the traditional goals of Soviet diplomacy.

As for the military, constraints were in store from the beginning. The assertive Ogarkov had been distanced from the center of power in September 1984, and the military had its political status symbols further reduced in dramatically demonstrative fashion immediately after Chernenko's death. With the help of Sergey Akhromeyev, who was already advancing war prevention to priority status in Soviet military doctrine, Gorbachev began to dampen international tensions and undermine the arguments of those urging a speed-up in military spending. Gorbachev would apparently spell out the new line, stressing priority attention to civilian industrial modernization and technological revitalization at a gathering of the high command in Minsk in July 1985, just after the ouster of defense sector booster and Gorbachev rival Grigoriy Romanov from the leadership. However, not a weaker but a stronger army was presented as the ultimate goal, and *perestroika* would not really hit the defense establishment and military thought hard for nearly two more years.

NOTES

1. Zdenek Mlynar, "My School Companion Mikhail Gorbachev," *L'Unita*, April 9, 1985.

2. *La Repubblica*, June 26, 1985 (Foreign Broadcast Information Service, *Daily Report, Soviet Union* [FBIS-SOV], July 2, 1985, R 7).

3. *Pravda*, February 8, 1986 (FBIS-SOV, February 10, 1986, CC 1).

4. TASS, March 13, 1985 (FBIS-SOV, March 13, 1985, R 3). Except for Gorbachev's speech on December 10, 1984, the "force of example" rhetoric had not been heard during Chernenko's 13 months in office.

C hernenko was reported to have died March 10, 1985, at 7:20 p.m. Moscow time. His physical remains and political legacy were disposed of with record speed. Less than 23 hours after his death at age 73, and only five hours after its official announcement, TASS reported at 6:18 p.m. on March 11 that the Central Committee had elected Mikhail Sergeyevich Gorbachev, age 54, the new general secretary.[1] By early afternoon on March 13 Chernenko was buried.[2]

The outward efficiency of the transition left the impression of solid support for Gorbachev. The accelerated takeover, however, may have reflected tactical wariness rather than confidence; the Gorbachev group seemed intent on denying the opposition any time to organize. Whatever deal Gorbachev and his backers had struck with the Chernenko group after Andropov's death could easily become unstruck, as Chernenko's efforts to bolster Romanov's stock the previous fall had demonstrated.

According to one account, when the Politburo first met three hours after Chernenko's death, three full members were not present: Ukrainian party leader Vladimir Shcherbitskiy, traveling in the United States; Russian Republic Premier Vitaliy Vorotnikov, on a trip to Yugoslavia; and Kazakhstan party boss Dinmukhamed Kunayev, too far away in Alma Ata to make it back to Moscow on such short notice. When the Central Committee met the next day, only two-thirds of its 300-odd members were on hand.[3] Gorbachev's supporters were apparently able to present the Central Committee with a fait accompli in the Politburo itself—although, as we shall see, it had been a close vote. Perhaps because of the substantial number of absences at the Central Committee session, the official report on the meeting said that Gorbachev had been elected *edinodushno*, by acclamation or in the spirit of unanimity, rather than *edinoglasno*, by unanimous vote.[4] Shcherbitskiy for one was not able to return to Moscow from the United States until the day after the Central Committee plenum.

ROMANOV'S GAMBIT

Half a year later, several months after Romanov's "retirement" in July 1985, rumors surfaced that in March 1985 Romanov had nominated

7

Viktor Grishin as an alternative to Gorbachev but had been blocked by opposition from Viktor Chebrikov and Ligachev—the first at that time only a candidate member of the Politburo and the second, only a Central Committee secretary. Grishin, it was said, then nominated Gromyko for the job, but the foreign minister turned it down.[5]

According to the scuttlebutt, KGB Chief Chebrikov had played the "Beria card" in undermining support for Grishin. The infamous Lavrentiy Beria had been Stalin's last and longest lasting police chief. After Stalin's death in 1953, Beria had been one of the leading contenders for power, only to be tried and executed by his mistrustful and nervous rivals. Beria had had a widely known, criminally roving eye, and even the judicial charges against him reportedly included rape.[6] Three decades later none other than Grishin's son reportedly was married to the daughter of one of Beria's best-known mistresses, whose spicy resumé would later include involvement with a big-time currency speculator executed in 1962 under Khrushchev. The younger Grishin couple had two children. This made the senior Grishin co-grandfather of at least a pair of what must have been a multitude of Beria's posthumous grandchildren. The younger Grishin couple's life-style apparently resembled that of the Galina Brezhneva-Churbanova set.[7]

The rumored last-ditch nomination of Gromyko was both intriguing and plausible. Gromyko's position was probably ambiguous, and his personal feelings toward Gorbachev likely ambivalent. Given the redirection by Gorbachev and Ustinov of Gromyko's handling of U.S. policy in August 1984, Grishin and Romanov may have hoped that Gromyko's vanity and pride had been sufficiently ruffled to predispose him to turn against Gorbachev. That Chernenko, while still alive, had courted Gromyko was suggested by the treatment accorded the foreign minister in October 1984: on his seventy-fifth birthday and then during the visit of Mongolia's Zhambyn Batmonh. Despite their differences, Chernenko may nevertheless still have viewed Gromyko as an honest broker and even confidant. Only three days before Chernenko died, according to Gromyko's memoirs, Cherneko telephoned him for advice. "Andrey Andreyevich, I'm not feeling well. I've been thinking that maybe I should resign." "There's no need to hurry," Gromyko claimed he counseled the ailing general secretary. "That would be unjustified."[8] Nevertheless, Gromyko's head had not been turned in October 1984, and in March 1985 he cast his vote for Gorbachev once Chernenko had passed from the scene. But in the future, after being turned out from the Foreign Ministry, Gromyko as president would raise eyebrows by sheltering both Grishin and Nikolay Tikhonov, giving them sinecures and the perquisites of "state counselors" in the apparatus of the Presidium of the Supreme Soviet.

Two years after Chernenko's death, playwright Mikhail Shatrov would go public with yet another angle on the critical role played by Gromyko in the debate over Gorbachev's ascension. The voting between Grishin and Gorbachev had been deadlocked four to four. Gromyko, who presided over the deliberations, according to Shatrov, had to break the tie.[9]

Shatrov's arithmetic is plausible. His assertion that nine of the ten full members of the Politburo were involved in Gorbachev's selection implies, however, that Kunayev and Vorotnikov were either present in Moscow for the decisive meeting of the Politburo or were able to cast their votes via secure communications: Kunayev from Alma Ata; and Vorotnikov from Titograd, capital of the republic of Montenegro in Yugoslavia. Shcherbitskiy may not have been able to do likewise, receiving word of Chernenko's death only after landing in San Francisco from Austin, Texas, by which time the Politburo deliberations may even have been over.

In any event, in Shatrov's nine-players scenario it can safely be assumed that Grishin was joined by Romanov and Tikhonov, whereas Vorotnikov and Solomentsev were solid supporters of Gorbachev. Three years later, in fact, Ligachev would confirm that Solomentsev, as well as he himself (though still only a Central Committee secretary), Gromyko, and Chebrikov (not yet a voting member of the Politburo) had been in Gorbachev's camp.[10] This leaves only two others—Aliyev and Kunayev—who, if there was indeed a four-four tie, must have cast their votes in opposite directions. The Gorbachev faction's subsequent hounding and ouster of Kunayev strongly suggests that Kunayev opposed Gorbachev in March 1985. As for Aliyev, he did not prosper under Gorbachev, but at least he was not publicly disgraced when he retired from the Politburo in October 1987. He therefore may well have supported Gorbachev in March 1985. In 1988 Aliyev would be referred to as a "recently appointed . . . State Advisor" when he was mentioned as attending a session of the Council of Ministers.[11]

Yet another alleged twist on the events of March 1985 is so implausible that it can be dismissed. According to *Washington Post* reporter Bob Woodward, the CIA received a report several days before March 10 that Chernenko was already dead but that the leadership was so embroiled in debate on a successor that it was withholding an announcement until the election of a new general secretary.[12] Leadership travel in early March 1985, however, makes this account wholly suspect. All seemed in order, with no expectation that Chernenko would die momentarily, well into the day on March 10. Moreover, Gromyko, as already mentioned, has written that he spoke by telephone with Chernenko three days before the latter's death—in other words, on or about March 7.

In any event, the public record shows that Shcherbitskiy left Moscow for the United States on March 3. Vorotnikov, also a full member of the Politburo, departed for Yugoslavia the following day. This impression of normalcy continued through most of March 10, when Central Committee Secretary Mikhail Zimyanin left Moscow for West Germany. Only later on March 10 did the situation change. Shcherbitskiy abruptly announced that he would be returning the next morning to Moscow via New York from San Francisco, where he had just landed on his tour of the US; he would not arrive in the Soviet capital until March 12. Similarly, Vorotnikov did not leave Yugoslavia until March 10, when he unexpectedly ended his official visit in Titograd without returning to Belgrade for a scheduled meeting with the Yugoslav president.[13] Zimyanin, not a member of the Politburo, even spent the night of March 10 in West Germany but returned to Moscow the next day in time to attend the lying-in-state for Chernenko.

GROMYKO'S SUPPORT

Three years later, at the 19th Party Conference, Yegor Ligachev would describe the events surrounding Gorbachev's selection as Chernenko's successor as "very anxious" and claim that the results could have been "absolutely different." Whatever happened on March 10–11, however, the effort to block Gorbachev in the Politburo was obviously short-lived. In turn, opposition to Gorbachev in the Central Committee—where many of the remaining Brezhnevites must have feared for their futures under a new regime—was deprived of leadership. Moreover, according to Ligachev's account, "a large group of obkom first secretaries" supported Gorbachev.[14] As a consequence, the Central Committee dutifully, if with what must have been extreme unease for some, went along with the decision of the Politburo.

It was under these circumstances that Gromyko delivered his apparently unscripted speech in support of Gorbachev at the Central Committee plenum on March 11. The previous fall, as Ustinov faded from the scene, Gromyko had apparently replaced him as the senior Politburo elder courted by all factions. Chernenko's early March 1985 phone call to Gromyko reinforced this impression, as did Gromyko's chairing of the Politburo session only a few days later, according to Shatrov, which settled on Gorbachev as Chernenko's successor. It was thus as something of an interregnum party chairman that Gromyko addressed this crucial audience.

The foreign minister's speech was not immediately published. When it finally appeared in pamphlet form, it differed markedly in style and content from the nomination speeches of earlier successions. It was highly emotional, as if meant to convince a substantial core of skeptics in the Central Committee of Gorbachev's qualifications to be the new party leader. It also completely avoided praising Chernenko, which was most unusual. In November 1982 Chernenko had lauded the Brezhnev legacy in nominating Andropov as the new general secretary; Tikhonov had similarly praised both Andropov and Brezhnev when nominating Chernenko to the top post in February 1984.[15] But now Chernenko would not even be buried shoulder to shoulder among his predecessors as general secretaries but, rather, off to one side.[16]

In contrast, the foreign minister praised Gorbachev for his uncommon "gift" of a "great ability to organize people and find a common language with them." He had "led" the Secretariat and, in Chernenko's absence, "brilliantly, without exaggeration," chaired the Politburo. Gromyko also reportedly said, though it did not appear in the official text, that Gorbachev had "a nice smile, but he has iron teeth."[17]

The top leadership obviously greatly desired to appear united before all and sundry outsiders. Gromyko spoke of "various telescopes" trained on the Soviet Union by people looking for "cracks of some kind in the Soviet leadership." The Politburo, he said, had been "unanimous" in its opinion that "we . . . will not allow our political opponents any satisfaction on this score."[18] But it was Gromyko himself who provided substantial new grist for the mill of telescopic speculation. His own hypersensitive warnings against betraying any disunity in themselves suggested something less than wholehearted unanimity.

NEW MAJORITY

The new party leader's support in the top echelons of the party was thus less than overwhelming. Although diminished, Tikhonov, Grishin, and Romanov still seemed entrenched and capable of mounting at least some rear-guard resistance to the Gorbachev faction and its program. Among full members of the Politburo residing in Moscow, however, Gorbachev could probably initially rely on the backing of Gromyko, Vorotnikov, Solomentsev, and apparently also Aliyev. Moreover, with Chernenko gone, Kazakhstan party boss Kunayev and Ukrainian leader Shcherbitskiy may have been more cautious about casting their lot consistently against Gorbachev.

Whatever the dynamics of power and policy within the Politburo, Secretariat, and Central Committee, Gorbachev was able to move quickly and spectacularly to obtain a working majority against what was left of the Chernenko faction. On April 23, at the first regular party plenum since Chernenko's death, KGB Chairman Chebrikov was promoted from candidate to full member of the Politburo, and Central Committee secretaries Ligachev and Nikolay Ryzhkov were simultaneously elevated to full membership in the Politburo without having first to serve as candidates.

In addition, Viktor Nikonov entered the Secretariat and took over the agriculture portfolio;[19] he presumably had impressed Gorbachev since being promoted to Moscow in 1979 to become a deputy agriculture minister and then, since 1983, agriculture minister for the Russian Republic.

Ligachev, Ryzhkov, Chebrikov, and Nikonov could all be considered close to Gorbachev. Of the now thirteen full members of the Politburo, therefore, Gorbachev's hard core of supporters numbered at least seven, including Gorbachev, and others—such as Aliyev—apparently were not inclined to cross him. In his speech to the plenum Gorbachev endorsed the policy of "stability" in cadres and of the "correct combination of experienced and young workers." But he warned against "stagnation" in promoting cadres and called for advancing women and young workers "with greater boldness."[20] A month later in Leningrad, the new party leader was even blunter about his intentions. "Those who do not intend to adjust and who are an obstacle to solving these new tasks must simply get out of the way—get out of the way, not be a hindrance."[21]

SOKOLOV SNUBBED

At the April plenum Defense Minister Sokolov was elected only a candidate member of the Politburo. On one level it was probably a factional slight, as Sokolov appeared to be close to Romanov and not a favorite of Gorbachev. Sokolov would return the affront by not referring in public to Gorbachev for almost six months after Chernenko's death.[22] But it went much further than this and was part of the evolving trend under Gorbachev of downgrading the military politically as an institution.

A year earlier, on May 28, 1984, Chernenko had stressed the "irreplaceable role" of Soviet armed might in guaranteeing peace. Now Gorbachev, in his speech at the landmark plenum on April 23, struck a different note, emphasizing that "vexing problems and conflict situations should be solved by political means—such is our firm conviction."[23] Gorbachev's change in emphasis set the stage for downgrading the military's representation in the Politburo. Though Sokolov's cooptation as a candidate member did have its face-saving aspects, his less than full status was on balance more a slap in the face after a dozen years during which the defense minister had been a voting member. The contrast between the full member status of the KGB's Chebrikov and Defense Minister Sokolov's candidate rank was striking.

Both Gorbachev and Gromyko, nonetheless, had played to the military galleries at the Central Committee plenum on March 11. In his nominating speech Gromyko underscored that "on very many occasions Mikhail Sergeyevich has expressed the opinion—and he has done so in the Politburo—that we must, so to speak, keep our powder dry. . . . He always upholds the view that the holy of holies for all of us is to struggle for the cause of peace and maintain our defense at the necessary level."[24] "In a complicated international situation," the new general secretary said in accepting the post, "it is important now as never before to maintain the defense potential of our socialist homeland at such a level that potential aggressors will know well that any encroachment on the security of the Land of the Soviets and its allies, on the peaceful life of the Soviet people, will be met with a shattering retaliatory blow."[25]

Despite the fine oratory at the plenum, recent tradition in civil-military relations was shattered two days later at Chernenko's burial. He was, to be sure, given a military funeral on March 13, his coffin placed on a gun carriage towed by a military combat vehicle. But the leadership reviewing stand on top of the Lenin Mausoleum was totally bereft of the presence of any military personalities, and their absence was widely noted.[26] Coming as it did only six months after Ogarkov's abrupt dismissal, it did not seem to have been an unintended or accidental signal, and the subsequent history of the Gorbachev era would reinforce this view.

Below Sokolov, the beginning of an attention-grabbing shuffle and moderate rejuvenation of the high command coincided with an important trip by Gorbachev to Minsk. There the new general secretary delivered a speech to a "training assembly of high-ranking commanding officers" on July 10, which will be dealt with more extensively in the next chapter.[27] The personnel changes that soon came to light included the naming of a new editor for Red Star;[28] the replacement of long-time head of the Main Political Administration A. A. Yepishev by A. D. Lizichev;[29] and the appointment of Y. P. Maksimov to succeed V. F. Tolubko as head of the Strategic Rocket Forces—all in July.[30] In December, furthermore, V. N. Chernavin would replace Admiral Sergey Gorshkov as commander of the Navy.[31] Nevertheless, it was not what could be called an extensive purge, and Defense Minister Sokolov stayed in place.[32]

As for Ogarkov, a review in Red Star of a new booklet authored by the marshal suggested that he still retained high-level political support.[33] After Ogarkov's ouster from the General Staff, the Moscow rumor mill had it that he and Romanov were close. But Romanov had disappeared after May 9, so Ogarkov's backing must have extended well beyond Romanov. At a minimum it probably included not only Shcherbitskiy but also Defense Minister Sokolov. In addition, Premier Nikolay Tikhonov and other still-lingering members of the Chernenko coalition probably continued to provide Ogarkov with enough backing to keep alive speculation about a comeback. But this support may even have extended into Gorbachev's own coalition, to Gromyko in particular, who together with Ogarkov had provided so many of the hard-line accents of Soviet national security policy and diplomacy in recent years.

In any event, Romanov was long gone by mid-July when a report surfaced that Marshal Kulikov would become rector of the General Staff Academy, thus opening the way for Ogarkov to replace him as commander in chief of Warsaw Pact forces.[34] Nevertheless, whatever Ogarkov's support, the story fed Western reporters about his impending promotion did not seem plausible under the circumstances. Gorbachev had been riding high in September 1984 when Ogarkov was removed from the General Staff. Gorbachev's position was now immensely stronger and Ogarkov's weaker. Moreover, the two, as we shall see in chapter 2, had just clashed in their assessments of the foreign environment. In fact, by early September it became possible to discount the "leak" totally when Kulikov, still identified as commander in chief of Warsaw Pact Joint Forces, authored an article commemorating, of all things, VJ Day.[35] But even had the rumor been true, Ogarkov as head of the Warsaw Pact would still not have restored to his previous prominence. The new position would still have kept him outside the inner circle of power in the Kremlin.

The Ogarkov "comeback" brouhaha came on the heels of Gorbachev's speech in Minsk on July 10, which was the first such publicized high-ranking civil-military meeting since Brezhnev's major address of October 27, 1982. Accompanying Gorbachev were Defense Minister Sokolov and Central Committee Secretary Lev Zaykov, whom Gorbachev presumably introduced as Romanov's replacement in charge of defense industries.[36] Several weeks later, Zamyatin confirmed that Gorbachev was chairman of the Defense Council.[37]

CHERNENKO'S TROIKA BANISHED

Gorbachev quickly carried the battle over power and policy into his enemies' very own backyards. In mid-April he made his first widely publicized walking tour, a two-day extravaganza centered on the Proletarskiy district in Grishin's Moscow.[38] After the April plenum he visited Romanov's Leningrad in mid-May, demonstrating not only his flair as a sidewalk populist but also his remarkable talents as a telegenic orator.[39] And then in late June he traveled to Dnepropetrovsk in the Ukraine, the home base of Brezhnev's "mafia."[40]

Gorbachev wasted no time in moving against Romanov, who disappeared from public view after his attendance at the VE Day parade on May 9. In Leningrad on May 17 Gorbachev praised Romanov's successor Zaykov, but never mentioned Romanov directly, instead sprinkling his major speech with negative allusions to Romanov's penchant for traffic-disrupting motorcades.[41] As the new general secretary pushed his assault, the former Leningrad party boss even missed a major Central

Committee conference on science and technology on June 11–12.[42] By the time Romanov "retired" for "health" reasons at the Central Committee plenum on July 1, his departure was anticlimactic.[43]

Romanov's ouster was a major benchmark — the first removal of a living member from the ruling Politburo since Kirilenko had been forced out in 1982 in Brezhnev's final months. It marked the end of the long succession struggle in yet another sense: there were now no credible rivals left to challenge Gorbachev's ascendancy from what remained of the Brezhnev-Chernenko faction. On the eve of the July plenum *Pravda* for the first time recorded the ceremonial election of an honorary presidium consisting of the Politburo "headed" by Gorbachev.[44] Although this type of accolade would hereafter be spurned by the new leadership, *Pravda's* signal marked the beginning of a new chapter in Soviet politics. About the same time, the Politburo also "approved" Gorbachev as chairman of the commission that would update the Party Program to be adopted at the 27th Party Congress early the next year.[45]

The July 1 plenum also promoted Leningrad party First Secretary Zaykov and his recent Sverdlovsk counterpart, Boris Yeltsin, to the Secretariat, and advanced Georgian party leader Eduard Shevardnadze from candidate to full member of the Politburo.[46] When Zaykov accompanied Gorbachev to Minsk a week later to meet with military leaders, it became clear that he had taken over Romanov's responsibilities in the Secretariat for defense industry.[47] Yeltsin hailed from Kirilenko's Sverdlovsk stronghold, where he had worked as regional party first secretary from 1976 until April 1985, at which time he moved to Moscow to head up the Central Committee's Construction Department. As Central Committee secretary he would continue to supervise the work of this department until late December. Two years later, of course, Zaykov would supplant Yeltsin as Moscow city party boss.

At the meeting of the Supreme Soviet the day after the July plenum, there were even more spectacular personnel fireworks. Fifty-seven-year-old Georgian party boss Shevardnadze, just elevated to full member of the Politburo, replaced Gromyko as foreign minister. Gromyko, in turn, was elected chairman of the Presidium of the Supreme Soviet. In nominating Chernenko for the same position in April 1984, Gorbachev had argued the need to combine the functions of party leader and head of state. Now Gorbachev said that "new tasks" called for "amendments" to this arrangement. As a result, the Central Committee had found it "advisable" that he concentrate on his responsibilities as party leader and on the task of "pooling the efforts of all party, state and public organizations for a successful implementation of the charted course."[48]

The Supreme Soviet session on July 2 also formalized the new leadership's pecking order. Ligachev was named chairman of the Foreign Affairs Commission of the Council of the Union, thus replacing

Gorbachev in that position and firmly establishing Ligachev as the second in command in the party. Judging from his public appearances, Ligachev continued to retain oversight of cadre matters and added the number two man's traditional portfolio for ideology. Ryzhkov in turn replaced Ligachev as chairman of the Legislative Proposals Commission.[49]

Despite Gorbachev's show of strength, there were rumors that he tried but failed to oust Premier Tikhonov at the party plenum on July 1. An unannounced symphony concert was used as filler that evening after the news show *Vremya* failed to use a scheduled extra 90 minutes of air time, reportedly allotted in anticipation that speeches from the plenum might be broadcast.[50] Despite the new regime's policy of greater openness, the party leader's speech at the plenum was not published, suggesting that not everything had gone according to script.

Whatever was going on behind the scenes, in public Tikhonov's physical decline was now painfully apparent. At the Supreme Soviet sessioh on July 2, he tripped and would have fallen had Gorbachev not held him up. A week earlier Soviet TV had showed him dragging a leg and with his left arm immobilized as he departed from Moscow for Warsaw.[51] By August Tikhonov may no longer have been able to work. It was later asserted that Boris Gostev had taken over the Central Committee's Economics Department sometime that month.[52] This suggested that Ryzhkov, who had headed the Economics Department since its establishment in November 1982, had by August 1985 assumed the functions of acting premier. In any event, the 80-year-old Tikhonov formally resigned on September 27 after his doctors "urgently" suggested he end his "active work", and Nikolay Ryzhkov, age 54, clearly took over as premier.[53] The promotion of Ryzhkov, former head of the Uralmash plant in Sverdlovsk epitomized the ascendancy of the Urals-based Kirilenko network — first under Andropov and now under Gorbachev.

The next plenary meeting of the Central Committee on October 15 formally retired Tikhonov from the Politburo and released Ryzhkov from his duties in the Secretariat. The day before, another sequence of notable changes had begun when Nikolay Baybakov was retired as chairman of Gosplan; deputy premier Nikolay Talyzin was named to replace him and was promoted to first deputy premier.[54] At the plenum Talyzin was elected a candidate member of the Politburo, the highest status attained by the head of Gosplan since May 1955, when Baybakov's tenure began.[55] Within a month, Finance Minister Garbuzov died at 74 "after a serious and prolonged illness" and Boris Gostev replaced him. This meant a clean sweep of the Baybakov and Garbuzov team, which for years had delivered tandem reports on the plan and budget to end-of-year sessions of the Supreme Soviet.[56]

The next major leadership move came on December 24, when Yeltsin replaced Grishin as head of the Moscow city party organization.[57] Vladimir Promyslov shortly after this was also retired from chairman of the Moscow city executive committee, and Valeriy Saykin, general director of the Moscow I. A. Likhachev automobile works, became Moscow's new "mayor."[58] Yeltsin's promotion was replete with political irony, looking both backward and forward. It had been one of Grishin's newspapers, *Vechernaya Moskva*, which in 1979 had cropped Kirilenko, head of the Sverdlovsk clan to which Yeltsin belonged, out of the May Day leadership photograph. Now Yeltsin, who only in April had moved to the Central Committee Secretariat from Sverdlovsk, took over Grishin's job in Moscow.

On February 18, 1986, there was one last Central Committee plenum before the opening of the 27th Party Congress. Grishin was retired from the Politburo and Konstanin Rusakov from the Secretariat, where he had supervised the Central Committee's Bloc Relations Department. Yeltsin was named a candidate member of the Politburo and formally released from the Secretariat.[59] Although popularly perceived as one of Gorbachev's most ardent supporters, Yeltsin would rise no higher, suggesting a more distant relationship with Gorbachev than supposed. Within two years Grishin would have the satisfaction of seeing Yeltsin self-destruct amid criticism from Gorbachev himself. Ligachev, moreover, would ruefully claim to have sponsored Yeltsin's move to Moscow and into the party leadership ranks.[60]

POLICY OF REVENGE

At lower levels the Gorbachev crowd steadily began to mete out retribution against especially dyed-in-the-wool Chernenkoites. At the center, V. V. Pribytkov and V. A. Pechenev, assistants to the deceased party leader, were quickly demoted and eventually even lost their seats as Supreme Soviet deputies.[61] Boris Yakovlev, head of the Central Committee Letters Department and long associated with Chernenko, was no longer mentioned in the media after Chernenko's death. The Letters Department itself, a creation of Chernenko, likewise ceased to exist and apparently was reabsorbed into the General Department, where it had resided as a sector prior to 1979.

The Moldavian chapter, whose ups and downs had long been a barometer of the factional struggle between the Brezhnev-Chernenko and Andropov-Gorbachev camps, was hard hit. Former republic party boss Ivan Bodyul lost his post as deputy premier in Moscow at the end of May 1985.[62] Republic premier I. G. Ustiyan, who together with republic party boss Semen Grossu had been honored by the East German ambassador in Moscow in late October 1984 as Chernenko sought to reassert himself against Gorbachev, was ousted in December 1985.[63]

While Chernenkoites fell, Gorbachevians rose. In early June Razumovskiy left Krasnodar for Moscow, where he took over the Cadres Department in the Central Committee.[64] By early August Gorbachev confidant Aleksandr Yakovlev was said by his secretary to have replaced Boris Stukalin as head of the Central Committee's Propaganda Department.[65] In early November Stavropol's Vsevolod Murakhovskiy became a first deputy premier and was then named head of the new State Committee for the Agro-Industrial Complex.[66] His appointment meant that a close associate of Gorbachev was now in charge of the entire agricultural sphere.

NOTES

1. TASS, March 11, 1985 (FBIS-SOV, March 11, 1985, R 7).

2. TASS, March 13, 1985 (FBIS-SOV, March 13, 1985, R 7).

3. Christian Schmidt-Hauer, *Gorbachev—The Path to Power* (Topsfield, MA: Salem House, 1986), 112–13.

4. *Pravda*, March 12, 1985.

5. Dev Murarka, "The Ascendency of Gorbachev," *Frontline*, October 19–November 1, 1985; and Zhores A. Medvedev, *Gorbachev* (New York: W. W. Norton, 1984), 15.

6. See in "Stalin—Man and Symbol," *Novoye Russkoye Slovo*, June 12, 1987; and the recollections of I. Zub, one of six officers who arrested Beria, in *Red Star*, March 18–20, 1988 (FBIS-SOV, March 24, 1988, 57–63).

7. Medvedev, *Gorbachev*, 172–3.

8. *New York Times*, February 21, 1988.

9. AFP, March 11, 1987 (FBIS-SOV, March 13, 1987, R 1).

10. See Ligachev's speech at the 19th Party Conference, Moscow Domestic Service, July 1, 1988 (FBIS-SOV, July 5, 1988, Supplement, 103).

11. *Izvestiya*, May 15, 1988 (FBIS-SOV, May 20, 1988, 35).

12. *Washington Post*, September 30, 1987.

13. *Washington Post*, March 11 and 12, 1985.

14. Moscow Domestic Service, July 1, 1988 (FBIS-SOV, July 5, 1988, Supplement, 102–3).

15. TASS, November 12, 1982 (FBIS-SOV, November 12, 1982, R 4–5); and TASS, February 13, 1984 (FBIS-SOV, February 13, 1984, R 9–11).

16. Behind the Lenin Mausoleum lie the busts and graves of the following notables, including all party leaders except Khrushchev: starting from the middle and going out to the left from the mausoleum as it is faced from Red Square: Brezhnev, Dzerzhinskiy, Andropov, Kalinin, Stalin, and Suslov; to the right: Frunze, Zhdanov, Voroshilov, Budyenniy, and Chernenko. Chernenko's grave is thus symbolically distant from those of Stalin, Brezhnev, and Andropov. Khrushchev, of course, who did not die in office, lies in posthumous political exile in the cemetery at Novodevichyy Monastery.

17. Medvedev, *Gorbachev*, 17.

18. *Materialy Vneocherednogo Plenuma Tsentralnogo Komiteta KPSS, 11 marta 1985*. (Moscow: Politizdat, 1985, signed to press March 14, 1985).

19. *Pravda*, April 24, 1985 (FBIS-SOV, April 24, 1985, R 1).

20. *Pravda*, April 24, 1985 (FBIS-SOV, April 24, 1985, R 12).

21. Moscow Domestic Service, May 22, 1985 (broadcast of speech on May 17; FBIS-SOV, May 22, 1985, R 10).

22. Bruce Parrott, "Soviet National Security under Gorbachev," *Problems of Communism* (November-December 1988): 7.

23. *Pravda*, April 24, 1985 (FBIS-SOV, April 24, 1985, R 16).

24. *Materialy Vneocherednogo Plenuma Tsentralnogo Komiteta KPSS, 11 marta 1985*.

25. *Pravda*, March 12, 1985 (FBIS-SOV, March 12, 1985, R 5).

26. *Pravda*, March 14, 1985.

27. TASS, July 10, 1985 (FBIS-SOV, July 11, 1985, R 1).

28. I. M. Panov vice N. I. Makeyev, as noted in *Red Star*, July 13, 1987.

29. Lizichev was first identified in this position in *Red Star*, July 24, 1985. The 74-year-old Yepishev was formally transferred to the Main Inspectorate of the Ministry of Defense but soon died after a "serious and prolonged illness" (TASS, September 16, 1985 [FBIS-SOV, September 17, 1985, V 1]).

30. At a press conference in Moscow on July 25, Nickolay Chervov confirmed that Vladimir Tolubko had been transferred to the Main Inspectorate. *Red Star* the next day identified Maksimov as a deputy defense minister, thus seeming to confirm rumors that he had replaced Tolubko.

31. Chernavin's promotion was revealed by *Red Star* on December 11, 1985, when it identified him as commander in chief of the Soviet Navy in its report on his visit to Tunisia.

32. See Edward L. Warner III, Josephine J. Bonan, and Erma F. Packman, *Key Personnel and Organizations of the Soviet Military High Command*, RAND/N-2567-AF (Santa Monica: RAND Corporation, April 1987), for high command changes through February 1987.

33. *Red Star*, June 11, 1985 (FBIS-SOV, June 11, 1985, V 1–2).

34. *Washington Post*, July 18, 1985.

35. *Izvestiya*, September 3, 1985 (FBIS-SOV, September 4, 1985, V 1–5).

36. TASS, July 10, 1985 (FBIS-SOV, July 11, 1985, R 1).

37. DPA, August 1, 1985 (FBIS-SOV, August 1, 1985, R 6).

38. *Red Star*, April 18, 1985 (FBIS-SOV, April 18, 1985, R 1–2).

39. Moscow Domestic Television Service, May 16, 1985 (FBIS-SOV, May 17, 1985, R 3–5); and Moscow Domestic Service, May 21, 1985 (FBIS-SOV, May 22, 1985, R 1–12).

40. Moscow Domestic Television Service, June 26, 1985 (FBIS-SOV, June 27, 1985, R 1–14).

41. Medvedev, *Gorbachev*, 176.

42. Moscow Domestic Television Service, June 11, 1985 (FBIS-SOV, June 11, 1985, R 1).

43. TASS, July 1, 1985 (FBIS-SOV, July 1, 1985, R 1).

44. *Pravda*, June 30, 1985 (FBIS-SOV, July 3, 1985, R 8).

45. TASS, June 29, 1985 (FBIS-SOV, July 1, 1985, R 2).
46. TASS, July 1, 1985 (FBIS-SOV, July 1, 1985, R 1).
47. TASS, July 10, 1985 (FBIS-SOV, July 11, 1985, R 1).
48. TASS, July 2, 1985 (FBIS-SOV, July 2, 1985, R 1–4).
49. Moscow Domestic Service, July 2, 1985 (FBIS-SOV, July 3, 1985, R 3).
50. *Daily Telegraph*, July 7, 1985.
51. AFP, July 3, 1985 (FBIS-SOV, July 3, 1985, R 15).
52. TASS, December 14, 1985 (FBIS-SOV, December 16, 1985, R 4).
53. *Pravda*, September 28, 1985 (FBIS-SOV, September 30, 1985, R 1–2).
54. Moscow Domestic Service, October 14, 1985 (FBIS-SOV, October 15, 1985, R 1).
55. TASS, October 15, 1985 (FBIS-SOV, October 16, 1985, R 1–2).
56. Moscow Domestic Service, November 13, 1985 (FBIS-SOV, November 13, 1985, R 18); and TASS, December 14, 1985 (FBIS-SOV, December 16, 1985, R 4).
57. TASS, December 24, 1985 (FBIS-SOV, December 24, 1985, R 1).
58. TASS, January 3, 1986 (FBIS-SOV, January 6, 1986, R 5).
59. TASS, February 18, 1986 (FBIS-SOV, February 18, 1986, R 1).
60. Ligachev told *Le Monde*, "I, together with other comrades, recommended" Yeltsin for the Moscow party job (*Le Monde*, December 4, 1987 [FBIS-SOV, December 4, 1987, 44]). Later, at the 19th Party Conference, Ligachev was even more personal, declaring that "it was I who recommended [Yeltsin] for inclusion in the Central Committee Secretariat and the Politburo" (Moscow Domestic Service, July 1, 1988 [FBIS-SOV, July 5, 1988, Supplement, 101]).

Inferentially at least, it had been possible in April 1985 to ascribe some role to Ligachev in Yeltsin's transfer to Moscow from Sverdlovsk, as Yeltsin had been replaced in Sverdlovsk by Yu. V. Petrov (*Pravda*, April 19, 1985). Petrov had earlier been regional party secretary for industry in Sverdlovsk under Yeltsin, but since January 1984 he had been identified as deputy head of Ligachev's Cadres Department in the Central Committee.

Nevertheless, Yeltsin years later somewhat implausibly denied Ligachev's claims of patronage in 1985. "It is untrue. When the Politburo decided that I should transfer from Sverdlovsk to Moscow in 1985 I was informed of it by telephone by Dolgikh. I said 'no.' So the next day Ligachev phoned me on Gorbachev's instructions. I repeated my 'no' so he invoked party discipline" (interview with Ezio Mauro in *La Repubblica*, January 7, 1989 [FBIS-SOV, January 12, 1989, p. 60])

61. On March 20, 1985, Pribytkov was appointed deputy head of Glavlit, the censorship office, according to *Sobraniye Postanovleniy Pravitelstva SSSR*, no. 14 (1985). Pechenev was named deputy editor of *Politicheskoye Samoobrazovaniye* at about the same time (see *Zhurnalist*, no. 6, 1985).
62. Moscow Domestic Service, May 30, 1985 (FBIS-SOV, May 31, 1985, R 2).
63. Moscow Domestic Service, December 24, 1985 (FBIS-SOV, December 26, 1985, R 7–8). A Central Committee decree in October 1986 would criticize Grossu by name for permitting phony reporting of production figures, and Moldavia would be denied "socialist competition" prizes, but Grossu

somehow hung onto his job until late 1989 (*Pravda*, October 22, 1986, and Moscow Television Service, November 3, 1986 [FBIS-SOV, November 4, 1986, R 1]).

64. *Pravda*, June 4, 1985 (FBIS-SOV, June 4, 1985, R 1).

65. AFP, August 6, 1985 (FBIS-SOV, August 7, 1985, R 1).

66. *Pravda*, November 5, 1985 (FBIS-SOV, November 5, 1985, R 6–7); and TASS, November 22, 1985 (FBIS-SOV, November 25, 1985, T 1).

Chapter 2

Accent on Investment

With his support bolstered in the Politburo, Gorbachev began to push more forcefully on policy. Although there was already speculation about differences between Gorbachev and Ligachev, their public statements sounded much alike. Programmatically, these amounted to a resounding triumph for the ideas long espoused by Kirilenko and Kosygin. But in a world that would not stand still in order to let the USSR catch up, these would prove too little, too late, and even counterproductive, perhaps appropriate for the 1960s but certainly not for the 1980s and beyond.

Besides cadres, the effort to increase investment, particularly in machine building, dominated the domestic politics of Gorbachev's first year in office. The new regime began to try to subordinate the military's maximalist near-term demands, so ardently pressed until recently by Ogarkov and his followers, to its own unfolding economic modernization program. In relative terms the efforts of the new administration on economic reform were cautiously incremental, basically aimed only at expanding Andropov's "five ministries" experiment.

KIRILENKOISM TRIUMPHANT ON INVESTMENT

From the start there could be no doubt where Gorbachev's resource priorities lay. Even before Chernenko's death, Gorbachev in December 1984 had announced that the next Central Committee plenum would be devoted to "questions of accelerating scientific and technological progress."[1] On taking over as general secretary, Gorbachev in his acceptance speech on March 11 emphasized his domestic goal of a "decisive turning point" in the "intensive" development of the economy. "We must, we are committed," he told the Central Committee, "to move to the most advanced scientific-technical positions in a short span of time and to a supreme world level in productivity of social labor."[2] Chernenko's death and Gorbachev's desire to set out broad policy themes at the April plenum apparently led to the decision to hold a

Central Committee conference rather than a plenum, as had been the earlier intention, on science and technology. Nevertheless, Gorbachev would later state that many of the materials that had been drafted in preparation for such a plenum were used in the conference that eventually took place on June 11–12, 1985.[3]

As recently as ten years into the Brezhnev era, comparisons with other countries could still be made in terms of refrigerators, televisions, and cars. Now the coin of comparison was computer microprocessors and industrial robotics. In this area the Soviet Union was not only lagging after the West but slipping farther and farther behind as Western development accelerated. A year into the Gorbachev era, Premier Ryzhkov would cite figures that dramatically underscored Soviet technological stagnation. "According to USSR Construction Bank [Stroybank] data," Ryzhkov told the 27th Party Congress, "25 percent of projects carried over into the 12th Five-Year Plan period [1986–90] which, according to ministries' conclusions, correspond to the modern level of scientific and technical progress, were elaborated 10–20 years ago."[4]

Thus it came as no surprise when at the April 1985 plenum Gorbachev pronounced the "cardinal acceleration of scientific-technical progress" the "main strategic lever."[5] Completely gone was the back and forth of the Brezhnev era over what constituted the "main lever" propelling economic growth. Kirilenko's proinvestment line had finally won out. To generate popular support for it, Gorbachev on occasion even evoked Stalin's arguments for rapid industrialization. "The history of old Russia in one unbroken record of the beatings she suffered for falling behind, for her backwardness," Stalin told the First Conference of Industrial Managers in February 1931. "We are fifty or a hundred years behind the advanced countries. We must make good this distance in ten years. Either we do it, or they crush us."[6] In May 1985 Gorbachev asked an audience in Leningrad to "remember how before the war the older generations resolved the task of how to travel in a matter of decades a path other countries had covered over the course of centuries in order to ensure that our country did not find itself in a critical situation. . . . In the same way, we now have to cover another long path once again in a short time."[7] There could not be, he said, any "quiet life" or "banking on relaxation."[8]

In January 1985, while Chernenko was still alive, Tikhonov had spoken as though the draft guidelines for the next five-year plan were already substantially worked out. In early April, less than a month after he replaced Chernenko, even Gorbachev told a meeting of managers in the Central Committee that "work is coming to an end" on the draft guidelines.[9] But in late May, after a working majority in the Politburo at the April plenum was obtained and with Romanov already out of sight, a report on a Politburo meeting suggested that the draft had been sent back for more work.[10] Gorbachev later told the Central Committee conference on science and technology in June that "serious observations were expressed which require the revision of the draft."[11] It was not approved by the Politburo for submission to the Central Committee until September 26, 1985—the day before the announcement that Tikhonov had resigned.[12]

Gorbachev told the June conference that a "drastic change in investment and structure policy" was necessary. In remarks clearly bearing Abel Aganbegyan's imprint, the general secretary said that investment targets had to be increased even further, particularly in civilian machine building. In the 1981–85 planning period, he said, only 5 percent of all capital investment in production had gone to the civilian machine-building sector. Investment targeted on this sector during the 1986–90 plan period had to be nearly doubled—"increased by 1.8 to 2 times."[13]

By August the Politburo approved a party-state resolution on measures designed to "dramatically raise" the quality and technical standards of the output of the machine-building sector. Capital investment in the development of machine building in the forthcoming five-year plan was to be 80 percent greater than that in the 1981–85 time frame.[14] By October the Politburo authorized the setting up of a permanent Bureau for Machine Building in the Council of Ministers.[15] In November new State Planning Committee (Gosplan) Chairman Talyzin reported to the Supreme Soviet on the one-year plan for 1986. State capital investment would increase 8.2 percent over 1985, Talyzin told the deputies. Capital investment for machine building would increase more than 30 percent over that "anticipated" for 1985.[16]

For the time being, Gorbachev pledged at the June conference on science and technology that spending on social programs and the military would not be cut to meet investment needs even though "immense funds" were going to defense.[17] But he seemed to imply, in his earlier speech in Leningrad, that a no-cuts policy could be adhered to only if the economy grew at a rate of at least four percent per year.[18] Moreover, though by no means for the first time, the Politburo was calling on the management expertise and production capacity of the defense sector to help meet its targets for the civilian sector.[19] Gorbachev told the conference that it was necessary to use the experience of defense industries to bolster civilian machine building. Under Andropov, as we have seen, S. A. Afanasyev had been transferred from the General Machine Building to the Heavy and Transport Machine Building Ministry in anticipation of the upcoming ministerial management experiment.

Under Gorbachev a fresh stream of defense managers would be assigned to the civilian sector. At the very top, soon-to-be-premier Ryzhkov had been a spectacular success earlier in his career in the defense industrial complex of Sverdlovsk. Two future new deputy premiers, Lev Voronin and Yuriy Maslyukov, appointed in mid-November 1985 to the chairmanship of State Supply (Gossnab) and the Military-Industrial Commission, respectively, also had prior experience in the Defense Industry Ministry. Aviation Industry Minister Ivan Silayev, furthermore, would also be appointed head of the new Council of Ministers' Bureau for Machine-Building in November.[20] And there would be more such transfers in the future—including the appointment of First Deputy Minister for defense industry Boris Belousov to the post of minister for machine building—to support the new regime's priorities.[21]

In the long run, however, apart from such talent transfers, the leadership appeared to be counting on the modernization of industry to pay for itself. In the short term, therefore, it embarked on a "squeezing" policy. "At the first stage of the fight for our economy's more rapid development," Gorbachev said in Leningrad in May, "we can and must squeeze more out of the economy by imposing more order and increasing labor, technological and state discipline."[22] Until modern new machinery could be produced and installed in numbers great enough to make a difference—a matter of "not one or two years," according to Gorbachev—a renewed discipline campaign was needed to boost production immediately.

Politically and economically, however, the new Gorbachev leadership would not be able to "squeeze" the population beyond three to four years. By 1988, as its investment policy foundered and the perception hardened among the population that the economy was actually declining rather than reviving, the Gorbachev regime would be forced to devote more resources directly to consumption. In fact, the new leadership's accent on investment and squeeze on consumption both contributed to rising inflation and a steadily worsening budget deficit, the latter estimated in the West to have quadrupled from roughly two percent of Soviet GNP in 1984 to nine percent in 1988.[23] By 1989 some leading Soviet intellectuals would declare, "The 1985 decision to accelerate industrial growth was an error."[24]

For all its good intentions, moreover, over the long run the new leadership did not make itself popular when it added to its discipline campaign a widely resented, harsh crackdown on the consumption of alcohol. In October 1984 Chernenko had for the first time focused public leadership attention on the serious nationwide problem of alcohol abuse. Now in early April 1985, under new General Secretary Gorbachev, the Politburo approved plans for "overcoming this ugly phenomenon" and called the battle against drunkenness and alcoholism "a social task of great political importance."[25] Initially most citizens wholeheartedly agreed, but then they began to complain with increasing bitterness about the way in which alcoholic beverages were made extremely difficult for even moderate imbibers to obtain.

Two years later Gorbachev would reveal and condemn the fact that from 1966 to 1985 the state's turnover tax receipts from the sale of alcoholic beverages had increased from R67 billion to R169 billion.[26] Shortly before, a Central Committee decree boasted that "consumption of liquor in 1986 was almost halved by comparison with 1984. Losses of work time owing to absenteeism were reduced. The number of persons taken to medical sobering-up stations fell by one-third, and there was a 26 percent reduction in the number of drink-related crimes." Moreover, according to this decree, "the accident rate at work and in the home fell. There was a significant reduction in the number of road accident victims. The death rate among the country's people fell for the first time in many years."[27]

But the loss of state revenues from the decreased sale of alcoholic beverages, together with the drop in world oil prices and increased spending on investment, would greatly aggravate the Soviet budget deficit. In early 1989 Gorbachev put the 1985–88 decline in state income from alcohol at R49 billion and from oil at R37 billion.[28] In addition, it turned out that after an initial drop in consumption due to the reduced state production of vodka and other alcoholic beverages, moonshiners quickly rose to the challenge, soon making up the deficit in alcohol while creating a new one in sugar, essential in the home distillation process. In fact, based on increased sugar sales, a state financial expert estimated in late 1988 that "there has been no real reduction in the nationwide consumption of alcohol," and an economist asserted that "the full per capita consumption of alcohol in 1987 was 14–17 liters of ethyl alcohol (absolute alcohol)—which is approximately five times higher than sales through state and cooperative trade—and it is with respect to this indicator that we remain the world 'leader.'"[29]

KOSYGINISM TRIUMPHANT ON REFORM

The main rallying cry of the Kosygin reform effort in 1965 had been the need to change from administrative to economic methods of economic management. Soviet reformers had long sought to engage the locomotive of individual self-interest while preserving the dominance of collective state interest. As general secretary, Gorbachev wholeheartedly embraced this essence of the legacy of Kosygin and earlier reformers. Nevertheless, though clearly determined to overcome the economic limitations and political inhibitions of the Kosygin formula, the Gorbachev leadership's efforts over the next several years would suggest that it was no longer adequate (if it ever was) to the task of pulling the USSR abreast of an ever more competitive world. And in the absence of effective economic reform, raising investment in industry would result in producing more goods than ever of little value to anyone—a point that three years later would be made in radical critiques of the Gorbachev regime's economic policies.

As had been true of Kosygin, Gorbachev and his allies were careful to insist that their intent was to strengthen the planned nature of the Soviet economy, not to switch to some sort of market economy. Gorbachev's speech at the June 1985 conference on science and technology reflected his continued adherence to what seemed the relatively conservative but proinvestment compromise hammered out a year earlier. "The advantages of the socialist method of production are inexhaustible," the new general secretary told conference attendees. "Unlike any other country we can mobilize the huge reserves we have, and concentrate funds on general directions of scientific-technological progress."

To carry out the redistribution of allocations to investment, and within investment to machine building, the leadership in fact could not dispense with a centrally planned economy, whatever its inefficiencies. Given entrenched bureaucratic self-interests and "inertia," any radical shifting of economic priorities in the Soviet setting would be impossible without an authoritarian mechanism at the center to enforce the new order. Not only was Gorbachev's early espousal of central planning politically necessary, but in the conditions he faced they were probably economically imperative also. But as time went on it became increasingly clear that in this short-run necessity lay the long-run downfall of his leadership's compromises on economic reform.

Gorbachev's program for management reform in industry at this stage was quite modest. At the bottom and peripheries, the goal was to expand the operational flexibility of managers of production associations and enterprises vis-à-vis their parent ministries in Moscow. Programmatically, however, all that this translated into for now was expanding the "five ministries" experiment launched at the beginning of 1984 under Andropov—though with the promise of even more to come.

In the Soviet context, however, implementing even this cautious program represented a monumental political challenge. It was not a simple case of confrontation between party and state representatives, with pragmatic state managers struggling to enhance their operational autonomy from the "petty tutelage" of hidebound party *apparatchiks*. The locus of resistance to change was the state ministerial apparatus itself. Each "ministry, with the aid of the State Committee for Labor, of the Ministry of Finance, and in some cases of the State Planning Committee," Gorbachev complained at the June 1985 conference, "has vast experience and the ability to keep a tight rein on everybody and interpret the decisions of the Central Committee and the government in such a way that, after their application and all the recommendations, nothing is left of these principles." As a result, Gorbachev called on the party organizations within each ministry to "sharply exert themselves" as "plenipotentiary representatives" of the party's economic line. Even at the enterprise level, liberal economists such as Leonid Abalkin noted that many managers no longer wanted more rights because of the additional responsibility that came with them. According to Abalkin, the managers turned out to be "unprepared for fully using the new rights granted to them," and as such to be an unexpected obstacle to reform.[30]

LIGACHEV AND GORBACHEV

A profile of Ligachev filed by a Western correspondent at about this time pictured him as a "confirmed teetotaller . . . something of a puritan in his personal life," and "the driving figure behind the new anti-alcoholism campaign." Ligachev was said to be a health enthusiast, a strong family man, and a bibliophile. His impact, according to this account, was already being felt in Moscow. "Literary sources say that in recent weeks there has been an almost tangible easing of the atmosphere, that the administration is now run by men who love books and enjoy the company of writers."[31]

As the new leadership began to try to impose its economic policies, however, Ligachev was portrayed by some as a leader of resistance to Gorbachev's economic line within the party hierarchy. It was an important issue, for by this time Ligachev was widely recognized as the new "second secretary." Several years later Ligachev would reveal that he organized and chaired the Secretariat while Gorbachev did the same for the Politburo.[32] It is likely that this arrangement was already in place by this time.

Even in his most conservative public pronouncements, nevertheless, during 1985 Ligachev appeared to be essentially on the same wavelength as Gorbachev. It is worth noting that Ligachev especially had long-standing ties to Aganbegyan, whose recommendations were now being turned into policy. Aganbegyan would later say that he had gotten to know Ligachev very well when the latter had worked in Novosibirsk and Tomsk, and that Gorbachev had personally summoned him to Moscow in summer 1985.[33] According to the Swedish diplomat-economist Anders Aslund, Aganbegyan probably met Ligachev in 1961 in Novosibirsk, and Gorbachev only much later in 1979.[34]

In any event, a textual comparison of key remarks by both leaders on the "market" in summer 1985 revealed striking similarities rather than differences. In late June 1985, for example, Ligachev told the graduating class of the Central Committee's Academy of Social Sciences that "the changes that the [June 11] conference outlined in the sphere of the economy will take place within the framework of scientific socialism without any divergence toward a 'market economy' or private enterprise."[35] This passage was interpreted by some as demonstrating Ligachev's conservatism and his alleged opposition to Gorbachev's reformism. Yet only the day before, Gorbachev had told a meeting of the Ukrainian party *aktiv* in Kiev that "not the market, not spontaneous forces, but primarily the plan should determine the main aspects of economic development."[36]

Ligachev, moreover, endorsed Gorbachev's thesis that "our path lies through the all-around consolidation of centralized planning with the simultaneous expansion of independence and the enhancement of enterprises' responsibilities, through financial autonomy and the use of commodity-money relationships in accordance with the socialist method of production." As Gorbachev had been doing, Ligachev also highlighted the need for cadres with "the ability to find and implement innovatory approaches toward problems. People are needed who know how to find unorthodox, really creative solutions and, no less important, know how to implement them."[37]

Whatever their private opinions, their private statements suggested that Gorbachev at this time was more conservative on economic questions and Ligachev more reformist than some speculation suggested. If not, then both men at the very least displayed great self-discipline in synchronizing and harmonizing their public statements on the direction and pace of economic reform. On this issue it would not be possible to document what appeared to be dissent by Ligachev against the prevailing trend of leadership opinion until spring 1987, when the June 1987 plenum on economic reform was in preparation.

OGARKOV AND GORBACHEV

In early May Gorbachev used the events commemorating the fortieth anniversary of VE Day to evoke a number of themes and sentiments long popular among wide circles of the professional military. He told World War II veterans that the importance of a "military-patriotic" upbringing was growing.[38] In his centerpiece speech on May 8 he praised the "talent" of Soviet commanders—Marshal Yuriy Zhukov in particular—and Stalin's leadership of the wartime State Defense Committee. Gorbachev appeared to paraphrase Stalin's legendary victory toast to the Russian nation, delivered at the Kremlin reception for Red Army commanders on May 24, 1945. "Displaying mass heroism in battles and labor," Gorbachev told the nationwide live television audience for his speech on May 8, "Soviet people of different nationalities upheld and defended their socialist motherland. They were rallied and inspired by the great Russian people whose courage, perseverance, and unconquerable spirit were an inspiring example of unbending will for victory."[39] On May 9 there was a military parade in Red Square, unlike the civilian demonstration of ten years before.[40]

The speech and parade, however, came in the middle of a surprising between-the-lines polemic over how to characterize the contemporary external threat. On one side, the debate pitted Gorbachev and Akhromeyev; on the other side stood Ogarkov and at least Shcherbitskiy. Ogarkov's assessment again implicitly called for a stronger defense effort right away, rather than down the line after the economy as a whole had been reinvigorated. In contrast, Gorbachev was once more pointing to the need to retool the economy as the greatest priority, and in effect arguing that the external environment was safe enough to permit concentrating on the long-term overhaul of the civilian economy.

On May 8 Gorbachev stated that "the present world is absolutely unlike the world of the thirties." The party leader emphasized that the "main task" now was "substantially to accelerate the socioeconomic progress of Soviet society." It was on this "basis," he said, that Soviet prosperity and the nation's economic and defense potential would grow.[41] On several occasions in April and May Akhromeyev backed Gorbachev's line when he asserted that the world now was "radically" or fundamentally" different from that of the thirties.[42]

Ogarkov, however, argued the contrary, in typically stubborn fashion. In a booklet signed to press in April, the deposed chief of the General Staff claimed that the international situation was "to a certain extent reminiscent of the years preceding the second world war."[43] In Kiev Shcherbitskiy reinforced this assessment with the view that McCarthyite and neo-Nazi tendencies in the US and West Germany "remind world society of similar processes that occurred in the states of the fascist coalition on the eve of the [Second World] War."[44] The Ukrainian leader's support of Ogarkov reinforced this book's hypothesis of an Ogarkov-Chernenko coalition after Brezhnev's death. In November 1985 Shcherbitskiy would again assert his skepticism toward Gorbachev's foreign policy after the general secretary's first summit with Reagan in Geneva.

SECRET SPEECH IN MINSK

Gorbachev laid out his program for the military in a speech to a "training assembly of high-ranking commanding officers" in Minsk on

July 10.[45] No text, however, has ever been published of what Gorbachev told his military audience. Presumably he outlined at least the economic aspects of his domestic program and said some words about personnel policy in the armed forces. Major General Yuriy Lebedev, who claimed to have been in the audience at Minsk, later told an American newsmagazine that Gorbachev said, "We now need energetic leaders who can command and communicate, people with initiative who are competent in their work. The time has come to reconstruct our economy [and] pay attention to scientific and technical progress."[46] Nearly two years after Minsk, Sokolov would mention Gorbachev's speech in the context of the need for a "new standard of Army and Navy combat readiness."[47] Thus cadre reforms in the military establishment and the need to reinvigorate the civilian economy seemed to have been the main thrusts of Gorbachev's speech in Minsk.

Gorbachev's remarks may have been so frank as to preclude their direct publication. Nevertheless, press commentaries soon indicated their likely thrust, in many ways reminiscent of Brezhnev's implicit call on the high command in October 1982 to use its budgetary allocations more efficiently. Within weeks an editorial in *Red Star* once again argued that "it is important to create a barrier to the irrational expenditure of materials and goods, to take steps in the battle for economy and thrift."[48] At a major conference six months later, the complaint was noted that some naval commanders had failed to properly understand the need for "an intensification of combat training." They had instead "decided on an unnecessary increase in the number of sea exercises, which leads to overuse of engine capacities, overconsumption of fuel, and premature aging of equipment."[49]

Most directly, however, only a month after the Minsk address, *Pravda* printed what may have been intended as a sanitized version of Gorbachev's remarks: an article entitled "The People and the Army" by Major General A. Skrylnik and N. Tarasenko. On the personnel side, for example, Skrylnik and Tarasenko called for strengthening military discipline and individual accountability while still observing "the spirit of social justice, collectivism, Army and Navy comradeship, and the principles of communist morality." On the economic side, more interestingly, they emphasized the need for greater efficiency by the military in the use of resources supplied to their sector. But beyond this they made clear that the decision, adopted in March 1984 under Chernenko, to relieve the military from the obligation to help bring in the harvest had been reversed. "The USSR Armed Forces are the flesh of the people's flesh," intoned Skrylnik and Tarasenko. "That is why they have not stood and cannot stand apart from the people's creative deeds and accomplishments. . . . The routine life of the Army and the Navy abounds with examples of personnel, without detriment to their service, helping *kolkhozes* and *sovkhozes* to gather the harvest."[50]

Finally, on professional military matters, Akhromeyev by this time was demonstrably beginning to put his own stamp on doctrine—giving primacy to the task of war prevention—with a revision of the one-volume *Military Encyclopedic Dictionary*. The original edition had appeared in 1983 under the editorial direction of Ogarkov and had presumably been intended for a long shelf life.[51] By August 6, 1985, however, a second, revised edition had been sent to the typesetters under the authority of Akhromeyev, who as new chief of the General Staff was now listed as head of the editorial commission.[52] The new volume, however, was not sent to the printers until April 21, 1986, apparently held back to reflect the decisions of the 27th Party Congress, and will be discussed more extensively later in this book.

NOTES

1. *Zhivoye Tvorchestvo Naroda*. Four years later Gorbachev would reveal that he was to give the main report at the plenum, had it been held (*Pravda*, January 7, 1989 [FBIS-SOV, January 9, 54]).

2. *Pravda*, March 12, 1985 (FBIS-SOV, March 12, 1985, R 3).

3. *Pravda*, January 7, 1989 (FBIS-SOV, January 9, 1989, 54).

4. *Pravda*, March 4, 1986 (FBIS-SOV, March 5, 1986, O 18).

5. *Pravda*, April 24, 1985 (FBIS-SOV, April 24, 1985, R 7).

6. Central Committee of the Communist Party of the Soviet Union, *History of the Communist Party of the Soviet Union (Bolsheviks). Short Course.* (Moscow: Foreign Languages Publishing House, 1939), 314.

7. Mikhail S. Gorbachev, *To Move Forward Persistently*, Speech at May 17, 1985 Leningrad Party Organization Aktiv Meeting (Moscow: Politizdat, signed to press May 24, 1985).

8. Moscow Domestic Service, May 21, 1985 (FBIS-SOV, May 22, 1985, R 4).

9. TASS, April 8, 1985 (FBIS-SOV, April 9, 1985, R 1–2); and *Pravda*, April 12, 1985 (FBIS-SOV, April 12, 1985, R 2).

10. *Pravda*, May 25, 1985 (FBIS-SOV, May 28, 1985, R 1).

11. This quote and all the references that follow to Gorbachev's speech at this conference are from Moscow Domestic Television Service, June 11, 1985 (FBIS-SOV, June 12, 1985, R 2–19).

12. TASS, September 26, 1985 (FBIS-SOV, September 27, 1985, R 1).

13. Moscow Domestic Television Service, June 11, 1985 (FBIS-SOV, June 12, 1985, R 2–19).

14. TASS, August 1, 1985 (FBIS-SOV, August 1, 1985, R 1).

15. Moscow Domestic Service, October 17, 1985 (FBIS-SOV, October 18, 1985, R 11).

16. *Pravda*, November 27, 1985 (FBIS-SOV, November 27, 1985, R 19).

17. See also Gorbachev's speech in Dnepropetrovsk on June 26, 1985 (Moscow Domestic Television Service, June 26, 1985 [FBIS-SOV, June 27, 1985, R 4]).

18. Moscow Domestic Service, May 21, 1985 (FBIS-SOV, May 22, 1985, R 4). See also Gorbachev's Victory Day anniversary speech (Moscow Television Service, May 8, 1985 [FBIS-SOV, May 9, 1985, R 10–11]).

19. In 1971, for example, Brezhnev told the 24th Party Congress that "taking into account the high scientific-technical level of the defense industry, the transmission of its experience, inventions and discoveries to all spheres of our economy acquires the highest importance." Cited by David Holloway in *The Soviet Union and the Arms Race* (New Haven, CT: Yale University Press, 1984), 171.

20. AFP, November 29, 1985 (FBIS-SOV, December 5, 1985, R 3). According to AFP, Silayev's new job was identified in *Pravda's* weekly television schedule.

21. On Belousov, see TASS, June 7, 1987 (FBIS-SOV, June 8, 1987, R 1). For a survey of defense-to-civilian transfers, see Christopher Davis, "'Perestroika' in the Soviet Defense Sector, 1985–87: National Security Elite Participation and Turnover," paper prepared for the Conference on Elites and Political Power in the USSR, Centre for Russian and East European Studies, University of Birmingham, July 1–2, 1987, pp. 33–35.

22. Moscow Domestic Service, May 21, 1985 (FBIS-SOV, Mar 22, 1985, R 5).

23. United States Congress, Joint Economic Committee, "The Soviet Economy in 1988: Gorbachev Changes Course," paper presented by the United States Central Intelligence Agency and the Defense Intelligence Agency to the National Security Economic Subcommittee, April 12, 1989, pp. 11–12.

24. This was the opinion of Gennadiy Lisichkin, Vasiliy Selyunin, Anatoliy Strelyaniy, and other members of an Against Inflation group in a discussion piece titled "Stop the Paper Money!" published in *Moscow News*, no. 19, 1989.

25. *Pravda*, April 5, 1985 (FBIS-SOV, April 5, 1985, R 1). The measures were published in *Pravda*, May 17, 1985 (FBIS-SOV, May 17, 1985, R 5–9; and May 20, R 5–10).

26. *Pravda*, June 26, 1987 (FBIS-SOV, June 26, 1987, R 25).

27. *Pravda*, June 2, 1987 (FBIS-SOV, June 10, 1987, R 2).

28. *Pravda*, January 7, 1989 (FBIS-SOV, January 9, 1989, 55).

29. G. Vlasov, first deputy chief, Department for Financing the Agro-industrial Complex, USSR Ministry of Finance, and B. Isakov, head of the statistics department, Moscow G. V. Plekhanov Institute of National Economy, in a roundtable discussion reported in "The Alcohol Problem in the Mirror of Economics," *Voprosy Ekonomiki*, no. 12 (December 1988), 107–28.

30. *L'Unita*, October 25, 1985 (FBIS-SOV, November 12, 1985, S 2–3).

31. *The Guardian*, May 22, 1985.

32. *Le Monde*, December 4, 1987 (FBIS-SOV, December 4, 1987, 42).

33. *Dagens Nyheter*, January 10, 1987 (FBIS-SOV, January 15, 1987, S 1–3); and *Financial Times*, July 28, 1987.

34. Anders Aslund, "Gorbachev's Economic Advisors," *Soviet Economy* 3, no. 3 (1987): 259.

35. *Pravda,* June 29, 1985 (FBIS-SOV, July 5, 1985, R 4–5).

36. Mikhail S. Gorbachev, *Izbrannye Rechi i Stati,* Vol. 2 (Moscow: Politizdat, 1987) 317.

37. *Pravda,* June 29, 1985 (FBIS-SOV, July 5, 1985 R 4–5).

38. *Pravda,* May 6, 1985 (FBIS-SOV, May 6, 1985, R 3).

39. Moscow Television Service, May 8, 1985 (FBIS-SOV, May 9, 1985, R 5).

40. There had also been a military parade in 1965, but not in 1955 (*Washington Post,* May 10, 1985).

41. Moscow Television Service, May 8, 1985 (FBIS-SOV, May 9, 1985, R 5–15).

42. *Novyy Mir,* no. 5 (May 1985), signed to press April 4, 1985; *Neues Deutschland,* May 3, 1985 (FBIS-SOV, May 10, 1985, V 5); and *Izvestiya,* May 7, 1985 (FBIS-SOV, May 15, 1985, CC 4).

43. N. V. Ogarkov, *Istoriya uchit bditel'nosti* (Moscow: Voyenizdat, 1985, signed to press April 8, 1985), 93. The booklet was later reviewed in *Red Star,* June 11, 1985 (FBIS-SOV, June 11, 1985, V 1–2).

44. *Pravda Ukrainy,* May 8, 1985, as cited in Parrott, "Soviet National Security," 5.

45. DPA, August 1, 1985 (FBIS-SOV, August 1, 1985, R 6).

46. *Newsweek,* November 18, 1985, 50.

47. *Red Star,* March 18, 1987 (FBIS-SOV, March 20, 1987, V 1–5).

48. *Red Star,* August 1, 1985.

49. *Red Star,* January 10, 1986 (FBIS-SOV, January 14, 1986, V 3).

50. *Pravda,* August 16, 1985 (FBIS-SOV, August 21, 1985, V 1–6).

51. N. V. Ogarkov, chairman of the Main Editorial Commission, Institute of Military History, USSR Ministry of Defense, *Voyenniy Entsiklopedicheskiy Slovar* (Moscow: Voyenizdat, 1983, signed to press January 14, 1983).

52. S. F. Akhromeyev, chairman of the Main Editorial Commission, Institute of Military History, USSR Ministry of Defense, *Voyenniy Entsiklopedicheskiy Slovar* (Moscow: Voyenizdat, 1986, signed to press April 21, 1986).

Chapter 3

Easing Gromyko Out

*T*o attentive and variously committed insiders, what would later develop into Gorbachev's strikingly different profile on foreign policy was probably already a known quantity by March 1985—to be feared or welcomed, whatever might be the case. In August-September 1984 Gorbachev had been riding high when Ogarkov was sacked and Gromyko was directed to meet with Reagan in the White House. In December 1984 Gorbachev had boldly resurrected Andropov's "force of example" formula, so suggestive of the need to dampen tensions abroad in order to concentrate on reforms and economic recovery at home, and had hinted at dissatisfaction with Gromyko's inflexibility in the face of changing external realities.

Nevertheless, from the March to the April plenums of the party Central Committee, these verbal stirrings found little reflection in the world of concrete policy adjustments. After the late April plenum, however, at which Gorbachev called for a turn to "civilized" relations, this began to change almost immediately. The elevation of Ligachev, Ryzhkov, and Chebrikov to full membership in the Politburo gave Gorbachev a working majority at the pinnacle of the party; Aleksandr Yakovlev, meanwhile, though nominally still only director of IMEMO, was already providing the intellectual framework that would soon supplant Gromyko's deliberately confrontational approach to the West. On regional issues, for example, a subtle yet surprising and important shift in the Soviet approach occurred almost immediately, with Moscow accepting Washington's proposal for regular consultations; three years later Gorbachev would date the beginning of the Soviet reappraisal of its military presence in Afghanistan to this period. This was followed within a month, in late May, by a sharp turnaround in Moscow's posture toward the European Economic Community (EEC), with Gorbachev unexpectedly announcing that the USSR was now ready to establish official relations.

These shifts notwithstanding, Gromyko's transfer from the Foreign Ministry at the beginning of July 1985 still came as a surprise with unclear consequences. New evidence of further experimentation and reappraisal soon surfaced. Nevertheless, the concrete implications of Gromyko's shift to the presidency remained highly debatable for well over a year, at least until the Soviet positions in the negotiations on intermediate-range forces (INF) and strategic nuclear forces (START) finally began to change in a fundamental way. But even then the political-military objectives of Soviet negotiators in Geneva remained the same as under Gromyko: to diminish the U.S. nuclear presence in Europe and the political and military cohesion of NATO, especially the alliance's cross-Atlantic ties. But any hope of success would have to await significant shifts in Soviet political-military posture.

NEW TALKS IN GENEVA

The opening Soviet stance in Geneva was very Gromykoesque. The veteran foreign minister and new party leader appeared to be mutually supportive and extremely close allies. The two of them, and the two of them exclusively, sat together in the front row of the leadership section when the Russian Republic Supreme Soviet opened on March 26.[1]

In his first speech as general secretary, Gorbachev appealed on March 11 for "the immediate cessation of the arms race, primarily the nuclear race, and the nonallowance of it in space."[2] The formulation foreshadowed Moscow's opening proposal for an across-the-board freeze at the new Geneva talks which began the next day, presumably designed to underscore the "organic" connection among the three sets of talks.

Gorbachev quickly sought to reignite anti-INF deployment sentiment in Western Europe in tandem with the campaign against the Strategic Defense Initiative (SDI). In a message in late March to a peace group in the Federal Republic of Germany (FRG), he asked why missile deployments should continue in Europe now that the Geneva talks had started, and charged that U.S. cruise missiles were being installed in Belgium against the will of the "overwhelming" majority of the population.[3]

On Easter Sunday the new Soviet leader used his first "interview" with a *Pravda* editor to announce a freeze on deployment of Soviet medium-range missiles and other countermeasures in Europe. It was to last until November, when it would be reconsidered in light of U.S. actions. He also revealed officially that the USSR had put forward a comprehensive nuclear and space arms freeze proposal in Geneva, as had been foreshadowed in his March 11 speech to the Central Committee.[4] At the end of May Gorbachev revived the 1983 Soviet offer to freeze SS-20 deployments in Asia in the context of an INF agreement in Europe and on condition that there would be no substantial change in the Asian strategic balance.[5]

In the INF group in Geneva, the Soviet position on missiles was familiar. It still insisted on the complete removal of Pershing II and ground-launched cruise missiles (GLCM) deployments in Europe, and on equivalence between Soviet forces and those of the United Kingdom and France, thus leaving the USSR with a substantial long-range INF missile force deployed against Europe. The Soviet position on aircraft was similar. It proposed to reduce and limit Soviet and NATO "medium-range" aircraft to agreed levels. This would include U.S. carrier-based aircraft and would have the effect of making the level of U.S. aircraft in Europe a residual dependent on the number of British and French aircraft.[6]

The overall Soviet position in Geneva seemed designed to make the point that Moscow was ready for an active negotiation, but only if the United States would agree to halt SDI. In his May 31 dinner speech for Gustav Husak, Gorbachev reiterated the Soviet proposal for an immediate moratorium on nuclear and space weapons. He went on to suggest that the United States and the USSR should agree—within a month or two of actually introducing the moratorium—to table "practical" proposals on the whole range of issues under discussion in Geneva. Such proposals would include the reduction they would be willing to take in offensive arms should "attack space weapons" be banned.[7]

GROMYKO: UP AND OUT

The basic relationship between Gorbachev and Gromyko, I have argued, was probably cast in August 1984. Gorbachev and Ustinov seemed to have rejected Gromyko's policy of no contacts with the White House before the November elections and had prevailed on him to meet with President Reagan in late September in Washington. Nevertheless, within this overarching context, Gromyko still appeared to be the architect of Soviet tactics and atmospherics, which remained basically unforthcoming on the issues and acerbic in tone well into the first months of the new Gorbachev leadership.

To outsiders, therefore, the meaning of Gromyko's transfer to the presidency at the July 2, 1985, session of the Supreme Soviet was at first highly debatable. Gromyko had nominated Gorbachev to be general secretary at the Central Committee plenum on March 11. The foreign minister had spoken at Chernenko's funeral two days later. He sat next to Gorbachev at the Russian Republic Supreme Soviet session later in the month. Up to the very last moment before vacating his office at the Foreign Ministry, he still seemed (except for a few anomalies) the preeminent architect of Soviet foreign policy, a full member of the Politburo and presumably also of the Defense Council.

At the time of Chernenko's death, Gromyko had been the only member of the older generation in the leadership left with his reputation intact. His televised "conversation" in January on Geneva issues had been masterful, providing the main talking points of Soviet propaganda for months. His relationship with Gorbachev seemed close. And so one could make a good argument that student Gorbachev would follow the lessons of professor Gromyko, now perhaps enjoying even increased authority as president within the Defense Council, and that the essence of Soviet diplomacy and political-military aims would remain the same.

Gorbachev, it is true, mentioned only domestic affairs on July 2 in describing the tasks that would face Gromyko in his new Supreme Soviet job. But in nominating Gromyko for president, Gorbachev also described the outgoing foreign minister as an "eminent politician, one of the oldest party members," who "is making a considerable contribution to formulating and implementing our home and foreign policies."[8] And the TASS report on the first session of the Presidium chaired by Gromyko said that both the Supreme Soviet and its Presidium "constantly keep at the center of their attention the implementation of the CPSU's domestic and foreign policy."[9]

As time went on, however, signs of friction accumulated. It became clearer that Gromyko's promotion had been of the "up and out" variety. Despite Gorbachev's speech to the Supreme Soviet, the real justification for splitting up the responsibilities of head of state and party, it would increasingly seem, had been Gorbachev's desire to remove Gromyko from operational command of the Foreign Ministry. In retrospect, with Gorbachev's shift to personal summit diplomacy looming, it would appear that the new general secretary wanted not only a new foreign minister but also to remove all hindrances and inhibitions to his becoming in effect Gorbachev's own foreign minister.

A diplomat in Moscow would later tell me that the emphatic view expressed by all his contacts among Soviet officials had been that Gorbachev had found Gromyko's continued presence as foreign minister "inhibiting." Similarly, a "senior Kremlin official" told Dusko Doder that despite the "close personal relationship" between Gorbachev and Gromyko, there was an element of "natural irritation" on Gorbachev's part; apparently he had little patience for Gromyko's long and didactic explanations of policy options.[10]

In the annals of Kremlin politics it was a fascinating and highly unusual maneuver. Gromyko had been shunted aside, yet the outside observer at first could find little if any political blood on the floor. Gorbachev, it would seem, had not had to push Gromyko out—at least not very hard. The veteran foreign minister, now almost 76, in office since 1957 and perhaps simply not up to the grueling trips Gorbachev's pursuit of a more activist foreign policy would entail, was ready to go. And at first it looked as though his tactics at least toward the Geneva negotiations would stay intact.

THE RISE OF YAKOVLEV

Gorbachev, however, had already started experimenting with a new mix of formulations well before Gromyko's transfer from the Foreign Ministry. In his major speech on December 10, 1984, he pointed to "new centers" of power in the capitalist world beginning to circumscribe the influence of the United States. During his trip to Britain late the same month, the then-second secretary told Parliament that all people live in an "interconnected world." At the Central Committee plenum on April 23, 1985, he said the Soviet Union stood for "civilized relations" between states.[11]

The new formulations seemed to have been developed for Gorbachev by Aleksander Yakovlev. The former acting chief of the Propaganda Department had been exiled to Ottawa in 1973 after authoring a hard-hitting polemic against the extremist wing of Russian nationalism in a memorable piece in *Literary Gazette*. Evidently Gorbachev had been impressed by Yakovlev when he toured Canada in May 1983. By July 1983, as we have seen, Yakovlev had been recalled from Ottawa to become director of the Institute for World Economy and International Relations (IMEMO). By August 1985 he would be back at the Propaganda Department after a twelve-year absence, now as its head.

Right after his return from Ottawa to Moscow in late 1983, Yakovlev authored some of the most outrageous post-Korean Airlines disaster charges against Reagan, including the assertion that the U.S. president had "openly proclaimed his support for all fascist and terrorist regimes."[12] Gorbachev essentially repeated this charge in Smolensk in June 1984, thus becoming the only member of the Politburo leadership to sink so low in public statements about Reagan.[13] Yet Gorbachev argued at the same time that the situation was not hopeless, and several days later Yakovlev similarly wrote that détente was not over.[14] Yakovlev's inclusion in Gorbachev's entourage on the trip to England in December 1984 suggested that he was already a close confidant on international affairs to the future general secretary.

Gorbachev's major statements still showed evident reliance on Gromyko and his Foreign Ministry apparatus. But the new party leader's distinct stress on broader relations with Europe and Japan already suggested an intention to open channels that by-passed and at the same time put pressure on the United States. "We never forget for a minute that the world is not limited to that country alone, but is a much bigger place," Gorbachev said on February 20, while still second secretary. And in his first "interview" with *Pravda* in April as general secretary, Gorbachev issued his famous comment, "we do not look at the world solely through the prism" of U.S.-Soviet relations.[15]

Fifteen years before, in his report to the 24th Party Congress, Brezhnev had characterized the United States, Western Europe, and Japan as "basic centers of imperialist rivalry" which had become "clearly defined" at the beginning of the 1970s. While welcoming what at times was perceived as the growing independence of Japan and Western Europe from the United States, however, Moscow at the same time had been wary of any tendency toward Western European political unity and defense coordination. One of the successes of Brezhnev's policy of détente in the first half of the 1970s, subsequently undermined by Soviet SS-20 deployments, had in fact been its ability to encourage drift on the continent rather than movement toward further political unity and collective security.[16]

Some of these attitudes toward Western European unity now seemed to be changing under Yakovlev's influence. In February 1985 Yakovlev had argued for recognition that Reagan's policies enjoyed considerable support in Western Europe. Nevertheless, he wrote, there were also factors that acted to restrict Washington's freedom to maneuver.[17] Now, in elaborating his view that "new centers of strength" were emerging in the capitalist world, Yakovlev appeared to be outlining a long-term prescription for Soviet diplomacy aimed, at first only implicitly, at encouraging greater internal cohesion in Western Europe as well as, more traditionally, fostering Western European and Japanese independence from the United States.

As Yakovlev explained the matter, "Despite the similarity of the political-strategic aims of the United States and its allies, essential disagreements emerge here. . . . The US allies' increasing economic and military potential and the gradual increase on this basis of their political influence creates the possibility of a progressive increase in the allies' military-political role." By this time Yakovlev already had the self-confidence to tell his Western interviewer, "I will answer you the same way as Gorbachev would." According to Yakovlev, "The United States has to fear that an increased political-military autonomy of certain elements in the system could alter the balance of forces mainly determined at the moment by the presence of the US missile umbrella." He insisted that "the distancing of Western Europe, Japan, and other capitalist countries from US strategic military plans in the near future is neither an excessively rash fantasy nor a nebulous prospect."[18]

Twenty years earlier Yakovlev, as a mid-career Central Committee official, had taken time out to earn a doctorate from the party's Academy of Social Sciences. During this period he had been an exchange student in 1959 at Columbia University. Although Zbigniew Brzezinski would not move from Harvard to Columbia until 1960 and not become director of the university's Research Institute on Communist Affairs until the following year, Yakovlev's vision of international affairs seemed to have been formulated in reaction to that of Brzezinski. Brzezinski, of course, was to become a leading exponent of the foreign affairs philosophy of the Trilateral Commission, founded in 1973 and directed for several years by Brzezinski. According to this view, "US relations with Western Europe and Japan provide the strategic hard core for both global stability and progress."[19]

Now in early 1985 Yakovlev appeared to be the behind-the-scenes formulator of Gorbachev's emerging policy of, in effect, "counter-trilateralism." Yakovlev's recommendations seemed the other side of Brzezinski's trilateral coin. Moscow should work to ensure that the centrifugal forces of divergent self-interests of the three main capitalist poles became stronger than any centripetal impulses toward cooperation. To this end it should encourage common interests, even political and military ones, within each non-American pole, especially the Western European one, so as to frustrate Washington's management of trilateralism, at least over the long haul.

Psychologically at least, Yakovlev's vision gave hope for the future after the unproductiveness and stagnation of Gromyko's post-INF deployment tactics and the vicissitudes of the Chernenko period. Even in the short run, as Moscow and Washington came closer to agreeing to the venue for the Geneva summit, some Soviet commentators returned optimistically to the Nixon analogy. "At the risk of seeming paradoxical again, I would not link the normalization of East-West relations with the ebbing of the 'conservative wave,'" said the International Department's Vadim Zagladin in late June. "Moreover, certain conservative politicians may, under certain conditions, show more inclination for normalization and the development of civilized relations on the international scene than certain liberals. Let us recall Mr. R. Nixon once again."[20]

FIRST SHIFTS: REGIONAL DIPLOMACY

By May 1 U.S. Under Secretary of State for Political Affairs Michael H. Armacost was able to disclose that the new Gorbachev leadership had responded favorably to a suggestion by President Reagan for more regular exchanges with the United States on regional problems.[21] In his speech to the United Nations General Assembly on September 24, 1984, President Reagan had proposed "that our two countries agree to embark on periodic consultations at policy level about regional problems. We will be prepared, if the Soviets agree, to make senior experts available at regular intervals for in-depth exchanges of views."[22] There had been *ad hoc* talks on specific regions before this, most recently on the Middle East in February.[23] These now became more routine, beginning with the resumption of talks on Afghanistan in June.[24]

Three years later, in his February 18, 1988, speech to the Central Committee, Gorbachev would state that after the April 1985 plenum the Politburo had begun to conduct a "hard and impartial analysis" of the Afghanistan situation in search of "a way out."[25] He thus dated and associated the beginning of serious deliberations on the issue within the leadership with the ascension of Ligachev, Ryzhkov, and Chebrikov to full membership in the Politburo. Ligachev in fact would characterize Gorbachev's February 8, 1988, statement on the withdrawal of Soviet troops as "splendid proof" of the Soviet people's "peaceful disposition and striving for good relations with all states and all peoples."[26]

Gorbachev's initial signaling on Afghanistan, however, was ambiguous. Despite a cooling of Moscow's political affections for Babrak Karmal during Chernenko's last months, Gorbachev's reported remarks to the Afghan leader at Chernenko's funeral in March 1985 were more supportive than those of Chernenko and Andropov in February 1984 and November 1982, respectively.[27] At the same time, Gorbachev privately warned Mohammed Zia of the consequences of Pakistan's support for the Afghan resistance, after which Soviet-Afghan military and terrorist intimidation of Pakistan sharply increased.[28] Nevertheless, there was evidence that supported Gorbachev's February 1988 assertion. Four days after the April 1985 plenum, the Soviet message to Kabul on the anniversary of the 1978 People's Democratic Party of Afghanistan (PDPA) coup differed significantly from previous ones: it was published on page two instead of page one of *Pravda*; it did not praise the PDPA for carrying out social changes with public support; it dropped the previous year's assertion that the Kabul regime had "gained deserved prestige in the international arena"; and it did not include the usual formulation that the Afghan government could count on Soviet "internationalist assistance."[29]

In June 1985, in addition to the U.S.-Soviet talks on Afghanistan, there was also a fourth round of Afghan-Pakistan proximity talks in Geneva on June 20–25. UN mediator Diego Cordovez was later to recount that "from the time Gorbachev came in, things began to change."[30] The framework of a four-"instrument" settlement was worked out: noninterference and nonintervention; international guarantees; return of refugees; and "interrelationships" between the first three "instruments and the solution of the question of the withdrawal of foreign troops in accordance with an agreement" between Kabul and Moscow.

The two sides, however, remained far apart on the timing of the last instrument. The Afghans maintained that the withdrawal of Soviet forces could come only after outside interference had ceased and been guaranteed internationally. Pakistan, however, insisted on simultaneity and a specific timetable for the Soviet withdrawal.[31] The USSR continued to insist, as it had since the beginning of its armed intervention, that

Soviet troops could not be withdrawn until the armed challenge to its client regime in Kabul ceased and the PDPA was left firmly in control of political life in Afghanistan.

In general there did not appear to be any early retrenchment of Soviet military and economic commitments around the world, though there was no rush and no obvious targets of opportunity to extend them any further. Gorbachev's resurfacing of Andropov's theme of advancing the Soviet cause through the "force of example" rather than arms had, as under Andropov, sparked widespread speculation that a retrenchment of Soviet commitments in the Third World might be under way. Cuba's Fidel Castro had even stayed away from Chernenko's funeral, reportedly to register displeasure over what he judged as the weak Soviet reaction to U.S. pressure on Nicaragua.[32] But despite its more flexible approach, Moscow under Gorbachev did not seem to be signaling any readiness to come to terms with the United States on Third World issues.

Quite the contrary. Soviet policy seemed designed primarily to portray the USSR as a responsible power, equal to the US, and with its own widespread regional interests which the USSR fully intended to defend even while engaged in a more "civilized" dialogue with the United States over regional differences. In late April, for example, even as the Kremlin was showing interest in the Reagan administration's regional overtures, Nicaragua's Daniel Ortega made a widely publicized visit to Moscow. The trip provoked almost immediate passage in the U.S. Senate of a resolution citing Ortega's call on the Kremlin as clear evidence of the Sandinista regime's efforts to strengthen its ties with the USSR, and condemning what were said to be the Ortega government's policies of militarization, repression, and interference in neighboring countries.[33] By mid-June both the Senate and House had approved administration requests for nonmilitary aid to the Contras.[34] It was a good object lesson—and puzzling faux pas—for a new Soviet leadership already clearly attuned to the demands and potential gains to be had by mastery and exploitation of public relations. But perhaps the publicity given Ortega's meeting had been deliberately intended to balance or camouflage the coincidental Soviet acceptance of the Reagan administration's proposal for regular talks on regional issues, including Afghanistan.

There was other post-April plenum evidence that the new leadership was grappling at least with the public relations aspects of portraying itself as forthcoming and reasonable toward the West. During Rajiv Gandhi's visit to Moscow in May, Gorbachev briefly revived the essence of the April 1981 proposal by Brezhnev for a superpower "code of conduct" in the Third World. It called for the permanent members of the UN Security Council to abide by the principles of noninterference and nonuse of force or the threat of force, to respect the nonaligned status of individual countries, and to work toward the peaceful settlement of conflicts in

Africa, Asia, and Latin America.[35] Resurrection of the Brezhnev post-Afghanistan initiative seemed to betray a renewed sensitivity to the impact of regional conflicts on U.S.-Soviet relations. But it also seemed to underscore the lingering continuity of the new Gorbachev regime with the Brezhnev era, and it may have been intended simply as a debating point to use in the upcoming regional talks with the United States.

FIRST SHIFTS: EEC; ARMS CONTROL GLASNOST; AND CHINA

On May 29, in connection with Italian Premier Craxi's visit to Moscow, Gorbachev announced the Kremlin's readiness to deal with the European Economic Community (EEC), or Common Market, not only as an economic but also as a "political entity."[36] At the time of Craxi's visit, Italy held the rotating presidency of the EEC. After exploratory contacts in 1973–74, talks between the EEC and the Soviet-dominated Council for Economic Mutual Assistance (CEMA) on establishing official diplomatic and political relations had been initiated in 1975. They never went anywhere, however, and in effect had been suspended since the Soviet invasion of Afghanistan. In fact, until Gorbachev's statement during the Craxi visit, CEMA had not even responded to the EEC's last written offer to resume talks, made in March 1981.

The basic sticking point over the years had been CEMA's insistence on being recognized by the EEC as a negotiating partner equal to the EEC. This ran counter to the EEC's preference for dealing directly with individual East European trading partners rather than through the CEMA structure. Moscow in response had opposed official diplomatic relations between the EEC and individual CEMA members, including the USSR, as long as the EEC refused to recognize CEMA as an equal.[37] As recently as March 1984 Arbatov had raised only to reject the possibility of establishing political relations with the EEC.[38]

Now Gorbachev's statement finally gave the green light to the establishment of official relations between individual CEMA members and the EEC, as well as to official but essentially unequal relations between the EEC and CEMA. When it was all done, the EEC would have diplomatic relations and dealings with individual CEMA members on a bilateral basis; CEMA's dealings with individual EEC members, however, would be channeled exclusively through the EEC.[39] Talks between individual CEMA members and the EEC, and between the EEC and CEMA, began in 1986.[40] Formal EEC-CEMA relations were finally established with the signing of an agreement on mutual recognition in Luxembourg on June 25, 1988; diplomatic relations between the EEC and most CEMA countries, including the USSR, soon followed.[41]

Gorbachev's initiative toward the EEC bore then-IMEMO Director Aleksandr Yakovlev's imprint. "The formation of a West European center, whose nucleus is the EEC, and the expansion of its economic and political activity," explained Yakovlev a month later with a proprietary tone, "have turned West Europe into a special region in the system of present-day international relations that plays a role comparable to that of the United States in many spheres." At the same time, he realistically noted the "great role . . . played by the blinding commonality of class interests" spanning the Atlantic, "which prevents people from seeing the world the way it is."[42]

Coincidentally, the first instances of *glasnost* in the Soviet media on some previously taboo national security issues can also be dated to this time. A *Pravda* editorial on the first round of the new Geneva talks referred for the first time to the existence of a Soviet antisattelite weapon (ASAT).[43] Akhromeyev, in an article rebutting U.S. statements on the compatibility of SDI with the Anti-Ballistic Missile (ABM) Treaty, similarly raised for the first time in the Soviet media the issue of the Krasnoyarsk radar.[44] Finally, an "authorized" TASS statement criticizing President Reagan's June 10 statement on interim restraint and Soviet treaty noncompliance for the first time mentioned and defended the SS-X-25 as a modernized version of the old SS-13 and therefore fully compatible with the SALT II Treaty.[45] In each case the breaking of media mores long predating the Gromyko era gave Soviet spokesmen a chance to counter U.S. charges on arms control compliance issues somewhat more effectively. Two years later Soviet handling of Krasnoyarsk would be truly revolutionized when a U.S. congressional delegation would visit the radar installation for an on-site inspection.

There was also a noteworthy change in the Soviet posture toward China. Unlike his predecessors, Gorbachev began to court Chinese cooperation on antinuclear public diplomacy. During Gandhi's visit to Moscow in May 1985, Gorbachev for the first time drew attention to the PRC's no-first-use pledge— totally ignored by previous Soviet leaders—and to Beijing's opposition to the militarization of space.[46] Soviet commentary also began to praise the Chinese for ending nuclear testing in the atmosphere. Moscow's clients in Southeast Asia could not fail to note the shifting winds in the Soviet capital and at least sought to appear to be bending with them. In mid-August Vietnam and Cambodia announced that yearly "withdrawals" from Cambodia of Vietnamese "volunteer forces" would be completed with their "total" repatriation by 1990. The pledge, however, was hedged by the condition that no one take advantage of the withdrawals to "undermine the peace and security of Cambodia," and therefore it was worth very little in practice.[47] Nevertheless, perhaps more for the benefit of the new leadership in Moscow than for Beijing the statement was meant at least to appear to address one of what Beijing insisted were "three obstacles" to normalizing Sino-Soviet relations—the other two being the withdrawal of Soviet troops from Mongolia and the Sino-Soviet border, as well as from Afghanistan.

Indeed, from the beginning of his tenure as general secretary, Gorbachev seemed to have a strong personal interest in improving relations with China. Perhaps even more interesting, however, was the changed Chinese attitude. After the personal criticism of Chernenko in June 1984, the leader of China's delegation to the Chernenko funeral addressed Gorbachev as "comrade" and brought greetings to Gorbachev from Chinese party leader Hu Yaobang, the first such message in nearly 20 years.[48]

GORBACHEV JUGGLES TWO LINES

In retrospect it was clear that these various external overtures toward Washington, European capitals, and Beijing came as Gromyko's transfer from the Foreign Ministry was being engineered on the inside. At a minimum, Gromyko undoubtedly perceived that his role would diminish as Gorbachev moved to become, in effect, his own foreign minister. The veteran diplomat probably saw that his position, had he stayed on, would increasingly revert to what it had been under Khrushchev: chief technician and implementer of Soviet foreign policy, rather than its architect. In any event, the June 1 announcement that the Supreme Soviet would convene on July 2 came as these various shifts and adjustments became public, presumably by which point Gromyko's transfer had already been agreed within the Politburo.[49]

The harbingers of change imparted to Gorbachev's pronouncements on foreign policy a curious duality during the period from the April plenum of the Central Committee to the July session of the Supreme Soviet. On one hand, the general secretary touted what seemed to be Yakovlev's call for "civilized relations." On the other hand, he further developed Gromyko's warning—delivered in the foreign minister's January 13 television "conversation"—that the new Geneva negotiations would be "wrecked" were the United States to embark on violating the accords he and Secretary Shultz had reached during their January 7–8 talks in Geneva. The first round of the new negotiations had just ended, and in this connection Gorbachev now charged in a speech to the Central Committee on April 23, that the United States had violated the January agreement between Shultz and Gromyko on the interconnectedness of the three sets of issues being discussed in Geneva. "We would not," he warned, "want a repetition of the sorry experience of the previous talks."[50]

Gorbachev's statement at the April plenum was the first of several thinly veiled walkout threats that would climax with an article by Georgiy Arbatov in *Pravda* on July 1. On May 29, in his dinner speech for visiting Italian leader Craxi, Gorbachev warned that U.S. pursuit of SDI would "subvert" the Geneva talks.[51] On June 26 in Dnepropetrovsk, Gorbachev stated that the USSR would have to "reassess the entire situation" if the United States continued to play for time at the Geneva talks and to use them to mask its military preparations.[52] Finally, in a lengthy article in *Pravda* on July 1, Arbatov in effect elaborated the rationale for a Soviet walkout from the Geneva negotiations: according to the U.S. timetable, Washington would not be able to make a decision on the feasibility of an SDI type of ABM defense until 1993 at the earliest; the United States therefore did not intend to talk seriously in Geneva for at least the next eight years. In the meantime, the United States regarded the talks as an "instrument . . . for universal swindling"; and "extreme right-wingers" in the Reagan administration hoped to use them to foist their policies on U.S. allies and on the president's successor—whoever won the next election.[53]

During this period Gorbachev also charged in his VE Day anniversary speech on May 8 that U.S. policy had become "a constant negative factor" in international relations.[54] It was an assessment reminiscent both of Andropov's post-KAL, September 1983 statement dismissing the possibility that Reagan administration policy might evolve "for the better," and of Chernenko's denial in May 1984, as he turned on the "deep freeze", that "realism and rationality" were coming to the fore in Washington.[55]

For the most part, the hard-hitting rhetoric against the United States was probably designed to pressure Washington not only on Geneva and other arms control issues but also on the question of a summit. Ever since Vice President Bush had delivered a letter from Reagan to Gorbachev at Chernenko's funeral in which the new Soviet leader was invited to a summit in Washington, there had been dickering between the two capitals on the venue for the meeting.[56] Reagan, furthermore, was being subjected to stinging criticism over his May 5 visit to a cemetery in Bitburg, where former SS officers were belatedly discovered to have been interred, and to skepticism over SDI during other stops on his visit to Europe. Kremlin spokesmen joined the fray, and Gorbachev even referred in a speech on May 8 to "politicians . . . ready to forget or even justify the SS cutthroats and, moreover, pay honor to them."[57] In general, everything suggested that it must have looked like a good time, from Moscow's perspective, to try to apply more pressure on Washington to see if it might bring about some change in the American positions in Geneva.

It was about this time also that Gorbachev's apparent initial predisposition to treat Bonn less harshly than had Gromyko soured. "Don't you believe those who maliciously allege that we are using the 40th anniversary of the victory over fascism for fanning up anti-German sentiments," he wrote to a German peace organization in late March.[58] But in his speech in Moscow on May 8, commemorating that same fortieth anniversary, for the first time as general secretary Gorbachev spoke of "the increased danger of West German revanchism."[59] Kohl's mounting political troubles apparently had proved too tempting. Also at this time, the Kremlin presumably authorized the East German Socialist Unity Party (SED) to negotiate with the West German SPD over a framework agreement for establishing a chemical-weapons-free zone in Central Europe.[60] With its harsh rhetoric toward Helmut Kohl and its praise of Social Democratic Party (SPD) positions, Moscow evidently wanted to drive home the message to the West German electorate that relations with Bonn could be much more productive under an SPD administration than under Kohl's coalition.

Gorbachev probably judged that the harsh rhetoric against the United States and now against the Federal Republic of Germany would be useful, moreover, in protecting his flanks against any attempt by Romanov (who disappeared from public view after May 9) to resist his ouster from the Politburo by rallying hard-line elements in his support. Gorbachev's threats also served to cloud in advance any outside perception that Gromyko's upcoming removal from the Foreign Ministry may have been precipitated by policy differences, or that it might bring significant shifts in Soviet diplomacy.

ENTER SHEVARDNADZE

Gorbachev's walkout warnings may even have been intended, to some extent, to lull Gromyko into thinking that his policies would stay in place even after his departure from the Foreign Ministry. Gromyko may have been instrumental in drafting them for Gorbachev. The Foreign Minister in effect issued the first threat on January 13. And Gorbachev seemed to rely almost entirely on Gromyko's foreign ministry apparatus during his first months as general secretary. Whatever the case, the threats continued right up to Arbatov's piece in *Pravda* on July 1 and then tapered off, not to be further developed in any immediate sense by Gorbachev once Gromyko had left the Foreign Ministry.[61]

Presummit bargaining with the White House also may have explained the verbal pressure tactics, except that they continued even after the Kremlin had begun informally to signal acceptance of the plans for Geneva. Word began to leak out in Moscow that a summit had been agreed the day after Gorbachev's speech in Dnepropetrovsk.[62] In Washington on the afternoon of July 1, in other words, after the Central Committee plenum had concluded in Moscow, Dobrynin conveyed official acceptance to Shultz in Washington.[63] The public announcement of the impending summit in Geneva followed on July 3, together with that of Gorbachev's trip to Paris in October.

Over the next few years Gorbachev and Eduard Shevardnadze would give every indication of having been close personal and political friends for many years. They claimed to have known each other since the mid-1950s, when they headed Komsomol organizations in the adjacent Georgian republic and Stavropol kray, and could be observed to call each other "Misha" and "Edik" in semiprivate social settings.[64] Thus it was especially noteworthy that with Shevardnadze now representing the Soviet Union at the foreign minister level, there was a perceptible change in the tone, if not yet the substance, of Soviet pronouncements. The new foreign minister's first major addresses, at the tenth anniversary of the signing of the Helsinki agreement on July 30 and then at the UN General Assembly on September 24,[65] were for the most part bereft of the sarcasm and even sanctimonious posturing of which Gromyko was so fond.

Open, direct, and personal criticism of Gromyko's long stewardship of Soviet foreign policy was impossible to find in the Soviet media. Nevertheless, by late August 1985 political commentator Aleksander Bovin was telling a Hungarian radio interviewer—without, of course, any reference to Gromyko—that Soviet foreign policy would now be more "dynamic, active, and constructive."[66] In his October Revolution anniversary speech on November 6, furthermore, KGB Chief Viktor Chebrikov argued against "immobility and routine" and in favor of "flexibility and boldness" in Soviet diplomacy.[67]

As Gorbachev prepared to travel to Geneva in mid-November, Gromyko symbolically, it would seem, was sent in the opposite direction to the Volga river city of Gorkiy.[68] In Geneva Gorbachev said at his final press conference, "In recent decades radical changes have taken place in the world which require a new approach, a fresh look at many things in foreign policy."[69] And Leonid Zamyatin, when asked about Gromyko's absence from Geneva, sardonically replied, "We are dealing in policy here, not protocol."[70]

On the issues, the first of several inconsistent Soviet references to banning space weapons research came to light within days of Gromyko's transfer. Under Gromyko the standard formulation of the Soviet position was that the two sides must agree to a "ban on the development (including research), testing and deployment of space attack systems." On July 5, however, Gorbachev's reply to a letter from the Union of Concerned Scientists omitted the parenthetical reference to banning research.[71] Nevertheless, the Soviet position in Geneva had not really changed, and the parenthetical "(including research)" was more in than out of public statements of that position. The Soviet delegation in Geneva quickly issued a rare press statement on July 10 denying the report published the previous day in the *New York Times* that the USSR was no longer seeking a ban on SDI research: "Such reports do not reflect the current state of affairs in these negotiations."[72]

On a different, though related, subject, it is possible that Gromyko's transfer from the Foreign Ministry also removed an obstacle to Gorbachev's promulgation of a unilateral nuclear test ban moratorium. Announced on July 29, 1985, it was to begin on August 6 and run until January 1, 1986, unless the United States followed suit.[73] Since replying in April to a test ban proposal from Gene LaRocque and Eugene Carroll of the Center for Defense Information, the Soviet position had been that it would agree to a moratorium if the other nuclear powers also did so, or at least the United States.[74] There had been no hint that the Soviet Union might go it alone or that it would be willing, as it turned out, to extend its unilateral moratorium repeatedly past the initial five-month period until early 1987.

At the beginning Gorbachev probably viewed the test ban initiative as a good device with which to pressure Reagan during the run-up to their Geneva meeting, and then in 1986 during the sparring over their agreed second meeting. Along the way the moratorium also became a useful public relations device with which to ease the transition past the Chernobyl disaster of April 1986, particularly given the impact of the disaster in Europe.

FIRST FEELERS TOWARD ISRAEL

On an entirely different issue, Soviet ambassador to Paris Yuliy Vorontsov met privately with his Israeli counterpart, Ovadya Sofer, for more than two hours on July 15. The two reportedly had spoken briefly at the funeral of Marc Chagall on April 1, at which time Vorontsov suggested they get together "for more serious talks." A date for lunch at a Paris restaurant was subsequently changed at Vorontsov's initiative to a more discreet meeting at the apartment of Paris Orchestra conductor Daniel Barenboim. The meeting was by no means the first high-level Soviet-Israeli contact since the breaking of diplomatic relations after the 1967 Middle East war; Gromyko had met several times with the Israeli foreign minister in New York on the margins of the UN General Assembly. But the reported contents of the discussions in Paris appeared to signal a renewed and more flexible Soviet approach not only to Israel but to the wider problem of expanding Soviet diplomatic influence in the Middle East.

According to the media reports, Vorontsov explored an accommodation in two areas: Jewish emigration from the Soviet Union and the reestablishment of diplomatic ties. On the first, Vorontsov allegedly suggested that the USSR might allow greater emigration in return for Israel toning down its "anti-Soviet propaganda" and guaranteeing that new emigrés would settle in Israel rather than the United States. On the second, he suggested that diplomatic relations might be resumed if there were movement on the Golan Heights question, such as the opening of negotiations with Syria. This, according to the media reports, might be enough of a pretext for the USSR to reopen its embassy in Tel Aviv. Ultimately, in Moscow's view not all of the Israeli-occupied Golan Heights would have to be returned to Syria, and it was "no coincidence" that Vorontsov had not mentioned Judaea and Samaria.

On the Middle East peace process, Vorontsov reportedly reiterated the Soviet commitment to Israel's existence. He again proposed the convening of an international conference with Soviet participation, explaining that the USSR could not agree to negotiations sponsored only by the United States; but it was difficult to envisage a solution of the Palestinian problem which also satisfied Israel's security demands. Finally, Vorontsov apparently did not quash the notion that Anatoliy Dobrynin might be returning to Moscow soon and that he was a candidate to replace Vorontsov in Washington.[75]

While not denying that the Vorontsov-Sofer conversation had taken place, TASS dismissed the reports of Vorontsov's proposals as "mythical" and "groundless," and Israeli officials described them as exaggerated.[76] Nevertheless, there would be more contacts between Soviet and Israeli representatives on these issues, and these first reports of Moscow's thinking on the evolving relationship would serve as useful benchmarks for judging future progress. Vorontsov, meanwhile, left Paris in May 1986 but wound up in Moscow rather than Washington as a first deputy foreign minister and a leading diplomatic operative on behalf of Gorbachev and Shevardnadze's "new thinking."

NOTES

1. Moscow Television Service, March 26, 1985 (FBIS-SOV, March 26, 1985, R 1–2).
2. *Pravda*, March 12, 1985 (FBIS-SOV, March 12, 1985, R 4).
3. TASS, March 28, 1985 (FBIS-SOV, March 28, 1985, G 1–2).
4. *Pravda*, April 8, 1985 (FBIS-SOV, April 8, 1985, AA 1–3).
5. See Gorbachev's dinner speech for Craxi, Moscow Domestic Service, May 29, 1985 (FBIS-SOV, May 30, 1985, G 6).
6. *Pravda*, August 1, 1985 (FBIS-SOV, August 1, 1985, AA 4).
7. TASS, May 31, 1985 (FBIS-SOV, June 3, 1985, F 8).
8. TASS, July 2, 1985 (FBIS-SOV, July 2, 1985, R 2).
9. *Izvestiya*, July 4, 1985 (FBIS-SOV, July 5, 1985, R 1).

10. Dusko Doder, *Shadows and Whispers* (New York: Random House, 1986), 296.

11. *Pravda*, April 24, 1985 (FBIS-SOV, April 24, 1985, R 15). On June 26 *Literary Gazette* published a "roundtable" discussion on "East-West: Civilized Relations. Necessity? Reality? Utopia?" (FBIS-SOV, July 1, 1985, CC 13–21) featuring Zagladin, Burlatskiy, and Yakovlev. The latter probably coined the term "civilized relations."

12. *Izvestiya*, October 7, 1983 (FBIS-SOV, October 12, 1983, A 3).

13. *Pravda*, June 28, 1984 (FBIS-SOV, June 29, 1984, R 4–9).

14. *Pravda*, July 3, 1984 (FBIS-SOV, July 9, 1984, A 5).

15. *Pravda*, April 8, 1985 (FBIS-SOV, April 8, 1985, AA 1).

16. See Nils H. Wessell, "Soviet Views of Multipolarity and the Emerging Balance of Power," *Orbis*, 22, no. 4 (Winter 1979).

17. *Mirovaya Ekonomika i Mezhdunarodnyye Otnosheniya*, no. 3 (March 1985), signed to press February 13, 1985.

18. *La Repubblica*, May 21, 1985 (FBIS-SOV, May 24, 1985, CC 1–2).

19. Zbigniew Brzezinski, *Power and Principle* (New York: Farrar, Straus and Giroux, 1985), 289.

20. *Literary Gazette*, June 26, 1985 (FBIS-SOV, July 1, 1985, CC 18).

21. See the speech by Armacost delivered at the United States Air Force Academy, Colorado Springs, Colorado, May 1, 1985, "Reflections on US-Soviet Relations," Current Policy No. 700 (Washington, DC: U.S. Department of State, Bureau of Public Affairs, May 1985), 5.

22. Ronald Reagan, "Reducing World Tensions," address before the UN General Assembly, Current Policy no. 615 (Washington, DC: U.S. Department of State, Bureau of Public Affairs, September 1984), 4.

23. *Washington Post*, February 21, 1985.

24. *Washington Post*, June 22, 1985. For a chronology and discussion of the more than a dozen such exchanges from 1985 to 1988, see Wayne Limberg, "Moscow and Regional Conflicts: Linkage Revisited," paper presented at the National Conference of the American Political Science Association, Washington, D.C., September 2, 1988.

25. *Pravda*, February 19, 1988 (FBIS-SOV, February 19, 1988, 56).

26. Moscow Television Service, February 9, 1988 (FBIS-SOV, February 9, 1988, 1).

27. Henry S. Bradsher, *Afghanistan and the Soviet Union*, new and expanded ed. (Durham, NC: Duke University Press, 1985), 268–69.

28. Don Oberdorfer, "Afghanistan: The Soviet Decision to Pull Out," *Washington Post*, April 17, 1988.

29. Bradsher, *Afghanistan*, 269.

30. Oberdorfer, "Afghanistan."

31. Richard P. Cronin, "Afghanistan Peace Talks: An Annotated Chronology and Analysis of the United Nations Sponsored Negotiations," Congressional Research Report for Congress, 88–149 F, February 19, 1988, 18–20.

32. *Washington Post*, March 24, 1985.

33. TASS, April 29, 1985 (FBIS-SOV, April 29, 1985, K 2–4), and *New York Times*, April 30, 1985.

34. *New York Times*, June 7 and 13, 1985.

35. *Red Star*, May 22, 1985 (FBIS-SOV, May 22, 1985, D 5).

36. Moscow Domestic Service, May 29, 1985 (FBIS-SOV, May 30, 1985, G 6).

37. Werner Weidenfeld, "The European Community and Eastern Europe," *Aussen Politik* 38, no. 2 (1987), especially 136–38. For more extensive treatments of EEC and CEMA through the mid-1970s, see Peter Marsh, "The Development of Relations between the EEC and COMECON," Peter Jones, ed., *International Year Book of Foreign Policy Analysis*, vol. 2 (New York: Crane, Russak, 1975), 74–103; and Christopher A. P. Binns, "The Development of the Soviet Policy Response to the EEC," *Co-Existence* 14, no. 2 (October 1977), 240–65.

38. *Le Matin*, March 29, 1984 (FBIS-SOV, April 5, 1984, CC 6–11).

39. *The Guardian*, December 13, 1988.

40. CEMA-EEC experts meetings would begin in Geneva in September 1986 (AFP, January 16, 1987 [FBIS-WE, January 20, 1987, B 1]; and TASS, March 18, 1987 [FBIS-SOV, March 19, 1987, CC 1]). The first meeting of Soviet and EEC experts to discuss the establishment of official relations would take place in Brussels in January 1987 (TASS, January 16, 1987 [FBIS-SOV, January 21, 1987, CC 1]). A month later the Supreme Soviet would issue its first invitation to the Western European Union (WEU) to send a delegation of parliamentarians to Moscow (ANSA, February 18, 1987 [FBIS-SOV, February 18, 1987, G 1]); a five-day visit followed in April (AFP, April 10, 1987 [FBIS-SOV, April 13, 1987, AA 4–5]).

41. TASS, June 25, 1988 (FBIS-SOV, June 29, 1988, 8); and *Le Monde*, August 18, 1988 (FBIS-EE, August 26, 1988, 1).

42. *Literary Gazette*, June 26, 1985 (FBIS-SOV, July 1, 1985, CC 18–20).

43. *Pravda*, May 27, 1985 (FBIS-SOV, May 28, 1985, AA 1–6).

44. *Pravda*, June 4, 1985 (FBIS-SOV, June 4, 1985, AA 1–6).

45. TASS, June 11, 1985 (FBIS-SOV, June 12, 1985, AA 1–2).

46. *Red Star*, May 22, 1985 (FBIS-SOV, May 22, 1985, D 5). See also his speech to the Supreme Soviet reporting on the Geneva summit (Moscow Television Service, November 27, 1987 [FBIS-SOV, November 29, 1985, R 30]).

47. See the communiqué of the eleventh conference of foreign ministers of Cambodia, Laos, and Vietnam, Phnom Penh SPK, August 16, 1985 (FBIS-EA, August 16, 1985, H 1).

48. Xinhua, March 14, 1985 (FBIS-PRC, March 15, 1985, C 1); and *Pravda*, March 18, 1985 (FBIS-SOV, March 18, 1985, B 1).

49. TASS, June 1, 1985 (FBIS-SOV, June 3, 1985, R 1).

50. *Pravda*, April 24, 1985 (FBIS-SOV, April 24, 1985, R 18).

51. Moscow Domestic Service, May 29, 1985 (FBIS-SOV, May 30, 1985, G 5).

52. Moscow Television Service, June 26, 1985 (FBIS-SOV, June 27, 1985, R 13).

53. FBIS-SOV, July 1, 1985, AA 1–4.

54. Moscow Television Service, May 8, 1985 (FBIS-SOV, May 9, 1985, R 15).

55. *Pravda*, September 29, 1983 (FBIS-SOV, September 29, 1983, A 1); and TASS, May 4, 1984 (FBIS-SOV, May 7, 1984).

56. *Washington Post*, July 4, 1985.

57. Moscow Television Service, May 8, 1985 (FBIS-SOV, May 9, 1985, R 16). A TASS report in *Pravda* on May 10 went so far as to state that the Bitburg "visit became . . . synonymous with the US Administration's fraternization with the Nazi degenerates and their 'fuehrer'" (FBIS-SOV, May 13, 1985, A 1).

58. TASS, March 28, 1985 (FBIS-SOV, March 28, 1985, G 2).

59. Moscow Television Service, May 8, 1985 (FBIS-SOV, May 9, 1985, R 15).

60. When Willy Brandt visited the Kremlin in late May, Gorbachev expressed support for the SPD's idea of a Europe free of chemical weapons (Moscow Domestic Service, May 27, 1985 [FBIS-SOV, May 28, 1985, G 3–5]). When the SPD-SED framework accord was signed in June, Foreign Ministry press spokesman Vladimir Lomeyko almost immediately pronounced it "useful" (Bratislava Domestic Service, June 20, 1985 [FBIS-SOV, June 21, 1985, AA 2]).

61. Gorbachev dropped the threats, but his "reassess" warning in Dnepropetrovsk was repeated at least once, in a *Pravda* editorial on August 1, 1985, reviewing the first two rounds of the Geneva arms talks (FBIS-SOV, August 1, 1985, AA 1–6).

62. *Washington Post*, June 29 and November 17, 1985.

63. *New York Times*, July 3, 1985.

64. Related to me by an observer present at one such occasion during the Washington summit in December 1987.

65. *Pravda*, July 31, 1985 (FBIS-SOV, July 31, 1985, CC 1–6); and TASS, September 24, 1985 (FBIS-SOV, September 25, 1985, CC 1–11).

66. Budapest Domestic Service, August 31, 1985 (FBIS-SOV, September 6, 1985, CC 1–2).

67. *Pravda*, November 7, 1985 (FBIS-SOV, November 7, 1985, O 9).

68. *Izvestiya*, November 14, 1985 (FBIS-SOV, November 18, 1985, R 1–12).

69. *Pravda*, November 22, 1985 (FBIS-SOV, November 22, 1985, Supplement no. 14, p. 2).

70. *Los Angeles Times*, November 20, 1985.

71. TASS, July 5, 1985 (FBIS-SOV, July 5, 1985, AA 1–2).

72. TANJUG, July 10, 1985 (FBIS-SOV, July 11, 1985, AA 1–2).

73. *Pravda*, July 30, 1985 (FBIS-SOV, July 30, 1985, AA 1).

74. TASS, April 17, 1985 (FBIS-SOV, April 18, 1985, AA 1); and TASS, July 5, 1985 (FBIS-SOV, July 5, 1985, AA 2–3).

75. Jerusalem Domestic Service, July 19 and 20, 1985 (FBIS-SOV, July 19 and 22, 1985, H 1 and H 1–2, respectively); and *Le Matin*, July 20–21, 1985 (FBIS-SOV, July 24, 1985, H 4–5).

76. TASS, July 20, 1985 (FBIS-SOV, July 22, 1985, H 2); and *New York Times*, July 22, 1985.

Chapter 4 —————————————————————————

Paris-Moscow-Geneva

—————————————————————————————————————

With the summit dates announced in early July, Gorbachev returned to Moscow from vacation in late August and immediately began to lay the groundwork for his first trip abroad as general secretary, to Paris, and for his first encounter with Reagan, in Geneva. As a Soviet leader, his would be a novel approach to a U.S. president. Instead of rejecting Reagan's antinuclear rhetoric as an insincere cover for a continuing of U.S. military buildup, Gorbachev would agree with and appropriate much of it as his own, and then challenge Reagan to go much further.

Soon the seeds of all of Gorbachev's developments in political-military doctrine and diplomatic "new thinking" would be in place. All but unnoticed, for example, perhaps because of the tendency still to interpret and therefore to reject Gorbachev's declarations merely as part of his "charm" diplomacy, Gorbachev first used the phrase "reasonable sufficiency" in Paris. In addition, while vigorously defending the traditional Soviet view of the causes of regional conflicts, in his November address to the Supreme Soviet Gorbachev would warn of the danger of such conflicts escalating into nuclear ones, a point that would be taken much further by academic Yegor Plimak in *Pravda* a year later.

Without doubt Gorbachev's rhetoric was a crucial component of his already highly successful diplomacy. But equally important was Gorbachev's dynamic use of the impact of his peace message in the West and the support for it in Eastern Europe to further his program at home. After Paris the October plenum of the Central Committee approved the proinvestment draft "basic directions" of the Five-Year Plan for 1986–90 and the draft revisions of the Party Program and Party Rules. The draft program not only resuscitated the first stirrings of "new thinking" given voice by Andropov but began to develop them much further toward a deemphasis of the priority of class struggle over peaceful coexistence. After Geneva the Supreme Soviet approved the budget for 1986, which symbolically held defense spending at the same level it had been in 1985. Within two months Gorbachev would call for a nuclear-free world by the year 2000 but, more to the point, for the first time would agree to zero INF in Europe.

GORBACHEV READS REAGAN

At the end of August, when Gorbachev returned from vacation in the Crimea, he lost no time in beginning to signal some of the hallmark themes of his disarmament policy toward the United States and NATO. In essence it amounted to trying to use President Reagan's own frequently stated aversion to the policy of nuclear deterrence to undermine NATO's strategy of extended deterrence and flexible response. Rather than continuing to ignore or criticize Reagan's statements on nuclear war, Gorbachev made a point of agreeing with them and seeking to make common cause not only toward the goal of a nuclear-free world but also toward an SDI-free world. Reagan had used the horrors of nuclear war as the rationale for SDI; Gorbachev would argue the irrelevance of SDI in a world without offensive missiles.

On Saturday morning, August 24, a Soviet diplomat phoned Editor in Chief Henry Grunwald of Time Inc. to arrange for Grunwald to travel to Moscow over the weekend and interview Gorbachev in the Kremlin on Monday. The meeting with Gorbachev, of course, made the magazine's front cover. "Let me just say . . . that our attention certainly was drawn to certain positive elements contained in some of the President's remarks," Gorbachev told Grunwald. "We note some of his public statements in 1983 and 1984. . . . One . . . was that war was inadmissible, that nuclear war was not winnable. . . . Then we also paid due attention to his statement that the US was not seeking superiority over the Soviet Union." These and other "positive elements" in Reagan's outlook could give the two leaders "opportunities . . . to find a basis to overcome the present negative phase in the state of relations between the Soviet Union and the US." That was "indeed why we agreed" to the summit.[1]

In fact, Reagan had a long-documented vision of a world with radically fewer nuclear weapons, as well as an aversion to the doctrines of nuclear deterrence and mutual assured destruction, or MAD. In his October 28, 1980, campaign debate with Carter, for example, Reagan had attacked SALT II for limiting rather than reducing nuclear arms. "I would say to the Soviet Union," Reagan asserted during the televised debate, "we will sit down and negotiate with you as long as it takes, to have not only legitimate arms limitation, but to have a reduction of these nuclear weapons to the point that neither one of us represents a threat to the other."[2] According to Reagan adviser Martin Anderson, as recounted by long-time Reagan observer Lou Cannon, "Reagan surprised his strategists in 1980 by coming up with an idea 'far more radical than a nuclear freeze.' . . . Reagan's notion was that both sides were so strong they could afford to make large-scale reductions in their nuclear arsenals without damaging their security—and that the Soviets might be persuaded to do this if confronted with a continuing US military buildup." In Anderson's recollection, "Aides kind of humored him about this, which as best as I can determine was Reagan's idea."[3]

Entirely consistent with these early ideas, when President Reagan announced the development of the Strategic Defense Initiative on March 23, 1983, he called on the scientific community, "those who gave us nuclear weapons," to devise "the means of rendering these nuclear weapons impotent and obsolete." And then later that year, in his speech to the UN General Assembly on September 26, 1983, and then again in Tokyo to the Japanese Diet on November 11, 1983—at the very height of post-KAL Reagan-bashing by Soviet spokesmen—Reagan declared that "a nuclear war can never be won and must never be fought." On the latter occasion, and then again in his major speech on U.S.-Soviet relations on January 16, 1984, Reagan added that his "dream" was "to see the day when nuclear weapons will be banished from the face of the Earth."[4] Gorbachev would accept the first as the cornerstone of his Geneva summit with Reagan, and then challenge Reagan a year later to make the second come true immediately, rather than dreaming of it in the future.

PARIS: UNTYING GROMYKO'S KNOTS

Moscow made a point of both scheduling and announcing Gorbachev's impending visit to Paris before the Geneva summit with Reagan. On July 3 Vladimir Lomeyko gave relations with France top billing in briefing the press on the announcements earlier in the day that Gorbachev would visit Paris on October 2–5 and meet with Reagan in Geneva on November 19–20.[5]

Even before his arrival in Paris, Gorbachev began systematically to inaugurate or further develop most of the themes that would collectively come to be known as "new thinking." While still in Moscow, on September 30 Gorbachev told French TV viewers, "History is long enough to ensure that the peaceful competition between ways of life provides people with the opportunity voluntarily to make their choice themselves and to decide which social system is more to their liking."[6] "Ideological differences," he told his French interviewers, "are not an obstacle to cooperating in the solution of such topical issues as the question of war and peace." French and Soviet citizens "live in the same house," and so it was "natural that the Soviet Union attaches important significance to cooperation."[7]

Once in Paris, Gorbachev immediately launched the notion of "reasonable sufficiency," though it was little noticed or remarked on at the time. On his first evening in the French capital, at the dinner in his honor hosted by François Mitterrand, Gorbachev quoted the French author Antoine de Saint-Exupéry to the effect that "we are all passengers on the same ship, the earth." In the nuclear age it was the "primary duty" of the "navigators of this ship"—in other words, statesmen and politicians—to "adjust a course toward a peaceful future." If universal disarmament was not yet possible, "then at least there should be negotiation about a reasonable sufficiency of armaments, primarily nuclear ones, and about maintaining strategic stability at the lowest possible level of this sufficiency."[8]

The next day, in the major speech during his visit, the Soviet leader unveiled several more new themes when he met with French parliamentarians. "We hold that it is not by force of arms but only and exclusively by force of example that one must prove the correctness of one's ideology," he reiterated. But Gorbachev then dropped the first hints of his later full assault on deterrence. "Europe's security cannot be ensured by military means, by military force," he told the French deputies. "So far fear of unacceptable retribution is one of the obstacles to war, to the use of military force. But everybody understands, however, that it is impossible to build a lasting peace on fear alone. But the entire question is where to search for the alternative to fear or, to use military language, deterrence?" He also previewed the call to banish class struggle from state diplomacy that would soon be incorporated in the draft new Party Program. "Esteemed ladies and gentlemen, I believe that in the present situation it is especially important not to emulate medieval fanatics and not to spread ideological differences to inter-state relations." On this last point Gorbachev in essence paraphrased the Prague declaration from January 1983—one of the first inklings of "new thinking" under Andropov.

On arms control, Soviet positions on Geneva issues had not begun to change in any interesting way until Shevardnadze's late September visit to the White House, on the eve of Gorbachev's departure for Paris. In late May Gorbachev had in effect said that the Soviet Union would not fill in the details of its reductions proposals until the United States agreed to abandon SDI. The United States had not abandoned SDI, yet all the same Shevardnadze in Washington, Soviet negotiators in Geneva, and now Gorbachev in Paris began to give some specifics of the Soviet position, which included giving ground on Soviet "principles" and untying the first of several of Gromyko's tight knots.[9]

The Soviet Union now considered it possible, Gorbachev told the French parliamentarians, to conclude an agreement on "medium-range" nuclear weapons in Europe "separately, outside of direct connection with the problem of space and strategic arms." Gorbachev also announced that the Soviet Union had unilaterally cut back its SS-20s deployed in Europe to the level fielded in June 1984—that is, to 243 missiles on "standby alert." At the conclusion of his visit to Paris, Gorbachev explained at a press conference that the USSR would not increase its deployments in Asia unless the United States built up its armaments in the region.[10] Later in October, at the disarmament negotiations in Geneva, Moscow gave up another issue of "principle" when it proposed a temporary freeze on INF deployments, including in Asia, as the basis of nothing less than the previously much-maligned idea of an "interim agreement." Nevertheless, in Paris Gorbachev suggested it was time for Paris and London to begin a direct dialogue with Moscow on nuclear forces, and the Soviet position still called for subsequent reductions that would bring U.S. INF forces down to zero and allow Moscow compensation for British and French forces.[11]

In the strategic area, Gorbachev at last seemed to move the Soviet position forward from the 25 percent cuts proposed in the "old" START talks when he called on both sides "to reduce really radically, by 50 percent, the nuclear arms capable of reaching each other's territory." Several weeks later, an editorial in *Pravda* publicly spelled out the numbers Moscow had in mind: 1250 Soviet and 1680 US delivery vehicles, with 6000 "nuclear charges" on each side.[12] Akhromeyev then revealed that the USSR was proposing a sublimit or cap of 60 percent of the overall limit of 6000 warheads on any one leg of the strategic triad.[13] This had the effect of preserving the existing ratio of intercontinental ballistic missile (ICBM) warheads to the total Soviet strategic arsenal. Gorbachev, moreover, had drastically redefined strategic weapons to include all the weapons of one side which could reach the other side's territory, thus constraining U.S. INF arms in Europe but not the comparable Soviet "medium-range" weapons. And even then, Gorbachev told the French lawmakers, the 50-percent reductions could be only in the context of a "total prohibition of space strike arms."[14]

SUMMITRY AND CLASS STRUGGLE

In the early 1970s, at the height of the Nixon-Brezhnev period of détente, Nikolay Inozemtsev—Aleksandr Yakovlev's predecessor as director of IMEMO—had begun to stress the existence of global problems deriving "from contradictions in the development of the human race as a whole." Inozemtsev had focused on the "prime task" of preventing a new world war and on environmental problems.[15] Andropov had resurrected this line of analysis at the June 1983 plenum, where he stressed the growing importance of global problems common to all social systems, the necessity for long-term peaceful coexistence, and the need to reevaluate the activities of revolutionary parties in the nuclear age.

Now, little more than a week after Gorbachev returned from Paris, the Central Committee plenum on October 15 not only formally approved Premier Tikhonov's retirement "on health grounds" and his replacement by Gorbachev's ally Nikolay Ryzhkov but also approved draft revisions of the Party Program and Statutes and the draft "basic directions" of the Five-Year Plan for 1986–90.[16] On international relations, the draft program notably gave short shrift to class struggle, highlighting instead Andropov's and now Gorbachev's favored slogans of "force of example" and "peaceful coexistence." The new draft declared that the "historical dispute between the two opposed social systems . . . can and must be resolved peacefully. Socialism proves its advantages not by force of arms but by the force of its example in all areas of social life."

Two years later, in his book *Perestroika*, Gorbachev would explain how the new program differed from the old on the question of peaceful coexistence. The previous Party Program, approved in 1961, had stated that "peaceful coexistence serves as a basis for the peaceful competition between socialism and capitalism on an international scale and constitutes a specific form of class struggle between them." In its view, "peaceful coexistence affords more favorable opportunities for the struggle of the working class in the capitalist countries and facilitates the struggle of peoples of the colonial and dependent countries for their liberation." The new draft dropped these passages. The principle of peaceful coexistence was still to guide relations between "states with different social systems," but it was no longer "a specific form of class struggle between them." Echoing the January 1983 Prague Declaration and Gorbachev's remarks in Paris, it stated that the party "considers the spread of the ideological contradictions between the two systems to the sphere of these relations to be inadmissible." Also, as in the Prague declaration, it called for enhancing the role of the United Nations in "consolidating peace and in the development of international cooperation," a theme Shevardnadze would develop at greater length in his address to the General Assembly in September 1986. On these points, the language of the draft survived intact and would be approved by the 27th Party Congress in March 1986.[17]

Others soon pushed this new treatment of peaceful coexistence even further, suggesting that "class struggle" be subordinated to the "struggle for peace." Just two months after publication of the draft revision of the Party Program and only some five months since Yakovlev's transfer from IMEMO to the Propaganda Department, Yu. Krasin signed to press in IMEMO's own house journal an article paraphrasing Andropov, quoting Gorbachev in Paris and the new draft program, and perhaps for the first time stressing the "independent" nature of the struggle for peace and its "priority" over other goals—in other words, class struggle. Class struggle remained a reality, wrote Krasin, but socialism had the best chance of influencing the course of history through the "force of example" under conditions of peace. Therefore, the struggle for peace should not pose as its primary goal the transformation of capitalism. "Peaceful coexistence corresponds not to the interests of some single group of countries embodying a certain social system but to the interests of all countries and all peoples."[18] A year later, right after Reykjavik, Gorbachev himself would make this point.

The new draft, furthermore, as Gorbachev would point out in *Perestroika*, "'divorced' the revolution and war themes" by omitting a passage from the 1961 program which declared that if "imperialism" started a new world war, "the peoples" would "sweep imperialism away and bury it."[19] Deletion of this language was at the very least consistent with Gorbachev's underscoring at the Supreme Soviet in November, as we shall see, of the dangers of regional conflicts spreading in the nuclear age. This point would then be developed much further by historian Yegor Plimak in *Pravda* a year later.

For now, in his speech to the October plenum on the domestic side, Gorbachev stressed that *uskoreniye*, or acceleration, was the "pivot" of the three draft documents placed before the Central Committee. Although *perestroika*, or restructuring, had still not risen in his lexicon to become a leading slogan, he emphasized the need for "extending and deepening socialist democracy in every way" and for "widening *glasnost*, strengthening control from below, deepening democratic principles in the work of all state and public organizations." On the international side, Gorbachev pointed to the "very dangerous turn that has appeared in the policy of the major capitalist powers." It could not be diverted, he maintained, "without making decisions at the highest level of responsibility directed toward putting a limit to the arms race and halting the slide toward war."[20]

Two days after the plenum, the same *Pravda* editorial that had given the specifics of the new Soviet START proposal also reiterated the basic premises of Gorbachev's diplomatic activism. "In the nuclear missile age peace cannot be based only on military force, on the constant buildup of mountains of weapons. What is needed is a different, bold view of things that accords with the realities in both the military and the political spheres." "Active political dialogue" was "especially necessary now" in the struggle against the threat of nuclear war.[21]

On November 6 KGB Chief and Politburo member Viktor Chebrikov followed this up in his October Revolution anniversary speech on behalf of the leadership. With the Paris summit an accomplished fact and the Geneva summit coming fast, Chebrikov pointedly laid "special emphasis" on the "alien" nature of "immobility and routine" in the party's foreign policy. Its distinguishing features should rather be, he said, "flexibility and boldness of initiatives, firmness in defending our people's interests, and parallel to that a deep understanding of the security requirements of other peoples, of the whole world." Whichever way the Geneva summit went, Chebrikov stated that Soviet diplomacy would "continue persistently to steer towards the expansion of mutual understanding and cooperation in all fields" with states around the world.[22]

GENEVA: EMBRACING REAGAN

With the Geneva summit at hand, the U.S. connection regained its primacy. Actually, it had never really lost it. For even at the height of Moscow's accentuation of the importance of Europe earlier in the year, Gorbachev had continued to stress the centrality of relations with Washington. Now after Paris, Moscow reverted to its habit of treating Western Europe as a potential lever for pressuring Washington rather than as an increasingly independent "political entity" in a trilateral Western world. Moreover, Moscow's ouster in September of several dozen British diplomats, businessmen, and journalists in retaliation for the expulsion of an equal number of Soviet spies from Britain,[23] together with its continued punitive line toward Helmut Kohl's government in Bonn, underscored what seemed to be the Kremlin's diminished interest in good relations with at least two major European powers.

Moscow's rhetoric on contacts with Washington came full circle since the dark days of INF. Soviet spokesmen all the way up to Gorbachev appropriated one of Honecker's key phrases as their own. "Why should we fly to Geneva?" Bovin asked rhetorically in October. "The Americans . . . will do their darndest to retain a free hand to militarize space and continue the arms race on earth. In general, there is little chance of a marked shift in Soviet-American relations. . . . However, . . . so long as there is even the slightest chance, it must be taken. If things do not work out, it will be necessary to seek new chances, to create them. That is what politics is about."[24]

In fact, the Geneva summit was not without progress on the arms control front. The two sides agreed to set up expert groups to pursue the question of establishing nuclear risk reduction centers in their two capitals, and such centers would eventually be inaugurated during Shevardnadze's visit to Washington in March 1988. And on the more central question of INF, the Joint Statement called for "early progress" on an "interim agreement" on missiles in Europe, thus going beyond the Soviet concession registered at the arms talks in Geneva a month earlier, which had proposed a temporary freeze on deployments as the basis for an "interim agreement."

In his lengthy press conference following the summit talks with Reagan, however, Gorbachev did not bother to mention this particular aspect of the Joint Statement.[25] Instead, in seeking to put the onus on the United States for the lack of greater tangible achievements, Gorbachev asserted to the assembled press corps that "the US side was not yet ready for major decisions." The idea of SDI appeared to have "captivated" the U.S. president "as a man." Nevertheless, Gorbachev was not ready to give up on Reagan as a statesman. The general secretary hoped this was not Reagan's "final word" and that the United States would "weigh most responsibly everything that we said on this subject." Gorbachev regarded Reagan's willingness to reaffirm the January 1985 agreement on the aims of the Geneva arms negotiations as "a certain signal and hope."

Soviet rhetoric surrounding the summit bore the imprint of Yakovlev, who that summer had been appointed head of the Central Committee's Propaganda Department and would soon be co-opted into the Secretariat at the 27th Congress. Thus Gorbachev emphasized that the meeting was "too important" for its productiveness to be judged "in oversimplified terms." It was widely noted that Gorbachev included Yakovlev, but not Gromyko, in his official party, and that Yakovlev sat next to Gorbachev at the postsummit press conference. This seemed to confirm not only that Yakovlev was among Gorbachev's closest confidants, but also that his influence extended far beyond propaganda and media affairs.

Gorbachev also echoed Erich Honecker and the Hungarians when he told his news conference in Geneva that "we were well aware that the situation in the world is too dangerous to neglect even the slightest chance of rectifying the situation and advancing toward a more stable and lasting peace." It was true, he admitted, that there were just as many weapons after the summit as before. Nevertheless, he insisted, "the world has become a safer place." The summit was "undoubtedly a significant event in international life." His talks with Reagan, Gorbachev asserted, represented "the start of the path to dialogue, to understanding—that is, to what helps to strengthen security." According to the Joint Statement, Reagan and Gorbachev had "agreed to meet again in the near future." They also assessed the exchanges on regional problems at the experts' level to be useful, and agreed that they should be continued "on a regular basis."

Above all Gorbachev hailed the two sides' agreement that "a nuclear war cannot be won and must never be fought." He said the Soviet side had taken note of Reagan's assurances that the United States was not striving for military superiority and did not want nuclear war. The Joint Statement underscored the importance of both sides preventing war in general, "whether nuclear or conventional." Gorbachev hoped the talks had made it "possible to dismiss . . . certain biased opinions about the

USSR and the policy of its leadership and remove some of the prejudices that have built up." In any event the summit had "revealed and stimulated world public interest in the problems of Soviet-US relations, the danger of the arms race, and the need to normalize the situation."[26]

Gorbachev's attitude toward nuclear weapons, however, was for the most part unremarkable; at least rhetorically there was no break with the Brezhnev-Gromyko legacy. In his Geneva press conference Gorbachev continued the practice of rejecting superiority on either side, just as Brezhnev had done most notably at Tula in January 1977. And again, as Brezhnev had done on numerous occasions, Gorbachev sought to enshrine strategic parity between the United States and the USSR as the natural state of affairs while calling for mutual efforts to lower that level of parity. Nevertheless, there was a first hint of what would in January be developed into Gorbachev's plan for a nuclear-free world by the end of the century. "We will seek a solution in order to stop the arms race and achieve a radical reduction in nuclear arms, so that at some subsequent stage we can really approach the elimination of nuclear weapons with the participation of all nuclear powers." But this would only be possible, Gorbachev asserted, if the "door is firmly closed on the development of an arms race in space."

SUMMITRY AND THE DEFENSE BUDGET

The timing, atmospherics, and rhetoric Gorbachev elected to use in his summits with Mitterrand and Reagan were directly connected with his efforts at home to promote and defend the tilt toward civilian machine building, presumably against grumbling within the military-industrial establishment. Gorbachev wanted to use the summits to cool the international climate enough to deprive those such as Nikolay Ogarkov who wanted to spend more now for weapons rather than invest in the future. Agreements with Mitterrand and Reagan would have been nice, of course, but they were not necessary to accomplish this limited objective. A change in the Kremlin's rhetoric by itself could go far to do the trick. After all, it had been Moscow's own policies and propaganda that had contributed so much in recent years to increasing world tensions.

While Gorbachev's call for "reasonable sufficiency," first issued in Paris, carried a large and obvious propaganda charge, key precedents suggested that it actually had concrete programmatic import for Soviet defense spending. In January 1960 Khrushchev had used the idea of "sufficiency" to justify a force reduction of 1.2 million men in a benchmark speech to the Supreme Soviet. Similarly Brezhnev's Tula speech in 1977 had implicitly justified the reduction in defense spending growth which began in 1975–76 but which would not be fully recognized in the West until about 1983. Gorbachev's line on defense spending appeared to be in this mold, designed to deflate pressure for greater priority for defense spending.

Gorbachev's deliberate easing of East-West atmospherics coincided with framing the draft guidelines for the next five-year plan. It all suggested a carefully choreographed scenario designed to undermine the arguments of those suggesting that the priority accorded defense spending be undiminished in the new plan. On October 15, as we have seen, the Central Committee plenum approved the draft basic guidelines for the 1986–90 Five-Year Plan to be submitted to the 27th Congress.[27] *Pravda's* lead editorial on October 17 echoed Gorbachev's assertion in Paris: "In the nuclear missile age peace cannot be based only on military force, on the constant buildup of mountains of weapons."[28]

After the Geneva summit and before heading home, Gorbachev stopped in Prague for a quick meeting of Warsaw Pact heads of state and party leaders. He seemed intent on using their support to bolster his position against any possible misgivings in Moscow over his dealings with Reagan. Predictably, his Eastern counterparts enthusiastically voiced their "full support" for the "fundamentally important" meeting.[29]

Once home, Gorbachev reported on his Geneva talks to the Politburo, which in turn also "fully approved" his conversations with Reagan and the Joint Statement the two had signed. Yakovlev's thesis that a change in atmospherics was good in and of itself was reflected in the Politburo's judgment that the summit "can have a positive effect on changing the political and psychological climate in present-day international relations and their improvement and lessen the risk of outbreak of nuclear war."[30] Gorbachev and the Politburo portrayed the Geneva Joint Statement's declaration that nuclear war was unwinnable and should never be started as a victory for Soviet diplomacy and world peace. Finally, the report on the Politburo session put forward the optimistic conclusion that "there are no contradictions which would inevitably doom the USSR and the US to confrontation, let alone war."

Gorbachev then delivered a major speech to the Supreme Soviet in which he returned to the theme of "sufficiency," first raised in Paris. "We will have to reach a common understanding of what level of weapons on each side could be considered relatively sufficient, from the point of view of its reliable defense. We are convinced," he declared, "that the level of this sufficiency is much lower than that which the USSR and United States in fact possess at the moment." Though defending the Soviet viewpoint on regional conflicts, he nevertheless pronounced them "a dangerous thing, particularly given the threat of their spreading in the nuclear age"—a thesis that would be developed in a radical direction to the detriment of national liberationists a year later by the historian Ye. Plimak in *Pravda*. In addition, Gorbachev once more echoed Honecker, reiterating that "we considered and still consider it necessary to adopt all measures to break the vicious circle of the arms race and not to lose a single chance to turn the course of events around toward an improvement." Jettisoned completely were any further ominous hints of a walkout from the arms talks or from any other high-level contacts with the US.[31]

Shcherbitskiy, who in May had supported Ogarkov's alarmist view of the world, appeared at the Supreme Soviet session to take issue with Gorbachev's assessment of the international scene and to spearhead the efforts of defense-firsters to register their less optimistic dissent. In commenting on Gorbachev's address, the Ukrainian leader told the Supreme Soviet that the Geneva summit had indeed been "necessary and useful." But the positions of the White House showed that "there is no real possibility at present of achieving mutual understandings on fundamental issues, particularly in the sphere of the so-called 'Strategic Defense Initiative' and arms reduction, or with regard to the SALT II treaty." Therefore, in light of the "real" international situation, Shcherbitskiy argued that it was necessary to "strengthen the economic might and the defense capability" of the USSR and the Warsaw Pact countries.[32]

Gorbachev, though, appeared to have the results of the parliamentary session wired. First Deputy Finance Minister Viktor Dementsev told the Supreme Soviet that the defense budget for 1986 would remain at R19.063 billion, unchanged from 1985. Even though the actual defense budget was much higher than the announced one, a well-established fact that the USSR would officially acknowledge two years later, the political symbolism of Dementsev's announcement was important. Under Chernenko the stated defense budget had gone up for the first time in years. Now at the end of Gorbachev's first calendar year in office, it stayed constant in absolute terms. And because the overall national budget projected for 1986 increased, the proportion going to defense actually decreased from that for 1985 from 4.9 percent to 4.6 percent.[33] A year later defense expenditures announced for 1987 would go up to R20.2 billion but remain at 4.6 percent of the total budget.[34]

In real terms the intent of the new leadership was probably to hold the growth rate of defense as close as possible to the approximately 2 percent per annum which had prevailed since the mid-1970s, rather than letting it rise back toward the 4–5 percent that had obtained in pervious years. According to one Western study, defense over the years has absorbed an ever-increasing proportion of the product of the machine-building sector, rising from 18 percent in 1960 to 44 percent in

1985. If Gorbachev was to have any chance of attaining his objective of retooling civilian industry, he had to slash the growth rate of defense machinery production from an estimated yearly average of 8.5 percent over the previous decade to about 4.0 percent.[35]

Even more agonizing choices, however, still lay several years down the road. In the last half of the 1980s, according to a joint assessment by the U.S. Central Intelligence Agency and Defense Intelligence Agency, the Soviet defense establishment could accommodate, if need be, a lessening of its demands on machine building: "Most of the weapons we expect to be delivered to Soviet forces through 1990 will be manufactured in plants already built, equipped, and operating. Although competition could be stiff for some basic materials and intermediate goods needed for both industrial modernization and weapons production—and might result in the delay or scaling back of some weapons systems—most major programs should go forward as planned."[36]

Although the crunch might not really hit with full force until sometime after 1990, Gorbachev could now make a good pitch—using arguments far different from those employed in his public diplomacy toward the West—that his program was not only in the best long-run interests of the military but also absolutely necessary. On October 3, 1985, for example, just as Gorbachev was unveiling the concept of "reasonable sufficiency," soldier-scholar Major General M. I. Yasyukov signed to press an article that laid out the main points of what was probably Gorbachev's appeal to the high command.

> Today it is difficult to overestimate the party's concern for the cardinal acceleration of scientific-technical progress in the matter of strengthening military-economic potential. After all, the leading directions of scientific-technical progress—the further, priority development of machine-building, particularly machine-tool building, robot technology, computer technology, instrument-making, and electronics—are simultaneously the basic catalysts of military-technical progress."[37]

JANUARY 1986 STATEMENT

In their talks in Geneva Gorbachev had taken his first face-to-face measure of Reagan as a man and politician. And it was in this context that Reagan's "dream" now appeared to begin to assume increasing importance in Soviet planning of arms control diplomacy and tactics. For Gorbachev embarked on a grand gamble to interest Reagan in bringing his dream dramatically closer to reality—but at the expense of substantially reining in SDI. Gorbachev's venture would climax (but not end) at Reykjavik in October 1986, but he began to lay the groundwork for Reykjavik shortly after Geneva with his statement of January 15, 1986.[38] This called for total nuclear disarmament by the year 2000 and thus marked the beginning of a new and sustained phase in Soviet international arms control diplomacy—Gorbachev the opponent of nuclear deterrence.

Gorbachev's statement was the most extensive Soviet program for disarmament since Khrushchev's proposals for "General and Complete Disarmament" 25 years earlier. As a utopian three-stage program for a nuclear-free world by the end of the century, it broke dramatically with the Brezhnev-Gromyko gradualist approach to arms control and harked back to Khrushchev. Khrushchev and Brezhnev, as we have seen, had both emphasized sufficiency and defense in benchmark speeches in 1960 and 1977, respectively. Khrushchev had had in mind slashing ground troops and the surface navy and relying on missiles for deterrence until the advent of General and Complete Disarmament. Brezhnev's notions were less utopian: a celebration of parity and a call for gradual and incremental strategic reductions. Gorbachev, in contrast, was now calling for the abolition of nuclear and other weapons of "mass destruction" by the year 2000 and the reduction of conventional weapons to levels making offensive operations either impossible or quickly detectable.

Soviet spokesmen, of course, portrayed the statement as a sincere expression of policy views. In practice, however, they used it as a propaganda platform to undermine the legitimacy of the West's reliance on mutual deterrence and flexible response. Beyond this, however, Gorbachev apparently saw it as a concrete guide to action intended to put Reagan's dream to the test. "If the US Administration—as it has repeatedly stated—is committed to the goal of completely eliminating nuclear weapons everywhere, it is being given a practical opportunity to actually do just that."[39]

Mixed with the airy call to denuclearize the world by the end of the century, however, was one more major concession on a long-standing concrete issue of "principle." Moscow not only agreed to the "complete liquidation" of U.S. and Soviet "medium-range" ballistic and cruise missiles from Europe, but it did so without demanding compensation for British and French nuclear forces, thus abandoning a long-standing central requirement of the Soviet position on INF as fashioned by Gromyko.

As usual, though, while giving up this point of principle, Moscow protected its core negotiating position and military requirements with a number of specific conditions, two in particular: the United States had to pledge not to transfer strategic and medium-range missiles to third countries (in other words, to any of its NATO partners); and Britain and

France had to pledge not to build up their corresponding nuclear forces any further. In addition, the proposed elimination of U.S. and Soviet medium-range missiles from Europe was to be just the "first stage" on the way to freeing Europe from all nuclear weapons, presumably to include the denuclearization of Britain and France.

Besides INF, but in part related to it, several aspects of the January 15 proposal were particularly noteworthy. In what in retrospect would assume a reality surprising even to Soviet propagandists, it stated that the USSR was prepared for treaty verification by national technical means, on-site inspection, and any other necessary additional verification measures. On the subject of SDI, it did not explicitly address the question of research. On strategic weapons, however, which it again defined to include all weapons that could reach the territory of either side, there was no change from the 50-percent reduction proposal of the previous October.[40]

Gorbachev's INF conditions—a freeze on French and British forces, a U.S. no-transfer pledge, and a freeze rather than reductions on Soviet INF deployments in Asia—were unacceptable to Washington and were unhesitatingly rejected. Nevertheless, the U.S. inclination to respond positively to the core thrust of what was Gorbachev's first offer of zero U.S. and Soviet deployments in Europe already provoked apprehension in European and Asian capitals. It was a dress rehearsal for the consternation and shock which Reagan's much wider-ranging bargaining with Gorbachev in Reykjavik later in the year would spark within the Western alliance. Having just spent a half-dozen years making the public argument that U.S. INF missile deployments were essential to preserve the integrity of NATO's flexible response strategy, European leaders were not prepared or anxious to execute a wrenching turn of direction on such short notice, even if it meant acceptance by the Soviet Union of NATO's original zero option position. Gorbachev's proposal was still far from that, but nevertheless NATO was already being drawn into an agonizing and very public dilemma.

Consequently, after consultations within NATO and with U.S. allies in Asia, Reagan proposed two variants of a plan to eliminate all INF missiles worldwide within three years. These were meant to assuage European concerns over hasty reductions to zero and Asian concerns over Soviet retention of a sizable force of INF missiles outside Europe. The variants were outlined in a letter to Gorbachev dispatched just before the opening of the 27th Party Congress and subsequently spelled out more fully by U.S. negotiators in Geneva. The first variant involved phased reductions in Europe and Asia down to zero over three years. There would be interim ceilings of 140 launchers in Europe at the end of the first year and 70 at the end of the second. In Asia there would be proportionate cutbacks. The second variant envisioned the elimination of all U.S. and Soviet INF missiles in Europe only. Elsewhere there would be a 50-percent reduction in the 170 Soviet SS-20 launchers in Asia, with the US retaining the right to deploy an equal number of comparable systems, presumably on U.S. territory.[41]

NOTES

1. *Time*, September 9, 1985, 5 and 27.

2. *New York Times*, October 29, 1980.

3. Lou Cannon, *Washington Post*, November 30, 1987.

4. United States Department of State, *Realism, Strength, Negotiation: Key Foreign Policy Statements of the Reagan Administration* (Washington, DC: Bureau of Public Affairs, May 1984), 43, 64, 108, 110.

5. TASS, July 3, 1985 (FBIS-SOV, July 5, 1985, A 1–2).

6. *Pravda*, October 2, 1985 (FBIS-SOV, October 2, 1985, G 2).

7. Moscow Television Service, October 1, 1985 (FBIS-SOV, October 2, 1985, G 6–7).

8. Moscow Domestic Service, October 3, 1985 (FBIS-SOV, October 3, 1985, G 4–5).

9. *New York Times*, October 4, 1985.

10. *Pravda*, October 6, 1985 (FBIS-SOV, October 7, 1985, G 4–5).

11. *Washington Post*, October 24, 1985; and *New York Times*, October 24 and November 4, 1985. Akhromeyev reiterated the demand for equality with British and French forces in *Pravda*, October 19, 1985 (FBIS-SOV, October 21, 1985, AA 4).

12. *Pravda*, October 17, 1985 (FBIS-SOV, October 17, 1985, AA 2–3).

13. *Pravda*, October 19, 1985 (FBIS-SOV, October 21, 1985, AA 5).

14. *Pravda*, October 4, 1985 (FBIS-SOV, October 4, 1985, G 6). Meanwhile, the Reagan administration was moving toward supporting the "broad interpretation" of the ABM Treaty, even though the first announcement by National Security Adviser Robert McFarlane on October 6, 1985, took many of its own officials by surprise. For a review of the development of this issue, see Raymond L. Garthoff, "The Making of the ABM Uproar," *Washington Post*, September 20, 1987; and idem, "History Confirms the Traditional Meaning," *Arms Control Today* 17, no. 7 (September 1987): 15–19.

15. N. N. Inozemtsev, "The Nature of Contradictions Today," *World Marxist Review* 16, no. 9 (September 1973): 18–19, as quoted in Morton Schwartz, *Soviet Perceptions of the United States* (Berkeley: University of California Press, 1978), 168.

16. TASS, October 15, 1985 (FBIS-SOV, October 16, 1985, R 1).

17. The draft CPSU Program was published in *Pravda*, October 26, 1985 (FBIS-SOV, October 28, 1985, Supplement 007). For a comparison of the draft and final language, which is identical on the points discussed in this paragraph, see FBIS-SOV, March 10, 1986, Supplement 051, P. Three, O 3–4. The citation from the 1961 Program is in Jan F. Triska, ed., *Soviet Communism: Programs and Rules* (San Francisco: Chandler, 1962), 66. For the

Prague Declaration, see TASS, January 6, 1983 (FBIS-SOV, January 6, 1983, BB 3–16).

18. Krasin also made another point later picked up by Gorbachev in *Perestroika* and in his speech on November 2, 1987: the possibility that capitalism might be able to wean itself from militarism. See Yu. Krasin, "A Strategy of Peace Is the Imperative of the Epoch," *Mirovaya Ekonomika i Mezhdunarodnyye Otnosheniya*, no. 1 (January 1986), signed to press December 13, 1985.

19. For Gorbachev's discussion of this and other points in the new Party Program, see Mikhail S. Gorbachev, *Perestroika*, new, updated ed. (New York: Perennial Library, 1988), 133–34.

20. Moscow Domestic Service, October 15, 1985 (FBIS-SOV, October 16, 1985, R 2–10).

21. *Pravda*, October 17, 1985 (FBIS-SOV, October 17, 1985, AA 1–5).

22. *Pravda*, November 7, 1985 (FBIS-SOV, November 7, 1985, O 9–10).

23. *Washington Post*, September 15, 1985.

24. *Izvestiya*, October 13, 1985 (FBIS-SOV, October 15, 1985, A 2).

25. For Gorbachev's press conference in Geneva and the text of the "Joint Soviet-US Statement," see *Pravda*, November 22, 1985 (FBIS-SOV, November 22, 1985, Supplement 14).

26. Ibid.

27. TASS, October 15, 1985 (FBIS-SOV, October 16, 1985, R 1–2).

28. *Pravda*, October 17, 1985 (FBIS-SOV, October 17, 1985, AA 1).

29. *Pravda*, November 22, 1985 (FBIS-SOV, November 22, 1985, Supplement, 5).

30. TASS, November 25, 1985 (FBIS-SOV, November 26, 1985, R 10–12).

31. Moscow Television Service, November 27, 1985 (FBIS-SOV, November 29, 1985, R 19 and 24).

32 *Izvestiya*, November 28, 1985 (FBIS-SOV, December 2, 1985, R 11–12).

33. TASS and AFP, November 26, 1985 (FBIS-SOV, November 26, 1985, R 9–10).

34. *Pravda*, November 18, 1986 (FBIS-SOV, November 20, 1986, R 17- 18).

35. Jan Vanous of PlanEcon, Inc., in *Washington Post*, August 17, 1986.

36. United States Congress, Joint Economic Committee, "Gorbachev's Modernization Program: A Status Report," paper presented by the United States Central Intelligence Agency and the Defense Intelligence Agency to the National Security Economics Subcommittee, March 19, 1987, p. 30.

37. *Kommunist Vooruzhennykh Sil*, no. 20 (October 1985), signed to press October 3, 1985. Yasyukov was identified as a doctor of philosophical sciences and a professor. He has also been listed as a member of editorial subcommissions for both editions of the one-volume *Military Encyclopedic Dictionary* and for the eight-volume *Soviet Military Encyclopedia*, and so may be on the staff of the Defense Ministry's Military History Institute. For a later, updated restatement by Yasyukov of his views, see *Red Star*, December 3, 1986 (FBIS-SOV, December 10, 1986, V 1–5).

38. *Pravda*, January 16, 1986 (FBIS-SOV, January 16, 1986, AA 2–3).

39. Ibid.

40. Ibid.

41. *Washington Post*, February 17 and 24, 1986.

Chapter 5

The 27th Party Congress

*T*he April 1985 plenum scheduled the 27th Congress of the CPSU to open on February 25, 1986, technically bending by a couple of days the party rule calling for congresses to take place every five years, given that the previous one had opened on February 23, 1981. While Chernenko was alive, his faction had wanted to move the opening forward in order to limit any further erosion of their position under the steady assault of Gorbachev and his allies. Once in power, the Gorbachev faction wanted the maximum possible time in which to work for the greatest possible turnover in the new Central Committee that would be elected at the Congress.

Given the spectacular, almost daily wave of purges and revelations of corruption that led up to it, the 27th Congress was almost anticlimactic except for newcomer Boris Yeltsin's impassioned attack on party privilege and Gorbachev's description of Afghanistan as a "running sore." Though Gorbachev and Ryzhkov called for "radical reform" and restructuring at the congress, the effort to infuse these slogans with real radicalism did not get under way in earnest until summer 1986. None other than the general secretary, when asked by *L'Humanité* in early February whether his leadership was embarking on a "new revolution," answered categorically, "Of course not."[1]

Programmatically, the new leadership's cardinal slogan remained *uskoreniye* (acceleration), which Gorbachev at the October 1985 plenum pronounced the "pivot" of the three draft documents approved for discussion in the runups to the congress: the new Party Program, Party Rules, and 12th Five-Year Plan (1986–90).[2] The concrete focus of domestic policy of Gorbachev and his supporters was on securing markedly higher rates of investment in industry—particularly in new technology—while seeking to lower tensions abroad in order to undercut proponents of greater priority for defense at the expense of investment and consumption.

The catchwords of *glasnost* (politically inspired and directed publicity, often misleadingly translated as "openness" but actually pushed to acquire some of this connotation by its radical supporters) and *demokratizatsiya* (democratization), to be sure, gained greater currency as Gorbachev endorsed them at the October plenum. But as they began to pick up an increasingly purposeful, anti-Brezhnevite tinge, they remained for the most part highly focused clubs with which to attack high-level, old guard opponents in the round of local and regional party meetings and elections preceding the 27th Congress.

"DE-BREZHNEVIZATION" IN HIGH GEAR

In general a purge atmosphere pervaded Moscow in the winter months of 1985–86. In June Andropov had been all but sanctified as a romantic poet and faithful family man in a full-length documentary film, *Yuriy Vladimirovich Andropov—Pages from a Life*.[3] Now the other side of the coin, de-Brezhnevization, became more explicit than ever. Moscow's Komsomol Theater staged a musical parody, *Noah and his Song*, lampooning the former leader.[4] On November 10, the third anniversary of Brezhnev's death, *Pravda* ran a review of letters critical not only of the "cult of personality" (in other words, Stalin) and "subjectivism and voluntarism" (that is, Khrushchev) but also of "unbridled praise for certain leaders" (clearly Brezhnev).[5]

The call for greater *glasnost*, or publicity, was grafted onto the drive against corruption. The general secretary and his allies used the *glasnost* and anticorruption themes to court public opinion, dent the pervasive culture of bribery that had increasingly dominated the economic landscape under Brezhnev, shake loose bureaucratic deadwood, and root out political opponents. The poet Yevgeniy Yevtushenko was allowed to attack abuses of power and opponents of change,[6] just as he had been permitted by Khrushchev to rail against "Stalin's Heirs" in 1962.[7] Gorbachev made clear that *glasnost* was a "weapon" and not a constitutional guarantee or inalienable human right. "We are resolutely struggling to ensure that deeds do not diverge from words," he told the French Communist party newspaper *L'Humanité* several weeks before the 27th Congress convened. "We are struggling with the weapon of criticism. We are also struggling with the weapon of publicity and the weapon of discipline."[8]

A major scandal again rocked the foreign trade network, this time resulting in the arrest of Deputy Foreign Trade Minister Vladimir Sushkov. In October 1985, Boris Aristov, reportedly a supporter of Gorbachev, had taken over the Foreign Trade Ministry. Two months later and with suspicious unexpectedness, Deputy Foreign Trade Minister Ivan Grishin died, on December 23. The next day Soviet sources disclosed that Sushkov—who as recently as December 11 had co-chaired a meeting in Moscow of the U.S.-Soviet Trade and Economic Council—faced criminal charges for corruption.[9] Later, in August 1986,

V. N. Bazovskiy, head of the Main Administration of State Customs Control, would confirm Sushkov's arrest.[10] Sushkov, who was charged with receiving almost R127,000 in bribes from foreign firms, eventually was sentenced to 13 years' imprisonment, with confiscation of property. His wife, who had been a senior employee with the State Committee for Science and Technology, was said to have extorted even more— R392,000—was sentenced to the slightly shorter term of 11 years.[11]

Sushkov had also served as liaison for trade with Japan. In this connection stories began to circulate in mid-February 1986 that Abrasimov, ambassador to Japan, had been forced to go through a customs examination at Moscow's Sheremyetyevo airport when returning from Tokyo to attend the 27th Congress. Twenty-nine items of electronic contraband were said to have been found in his luggage.[12] Abrasimov subsequently lost his seat on the Central Committee at the Party Congress and was replaced as ambassador in May.

CHEBRIKOV, VLASOV, AND LUKYANOV

At an even higher level, the personnel changes that began with Gorbachev's replacement of Chernenko in March 1985 showed no sign of abating as the Party Congress drew closer. On January 26 the press announced the replacement of MVD head Fedorchuk by Aleksander Vlasov.[13] Politically, of course, it was the end of the line for Fedorchuk, later reported to have been assigned to the Main Inspectorate of the Soviet Army—in effect, retired.[14] This seemed to confirm once and for all that Chebrikov, not Fedorchuk, had been Andropov's candidate to head the KGB in May 1982, when Andropov entered the Secretariat. Before 1982 ended, it will be recalled, Fedorchuk had been shunted from the KGB to the less powerful MVD as Andropov, having succeeded Brezhnev, was finally able to install Chebrikov in command of the KGB.

As for MVD Chief Vlasov, he had been party first secretary from 1975 to 1984 in the Chechen-Ingush autonomous republic bordering on Gorbachev's Stavropol region. In July 1984 Vlasov had been transferred to Rostov, where he replaced Gorbachev's reported regional rival Ivan Bondarenko. As Gorbachev thrust himself forward in Moscow, Bondarenko had been forced into retirement by (what else?) a burgeoning trade scandal. In 1986, just two weeks after Vlasov moved to Moscow from Rostov, *Izvestiya* reported that death sentences had been handed out to two defendants in the case.[15]

Georgiy Tsinev's fate, meanwhile, threw additional retrospective light on changes in the KGB in 1982. Tsinev, now 78, was last identified in the media as first deputy chairman of the KGB by *Izvestiya* on August

18, 1985. Tsinev, whose ties to Brezhnev went back to Dnepropetrovsk in the 1930s, presumably now at last had been retired, and at the 27th Congress he would not be reelected to the Central Committee. As with Fedorchuk's eclipse, Tsinev's fading from the scene seemed to confirm that Chebrikov indeed had been Andropov's candidate for the KGB post in May 1982.

In the meantime, Chebrikov, as already noted, gave the leadership speech on November 6, 1985, commemorating the sixty-eighth anniversary of the October Revolution. The KGB chief left no doubt that he solidly supported the Gorbachev line. On the domestic front, Chebrikov castigated those cadres who had "lost the taste for the timely implementation of reforms and innovations dictated by life" and called for a "radical improvement in the whole system of management." In foreign policy, as Gorbachev prepared for his Geneva summit with Reagan, Chebrikov criticized "immobility and routine"—presumably an allusion to Gromyko's failures—while endorsing "flexibility and boldness of initiatives."[16]

Other accounts were also squared at about this time. Richard Kosolapov lost his post of chief editor of *Kommunist* in late February. He would teach philosophy at Moscow State University, it was said.[17] *Sovetskaya Rossiya's* chief editor, Mikhail Nenashev, replaced Boris Pastukhov as chairman of the State Committee for Publishing Houses, Printing Plants, and the Book Trade.[18] Valentin Chikin, long a publicist for the Andropov-Gorbachev camp, moved up to become chief editor of *Sovetskaya Rossiya.*[19] Some moves, however, were puzzling. Konstantin Katushev, a former protégé of Brezhnev who had replaced Vorotnikov as ambassador *cum* political exile in Havana in 1982, was brought back to Moscow in late November 1985 to take up the post of chairman of the State Committee for Foreign Economic Relations.

Also initially curious was the case of A. I. Lukyanov, who was identified in late November 1985 as head of the Central Committee's crucial General Department.[20] Lukyanov, who had been appointed first deputy chief of the General Department by October 1983, now replaced Klavdiy Bogolyubov as head of the office that supervises the flow of documents to and from the Politburo. Lukyanov had worked for years under Chernenko in the Secretariat of the Presidium of the Supreme Soviet. Chernenko himself had served as head of the General Department under Brezhnev from 1965 to 1982, and had managed to turn over the post to his long-time deputy Bogolyubov even in the aftermath of Brezhnev's death and Andropov's succession.[21] Nevertheless, despite his long association with Chernenko, it was becoming increasingly evident that Lukyanov must have also had ties to Gorbachev, apparently dating from their days together studying law at Moscow State University.

TURNOVER AT THE TOP

In general, as it prepared for the election of a new Central Committee, the leadership appeared to be unified over the need to put an end to the public infallibility to which certain leaders and organizations had grown accustomed. In his opening speech at the 27th Congress, Gorbachev complained, "At some stage individual republics, *krays*, *oblasts*, and cities were removed from the sphere of criticism. In places this led to the appearance of untouchable *rayons*, collective and state farms, industrial enterprises, and so forth. From all this," he sternly intoned, "one must draw a hard conclusion: In the party there are not and must not be organizations outside control, closed to criticism. There are not and must not be leaders protected from party responsibility.[22]

The new leader made special reference to the party organizations in Uzbekistan and the city of Moscow. Yet it was a far more widespread problem, and the Gorbachev group showed itself determined to subordinate the many geographic and institutional fiefdoms—not only in the peripheries but in Moscow itself—which had evolved in almost autonomous fashion during the long period of Brezhnev's decline.

Even before the congress opened in Moscow, the results of elections of new leading organs at republic-level party congresses witnessed the extent to which Gorbachev had been successful in his campaign against the "untouchables." Of the 2125 full members of the newly elected central committees in the 14 outlying republics, 944—over 44 percent—were newcomers to the job. In Uzbekistan, a particular target of the campaign for renewal, nearly 73 percent of new central committee members were completely new to the position, and the republic's politburo and secretariat were almost completely revamped and purged of office holders from the Brezhnev period.[23]

The composition of the new Central Committee elected at the conclusion of the 27th Congress reflected the magnitude of the changes that Gorbachev's personnel policies had wrought. Nearly 41 percent of its 307 full members were new to the position. Of these 125 newcomers, 94 were new to the Central Committee, 23 had been candidate members, and eight had been members of the Auditing Commission. By comparison, only 25 percent of the 319 full members of the Central Committee elected at the 26th Congress had been newcomers, and of these 81, only 41 were new to the Central Committee.[24]

On the last day of the congress this new Central Committee in turn approved an influx of new members into the top party leadership. Lev Zaykov became a full member of the Politburo in addition to his responsibilities in the Secretariat. Yuriy Solovyov, Zaykov's replacement in Leningrad, was elected a candidate member of the Politburo, as was

Belorussian party First Secretary Nikolay Slyunkov. But it was the Secretariat that registered the greatest change, with the new Central Committee electing five new secretaries: Alexandra Biryukova, a trade union
official; Anatoliy Dobrynin, ambassador in Washington since 1962; and
Central Committee Department heads Vadim Medvedev (Science and
Educational Institutions), Georgiy Razumovskiy (Organizational Party
Work, or cadres), and Alexander Yakovlev (Propaganda).[25]

For those accustomed to the old gang under Brezhnev, the turnover
was massive. The cumulative changes since 1982 were more far-reaching
than anyone would have expected in March 1985 when Gorbachev took
over. All three of his clear opponents at that time had been retired by
the end of 1985: Romanov in July, Tikhonov in September, and Grishin
in December. Now there was a strikingly changed cast of leading and
supporting characters. Of the 12 full members of the Politburo, eight
were new to the position since Brezhnev's time, though not necessarily
to high-level jobs in Moscow. Of the seven candidate members, five
were new. Of the 11 members of the Secretariat, eight were new.

Examining specifically the personnel overseeing foreign policy from
the Secretariat, there were two key changes. Boris Ponomarev, long-
time head of the International Department, was retired and replaced
by Anatoliy Dobrynin, who returned to Moscow after more than 20
years as ambassador in Washington.[26] Konstantin Rusakov was also
retired even before the Congress, and Vadim Medvedev, who had been
Aleksandr Yakovlev's deputy in the Propaganda Department in the early
1970s, assumed the duties of head of the Bloc Relations Department. In
addition, Andrey Aleksandrov-Agentov, long-time chief foreign policy
aide to general secretaries from Brezhnev to Gorbachev, finally bowed
out on the eve of the congress, only to show up later as one of four
"wise elders" comprising a "Group of Counsellors" attached to the
Ministry of Foreign Affairs (MFA).[27] And in early May, Boris Yeltsin
revealed that Zamyatin's International Information Department had
been abolished.[28]

Finally, it was perhaps only coincidental, but nevertheless noteworthy, that the fortunes of Valentin Falin rose again, not long after
Gorbachev's January 15 disarmament statement dropped the Soviet
demand for compensation for British and French forces in INF. Falin's
demotion in early 1983, we speculated, may have been in some way
connected with Kvitsinskiy's willingness at least temporarily to cede
the point on British and French forces in his "walk in the woods"
with Nitze. Germanicist Falin may have argued that this was the best
deal Moscow would likely get, and was ousted from the International
Information Department for his pains. In any event, Falin, who had been
marking time since 1983 as a political observer with *Izvestiya*, was elected
a candidate member of the Central Committee at the 27th Congress and

then promoted in March 1986 to chief of the Novosti Press Agency.[29] In May 1986, after an absence of seven years, Falin would return on a short visit to Bonn, where Kvitsinskiy was now the ambassador.[30]

"RADICAL REFORM"?

On economic matters, Gorbachev went so far as to call for "radical reform" at the congress. He still emphasized, however, that what was involved was changing the "ways and means" of "planned management," rather than changing the very basis of the Soviet economy. But within this context what was needed was the "healthy function of commercial and monetary relations on a socialist basis," in effect the creation of "a new economic mechanism." Gorbachev gave barely perfunctory treatment to the old-time panacea of "socialist competition." "The major task is not the petty regulation of enterprises' activities," Gorbachev told the congress, "but economic stimulation, and the strengthening of the money circulation and financial autonomy, which is itself the best controller."[31] The "five ministries" experiment launched at the beginning of 1984 under Andropov was to apply to all enterprises throughout the economy by the beginning of 1987. The self-financing management of the Volga motor vehicle plant (VAZ), which Gorbachev would visit in April 1986, and of the SUMY machine-building works were held up for emulation.

These were still fairly tepid measures, however, and the most "radical reforms" approved in principle by the new leadership early on primarily concerned the countryside. At the congress Gorbachev endorsed nothing less than the concept of family links and work teams, long denounced by orthodox economists and ideologues as an opening wedge for the return to private farming.[32] Aganbegyan also continued to talk of experiments with small-scale, independent shops in the service sector.[33] But these would all be fiercely resisted, as we shall see, by entrenched lower-level interests and popular prejudices.

Gorbachev had better luck with his investment policy. The Basic Guidelines for the new Five-Year Plan (1986–90) approved by the congress targeted an 18–22 percent increase in capital investment over that attained in the previous five-year planning period. When the final five-year plan was approved by the new Central Committee at the June plenum, the planned growth in capital investment went up even further, to 23.6 percent, thus exceeding even the target range of the Basic Guidelines approved at the congress.

This was in direct contrast to what had happened five years earlier under Brezhnev. The Basic Guidelines for 1981–85 approved at the 26th Party Congress had called for an increase in investment of 12–15 percent over the previous five years. It was already the second consecutive five-year plan to cut the rate of growth of investment. But even so, when Brezhnev announced in November 1981 the actual 1981–85 plan figures, he said that it had been necessary to decrease investment even further by another 30 billion rubles. This would have meant only 10.4 percent growth over the five-year planning period. As it turned out, however, political pressures voided Brezhnev's projected low investment rates almost from the start, and investment actually grew 15.4 percent from 1981 to 1985.

Machine building was especially favored by the new plan. The previous five-year plan had designated only a 20-percent increase in investment for machine building. The 1986–90 plan, as foreshadowed by Gorbachev's speech at the June 1985 Central Committee conference on science and technology and by the Politburo's approval in early August 1985, called for investment in this sector to increase by 80 percent. The sector's growth rate was to exceed that of industry as a whole by 90 percent. By 1990, according to Aganbegyan, "half of the present machine-building industrial equipment will be abandoned and replaced by the equipment now under construction."[34] That the regime could actually accomplish this was doubtful, but at least its intentions were clear.

Both Gorbachev and Ryzhkov described in bitter terms the consequences of the Brezhnev era's technology policy. "The headlong pursuit of imported machinery and technology which obsesses many leaders has a demoralizing effect on collectives of researchers," Ryzhkov told the 27th Congress. "We are far from unwilling to utilize the results of the international division of labor and the exchange of scientific and technical knowledge, but we must rely first and foremost on our own vast scientific potential." Dissipation of investment funds was also still an enormous problem. "We have been talking about this for a long time and yet over 300,000 large and small projects are simultaneously under construction in the country." This number was "intolerably large," warned the premier, and "a number of nonpriority projects may have to be shelved."[35] Four months later Gorbachev would tell the June 1986 party plenum that 100 machine-building projects whose design was outdated would be frozen in an effort "to concentrate investments on the crucial lines of scientific and technological progress."[36]

The consumer did not fare well in the projected plan. In 1985 Gorbachev had argued that neither consumption nor defense spending should be cut. Now the overall share of consumption in national income was actually slated to decline while the proportion devoted to accumulation went up. The leadership, nevertheless, was calculating—erroneously—that in absolute terms the reduced share of consumption would be "largely compensated by the accelerated growth of national income."[37] In addition, the Politburo in September 1985 had approved a long-term consumer goods program, a project launched under Andropov in 1983 after the KAL shootdown.[38] Moreover, under the new five-year plan, one-third of all capital investment would still go to the agroindustrial complex, according to Premier Ryzhkov.[39]

"NEW THINKING" ON NATIONAL SECURITY

Gorbachev framed his discussion of foreign policy at the congress with a sober and conclusive assessment of the neoconservative wave in the West. "Any further substantial shift . . . to the right," he warned, presented a "serious danger." The consequences of such a shift were hard to predict and should not be underrated.[40] This implicitly self-critical judgment seemed to underlie the cardinal reorientation of at least the tactical modalities if not the strategic aims of Soviet diplomacy following Gromyko's transfer from the Foreign Ministry. It was in his congress report that Gorbachev introduced the idea of a "comprehensive system of international security." From now on this would become a flexible grab-bag for any and all Soviet external policies—in effect a device for the political, economic, and other components of Soviet foreign policy to submerge and overshadow its military aspect.

Gorbachev used his report to the 27th Party Congress to refine the military-political formulations he had begun to develop in 1985. "The nature of today's weapons leaves no state any hope of defending itself with military-technical means alone," he said. "Ensuring security is taking the form more and more of a political task and it can only be solved by political means." All the new or refurbished buzzwords, formulations, assessments, and debating flourishes developed by Yakovlev for Gorbachev over the previous year and a half were in it.

Rejection of nuclear deterrence had been implicit in Gorbachev's disarmament statement of January 15, 1986, but he now began to spell it out explicitly, picking up where he left off in Paris. "Security cannot be built forever on a fear of retribution," he told the Congress, "that is, on the doctrine of restraint or deterrence, to say nothing of the absurdity and immorality of a situation when the whole world becomes a nuclear hostage and these doctrines encourage the arms race, which sooner or later is capable of getting out of control."[41] Nevertheless, Gorbachev made it explicitly clear in his Congress speech that the Soviet Union would not engage in unilateral disarmament. "The nature and level" of "reasonable sufficiency," he explained, would "continue to be limited by the positions and actions of the United States and its bloc partners." Thus, "we repeat again and again: The Soviet Union lays no claim to greater security, but will not settle for less."[42]

Gorbachev dealt only briefly with defense needs at the 27th Congress. The party leadership was "devoting unremitting attention to the country's defense capability," he said, and the armed forces had "modern weaponry and technology at their disposal." Then, "We can say today with full responsibility that the USSR's defense might is maintained at a level which allows it to reliably protect the peaceful labor and peaceful lives of Soviet people."[43]

Against this trend in "new thinking," there had been some signs of unease from members of the officer corps. In late 1985 Major General I. Sidelnikov had proposed to strengthen one passage in particular in the draft new Party Program. The language Sidelnikov wanted to amend stated with some restraint that the party "will make every effort to ensure that the USSR Armed Forces are at a level excluding strategic superiority on the part of imperialism's forces." Sidelnikov proposed that it be reworded to state that the "CPSU will continue to take unfailing care to ensure that the Armed Forces possess all the modern means for the motherland's defense."[44] The document finally approved by the 27th Party Congress, however, ignored Sidelnikov's suggestion and stuck to the draft language. Nevertheless, both the draft and final Party Program called for the party to "pay unremitting attention to reinforcing the USSR's defense might and strengthening its security." To this, the final version added the obligation to do the same for the "readiness of the Armed Forces to rout any aggressor."[45]

Significantly, it was these passages which Defense Minister Sokolov chose to cite in his speech to the congress, rather than those in Gorbachev's report. Sokolov ignored Gorbachev's emphasis on political efforts to enhance Soviet security, stating instead that since World War II the Soviet "armed forces have always been and remain the reliable guarantor of peace and the socialist fatherland's security."[46] But there was some ambiguity in the defense minister's stance. His Order of the Day on Armed Forces Day on the eve of the congress spoke only of "maintaining" defense capabilities and combat might "at the requisite level," rather than "strengthening" them. But on Victory Day in May, Sokolov would revert to "strengthening."[47]

THE AFGHAN "SORE"

Gorbachev drew widespread attention to the issue of Afghanistan at the congress by graphically describing it as a "running sore." It was not Soviet troops, of course, which had infected the wound, but the forces of "counterrevolution and imperialism." Nevertheless, Gorbachev declared that "we would like in the near future to bring the Soviet forces—situated in Afghanistan at the request of its government—back to their homeland." According to the general secretary, "The time scale for their step-by-step withdrawal has been worked out with the Afghan side," and it could go into effect "as soon as a political settlement has been achieved which will provide for a real end to and reliably guarantee a non-renewal of the outside armed interference in the internal affairs of the DRA."[48]

Gorbachev's comments capped a number of significant though seemingly contradictory moves since his takeover as general secretary and set the stage for more. Diplomatically, the fifth round of talks in Geneva, held August 26–30, 1985, had not broken the procedural impasse over the timing of when of the four "instruments" of the peace accords under negotiation would come into force. On December 10, 1985, however, after the summit in Geneva between Reagan and Gorbachev, the United States had expressed its willingness in principle to guarantee an Afghan accord—as long as the issue of the withdrawal of Soviet troops and its interrelationship with the other instruments of the accord on noninterference and the return of refugees were resolved. Following this, at the brief sixth round of Geneva proximity talks, December 16 and 19, 1985, the Afghans reportedly gave Cordovez a withdrawal timetable—presumably the one alluded to by Gorbachev in his congress speech. They insisted, however, that they would discuss it with Pakistan only in direct negotiations, which Pakistan refused to do lest it imply official recognition of the Kabul regime.[49]

Militarily, Gorbachev in July 1985 had appointed General Mikhail Zaytsev as commander of the Southern Theater of Military Operations (TMO). At about the same time apparently, Lieutenant General Boris Gromov was named commander of the "limited contingent of Soviet troops in Afghanistan"—in other words, of the 40th Army.[50] The transfer of Zaytsev from the Group of Soviet Forces in Germany (GSFG) to Tashkent was only one of several major moves in Gorbachev's reshuffle of the high command after his meeting with the military in Minsk. It therefore attracted far less attention than the appointment of Maksimov, Zaytsev's predecessor at Southern TMO headquarters, to replace Tolubko as head of the Strategic Rocket Forces (SRF).

Later there would be reports that Gorbachev had given Zaytsev only one or two years to turn the situation around in Afghanistan.[51] Indeed, escalated cross-border attacks against Pakistan appeared to presage more rather than less violence in the region. It was easy to conclude that the new Gorbachev leadership thought military victory was still possible. But Zaytsev's efforts more likely camouflaged the rethinking and preparation of diplomatic alternatives that was probably going on in the Kremlin.

With the benefit of hindsight it seems plausible to argue that Gorbachev and his supporters had already embarked on a multipronged effort designed to extricate the USSR from Afghanistan. The military campaign was aimed at intimidating Pakistan, slowing the flow of arms to the *mujahidin*, and sapping the strength and morale of the resistance. Attainments of these goals, in turn, would provide cover and buy time for Moscow to achieve the removal of Afghan leader Babrak Karmal and his replacement (by May 1986) by the more flexible Najib. Najib would then have some breathing room to consolidate his power and court potential collaborators with a strengthened PDPA. If successful, Moscow and Kabul would end up in a much better position for eventual accelerated bargaining designed to assure the PDPA a dominant role in Kabul even after a Soviet troop withdrawal. And if the effort failed, the Gorbachev leadership would at least have protected itself from the charge that it had not explored the military option fully before getting out with whatever diplomatic deal it could get.

Indeed, for all its professed desire to get out, the Gorbachev leadership was still insisting on the legitimacy of the Kabul regime and the correctness of the Soviet intervention. It was also still insisting on a veto power over the composition of any future regime in Kabul, and—although not a formal part of one of the four instruments of the peace accord under discussion—demanding that the internal conflict in Afghanistan be resolved to Soviet satisfaction and that outside interference cease before any Soviet withdrawal begin. Nevertheless, Gorbachev's "running sore" imagery at the congress and his mention of a timetable for withdrawal for the first time suggested at least a glimmer of urgency—altogether nonexistent in Soviet public statements up to this time.

"PURIFICATION": HOW DEEP, HOW MUCH, HOW FAST?

On two key domestic issues the congress exposed sharply divergent viewpoints within the leadership: the morality of party privileges, and the extent of the corruption of the apparatus and therefore the prospects of reforming it. More than two years later, well after Yeltsin's October 1987 clash with Ligachev and his November 1987 ouster from the leadership, the journalist and Yeltsin ally Mikhail Poltoranin would explain the core of their differences. Ligachev believed that "existing privileges [of the party *nomenklatura*] must not be touched, but the conditions of those who, as yet, do not enjoy certain opportunities must be improved." Ligachev was the "custodian" of the party apparatus. "He believes that the apparatus can constitute the motive force behind *perestroika*," according to Poltoranin. "Yeltsin, on the other hand, feels that the party apparatus—and not just in Moscow—is too compromised and argues that it must be removed, just as you do with topsoil contaminated by radiation."[52]

In 1985–86, while moving with almost breathless ruthlessness on the cadre front as it prepared for the congress, the Gorbachev leadership defined its targets largely on an individual basis and drew back from making wider generalizations about the degradation of the bureaucratic apparatus as a whole. But the more fundamental backstage pulling and hauling over how to assess and attack the corruption endemic in the entrenched bureaucracies was exposed shortly before the opening of the 27th Party Congress, and then with Boris Yeltsin's fiery speech spilled over into the congress itself.

On February 13, under the headline "Purification," *Pravda* printed a trenchant review of letters by correspondent T. Samolis. Several of the letters suggested there should be a "purge" of what one writer (V. Ivanov from Tula) described as the "immovable, inert, and flabby 'party-administrative stratum,'" which was not ready for "radical changes" and was addicted to privileges.[53] In commenting on the letters, Samolis rejected the notion of "mass purges" in favor of "purification" on a "strictly individual" basis. Nevertheless, her article provoked strong reactions, many of them negative. Two days later *Pravda's* editorial board felt compelled explicitly to side with a reader who criticized V. Ivanov's letter for making "generalizations on the basis of individual impressions." The editorial board said it was determined in the future to write more about the "best" party, soviet, and managerial cadres.[54]

When the congress finally opened with Gorbachev's report on February 25, the general secretary dealt gingerly with the purification issue. Gorbachev contended that the party was "freeing itself of persons who have compromised themselves by their poor work and unworthy behavior," and asserted that "I do not think there is any need for a special campaign to purge the ranks of the CPSU." New Moscow Party Chief Yeltsin, however, clearly alluded to and strongly endorsed V. Ivanov's unflattering description of the party-state apparatus that Samolis had quoted in her article. "Why even now does the demand for radical changes get bogged down in an inert stratum of time-servers with party cards?" Yeltsin asked, paraphrasing Ivanov. It was necessary, Yeltsin continued, at "all levels" of the apparatus to do away with any "unjustified" benefits, revive collegiality in party work, and not allow to develop "even the beginnings of a boss syndrome."[55]

Volgograd party leader Vladimir Kalashnikov, however, who had worked under Gorbachev in Stavropol in the 1970s as a regional secretary, disputed Yeltsin-Ivanov though without mentioning either directly. The party was already purging itself, asserted Kalashnikov. Yet "on the pretext of holding a 'frank discussion,'" he complained bitterly, "the cadres of some 'immobile, inert, and unprogressive party-administrative stratum' must be vilified simply for sensation's sake. (applause) It is not hard to see what some writers have in mind when they do that."[56] Gromyko, like Kalashnikov, drew the distinction between "criticism" and "vilification of honest communists." Just as he had done when nominating Gorbachev for general secretary a year earlier, Gromyko warned against resorting to the "fantasy of cracks in our party and in Soviet society."[57]

Ligachev was more restrained than Kalashnikov and Gromyko yet clearly on the same side of the divide. While encouraging further criticism and self-criticism, Ligachev in his congress speech commented that some newspapers, including *Pravda*, had "unfortunately . . . permitted lapses."[58] Although made almost in passing, Ligachev's negative allusion to the Samolis article was unmistakable. Aliyev, interestingly, probably endeared himself to Ligachev by denying at a press conference that party leaders enjoyed any special privileges.[59]

A year after the congress, *Pravda* editor Viktor Afanasyev told an Italian interviewer, "we were criticized not for talking about privileges but for unskillful editing of the item. There appeared to be a huge stratum of bureaucrats between the Central Committee and the working class."[60] Two years later, however, in the wake of the affair over the neo-Stalinist letter Nina Andreyeva to *Sovetskaya Rossiya* and the decline in Ligachev's fortunes, Afanasyev would portray the contretemps over publication of "Purification" more as a result of principle and civic courage than of sloppy editing. "That was a critical article based on letters from readers," he would say in an interview on Press Day. "What a dressing-down I got for that 'purification'! At the 27th Congress *Pravda* was criticized and very high-level bosses really raked me over the coals on that occasion. However, that was an article of principle; in fact it was the beginning of *glasnost*."[61]

Meanwhile, on a different issue, Ligachev some months before the 27th Congress had struck what appeared to be a rather conservative note when he expounded in the journal *Kommunist* on the draft Party Program and Rules approved by the October plenum for public discussion. On what would become a key issue over a year later at the January 1987 plenum on cadres and democratization, Ligachev endorsed the extension of voting by show of hands, rather than by secret ballot, of leadership organs throughout the party and not just in its grass-roots organizations. This, he said, would "contribute to the establishment of frankness and principledness in relations between communists."[62] Although this was interpreted by some as indicative of Ligachev's antireform bias, in the atmosphere leading up to the Party Congress, with heads rolling right and left day after day, Ligachev's proposal would have taken the shield of secrecy away from the old guard seeking to frustrate the new regime's cadre preferences. Ligachev's article, moreover, had somewhat of an *ex officio* rather than purely personal character. It appeared in the same issue of *Kommunist* which published the draft program and rules and thus was intended as an authoritative explication of them.

For now, the focus of the contretemps at the congress was clear, yet the dispute was replete with ambiguities, unanswered questions, and what would be for the next several years an enduring pattern. Yeltsin had thrown down the gauntlet before the party-state apparatus on the cardinal question of its readiness to engage in radical reform for the benefit of the country, rather than subverting reforms in order to protect its self-interests. But Yeltsin had been opposed by Ligachev and not supported, at least in public, by Gorbachev. Ligachev, furthermore, would subsequently claim to have sponsored Yeltsin's move to Moscow from Sverdlovsk and his recent elevation into the central party leadership. Yet Yeltsin was already crossing swords with Ligachev, and the latter was already emerging as the radical Yeltsin's chief nemesis. Ligachev, however, was not opposed to a vigorous shake-up of the party apparatus; but he fundamentally resisted any questioning of the right of the party to occupy the leading role in Soviet political life. And Gorbachev, while probably working behind the scenes to push the spectrum of leadership opinion in Yeltsin's direction, in public displayed party discipline by adhering to a centrist consensus closer to Ligachev's views.

The leadership's caution (except for Yeltsin) in its diagnosis of the ills besetting the party apparatus—and thus in its prescription and prognosis for recovery—clearly risked disaffecting a key source of support for radical change: the creative and scientific intelligentsia. A "manifesto" put together in November 1985 by a group calling itself the Movement for Socialist Renewal urged drastic rather than incremental change. "The crisis of the economic system is closely connected to the political crisis, which concerns such fundamental constitutional principles of the socialist state as the freedom of speech, press and assembly, of personal immunity, private correspondence and telephone calls, and the freedom to join organizations," declared the as-yet-unpublicized document. "It is necessary, before it is too late, for the country and the Soviet people to take urgent measures of a revolutionary nature to rebuild the economic foundations of the socialist structure, and to carry out the necessary changes in its superstructure which can lead Soviet society from its blind alley."[63]

Gorbachev, it would later be reported, was well acquainted with the "manifesto." Its analysis was said to have resulted from discussions within consultant groups which the general secretary had himself promoted. But Gorbachev would shy away from endorsing anything resembling its ideas until mid-1986, when the document coincidentally and probably not accidentally found its way into the public domain as the Gorbachev leadership embarked on a new stage of radicalization.

NOTES

1. *Pravda*, February 8, 1986 (FBIS-SOV, February 10, 1986, CC 1).

2. Moscow Domestic Service, October 15, 1985 (FBIS-SOV, October 16, 1985, R 3).

3. Moscow Domestic Service, June 10, 1985 (FBIS-SOV, June 11, 1985, R 9). For the FBIS Editorial Report on the June 15, 1985, Moscow Television Service broadcast of the film, see FBIS-SOV, June 20, 1985, R 3–13.

4. AFP, November 11, 1985 (FBIS-SOV, November 12, 1985, R 10–11).

5. *Pravda*, November 10, 1985 (FBIS-SOV, November 13, 1985, R 9).

6. "Taboo," *Novyy Mir*, September 1985; and "Suppose-Something-Goes-Wrongers," *Pravda*, September 9, 1985.

7. In *Pravda*, October 21, 1962. See Michel Tatu, *Power in the Kremlin* (New York: Viking, 1970), 248–49.

8. *Pravda*, February 8, 1986 (FBIS-SOV, February 10, 1986, CC 5).

9. *Mainichi Shimbun*, December 25, 1985, and AFP, January 6, 1986 (FBIS-SOV, January 8, 1986, R 6–7).

10. *Izvestiya*, August 22, 1986 (FBIS-SOV, August 26, 1986, R 11).

11. TASS, June 15, 1987 (FBIS-SOV, June 15, 1987, R 7–8).

12. Kyodo, February 20, 1986 (FBIS-SOV, February 21, 1986, R 3).

13. *Izvestiya*, January 26, 1986 (FBIS-SOV, January 27, 1986, R 1).

14. AFP, March 9, 1986 (FBIS-SOV, March 11, 1986, S 1).

15. *Izvestiya*, February 6, 1986 (FBIS-SOV, February 7, 1986, R 4).

16. *Pravda*, November 7, 1985 (FBIS-SOV, November 7, 1985, O 1–11).

17. AFP, February 24, 1986 (FBIS-SOV, February 24, 1986, R 2). *Kommunist*, no. 4 (1986), signed to press on March 11, listed I. T. Frolov as the new chief editor.

18. *Izvestiya*, February 25, 1986 (FBIS-SOV, February 25, 1986, R 1).

19. First identified as such in *Moskovskaya Pravda*, April 23, 1986.

20. *Pravda*, November 29, 1985.

21. AFP, November 29, 1985 (FBIS-SOV, December 5, 1985, R 3).

22. Moscow Television Service, February 25, 1986 (FBIS-SOV, February 26, 1986, Supplement no. 41, O 36).

23. AFP, February 17, 1986 (FBIS-SOV, February 18, 1986, R 2).

24. See Martin McCauley, "Gorbachev as Leader," in Martin McCauley, ed., *The Soviet Union under Gorbachev* (New York: St. Martin's, 1987), Table 1.2, p. 22.

25. TASS, March 6, 1986 (FBIS-SOV, March 6, 1986, O 17). No one was dropped from the Politburo except for candidate members Vladlem Kuznetsov, age 85, and Boris Ponomarev, age 81. Ponomarev also left the Secretariat, as well as Ivan Kapitonov, who became chairman of the party Central Auditing Commission. Rusakov had already been retired from the Secretariat at the pre-Congress plenum on February 18.

26. Dobrynin was first identified as head of the International Department when he and Zagladin met with an Italian Communist Party (PCI) delegation (TASS, June 9, 1986 [FBIS-SOV, June 10, 1986, G 3–4].

27. *Vestnik Ministerstva Inostrannykh Del SSSR* [Herald of the USSR Foreign Ministry], no. 1 August 5, 1987, 68.

28. *Die Zeit*, May 9, 1986 (FBIS-SOV, May 8, 1986, G 6). By this time Zamyatin had been appointed ambassador to the United Kingdom (TASS, April 25, 1986 [FBIS-SOV, April 28, 1986, G 3]).

29. TASS, March 10, 1986 (FBIS-SOV, March 11, 1986, S 1).

30. *General-Anzeiger*, May 31/June 1, 1986 (FBIS-SOV, June 6, 1986, CC 2).

31. Moscow Television Service, February 25, 1986 (FBIS-SOV, February 26, 1986, Supplement no. 41, O 15–19).

32. Moscow Television Service, February 25, 1986 (FBIS-SOV, February 26, 1986, O 14).

33. *Asahi Shimbun*, March 14, 1986.

34. Ibid.

35. *Pravda*, March 4, 1986 (FBIS-SOV, March 5, 1986, O 16 and 18).

36. *Pravda*, June 17, 1986 (FBIS-SOV, June 18, 1986, R 15).

37. G. Sarkisyan, *Sotsialisticheskaya Industriya*, April 4, 1986 (FBIS-SOV, April 10, 1986, R 9).

38. Moscow Domestic Service, September 19, 1985 (FBIS-SOV, September 20, 1985, R 1).

39. *Pravda*, March 4, 1986 (FBIS-SOV, March 5, 1986, O 17).

40. Moscow Television Service, February 25, 1986 (FBIS-SOV, February 26, 1986, Supplement no. 41, O 6).

41. Moscow Television Service, February 25, 1986 (FBIS-SOV, February 26, 1986, Supplement, O 30).

42. Moscow Television Service, February 25, 1986 (FBIS-SOV, February 26, 1986, Supplement, O 30). Deputy Defense Minister for armaments V. Shabanov elaborated in great detail on the hardware implications of this point in *Red Star*, August 15, 1986 (FBIS-SOV, August 25, 1986, V 1–6).

43. *Pravda*, February 26, 1986 (FBIS-SOV, February 26, 1986, Supplement no. 41, O 28).

44. *Red Star*, December 25, 1985 (FBIS-SOV, January 8, 1986, R 1–3).

45. *Pravda*, March 7, 1986 (FBIS-SOV, March 10, 1986, Supplement no. 51, O 12).

46. *Pravda*, March 2, 1986.

47. *Red Star*, February 23 and May 9, 1986 (FBIS-SOV, February 24 and May 15, 1986, V 4 and R 2, respectively).

48. Moscow Television Service, February 25, 1986 (FBIS-SOV, February 26, 1986, Supplement no. 41, O 31).

49. Cronin, *Afghanistan Peace Talks*, 18–23.

50. In an interview in the Bulgarian paper *Rabotnichesko Delo*, May 20, 1988 (FBIS-SOV, May 27, 1988, 29–30), Gromov was said to have held this position "for the last 3 years."

51. Oberdorfer, "Afghanistan."

52. *Corriere della Sera*, May 12, 1988.

53. *Pravda*, February 13, 1986 (FBIS-SOV, February 14, 1986, R 11–13).

54. *Pravda*, February 15, 1986.

55. *Pravda*, February 27, 1986 (FBIS-SOV, February 27, 1986, Supplement 042, O 19–21).

56. *Pravda*, March 2, 1986 (FBIS-SOV, March 5, 1986, O 4–6).

57. *Pravda*, February 27, 1986 (FBIS-SOV, February 28, 1986, Supplement 043, O 9–13).

58. *Pravda*, February 28, 1986 (FBIS-SOV, February 28, 1986, Supplement 043, O 20–23).

59. AFP, February 27, 1986 (FBIS-SOV, February 28, 1986, Party Congress Supplement, O 33).

60. *La Stampa*, February 24, 1987.

61. Moscow Domestic Service, May 5, 1988 (FBIS-SOV, May 6, 1988, 39).

62. *Kommunist*, no. 16 (November 1985): 82–83, (signed to press November 4).

63. The "Manifesto" was signed November 21, 1985. It was first publicized in July 1986 by the American television correspondent Steve Hurst and by Martin Walker in *The Guardian*, July 22, 1986.

Part II

Gorbachev: Radicalization

Overview

Had Gorbachev's grand coalition collapsed after the 27th Party Congress, Gorbachev would probably have gone down in history as a young and dynamic leader who might have been able, had he survived, to inject new life into familiar and oppressive Soviet structures—but not much more. Instead, a year after coming to power, Gorbachev and his supporters began to move beyond the narrow scope of everyday politics and set their sights on truly revolutionary goals.

To this end, Gorbachev's first year in power had been more critically important than at first apparent. Its widespread cadre changes and basic new themes and ideological formulations justified and set the stage for a new era in Soviet politics and diplomacy. Just months after the conclusion of the Party Congress, the Gorbachev regime began to effect the great turn in contemporary Soviet politics, the subject of Part II: democratization, economic reform, and the first parliamentary elections with a choice since 1917; the Reykjavik, Washington, and Moscow summits; and the INF Treaty, withdrawal from Afghanistan, and unilateral defense cuts. These monumental undertakings were virtually unimaginable when Gorbachev succeeded Chernenko in March 1985, and staggering in the political energies and will power they demanded in order to be accomplished.

Observers of this period often fell into the trap of ascribing every reformist initiative to Gorbachev and all submerged resistance to Ligachev. Branding Ligachev a "conservative" and even a "neo-Stalinist," however, greatly clouded and misleads analysis of the real situation. Ligachev in fact was a key pillar and locomotive of the new regime as it entered its more radical phase. There were differences between Ligachev and Gorbachev, to be sure. But to be blinded by them was as big a mistake as being blind to them. In the short run, at least, their divergent views on the ultimate ends of the revolution they were making did not preclude close cooperation on pressing, immediate tasks. The immensity of the morass left by the Brezhnev era meant there was much Ligachev and Gorbachev could do together before having to face up to their growing differences, of which they may not even have been fully aware at the beginning.

95

Publicly, at least, Ligachev and Gorbachev managed to harmonize their positions rather successfully until some months past the January 1987 plenum on cadres and democratization. In July 1986 in Voronezh Ligachev called on party secretaries to take the initiative and get closer to the people, and Gorbachev appealed to the population in Khabarovsk to pressure local officials to heed the new winds from Moscow. At the time, these were probably simply two sides of the same coin. But as time went on, they developed into two different, competing coins. Increasingly both leaders strove to define in their own way the mandate of the January plenum and to control the attendance at and agenda of the 19th Party Conference, scheduled to open in late June 1988. Both politicians stressed the need for a revitalized and reformed party within the context of greater democratization. But while Gorbachev eventually argued for a substantial redefinition and reconfiguration of decision-making prerogatives away from the party apparatus and toward the ministerial and Supreme Soviet structure, Ligachev began ever more insistently to defend the party's leading role.

As the differences on this key point opened up and created tensions, they did not necessarily spill over into other areas. In foreign policy, even as Gorbachev and Ligachev became estranged in 1987, the Soviet leadership approved a global double-zero INF Treaty with the United States and, even more remarkably, worked its way toward the April 1988 accords on the pullout of Soviet troops from Afghanistan. It was only in August 1988 that Ligachev decided to challenge publicly the Gorbachev view that "class struggle" was increasingly of secondary importance to common global problems. Even on the domestic issues of *glasnost* and economic reform, though there were definite shades of differences over how much to loosen the system, the spectrum of leadership opinion stretching from Ligachev to Yakovlev was in basic agreement on the need for fundamental changes from the previous era.

In both domestic and foreign affairs, Gorbachev's modus operandi was to insist on putting uncomfortable but pressing issues on the agenda and then persistently to work to develop a leadership consensus on a solution. In the context of a political culture in which a change in policy is traditionally first signaled by a change in rhetoric, the language of Gorbachev's early charm diplomacy was actually part of the process of putting down markers for internal debate and laying the groundwork for many of the changes that would later take the world by surprise. Even during his first year in power, Gorbachev had forced issues rather than let them fester, albeit doing so with careful consideration not to overload the agenda and provoke more opposition than support for his evolving ideas.

As with democratization on the domestic side, outside observers were continually caught up short by the inability to realize or believe just how radical the Gorbachev leadership's foreign policy goals were. But to insiders, the lines of continuity with politics as they had evolved since the time of Andropov must have been much more apparent. Even at the height of the INF crisis in 1983, there had been indications of schools of opinion within the Soviet leadership—both civilian and military—that would have supported markedly different policies. On both domestic policy and diplomacy, it was astonishing to reread dissident historian Roy Medvedev's *On Socialist Democracy*, written in 1970–71, and to discover the expanse of common ground between what Medvedev then advocated and what the Gorbachev leadership now appeared intent on putting into place.[1]

As ragged as it appeared to some observers, the evolution of foreign policy under Gorbachev was fairly logically structured, given the Soviet and American political calendars. The ideological underpinnings for new policies had to be blessed by the 27th Party Congress, and only after that could they be operationalized. The INF Treaty stood the best chance of being concluded and ratified if all this could be accomplished before the U.S. presidential conventions in summer 1988. After that there would be at least a year of uncertain decision making in Washington, first because of the distractions of a presidential campaign and then because of the time needed by a new administration to sort itself out and become organized for business. By the same token, once the decision to withdraw Soviet forces from Afghanistan had been made in principle, it was best to conclude the Geneva accords with the United States while Reagan was still the commanding presence in American politics. And a unilateral reduction of Soviet troops made the most sense economically if its outlines were decided in time for drafters of the next five-year plan to take them into account.

The new leadership's freedom to maneuver proved far less on domestic economic issues than on foreign policy. After the 27th Party Congress its intention was apparently to focus attention first on formulating the substance of "radical reform" of economic management. Finding the resistance to change even more tenacious than it had assumed, however, the leadership launched a campaign over the heads of its own bureaucrats in order to pressure them from below as well as from above. Two campaigns developed along parallel tracks, but with the cadre reform *cum* democratization campaign pushed ahead of the effort aimed at developing a comprehensive program for "radical" restructuring of economic management.

Democratization and *glasnost* became the order of the day; after the opposition had been softened, the leadership would switch back to concentrating on economic reform. *Glasnost* and democratization were at first intended by Gorbachev and his supporters strictly as social engineering, feedback mechanisms enabling the central leadership better to control, monitor, and pressure the peripheries. Khrushchev had taken some tentative steps toward replacing Stalin's methods of mass terror and permanent purges with a measure of *glasnost* and democratization. But Brezhnev then built his power on a policy of cadre stability which tolerated widespread hoodwinking of the center by local party organs in return for an unending stream of tribute and the semblance of control. After the Brezhnev era there was a pressing need to break the grip of the apparatus with political reform in order to clear the way for economic reform.

Another way to understand the shift to radicalism was to compare the Soviet experience with that of China under Mao Zedong and then Deng Xiaoping—putting aside for the moment the June 1989 Tiananmen Square massacre and suppression of the Chinese prodemocracy movement. Although of a vastly more humane and different order of magnitude, Gorbachev's democratization was intended as the functional equivalent of the shake-up of officialdom achieved by Mao's Cultural Revolution but with Deng's reformist economic goals ultimately in mind. Unfortunately, Gorbachev had to embody both Mao and Deng, and to do so not sequentially but simultaneously. The Brezhnev era of "stagnation," to be sure, had generated a strong desire for change but had left the apparatus more entrenched than ever and well positioned to block reforms. The very stability of the Brezhnev period assured that the unsettling nature of reforms would be less well received in the post-Brezhnev USSR than in post-Mao China, where after the chaos of the Cultural Revolution the Deng reforms had meant not only welcome stability but also more to eat. In China, moreover, the habits of a market economy had still not been extinguished after 30 years of communist rule. In contrast, Gorbachev's attempts at radical reform came 70 years after the Russian Revolution, and they meant the unleashing of turmoil rather than the restoration of normalcy. Much pent-up desire for change quickly dissipated when confronted with the confusion, uncertainty, and fear for the future spawned by the reality of change.

As a result, Gorbachev was forced to maneuver. Tinkering had no chance of solving the country's fundamental economic imbalances, but going too far in pressing for change courted disaster by destabilizing not only the structure of state power but also the comfort of traditional belief systems. Gorbachev proved a brilliant tactician, never pressing his luck too far, inventing repeated tests and challenges designed to wear down his detractors while advancing his own program, and when necessary always pulling back to a centrist position from which to rebuild a more radical consensus for change. Nevertheless, after four years of pressure from Gorbachev, the bureaucracies in 1989 still seemed remarkably adept at co-opting and smothering economic *perestroika*, and the sense of economic crisis seemed more acute than ever.

Gorbachev and his supporters were sometimes faulted for not starting economic reform in the countryside. If the Chinese model had been followed, went the argument, a liberalization of Soviet agriculture could have quickly increased food production and soon won the Soviet population over to *perestroika*. Given a choice, Gorbachev probably would have done just that. But it was precisely in the countryside that the opposition from the regime's own officials was most tenacious and most difficult to neutralize. And as for the population, five decades after the brutalities of collectivization, Soviet poll takers not surprisingly found that "on domestic issues, . . . the rural population and smaller cities tend to be more conservative."[2] It was far easier at the beginning for Gorbachev to gain the support of conservatives for a program aimed at revitalizing industry on the essentially Stalinist basis of raising the rate of investment. A major push on agriculture would have to be put off until the Gorbachev leadership felt itself more secure.

The leadership thus gambled on a new political dynamic generating grass-roots pressure on local officials. But there was an inherent tension between Gorbachev's attempts to use the population and the intelligentsia to goad the apparat, and his need during this transition period to use this same apparat to pursue and implement his programs. Like it or not, nearly twenty million bureaucrats could not be replaced overnight, and Gorbachev and his colleagues were compelled to work through them even while going around them in order to stimulate pressure from below. Nationality tensions in the Caucasus and movements toward regional autonomy in the Baltics, moreover, soon faced the leadership squarely with the question of whether the permissiveness of democratization was simply inflaming old disputes and divisions rather than leading to a new age of consensus politics. Local leaders quickly learned to use Moscow's fears of inflaming local nationalistic sentiments to deter or postpone attempts by Moscow to impose its will.

Until the political process was finally opened to the public through elections to a reformed Supreme Soviet structure in 1989, most citizens remained either apathetic or cynical, and in either case on guard about the whole process. Rather than enthusiastically embracing reform, they perceived themselves to be the utilitarian object of Gorbachev's pitch who would quickly be abandoned and exposed to the revenge of local officialdom should it fail, or who would have to pay with the unrecompensed sweat of their brows to make economic *perestroika* succeed. In this regard, the landmark elections were remarkable but possibly misleading. Yeltsin's resounding victory and the defeat of scores of regional party secretaries certainly reflected widespread distaste for apparatchiks and their privileges but probably little taste for real economic reform. Nevertheless, the elections marked the beginning of a new political process that, if allowed to continue, might conceivably change even this.

NOTES

1. Roy A. Medvedev, *On Socialist Democracy* (New York: Alfred A. Knopf, 1975).

2. *New York Times*, May 27, 1988.

Chapter 6 ───────────────────

No More "Mr. Nyet"

───────────────────────────

After the 27th Party Congress, Gorbachev launched the radicalized second phase of his tenure in office with new movement in foreign and security policies—well in advance of kicking off a new campaign on cadres on the home front. By now Gorbachev's dynamic use of initiatives abroad and at home to reinforce each other was becoming a pattern. In October-November 1985 the general secretary shuttled back and forth between summits in Paris and Geneva and a Central Committee plenum and Supreme Soviet session at home. As Gorbachev prepared for the upcoming party congress, he used the atmospherics generated by the summits as a backdrop for the release of a significantly revised new edition of the Party Program and a proinvestment, "hold the line on defense" 12th Five-Year Plan (1986–90).

Following this same formula, Gorbachev again set in motion some significant departures from the foreign policies of the Gromyko era, and then only later against this background launched what would turn out to be the key political and economic reforms of this "radicalization" phase. The beginning of this second phase probably would have come a month or so earlier had it not been for the April 26 nuclear power plant disaster in Chernobyl, not far from the Ukrainian capital of Kiev. Nevertheless, it finally got under-way with a speech by Gorbachev on May 23 at the MFA.

A short TASS report at the time made clear that Gorbachev had been critical of Soviet diplomacy under Gromyko. But the decision not immediately, if ever, to release the text of Gorbachev's remarks was already an indication—against the background of the emphasis on *glasnost*—that something truly serious was afoot. Only a year later would it be revealed how truly stunning and predictive the speech had been. In the operational sense it marked the beginning of a determined entering into a post-Gromyko phase of Soviet foreign policy. In his first year Gorbachev had put in place the new ideological principles and justifications of "new thinking," but skeptics could still maintain that the changes in Soviet foreign policy were only charm diplomacy deep. Now real movement in Soviet positions on major issues finally showed conclusively that the days of Gromyko's tight grip on the Foreign Ministry had come to an end.

Soviet foreign policy at last began to acquire an activism that extended well below the activities of only Gorbachev and Shevardnadze at the top. Even without the immediate availability of the text of Gorbachev's speech, its policy ramifications began to be apparent with the unveiling of new disarmament proposals in Geneva in late May and June; with Gorbachev's speech in Vladivostok in the Far East in late July; and with Shevardnadze's speech at the UN General Assembly that fall.

At the same time, a major reorganization got under way at the Foreign Ministry and in the two Central Committee departments primarily responsible for foreign affairs. Moreover, encroaching on what previously had been the prerogatives primarily of the Defense Ministry and General Staff, Dobrynin and others now gave the green light to civilian experts to involve themselves in the formulation of national security and military-political options.

BAITING GROMYKO

The first inkling of major, across-the-board changes in Soviet diplomacy going beyond the new rhetorical formulations and the tentative testing of the waters of Gorbachev's first year in power came on May 23, 1986, when Gorbachev delivered a "major" speech at the Foreign Ministry. The conference the general secretary addressed was attended not only by diplomats but by trade-and-aid officials—in other words, by representatives of the entire bureaucratic empire Gromyko had headed since his elevation to first deputy premier in March 1983. Now, however, the former foreign minister seemed more than ever in eclipse, even physically: on a trip to Sverdlovsk the month before, he had caught a "chill"[1]; and he was subsequently the only member of the leadership to miss the Lenin Day ceremonies on April 22 at which his successor, Shevardnadze, was the featured speaker.

The year before, in his February 20, 1985, election speech, Gorbachev had praised Soviet diplomacy for its role in securing favorable shifts in world politics over the previous four decades—that is, during Gromyko's long career as a top-ranked diplomat and foreign minister. This time he was much less complimentary. Although the text of Gorbachev's speech was not made public, and excerpts of its main points would not be published until mid-1987, TASS at the time reported that the general secretary had examined "Soviet diplomacy in recent years . . . critically and with party-style exactingness."[2]

Several days before, Dobrynin had given what was in effect a preview of one of the main themes of Gorbachev's upcoming remarks.

Speaking in Alma-Ata, Dobrynin said, "In foreign policy matters, as in domestic matters, what is required is the growing dynamism, intensive activity and the increased effectiveness of the measures being implemented in support of peace and disarmament."[3] Later, after the convocation at the Foreign Ministry, Burlatskiy was more to the point. Gorbachev had stressed the need for "revitalization of diplomatic activity, overcoming the present blind alley state of Soviet diplomacy and strengthening diplomatic activity to actually achieve specific results." Burlatskiy told interviewers in Japan that "in all areas, a fresh breeze is necessary."[4]

Extensive portions of Gorbachev's speech were finally published in August 1987. They confirmed the intimations of Dobrynin and Burlatskiy. "Soviet diplomacy must help the country's domestic development," Gorbachev told his Foreign Ministry audience. At the same time, "the key to success in foreign policy matters lies in . . . the health of Soviet society and our economy." The general secretary demanded that the "forms and content" of Soviet diplomacy be "modernized," and he warned that the Central Committee would "monitor strictly" the progress of restructuring in the foreign service.

In his *tour d'horizon*, Gorbachev had again underscored the priority of relations with "socialist" countries, singling out China. He pointedly emphasized that "it should not be felt that we can teach all of them. No one has given us that right." And he called for greater consideration of the views of Soviet allies and their greater involvement in the formulation of bloc foreign policy.

Gorbachev next turned to arms control issues, mentioning the idea of a "comprehensive system of international security" and his January 15, 1986, proposals. Judging from the excerpts later published, it could be speculated that he had intimated a radically new approach to disarmament when he said, "It is necessary to keep a careful watch to assure that our fundamental proposals aimed at disarmament and the limitation of the arms race are reinforced within the shortest possible periods of time by concrete recommendations at the appropriate negotiations." But those excerpts left out the most policy-predictive passage, revealed only two years later by Shevardnadze, who asserted that Gorbachev had called for an end to the "absolutely groundless" notion that "the Soviet Union could be as strong as any possible coalition of states opposing it."[5] With that injunction, Gorbachev clearly gave the go-ahead for the movement in Soviet arms control positions that would soon begin in Geneva and within two years almost to the day yield the INF Treaty, whose ratification instruments would be exchanged by Reagan and Gorbachev at the Moscow summit.

Europe came next, with Gorbachev pointing to "shortcomings" and the necessity of overcoming "inertia" in Soviet thinking on relations with the continent. He drew attention to Soviet movement away from earlier "dogmatic positions" in regard to the EEC. He repeated his earlier line that Moscow did not look at Europe "through the prism" of Soviet relations with the United States, as well as the caveat that this did not mean a lessening of the perceived importance of the United States.

On other issues Gorbachev underscored the importance of relations with countries in Asia and the Pacific, as he had at the 27th Party Congress and as he would later do in Vladivostok. (But curiously, especially given the attention Gorbachev had drawn at the party congress with his "running sore" imagery, the published excerpts of his speech at the Foreign Ministry contained absolutely no reference to Afghanistan.) In addition, he said that "fundamental reforms" were necessary in Soviet policy on foreign economic ties. It was time for a "comprehensive" review of Soviet trade-and-aid ties and obligations to the "Third World," and to improve coordination among all Soviet economic representatives abroad. Turning to human rights and foreign policy, the general secretary said that the time had come for a "fundamental reinterpretation" of the Soviet approach, and he urged Soviet diplomats to display "boldness" at the upcoming Vienna Conference on Security and Cooperation in Europe (CSCE) review conference. Soon, on the eleventh anniversary of the signing of the Helsinki Final Act, the USSR would announce the establishment, "within the framework" of the Soviet CSCE committee, of a new public commission on humanitarian issues.[6] (Even before the 27th Party Congress, the USSR on February 11, 1986, had released long-imprisoned Jewish dissident and human rights activist Anatoliy Shcharanskiy in a prisoner exchange on Glienicke Bridge in Berlin.)

Finally, Gorbachev unmistakably and bluntly alluded to the core shortcoming of at least the latter part of the Gromyko era. "One of the decisive forms of diplomacy is the conducting of negotiations," he said. "When conducting them, it is necessary for us to be well aware of what we want, in order not to create any impasses either for ourselves or for the other side." Then came the clearest and most audacious shot at Gromyko: "It is inadmissible to think that our partner is more stupid than we are. We must not allow persistence in defending a particular position to develop into senseless stubbornness, so that the Soviet representatives will be called 'Mr. Nyet'"—a sobriquet decades earlier also applied to Molotov as Stalin's foreign minister.

The party leader did not let the matter drop at that. He even went on to raise the issue of corruption within the foreign relations establishment, though somewhat delicately referring to it as the appearance of "petty-bourgeois phenomena."[7] Over the winter there had been the extortion and contraband scandals involving Deputy Foreign Trade Minister Vladimir Sushkov and ambassador to Japan Petr Abrasimov.

Now, in May-June, according to Shevardnadze a year later, the Foreign Ministry's International Relations Institute and Diplomatic Academy were under scrutiny for low academic standards and noncompetitive admissions, presumably influenced by bribery and connections. The seriousness of the situation was indicated by the fact that the Central Committee Secretariat had issued a "special decision" on the Diplomatic Academy, and the Party Control Committee had launched an investigation of "incoming warning signals."[8]

After Gorbachev's speech at the Foreign Ministry, Ligachev would publicly renew the general secretary's implicit attack on the integrity of Gromyko's management of the Foreign Ministry. Even before Gorbachev's speech Ligachev had already criticized the conduct of foreign policy under Gromyko. "The foreign policy activity of the party and the state has recently been stepped up in all areas," he told a group of leading figures from the world of theater in a meeting on April 19, 1986. "To be honest, there was a time when our enterprise had begun to slacken in this main area of foreign policy. Now the situation is changing decisively."[9] Five months after Gorbachev's lecture at the Foreign Ministry, the second secretary, in an October joint appearance with Gorbachev to open a national conference on the social sciences, would hold up the International Relations Institute and the Diplomatic Academy as singular examples of negative phenomena.

According to Ligachev, the institute and the academy were both redolent with the "practice of deciding questions in a narrow circle, nepotism in the selection of cadres, the cultivation of toadyism and lack of principles, the reluctance to heed the healthy voice of the collective." Matters had gotten so bad at the institute that its rector had even been expelled from the party. Significantly, the institute and the academy were the only two organizations singled out by Ligachev for criticism in this context, and both were subordinated to what had been Gromyko's Foreign Ministry. Ligachev's attack, furthermore, came just as the meeting in Reykjavik between Reagan and Gorbachev was being announced. If Gromyko had doubts about the upcoming summit and the surprisingly new positions Gorbachev was formulating for it, then Ligachev's criticisms of Gromyko's past management practices could have been meant to silence them.[10]

PERESTROIKA AT THE ID AND IN THE MFA

Beyond Shevardnadze's replacement of Gromyko, the changes at the MFA before the Party Congress had been few in number but similarly portentous of more to come.[11] In December 1985 Vadim Loginov had been promoted from within the Foreign Ministry to become a new deputy foreign minister responsible exclusively for the first time for Eastern Europe;[12] and Valentin Nikiforov had been transferred from the Central Committee's Cadres Department to oversee personnel matters at the Foreign Ministry, also as a deputy foreign minister. Elsewhere, Anatoliy Chernyayev had left his position as deputy head of the International Department (ID) in February 1986 to join Gorbachev's personal secretariat.

A much more extensive renewal and reshuffling of the foreign affairs establishment began at the party congress and greatly accelerated after Gorbachev's speech at the Foreign Ministry. Gorbachev confidant Aleksandr Yakovlev, clearly an adviser to Gorbachev not only on ideology and propaganda but also on domestic and foreign affairs generally, became a Central Committee secretary at the congress. Also entering the Secretariat, as we have already seen, was Vadim Medvedev, who had worked for Yakovlev in the early 1970s in the Propaganda Department and who now replaced the retiring Konstantin Rusakov both in the Secretariat and as head of the Central Committee's Bloc Relations Department.

In addition, Boris Ponomarev, who had headed the ID since 1955, left the leadership when he lost his candidate membership in the Politburo and his Secretariat seat at the congress, and ceded his place both in the Secretariat and at the International Department to Anatoliy Dobrynin. In April Georgiy Korniyenko transferred from first deputy foreign minister to first deputy chief of the International Department, where he began to work for Dobrynin along with the veteran ID staffer Vadim Zagladin, also a first deputy chief. Later in the year Andrey Urnov (in July) and Yuriy Zuyev (in December) would replace two removed deputy chiefs at the ID, joining at this level the better-known Karen Brutents, Ivan Kovalenko, and Vitaliy Shaposhnikov.

At the Foreign Ministry, an extensive reorganization and personnel shuffle began on May 21—two days before Gorbachev's conference speech—with the appointment of two new first deputy ministers, Anatoliy Kovalev (Western Europe) and Yuliy Vorontsov (arms control and the Middle East), and new deputy minister Boris Chaplin (protocol and consular affairs). After the conference the ministry's 18 tradition-bound regional departments were reorganized into 16 departments or administrations reflecting contemporary rather than nineteenth-century international affairs, and five new functional administrations or departments were created, including one for arms control and disarmament.

Of the changes in the regional offices, those affecting the socialist countries were perhaps the most significant, seeming to foreshadow greater involvement by the MFA in managing relations with them instead of these affairs being handled for the most part out of the Central Committee's Bloc Relations Department. Previously those in

Eastern Europe had been parceled out among three of the five European departments, while those in the Far East had been handled through two separate Far East departments. Now, after the reorganization, relations with all Eastern European countries were consolidated into a single administration for Socialist Countries of Europe, and a parallel administration was created for the Socialist Countries of Asia. Deputy Foreign Minister Loginov would be replaced by Ivan Aboimov in spring 1988, but Aboimov would also devote full time to Eastern Europe. New Deputy Foreign Minister Igor Rogachev would similarly concentrate exclusively on the Asian socialist countries.[13] The greater management clarity that resulted from this reorganization, plus the 1988 absorption of the Central Committee's Bloc Relations Department into the International Department, all suggested an effort by Gorbachev and Shevardnadze to put the day-to-day management of relations with socialist countries on more normal state-to-state footings through the MFA, while the Central Committee remained in control of the ultimate political decisions.

By May 1987, in any event, the turnover in personnel at the Foreign Ministry had been massive. In the year following Gorbachev's denunciation of "Mr. Nyet" diplomacy, three new deputy ministers were appointed; seven (of ten) new ambassadors-at-large were named; six of the 16 regional department chiefs were replaced; five new functional offices acquired their first-time heads; and of the 13 preexisting functional offices that were unchanged by the reorganization, five acquired new leadership. Abroad, 41 of Moscow's 115 ambassadors were replaced from May 1986 to May 1987. Except for Shevardnadze and Deputy Minister Nikiforov, however, all of these changes involved in-house promotions of career diplomats.

Both Dobrynin and Korniyenko, of course, had long experience in U.S.-Soviet affairs. Dobrynin, furthermore, may have had a powerful patron in Ligachev, with whom he had attended the Ordzhonikidze aircraft construction institute in Moscow, graduating in 1942, a year ahead of Ligachev. Given Dobrynin's breadth of experience in foreign affairs, it was widely (though incorrectly) presumed that he would be calling the shots for Shevardnadze. The transfers of Dobrynin and Korniyenko to the International Department led some observers to speculate at the time that they would establish a counterpart to the U.S. National Security Council in the Central Committee, an interministerial focus for decision making on external security policy headed by Dobrynin. (Dobrynin's early encouragement of civilian involvement in the formulation of military-political options, discussed in a later chapter, certainly fit with this speculation.) This would have been a far cry from the ID's earlier more narrowly sectarian, almost exclusive focus under Ponomarev on CPSU relations with nonruling communist parties. The personnel moves at the ID seemed to go hand-in-glove with the deemphasis under Gorbachev of "class struggle" in diplomacy, and his frequent calls for "civilized relations."

BUDAPEST APPEAL AND GENEVA SHIFT

In any event, there were now two leading personalities in the Secretariat overseeing the formulation of Soviet policy; though they did not share Western values, each had long and intimate knowledge of them: the veteran Americanist ambassador Dobrynin, home after more than two decades in Washington, and Aleksandr Yakovlev, former exchange student at Columbia and ambassador to Canada. It was the first time such a situation occured since the passing of the Old Bolshevik generation. Dobrynin had played an important back-channel role in previous Geneva negotiations, on strategic weapons in particular. Perhaps Gorbachev wanted him back in Moscow to oversee the development of the Kremlin's next move at the talks, though the extent of Dobrynin's impact was unclear. In any event, Moscow's positions in the Geneva arms talks—in terms of the advancement of new negotiable numbers rather than just the abandonment of old unacceptable principles—finally began to catch up with its public rhetoric. And these new departures were accompanied by new approaches to current and future negotiations on conventional arms.

Had it not been for the Chernobyl nuclear power plant disaster on April 26, Moscow's new initiatives in late May and June 11 on both conventional and nuclear weapons might have come even earlier. On April 18 Gorbachev had first suggested at the SED Congress in East Berlin that there be negotiations aimed at reducing conventional forces, tactical aircraft, and "operational-tactical" nuclear systems in Europe "from the Atlantic to the Urals." If put in a broader context, it might be possible to cut the Vienna MBFR "knot."[14] On June 11 the Warsaw Pact summit's Budapest Appeal more formally called for cuts of "land forces and tactical strike aviation" from "the Atlantic to the Urals." The proposed reductions could be dealt with either in expanded Mutual and Balanced Force Reductions (MBFR) talks, the second phase of the Conference on Disarmament in Europe (CDE), or in entirely new talks.

In addition, the Budapest Appeal stated that "operational-tactical nuclear arms with a range of up to 1,000 km would be reduced along with conventional armaments."[15] This meant that Moscow at this point preferred to negotiate on short-range INF missiles (SRINF) in a multilateral European context rather than in the ongoing bilateral negotiations with the United States on long-range INF (LRINF). This was a point that would gain increasing significance in 1987 as Gorbachev moved to accommodate and then trump Washington's insistence that SRINF be constrained within a treaty on LRINF rather than be dealt with separately and most likely unproductively in a long, drawn-out multilateral negotiation on forces in Europe.

The same day as the Budapest Appeal, the USSR also made a move of major consequence at the Geneva disarmament talks, which Gorbachev then outlined to the Central Committee plenum on June 16. Moscow's definition of strategic weapons reverted to the traditionally accepted one. No longer would it include, as it had since Gorbachev's initiative in Paris in October 1985, U.S. nuclear forces in Europe. The call for 50-percent reductions, however, was dropped and replaced by numbers closer to 30 percent—1600 strategic delivery vehicles on each side and 8000 instead of 6000 warheads—and there was no mention of the earlier 60-percent warhead sublimit on any one leg of the triad. A separate agreement on "medium-range" weapons was still said to be possible. Moreover, a week and a half earlier, on May 29, the Soviets had also begun to address the question of space weapons research more seriously. Instead of an outright ban on all SDI research, they now called for it to be limited to "the level of laboratory tests," and for both sides to pledge not to withdraw from the ABM Treaty for at least 15 years, rather than indefinitely.[16]

It was still far from a satisfactory and clinching set of proposals. Nevertheless, it marked the beginning of a new, potentially more productive stage in the Geneva negotiations. Although Moscow still preferred an outright ban on SDI, it had begun to suggest ways to limit it rather than outright killing it. On START, the two sides were drawing somewhat closer on their proposed total weapons limits, even if they were still far apart on their distribution among each component of their respective strategic triads. Mixed bag as though they were, the changes in the Soviet position were at last beginning to make the talks more interesting to the United States, if not yet anywhere close to an agreement.

SPEECH IN VLADIVOSTOK

Soviet diplomacy carefully balanced its efforts to improve relations westward with renewed attention to Sino-Soviet relations. At the 27th Party Congress Gorbachev had reported "satisfaction" with a "certain improvement" in the USSR's relations with its "great neighbor, socialist China."[17] Now in Vladivostok on July 28, 1986, Gorbachev made his first major overture toward Beijing. The speech underscored the change since 1982, when Soviet commentary on occasion had charged Beijing leaders with "hatching plans" for an anti-Soviet "China-US-Japan-NATO bloc."[18] Now Gorbachev left Beijing out of the equation, asserting that it was a "militarized Washington-Tokyo-Seoul triangle" that was taking shape under U.S. pressure. Soviet and Chinese priorities were similar, stressed Gorbachev: "the acceleration of socioeconomic development." So "why not support one another and cooperate in realizing our plans where this is evidently to the benefit of both?"

China had nevertheless continued to insist on Soviet movement on the "three obstacles" to improved relations: the Soviet military buildup on the Sino-Soviet border, including in Mongolia; the Soviet occupation of Afghanistan; and Soviet support for the Vietnamese occupation of Cambodia. Although Gorbachev sidestepped the Cambodian question, he signaled at least some movement on the other two. With the balky Yumzhagiyn Tsedenbal having been replaced in August 1984 by the more cooperative Zhambyn Batmonh in Ulan Bator, and with Tsedenbal's protectors in Moscow presumably weakened by the purges of the ranks of the Brezhnev-Chernenko camp, the Soviet leader at last announced that the withdrawal of "a considerable number of Soviet troops from Mongolia is being examined with the leadership of the Mongolian People's Republic"[19]—a move Andropov may have wanted to take, as argued earlier, as far back as 1983. Gorbachev, in addition, reiterated Soviet willingness to accept the main channel of the Amur river as the official border,[20] and also said that the USSR was prepared to discuss the question of thinning out forces along both sides of the long Sino-Soviet border. And he announced the withdrawal of six regiments from Afghanistan by the end of the year.[21]

Several weeks later, as part of the vast reshuffle at the MFA in Moscow, Igor Rogachev would be appointed deputy foreign minister and take over from Leonid Ilichev the portfolio for conducting talks with Beijing.[22] Evidently the change in faces was intended to underscore Moscow's determination to improve Sino-Soviet relations. At the end of the year, in another positive signal, the USSR would turn off two radio stations that had catered to potentially disgruntled elements in Chinese society, including the armed forces, in broadcasts beamed to China from Siberia.[23]

A Foreign Ministry spokesman in Beijing conceded that Gorbachev in Vladivostok had made "new remarks" on improving Sino-Soviet relations. But China reacted coolly to Gorbachev's declaration of a missile freeze in the Far East. Commenting on Gorbachev's call for a Pacific conference, the Foreign Ministry spokesman said that "to guarantee" the security of the region it was "essential, first of all, to take concrete actions by greatly reducing nuclear weapons and missiles already deployed and easing the tension in the region and removing the hot spots of Afghanistan and Kampuchea."[24] After the Reykjavik summit in October, China would continue to pressure Moscow to waive its demand to retain 100 medium-range warheads in the Far East. Beijing, moreover, would also dismiss the announced Soviet troop withdrawals from Afghanistan as a sham—which they were, at least partly.[25]

Nevertheless, in September 1986, when Chinese Foreign Minister Wu Xuequian met with Shevardnadze at the UN, he agreed to resume border talks, suspended by Beijing after the Soviet invasion of Afghanistan.[26] The first round took place in February 1987 in Moscow,[27] the second round, in Beijing in August. After the latter session the two sides announced the establishment of a working group of experts to consider technical issues concerning the "course of the whole length" of the eastern border.[28] Meanwhile, Chinese Premier and Acting Party Chief Zhao Ziyang's tour of Eastern Europe in June seemed to foreshadow the eventual reestablishment of party-to-party relations with Moscow, broken off in 1966.[29]

EUROPE: EAST AND WEST

Upon becoming general secretary, Gorbachev gave pride-of-place in his remarks on foreign policy to the need to improve and strengthen Soviet–East European unity and cooperation. In mid-1985, mirroring the essentially still very conservative post-Chernenko stance, Moscow had insisted on greater solidarity within the Warsaw Pact and allegiance to the Kremlin line.

In spring 1984 Central Committee official Oleg Rakhmanin, long-time first deputy head of the Bloc Relations Department, had polemicized with the Hungarian and East German thesis of the special role of small countries as mediators between the great powers. In summer 1985 the Central Committee official once again threw down the gauntlet. Under the pseudonym "O. Vladimirov," Rakhmanin in *Pravda* attacked East European deviations not only in foreign policy but also on the domestic side, condemning "quests" to expand the private sector, weaken central planning, and increase the role of market competition. In addition, he took after Russophobia, anti-Sovietism, and any aspersions on "proletarian internationalism" in favor of "some kind of 'new unity.'"[30]

Rakhmanin's fulminations notwithstanding, Gorbachev was giving leaders such as Erich Honecker and Janos Kadar something they greatly wanted: a return to arms talks with the United States and a resumption of contacts at the highest level. After the Geneva summit, as we have seen, Gorbachev had formally sought the "full support" of his Warsaw Pact counterparts in Prague before heading home. For them an improvement in the superpower relationship held out the hope of greater room to pursue their own individually tailored external policies.

By the time Gorbachev gave his report at the 27th Party Congress, he stressed that "there cannot be an identity of views on all issues without exception" among communist parties. Although "variety in our movement is not a synonym for disjointedness," the general secretary declared, "unity has nothing in common with uniformity, with a hierarchy, with interference by some parties in the affairs of others, with an aspiration by any party for a monopoly on truth."[31] Three months later, in his speech at the Foreign Ministry, Gorbachev reinforced the point by warning that no one had given the Soviet Union the "right" to "teach" other socialist countries.

Moscow under Gorbachev, however, did not abandon pressure on its bloc allies, but rather replaced one form of it with another: the need to confront rather than ignore or postpone pressing domestic problems. As with profligate Third World clients, the Gorbachev leadership began to lean on its Eastern European allies to engage in restructuring. In foreign policy, nevertheless, Moscow's Warsaw Pact allies now definitely seemed the beneficiaries of a somewhat longer and more rational leash. Rakhmanin began to fade and finally headed into retirement. By early October 1986 Bloc Relations Department Deputy Chief Georgiy Shakhnazarov, a veteran of Andropov's group of consultants in the 1960s and a future aide to Gorbachev, was promoted to first deputy chief as Rakhmanin's replacement. Meanwhile, as we have seen, the reorganization at the MFA had consolidated Eastern European affairs within a single administration, and there was now a deputy foreign minister whose exclusive function was to oversee relations with Eastern Europe.

Toward Western Europe, one of the by-products of this shifting attitude in Moscow seemed to be a somewhat warmer posture even toward Bonn beginning in late June 1986. By October, however, the relatively more civil approach appeared to be a casualty of backstage, post-Reykjavik recriminations in Moscow. Federal elections were soon coming up in West Germany, to be sure, and so the Soviet leadership had cause for reverting to a cooler stance in order not to undermine opponents of the Christian Democratic Union/Christian Socialist party (CDU/CSU). But these elections had been scheduled long ago for January 1987.

In late October the Soviet tone began to border on the vengeful, rather than merely cooler, when it latched onto Kohl's comparison of Gorbachev's public relations talents with those of the Nazi Goebbels.[32] A new chill set in. An unsigned article in *Pravda* called Kohl's "pronouncements . . . unprecedented in the history of . . . all relations between states maintaining diplomatic relations." The "boil of revanchism" had "clearly burst," charged the newspaper. The article concluded with the hope that Bonn would "purge" its relations with the USSR of "political dirt and start thinking about the advantages of a healthy and clear-cut future."[33]

With the victory of Kohl's coalition in the January 25 elections, however, it was up to Moscow to rethink its relations with the FRG. Before long, on February 9, Ambassador Kvitsinskiy reportedly confided to Bonn, "We must get going eventually." West German President Richard von Weizsaecker would be invited to make a state visit later in 1987. Soviet Deputy Premier Antonov would visit the FRG April 2, the first high-ranking trip between the two countries not canceled since Kohl's *Newsweek* interview.[34]

REDEFINING REGIONAL POLICIES

Elsewhere in the world, Soviet policy still seemed designed primarily to portray the USSR as a power equal to the United States, defending its own widespread regional interests but doing so with a greater sense of responsibility for upholding the peace than the militaristic "neo-globalist" United States. For the future it could not be ruled out that Moscow's new-found tactical flexibility might eventually lead to a fundamental reappraisal of its regional aims. But for now Gorbachev's call in Vladivostok for a "Pacific Ocean conference along the lines of the Helsinki conference," hints of flexibility on Afghanistan, expanding diplomatic contacts in the Middle East and the Persian Gulf, and visits by Shevardnadze to Latin America and swings through Southeast Asia all seemed to have a similar and more limited goal in mind: a hope that tactical moderation would in the end better serve strategic consolidation and expansion.

There were, however, important and novel nuances, including a budding campaign to wrap Soviet regional diplomacy in the UN flag. The new Party Program already included a call for enhancing the role of the United Nations. But the Soviet intention was signaled most clearly for the first time by Shevardnadze in his speech to the General Assembly on September 23, 1986: "Whatever the area of international relations we turn to, everywhere the role of the United Nations is indispensable and its responsibility is great. Today, ... enhancing the authority and prestige of this organization and the effectiveness of its decisions becomes more than ever a common concern for all its members."[35] The new Soviet approach, however, appeared at least partly designed to use the UN as a buffer to absorb negative repercussions from Soviet regional initiatives, as well as to gain leverage on the United States in the "democratic" UN community. The USSR was not abdicating its role in the world or forfeiting the competition for the ultimate judgment of history. Rather, the Gorbachev leadership's policy of consulting with the

United States and other major powers as well as working through the good offices of the UN secretary general was intended to have the effect of legitimating its Third World interests even as it began to redefine the Soviet presence by toning down its military profile.

In fact, Soviet diplomacy under Gorbachev and Shevardnadze, nonetheless, began to show what appeared to be some genuine concern with the need to dampen regional hot spots, particularly in the Middle East. In his November 1985 speech to the Supreme Soviet Gorbachev had begun to resurrect earlier warnings—which had fallen into disuse in the last half of the 1970s—of the dangers of regional conflicts escalating into nuclear conflicts. A year later Ye. Plimak's striking essay in *Pravda* warned that "any local conflict has a tendency to expand into a regional, even world conflict."[36] Then, remarkably, Gorbachev in April 1987 stated in the presence of none other than Syrian leader and Soviet weapons client Hafiz al-Assad, "The stake on military power in settling the [Middle East] conflict has become completely discredited."[37]

During the Assad visit, Gorbachev also declared that the lack of diplomatic relations between the Soviet Union and Israel "cannot be considered normal." Somewhat softening the usual Soviet insistence that diplomatic ties could be restored only after Israeli withdrawal from territory occupied in 1967, Gorbachev declared that "changes in relations with Israel are conceivable only in the mainstream of the process of settlement in the Middle East."[38] Since the Vorontsov-Sofer exploratory talks in Paris in 1985, there had been preliminary Soviet-Israeli consular discussions in Helsinki on August 18, 1986;[39] a meeting between Israeli then-Prime Minister Shimon Peres and Shevardnadze at the UN in September 1986; and three days of talks between Peres, now foreign minister, and Brutents and Zotov of the Central Committee's International Department in Rome in April 1987—shortly before Assad traveled to Moscow.[40] Finally, on July 12, 1987, a Soviet consular delegation arrived in Israel, the first official Soviet visit in 20 years.[41]

In the Middle East and elsewhere, consonant with Gorbachev's injunction at the Foreign Ministry conference, there was also the beginning of an effort to revamp trade-and-aid relationships with less-developed clients. At the 27th Congress Gorbachev had again seemed to suggest that Soviet economic needs would come first when he stated, "The CPSU sees as its main international duty the successful progress of our country along the path opened up and laid down by October."[42] Of course, Gorbachev's "force of example" rhetoric did not mean a precipitous pullback of Soviet involvement in the Third World.[43] Nevertheless, it clearly worried those like Castro, who called for "nerves of steel, a crystal-clear policy, and granite-like firmness" in rejecting attempts by "imperialists to impose on areas of the world local wars or 'low-intensity' conflicts" in exchange for world peace.[44]

Subsequently, and at least partly bearing out Castro's premonitions, the "force of example" line was to prove to have an increasingly evident external effect on at least some military and economic relationships. It was clearly not just a domestic theme aimed only at Soviet audiences and designed only to support Gorbachev's call for reform at home.

The impact on certain Third World clients was a mirror image of the Soviet domestic campaign for discipline, economic rationality, and more modern-thinking cadres. During the course of the next year the case of Vietnam was the easiest to document. None other than Ligachev attended the Vietnamese party congress in December 1986, which capped a year-long campaign of self-criticism over mismanagement of the economy and Soviet aid, and which for the first time chose somewhat an economic pragmatist to head the party.[45] In January 1987 Ligachev also held a Central Committee conference in Moscow to discuss "creative rethinking" of Soviet-Vietnamese economic ties.[46] In May 1987 the Vietnamese Politburo noted the frequent "irrational utilization of the extensive Soviet aid" and stated that it was "necessary to resolutely eschew old and obsolete theoretical administrative methods of running the economy."[47] In June 1987 Ligachev convened yet another Central Committee conference, this one to air the "serious shortcomings" in the management of Soviet economic ties with Cuba, Mongolia, and Vietnam—the three non-European members of CEMA.[48]

Finally, subsequent developments suggested that Gorbachev, in calling for a reform of trade-and-aid relationships, had in mind not only just Soviet relations with Third World clients but also a gradual Soviet integration into the world economy. Toward the West, the USSR in August 1986 signaled its interest in participating in the General Agreement on Tariffs and Trade (GATT), though not in the IMF or the World Bank.[49] A year later the June plenum of the Central Committee approved plans to make the ruble convertible within CEMA, and then later within the world economy. As this could happen only after successfully pushing through painful price reforms at home, however, it all remained in the distant future.

NOTES

1. AFP, April 19, 1986 (FBIS-SOV, April 21, 1986, R 1).
2. TASS, May 23, 1986 (FBIS-SOV, May 27, 1986, R 1).
3. *Kazakhstanskaya Pravda*, May 21, 1986 (FBIS-SOV, June 19, 1986, R 10).
4. *Asahi Shimbun*, June 6, 1986.
5. *Pravda*, July 26, 1988 (FBIS-SOV, July 26, 1988, p. 30).
6. TASS, July 31, 1986 (FBIS-SOV, August 1, 1986, R 1).

7. *Vestnik Ministerstva Inostrannykh del SSSR*, no. 1 (August 5, 1987), signed to press July 28, 1987, 4–6 (FBIS-SOV, September 2, 1987, 23–25).

8. See Shevardnadze's May 3, 1987, speech on restructuring in the Foreign Ministry, in *Vestnik Ministerstva Inostrannykh del SSSR*, no. 1 (August 5, 1987), signed to press July 28, 1987, 21 (FBIS-SOV, September 2, 1987, 30).

9. *Teatr*, no. 8 (August 1986), signed to press June 5.

10. *Pravda*, October 2, 1986 (FBIS-SOV, October 21, 1986, R 9).

11. This section draws heavily on the survey by Daniel S. Papp, "The Impact of the Shevardnadze-Dobrynin Apparatus on Soviet Foreign Policy," paper presented at the Airlie House Conference on Gorbachev's "New Thinking" and Soviet Foreign Policy, May 10–11, 1988, especially 3–13.

12. In recent years First (one of two) Deputy Foreign Minister Viktor Maltsev (1977–86) had been responsible for Eastern Europe as well as South Asia and China. At the deputy foreign minister level, Nikolay Firyubin had been responsible since 1957 for South and Southeast Asia and since 1966 had also acted as secretary general of the Warsaw Pact's Political Consultative Committee until his death in February 1983.

More important, Nikolay Rodionov, a former party official associated with Brezhnev, had been responsible for Eastern Europe and perhaps the Far East as well during his tenure at the Foreign Ministry from 1970 to 1978, when he was appointed ambassador to Yugoslavia (1978–86). After Rodionov's departure, however, no deputy foreign minister apparently covered Eastern Europe until Loginov's appointment in December 1985, though Maltsev presumably carried the load at the first deputy level. In 1986 Maltsev replaced Rodionov as ambassador in Belgrade, and Rodionov returned to the MFA as ambassador-at-large. This information is drawn from the various United States Central Intelligence Agency directories published over the years on the USSR Ministry of Foreign Affairs, as listed in the bibliography.

13. United States Central Intelligence Agency, *Directory of USSR Ministry of Foreign Affairs Officials*, CR 83–12416 (June 1983) and LDA 87–12484 (July 1987). On Aboimov vice Loginov, see the "new appointments" section of *Vestnik Ministerstva Inostrannykh del SSR*, no. 9 (May 15, 1988): 43–45, signed to press May 5, 1988.

14. TASS, April 18, 1986 (FBIS-SOV, April 18, 1986, F 8).

15. *Pravda*, June 12, 1986 (FBIS-SOV, June 13, 1986, BB 8–12).

16. *New York Times*, June 1 and 12, 1986; and TASS, June 16, 1986 (FBIS-SOV, June 17, 1986, R 3). The "full" text of Gorbachev's speech did not include all these details, which appeared only in this brief TASS dispatch.

17. Moscow Television Service, February 25, 1986 (FBIS-SOV, February 26, 1986, Supplement no. 41, O 33).

18. TASS, July 7, 1982 (FBIS-SOV, July 8, 1982, B 1).

19. On January 15, 1987, the Soviet Defense Ministry would announce that "one full-strength motorized rifle division and several separate units from the contingent of Soviet troops on temporary station in the territory of Mongolia will be returned to the Soviet Union next April through June" (TASS, January 15, 1987 [FBIS-SOV, January 15, 1987, C 1]). Of an estimated 75,000 Soviet troops in Mongolia, over 10,000 might be withdrawn given that a normal Soviet

division was thought to be made up of 11,000–12,000 personnel (Kyodo, January 15, 1987 [FBIS-SOV, January 16, 1987, CC 2]).

20. As already noted, this was a concession dating at least from March 1973, when the Soviets first claim to have submitted a draft proposal to this effect to the Chinese. See A. A. Gromyko and B. N. Ponomarev, *Istoriya Vneshney Politiki SSSR, 1945–1975*, vol. 2 (Moscow: Nauka, 1976), 579.

21. Moscow Television Service, July 28, 1986 (FBIS-SOV, July 29, 1986, R 1–20).

22. TASS, August 13, 1986 (FBIS-SOV, August 14, 1986, R 1).

23. Kyodo, December 25, 1986 (FBIS-SOV, December 29, 1986, B 1).

24. Xinhua, August 6, 1986 (FBIS-PRC, August 6, 1986, A 1). Beijing's reaction to Gorbachev's proposal for an Asian security conference was not surprising. The idea was actually an old one, dating form 1969, but had been dormant for some five years when Gorbachev first refloated it during Gandhi's visit to Moscow in May 1985. It was on that same occasion that Gorbachev also briefly raised the essence of Brezhnev's April 1981 notion of a "code of conduct" in the Third World for permanent members of the UN Security Council, of which the PRC is one.

25. *Renmin Ribao*, November 2, 1986. For details on the Soviet deception, see Craig Karp, "Afghanistan: Seven Years of Soviet Occupation," Special Report no. 155 (Washington, DC: United States Department of State, Bureau of Public Affairs, December 1986), 10–11.

26. *Washington Post*, September 26, 1986.

27. Moscow Television Service, February 23, 1987 (FBIS-SOV, February 24, 1987, B 2).

28. TASS, August 21, 1987 (FBIS-SOV, August 21, 1987, B 1); and *Washington Post*, August 22, 1987.

29. *Washington Post*, June 4, 1987.

30. *Pravda*, June 21, 1985 (FBIS-SOV, June 24, 1985, BB 2–7).

31. Moscow Television Service, February 25, 1986 (FBIS-SOV, February 26, 1986, Supplement no. 41, O 33).

32. *Newsweek*, October 27, 1986; and *Washington Post*, November 22 and 28, 1986. Shortly before, and presumably to enhance the West German SPD's vote-getting appeal, the East German SED had been authorized to join the SPD in a Bonn press conference to publicize an SED-SPD agreement on principles for a nuclear-free corridor in Central Europe. Unlike the Soviet rejection in 1982 of a 150-km-wide corridor on either side of the line separating NATO and the Warsaw Pact in the FRG, GDR, and Czechoslovakia, this now accepted it. It followed the similar SED-SPD draft agreement on a Chemical-weapons-free zone in Central Europe of June 1985 (*Pravda*, October 23, 1986 [FBIS-SOV, October 24, 1986, G 1–2]).

33. *Pravda*, November 27, 1986 (FBIS-SOV, November 28, 1986, G 1–4).

34. *Der Spiegel*, February 23, 1987 (FBIS-WE, February 24, 1987, J 2). Even before the elections, Dobrynin had visited East Berlin (January 19–21) and Warsaw (January 21–24), perhaps to do some anticipatory coordination of diplomacy toward Bonn on the assumption that Kohl would continue in office.

35. TASS, September 23, 1986 (FBIS-SOV, September 24, 1986, CC 9).

36. *Pravda*, November 14, 1986. For a historical survey of the ebb and flow of Soviet thinking on the dangers of regional escalation in the nuclear age, see Francis Fukuyama, "Soviet Civil-Military Relations and the Power Projection Mission," RAND/R-3504-AF (Santa Monica, CA: RAND Corporation, April 1987).

37. *Pravda*, April 25, 1987 (FBIS-SOV, April 28, 1987, H 7).

38. Ibid.

39. These talks, however, lasted only 90 minutes and were terminated when the Soviet delegation rejected the Israeli demand for a reciprocal visit to the USSR by an Israeli consular delegation (Helsinki Domestic Service, August 18, 1986, and *Ha'Aretz*, August 17, 1986 [FBIS-SOV, August 18, 1986, H 1–2]; and TASS and AFP, August 19, 1986 [FBIS-SOV, August 20, 1986, CC 1- 2]).

40. *New York Times*, April 10, 1987.

41. Jerusalem Domestic Service and Tel Aviv IDF Radio, July 13, 1987 (FBIS-SOV, July 13, 1987, E 8–9); and TASS, July 14, 1987 (FBIS-SOV, July 14, 1987, E 1).

42. Moscow Television Service, February 25, 1986 (FBIS-SOV, February 26, 1986, O 33).

43. For a number of case studies extending into the early period of the Gorbachev era, see Francis Fukuyama, "Moscow's Post-Brezhnev Reassessment of the Third World," RAND/R-3337-USDP (Santa Monica, CA: RAND Corporation, February 1986).

44. *Pravda*, February 27, 1986 (FBIS-SOV, March 13, 1986, Supplement, O 8).

45. TASS, December 17–18, 1986 (FBIS-SOV, December 18, 1986, E 6); and *Washington Post*, December 19, 1986.

46. Moscow Domestic Service, January 5, 1987 (FBIS-SOV, January 6, 1987, E 1).

47. *Izvestiya*, May 11, 1987 (FBIS-SOV, May 27, 1987, E 8–9).

48. *Pravda*, June 23, 1987 (FBIS-SOV, June 23, 1987, BB 1–2).

49. TASS, August 22, 1986 (FBIS-SOV, August 25, 1986, CC 1); and *Pravda*, September 1, 1986 (FBIS-SOV, September 5, 1986, CC 1).

Chapter 7

Turn to Radicalism

*A*ll along, Gorbachev and his closest supporters presumably were well aware that it would be necessary to loosen the grip of lower-level party and state officials in order to get the country moving again. But only beginning in late May 1986 did his leadership seem to begin to realize how tight was this grip. Local administrators still controlled the nation's breadbasket and thus had the power to demoralize the peasantry and, in turn, the populace over the prospects of perestroika improving the standard of living. From the vantage point of common citizens, all they saw in perestroika at the grass-roots level was increased disruption of the food supply and continued party tyranny.

In this sense Gorbachev and his colleagues were indeed radicalized by the unexpectedly strong reaction of the grass-roots apparatus against their still rather moderate agenda for change and reform. They fully expected opposition at the top from the remnants of the Brezhnev-Chernenko clan but probably thought there would be less at the bottom. But it was the realization that resistance to change was perhaps even stronger at the lower levels of the power structure that compelled the Gorbachev leadership abruptly to switch its immediate priorities from economic to political reform in mid-1986. It was headed in this direction already, but the opposition to reform accelerated and radicalized the process.

It is not too difficult to pinpoint the redirection of Gorbachev's agenda. In April 1986 in Prague Gorbachev suggested that the next item of business on the Soviet leadership's agenda was the elaboration of more concrete "recipes" for economic reform. At the end of May it began this process by issuing an unfortunate decree spelling out the bans on what was condemned as "unearned income." This led to several months of what liberal economist Nikolay Shmelev described as "administrative lunacy," during which local officials latched onto the decree's many prohibitionary clauses to clamp down on individual economic enterprise.

By mid-June, in remarks that did not surface until the fall, Gorbachev sounded remarkably like Yeltsin when he met with a group of leading writers. Some time in July Burlatskiy began composing a remarkable dialogue, which would appear in October in *Literary Gazette*, between an old-style and a new-style provincial party leader. By mid-July Gorbachev and Ligachev began cranking up what would develop into a radical push for democratization. Ligachev's remarks on the subject in Voronezh, unnoticed or ignored by most observers, were replayed in a lead editorial in *Pravda*. By the end of July Gorbachev's announcement in Khabarovsk of a Central Committee plenum on cadre policy finally caught the world's attention. After denying in February to *L'Humanité* that a revolution was under way, Gorbachev began to assert that this was exactly what was needed.

The new phase of the campaign against the entrenched bureaucracies was supported by Gorbachev and Ligachev working together as a team. In this lay its strengths as well as its tactical contradictions and pitfalls, but those would not come to a head until the next year. At the grass-roots level it tried to use grievances against local officials to pressure them for change. Among the intelligentsia it played to themes strikingly reminiscent of those in the November 1985 "manifesto" of the' Movement for Socialist Renewal, still circulating only privately but soon to be leaked.

LULL BETWEEN STORMS

At the congress in February Gorbachev had said that "acceleration in the development of society is unthinkable and impossible without further development of socialist democracy and of all its aspects and manifestations." But the emphasis still seemed to be on "acceleration," which Gorbachev stated "holds the key to all our problems in the near and more distant future—economic and social, political and ideological, and internal and external."[1] The leadership's attention seemed focused more on eradicating endemic corruption than on instituting systemic reform—economic or otherwise. The outspoken Yeltsin told a meeting of Moscow party *aktiv* that 800 trade officials had been arrested in the past few months and that "we are digging deeper and deeper and still cannot see the bottom of this well of corruption." The resistance to the anticorruption drive was fierce. One letter writer had warned Yeltsin that "Khrushchev once tried to dress us all in peasant clothes. He failed, and so will you. We have stolen and will continue to steal."[2]

In April Yuriy Brezhnev was finally forced out of his job as first deputy minister of foreign trade, though he was allowed to retire half-gracefully "on health grounds."[3] In general, however, the paroxysm of change either tapered off or was temporarily halted by the Chernobyl nuclear power plant disaster set off the night of April 26. The catastrophe preoccupied the leadership for some weeks and probably suspended decision making on all other matters. Gorbachev finally reported the situation on television on May 14, delivered his critique of Soviet diplomacy at the Foreign Ministry on May 23, and attended a conference at the KGB on May 27–28. While something seemed to be afoot on the foreign affairs front, on domestic affairs the leadership appeared to be catching its breath and in no haste to resume running.

In May, however, Yeltsin again revealed that Zamyatin's International Information Department and the Agricultural Machine Construction Department in the Central Committee had been dissolved. The apparatus of the Moscow party committee, he said, had also been reduced by 10 percent, some of its departments abolished, and some municipal administrations trimmed—in some instances such as the building administration and railroad authority, by letting go 3000 employees in each case.[4] But the only major streamlining of the vast ministerial baronies in Moscow and the republic capitals had been the November 1985 consolidation of five ministries and one state committee under the State Committee for the Agro-Industrial Complex.[5]

At the next Central Committee plenum, held on June 16, Gorbachev once again complained about "those who are trying to pull us backwards," warning that "we cannot and will not put up with this attitude." He also continued to wax rhetorically in favor of decentralization. "In today's conditions it is intolerable that all questions should be resolved in the center, and it is even practically impossible. Everyone must understand this truth," he told the Central Committee. "The main responsibility for the solution of practical questions must be borne by labor collectives in enterprises and associations." The June plenum, however, was the first under Gorbachev not to announce any movement of personnel into or out of the Politburo or Secretariat.[6] At the companion parliamentary session, nevertheless, Ligachev did announce several personnel shifts at the next lower level: Petr Demichev's transfer from the Culture Ministry to first vice president, replacing Vasiliy Kuznetsov, who had been retired at the Party Congress; and Grishin's release from membership in the Presidium of the Supreme Soviet.[7] (A year later Grishin would also give up his seat as a Supreme Soviet deputy.[8]) In August there were further ministerial changes. Vasiliy Zakharov became minister of culture.[9] In addition, Nikolay Panichev was appointed new minister for the machine tool industry, replacing Boris Balmont in the wake of a critical report by the CPSU Central Committee Party Control Committee.[10] And Valentin Pavlov replaced Nikolay Glushkov as chairman of the State Committee on Prices.[11]

Shortly after the June plenum, moreover, the veteran Kirilenkoite Yakov Ryabov, who in September 1984 had been promoted from chairman of the State Committee for Foreign Economic Relations to deputy premier status, was named ambassador to France.[12] The announcement came several weeks before Mitterrand's visit to Moscow and may have been intended to underscore the importance of Moscow's French connection. More likely, however, Gorbachev or Ryzhkov may have found Ryabov too ambitious or contentious; his removal from Moscow suggested that harmony had its limits even among members of Kirilenko's Sverdlovsk group. The same point would be made even more spectacularly in October-November 1987 with Yeltsin's ouster as head of the Moscow party organization. The examples of Ryabov and Yeltsin suggested that Sverdlovsk seemed to breed not only eminent politicians but also peppery ones.

More than any other issues, however, the main order of business at the June plenum seemed to be nailing down final approval of the proinvestment five-year plan before it was enacted as law by the Supreme Soviet.[13] It was easy to speculate that some in the leadership may have viewed accelerated investment in domestic technology more as an alternative than as a complement to reform—just as Brezhnev and his supporters years before had seen the importation of foreign technology as a way to avoid management changes. Boris Ponomarev, who had been retired from the leadership at the 27th Congress but nevertheless retained his seat on the Central Committee, was allowed in May to pen a major piece in *Pravda* presenting the case for conservative resistance to management reform. The article solidly endorsed renewed attention to industrial investment, science and technology, and labor discipline. But for Ponomarev, and no doubt many others, "the forms and methods of work employed by party, state, trade union, and youth organizations, the press, and the entire Soviet society" during the industrialization drive of the 1930s still contained "much that could be put to use with a view to accelerating the socioeconomic development of the USSR."[14]

What appeared to be a lull on the domestic reform front, however, was deceptive. Very little was as it seemed. Reformist sociologist Tatyana Zaslavskaya had predicted that reorganizing the Soviet economy—even under the best of circumstances—would be a "prolonged and complicated process" aggravating the "contradictory nature" of entrenched interests.[15] Even that judgment understated the veritable war about to break out as the Gorbachev leadership prepared to appeal to the intelligentsia and to the public to help apply pressure from above and below on the vast bureaucracies resisting the calls for change.

GORBACHEV AND THE WRITERS

The leadership's campaign of courting the intelligentsia began on June 19, days after the Central Committee plenum and Supreme Soviet session, when Gorbachev, Ligachev, and Yakovlev met with a group of leading establishment writers. *Pravda's* sanitized account of Gorbachev's remarks, however, did not reveal that this was the kick-off of the new, more radical phase of the leadership's efforts to bring the bureaucracies to heel.[16] Only in October, when unofficial transcripts of the meeting reached the West, was its import clear: Gorbachev and his colleagues were taking on "the apparat which broke Khrushchev's neck," and which now threatened to break their necks too.

Sounding much like letter writer V. Ivanov in T. Samolis's pre-Congress *Pravda* article, and like Yeltsin at the congress, according to one version Gorbachev complained that "between the people who want . . . changes, who dream about . . . changes, and the leadership, there is the management, the apparat: of the ministries, of the party, and they do not want changes, they do not want to be deprived of certain rights and privileges."[17] "The Central Committee," he appealed, "needs support. You cannot imagine how much we need the support of such a group of writers. . . . We have no political opposition." Therefore criticism, self-criticism, and glasnost were vital to establishing social self-control. "Most important of all," he emphasized, was glasnost. "There can be no democratic rule without openness. At the same time, however, democracy without a framework is anarchy. Therefore it won't be easy."[18]

The economy, Gorbachev said, "is in great disarray. We lag behind in every sphere. . . . The relationship between money and goods, income and goods, has been distorted." In general, he lamented, "we have forgotten how to work. Not simply have we forgotten how to work, but we have forgotten how to work within the framework of a democracy." Though it was true that there were many "drunkards, thieves and embezzlers," the greatest problem was the "loads of bureaucrats, people who do not wish to part with their privileges." According to Gorbachev, "many enterprise managers write to us: 'We don't need rights and independence. Let it all remain as it used to be, it was easier for us to work then, it was better.' They don't want it, they don't know how to deal with it. Generations need to pass before we will be able to change ourselves. Generations."[19]

Gorbachev revealed a clear, though soon to be revised, sense of tactical pacing. Clearly alluding to the still painful, unresolved question of Stalin's legacy, Gorbachev asked the writers for more patience. The general secretary evidently calculated that tackling the issue would create more trouble than gain. "If we were to get too involved with the past, we would lose all our energy. We would create internal strife. We have to go forward. We *will* sort out the past." But by October Gorbachev and his supporters apparently came to the conclusion that without a frontal attack on Stalinism and its tenacious legacy, they would be striking only glancing blows on the opposition.

For now, nevertheless, Gorbachev declared his leadership finally ready and agreed to go on a radical offensive. "About Politburo meetings. Clashes do occur, so do arguments. For 2–3 years we've been putting things off, now we want to act. Society is ready for an about-turn. If we retreat now, society will not agree to it. We have to make the process irreversible. If *we* don't do it—then who will? If not now—then when?"[20]

THE PARTY AND THE PEOPLE

Gorbachev and Ligachev soon started the open phase of this new campaign. On July 9 Ligachev addressed some of these issues at an awards ceremony in Voronezh. "The aim of changes," he said, "is to bring people into closer contact with party work, carry it out in an atmosphere of broad democracy, and eradicate from party practice such intolerable phenomena as bureaucracy, paper generation, and formalism. More light and as much openness as possible."[21] Though in agreement with Gorbachev's demand for a sea-change in the party's relationship with the Soviet public, Ligachev's remarks appeared more positive in their approach to the party apparatus and highlighted examples worthy of emulation. In the future, this difference in tone would acquire increasing significance. But for now Ligachev's greater solicitousness could be explained as dictated by the public nature of the ceremony, compared with the more confidential setting of Gorbachev's earlier meeting with the writers, and in subsequent public outings Gorbachev would sound much the same.

In any event, in Voronezh Ligachev said that everything ultimately depended on the party's cadre policy, and he asserted that the "profound, comprehensive reorganization" under way affected above all the work of party organizations. Calling for "more light and as much openness as possible," the second secretary said, "The reorganization of party work fills our party with new vitality, enhances its authority even more, and strengthens its leading role in society. And this is the guarantee of our country's steady progress."[22] Ligachev's assertion that it was a revitalized party which was the "guarantee" of progress was important to remember. It was precisely over this issue that he and Gorbachev would differ most fundamentally and publicly the following year: Gorbachev and his supporters would underscore democratization as the main "guarantee" of perestroika; Ligachev would dig in his heels and insist that it was the maintenance and nurturing of the party's vanguard role.

All that, however, was in the future. For now, Ligachev's hand was evident later in July in the wording of a lead editorial in *Pravda* entitled "First Secretary."[23] "The time that has elapsed since the 27th CPSU Congress," the piece declared, "has convincingly shown that it is impossible to turn the energy of schemes into the energy of actions without reorganizing the style and methods of party leadership." Ligachev had spoken of the need "to bring people into closer contact with party work, carry it out in an atmosphere of broad democracy." Now the *Pravda* editorial lifted this passage almost word for word. "The Congress directed leaders of party committees to master political methods of leadership. The purpose of the changes is to bring party work closer to the people and carry it out in an atmosphere of broad democratism."

The editorial was a veritable Rosetta Stone for understanding some of the critical personnel appointments of the past two years. "People speak well of the following first secretaries: Yefrem Yevseyevich Sokolov of Brest Belorussian Communist Party obkom, Gennadiy Vasilyevich Kolbin of Ulyanovsk CPSU obkom, Vasiliy Ivanovich Sitnikov of Irkutsk CPSU obkom, . . . , and of many other comrades who skillfully and conscientiously fulfill their duty to the party and the people."[24] Within five to seven months Sokolov and Kolbin would be promoted to head the Belorussian and Kazakhstan party organizations, respectively. This was the same Kolbin who got his start in Sverdlovsk during the heyday of Kirilenko's patronage of the region, who then served as second secretary in the Georgian republic under Shevardnadze and at whose installation as first secretary in Ulyanovsk none other than Ligachev had presided in December 1983.[25] Sitnikov, on the other hand, would lose his job in Irkutsk in April 1988 in the wake of a highly publicized airplane hijacking in March, just as rumors were swirling in Moscow of bitter leadership debates over Ligachev's reported sponsorship of publication of the famous "letter" from Nina Andreyeva to *Sovetskaya Rossiya*.

Several days after the "First Secretary" editorial, Gorbachev left Moscow for the far east, where he delivered his already discussed speech in Vladivostok and met future defense minister Dmitriy Yazov, to be dealt with more fully in a later chapter. In the context of this discussion, the key event of the trip was the general secretary's speech to the party aktiv in Khabarovsk kray. Here Gorbachev announced that the next plenum of the Central Committee would be devoted to cadre policy, and it was on this occasion that Gorbachev began unabashedly to equate the now all-important slogan of "restructuring" with "revolution."

"I will say bluntly," the general secretary told his audience in Khabarovsk, "that our cadres—party, local soviet, and economic—must learn to work in conditions of a widening of democracy and activation of the human factor, of an unfolding of the initiative of the people."

"Demagogues," to be sure, would exploit the "process of democracy." But they were "only a handful," and the "great majority of our people are in favor of having a healthy atmosphere in society, of the leadership being closer to the working people and consulting with them, being accountable and keeping them informed." Glasnost needed to become the norm. The same was true of criticism and self-criticism. "If we do not criticize ourselves, and subject ourselves to analysis—we do not have any opposition parties, comrades—that is why it is a requirement, it is simply an essential requirement for the normal functioning of both the party and society."[26]

In September Gorbachev repeated many of these points while on vacation in Krasnodar and Stavropol. "In the Politburo, the Central Committee, in the Soviet Government" there was "complete unanimity" on these tenets, Gorbachev claimed in Stavropol.[27] Although Gorbachev would publicly contradict his assertion of unanimity the following April at the Komsomol Congress, media reports on Politburo sessions in August-September 1986 claimed at great length that the ruling body had fully endorsed the "fundamental political significance" of what Gorbachev had said.[28] In addition, the Secretariat, which Ligachev would later claim to chair, adopted a special "decision" noting the "fundamental significance of the tenets and conclusions" of Gorbachev's remarks in Krasnodar and Stavropol.[29]

There was, however, a curiously dissonant note on the danger from demagogues in *Pravda's* lead editorial on the new campaign, "To Be the Master and Not a Guest in Your Own Home." Given future developments, it is fair to speculate that the anomaly was directed against none other than Moscow party leader Boris Yeltsin. In Khabarovsk and the Caucasus, Gorbachev had conceded that demagogues would make themselves felt under more democratic conditions, but he had minimized the threat and in any case clearly had in mind demagogues at the grass-roots level. *Pravda*, however, was troubled by the prospect of showboating demagogues in positions of authority. "We must go to the people," it stated. "Unfortunately, in some places 'going to the people' is passed off as the main sign of restructuring and broadening democracy, although sometimes these visits leave no practical trace. There still persist demagogues supposedly fighting for order in their own home. 'Yes, there are such people,' readers observe, 'and especially among those workers who hide their incompetence behind loud words. This is yet another danger on the path of radical change.'"[30] In retrospect, *Pravda's* warning foreshadowed some of the charges that would be leveled against Yeltsin little more than a year later.[31]

Otherwise, however, there seemed to be a solid leadership consensus to move forward with change in the directions outlined by

Gorbachev and Ligachev. In early August Yuriy Sklyarov left the editorship of *Problems of Peace and Socialism* and took over the position of chief of the Propaganda Department in the Central Committee from Gorbachev confidant Aleksandr Yakovlev, said to be on his way to reassignment to "a broader, more important post."[32] A decade and a half earlier, in a previous political incarnation, Sklyarov as well as Vadim Medvedev had worked for Yakovlev in the same department.[33] In addition, in late August Gromyko and Ryzhkov signed a decree outlining an extensive five-year program of legislative reform; many of the issues covered would be the focus of the upcoming plenums on political and economic reform.[34] At the same time, Valentin Falin told a Japanese interviewer that the Central Committee plenum on cadre policy was expected in October or November.[35]

IN SEARCH OF ECONOMIC RECIPES

For all the political blood spilled and heads cracked, what the new team under Gorbachev had accomplished in its first year was the easiest part of all the domestic challenges it faced after Chernenko's death. Retiring and firing burnt-out and compromised cadres and redirecting allocations toward investment were no mean accomplishments. But what lay ahead was an infinitely more difficult task: the need to accomplish no less than a profound revolution guided by a well-thought-out, comprehensive plan. And despite what would turn out to be the best harvest in years (210 million metric tons of grain)[36] and an increase in national income higher than planned (4.1 percent instead of 3.9 percent),[37] which under Brezhnev would have been cause for complacency, the Gorbachev leadership now seemed intent on forging ahead.

On economic issues, however, the leadership under Gorbachev was not much further along the path of economic reform than when Andropov stated in November 1982 that he had no "ready recipes." On a visit to Hungary in June 1986, Gorbachev had all but admitted as much. "The course, I repeat, is clear," he told a meeting at the Csepel Industrial Center. "But the tactics, methods, and forms of implementation of the course mapped out are still to be finally developed and specified, on the basis, of course, of everything that has been verified in practice in our country as well as in the fraternal countries."[38]

There was renewed speculation, moreover, of a leadership split on economic reform. Much of it was fueled by publication of Ligachev's brief remarks to a group of leading theater workers that, in reforming the economy, the Soviet Union would "continue to move forward within the framework of socialism. We will use the advantages of the socialist system. There is no question, nor will there be, of a market economy, which always and everywhere entails social injustice and social inequality."[39] But as had been the case the previous summer, Gorbachev soon said much the same thing in his key speech in Khabarovsk on July 31, 1986. "We must seek the answers to the questions posed by life not beyond the boundaries of socialism but within the framework of our system, revealing the potential of the planned economy. . . . Certain people in the West do not like this. They lie in wait for something that would mean a deviation from socialism, that we would go cap in hand to capitalism and would borrow its methods."[40] Nevertheless, in what seemed an allusion to the retired Boris Ponomarev's conservative piece in *Pravda* on May 10, in Khabarovsk Gorbachev rejected the advice of those who would "seek the answers to new questions in the economy and in technology by looking to the experience of the thirties, forties, fifties or even sixties and seventies." In response to his call at the Party Congress for "radical reform," said Gorbachev, leading economists were now at work on an "integral concept for improving the system of managing the economy." Among other central economic organs, the functions and status of the State Planning Committee (Gosplan), the State Committee for Material and Technical Supply (Gossnab), and the State Committee for Science and Technology would be "redefined."[41]

The main obstacle to the "radical reform" Gorbachev said he wanted was the immense Soviet managerial class in both the state and the party apparatus. Its entire life-style and method of operating had come to be regulated not only by "administrative methods" but also increasingly by connections and bribes. This way of doing business and running the Soviet economy could not be changed overnight. The second economy and the black and grey markets, after all, had flourished because the official economy could not function without the circumvention of its own rules and regulations, and had defaulted on providing what Soviet citizens wanted and needed. The system risked grinding to a halt if the lubricant of payoffs was abruptly taken away and not replaced by an equally efficient mechanism of imposing priorities in the public sector, and if self-initiative were discouraged in the private sector. Gorbachev had seemed to recognize this when he stated at the Party Congress that the "proposal concerning the regulation of individual labor activity must be studied attentively," and that "when stopping income not earned through labor one must not allow a shadow to fall on those who are receiving additional earnings by honest labor."[42]

Nevertheless, despite Gorbachev's congress emphasis on the need for caution, the regime now acted precipitously, and its short-term, quick-fix attempts to address the most pressing problems soon backfired. As foreshadowed by Gorbachev at the congress, two specific pieces of legislation were the focus of attention in 1986: a law on "unearned income," and a companion provision on "individual labor activity." The first amounted to a spelling out of all the "don'ts", the second, to a fairly circumscribed list of conditional "do's." It was the prohibitory measure against "unearned income" that was now pushed through on what seemed a priority and not fully thought-out basis.

On May 28, 1986, *Pravda* gave details of the Council of Ministers resolution, "On Measures to Step Up the Struggle Against Unearned Incomes." Most eye-catching were the measure's regulations forbidding cash transactions involving more than R5,000. Deals of this magnitude now had to be conducted through banks or savings institutions. If someone spent more than R10,000 at once or built a *dacha* worth more than R20,000, the individual had to be prepared to declare where the money came from. Even if no money was spent, citizens could be compelled to declare the source of their monetary holdings if requested to do so by a local executive committee or prosecutor. The good intention of the measure was clear: to close off graft as an incentive to economic activity while the official economy's system of material incentives was improved.

"LEFTIST" CHAOS

Of far greater and immediately negative impact, however, were certain other provisions in the new law. According to these, government authorities across the land were ordered "to step up the struggle against embezzlement of socialist property, bribe-taking, speculation, and other crimes of profiteering resulting in unearned incomes." While on the one hand vaguely encouraging garden plot enterprise, it also called for "intensified monitoring of the strict observance of the statutory norms and procedures for keeping livestock on citizens' personal subsidiary farms." In addition, the resolution ordered the drawing up of "procedures for registering persons engaged in the sale of agriculture produce at kolkhoz markets," and it stated that "the rights and responsibilities of the market administrations in monitoring the observance of trading regulations and the prevention and curtailment of speculation and other forms of obtaining unearned income must be expanded and increased."[43]

In an interview in June 1986, Prosecutor General Aleksandr Rekunkov defended the measure, asserting that there was nothing wrong with making "lots of money" as long as it was legal and taxed, and that the state had no intention of limiting the work or pay even of controversial *shabashniki* (moonlighters) or of "defaming" honest people. A "Law on Individual Labor Activity of Citizens," he said, was under preparation, and "its sense is not to forbid" such activity "but, on the contrary, to develop it."[44] Unfortunately, however, this second, more positive measure was not completed and published until mid-November.[45]

For now, the regime had bungled matters by coming out with the law against unearned income first and then only later with the law on individual labor activity. Local authorities, it later came to light, took advantage of the edict on impermissible income to repress private entrepreneurs foolhardy enough to engage in open commerce. Gorbachev, however, seemed totally unaware of the unfolding disaster when he called at the June plenum for "stepping up the war on unearned income" and asserted that the edict had been "welcomed by society with satisfaction."[46] When the law on permissible activity finally came out toward the end of the year, most individual operators must have been doubly resolved not to register their activities with the authorities.

By July, however, word of the disastrous impact of the unearned income measure apparently began to alarm reformers in Moscow. Burlatskiy would later reveal that he started to write his benchmark "Political Dialogue on Restructuring" in this month. As it appeared in *Literary Gazette* on October 1, the dialogue between the old-style local party secretary Streshnev and the new-style Shirokov opened with a discussion of the suspected suicide of a victim of the "excesses" which an unnamed but clear *ukaz* had generated. Local officials had seen the decree as giving them a mandate to move against *nazhiva*, or easy money-making. In this particular case they had taken a retired war veteran to court for raising and selling flowers without a permit. The veteran had subsequently died, leaving behind a note declaring "They have deceived me again." More generally, it turned out, two-thirds of the gardeners in Burlatskiy's allegorical region had been refused permits, all had been banned from shipping produce outside the oblast, and militiamen had been ordered by the local authorities to smash gardenplot greenhouses—an action Streshnev defended as in accord with the "decree" while conceding that "maybe they went too far."[47]

In his famous 1987 analysis of the nation's economic ills, reform economist Nikolay Shmelev would also vividly describe the "more than two months of rampant 'administrative lunacy'" that ensued after publication of the measure on unearned income. "It sometimes turns out once again that the right hand seems not to know what the left hand is doing," Shmelev complained. "Under the banner of the struggle for social justice, the most unbridled leftism and bungling is coming out against unearned income. . . . How are we to understand the signs which emerged in the summer of 1986 of a new onslaught on farmstead hothouses, orchards, and personal fattening plots? Was it not immediately apparent that this campaign is antistate and hostile to the country? Can it really be conceivable, in the end, to buy so much grain and meat abroad and at the same time, fearing that some individuals may earn a bit extra, to stifle the economic initiative of hundreds of thousands, millions of our citizens?" According to Shmelev, "food requisitioning" had been imposed instead of a promised "food tax." "[This] probably did agriculture more harm than any drought. Now people in the countryside are less concerned about the fate of the restructuring than people anywhere else. The authority of the raykoms and obkoms which were forced to implement 'food requisitioning' suffered a blow from which it will now be very difficult for many of them to recover."[48]

In addition, a third law on "State Acceptance" (*Gospriyemka*) was beginning to provoke widespread labor and managerial discontent. The measure was patterned on the long-standing practice of quality control in the defense sector whereby state inspectors posted in manufacturing plants could reject defective products on the spot.[49] As a result of State Acceptance, bonus pay for managers and workers alike began to drop in those plants first affected by the law, where defective products were unavoidable because workers had to rely on defective materials supplied by plants not yet covered by the law. Despite the howls of protest, the regime gritted its teeth, seeing no other way to stop the practice of manufacturing shoddy goods no one had an interest in buying but which nevertheless secured its producers hefty income bonuses.

Gorbachev and Zaykov defended State Acceptance at a Central Committee conference in November 1986.[50] The following spring Ryzhkov conceded that introducing State Acceptance had been a "harsh step," and revealed that in machine building in particular its progress was "painful." Nevertheless, he stated that the "problem of quality is an extraordinarily acute one for us" which had "developed from an economic problem into a political one."[51] Meanwhile, Shmelev called the law "a step forward" but warned that it "excludes from quality evaluation the most interested party—the consumer" and that "the fundamental defect of the present economic system—diktat by the producer—will basically remain inviolate."[52]

TROUBLED AUTUMN

A visitor to Moscow in the last half of 1986 could find the atmosphere vastly altered.[53] What seemed the nearly universal desire for change in Brezhnev's last years, and then during Chernenko's short rule, had given way to an equally widespread unease over the measures being implemented. Many had been initially pleased by the anticorruption campaign and the questioning of the perquisites of party and state functionaries. In general there was widespread and somewhat perverse pleasure in seeing big shots having something taken away from them. But the new leadership as yet did not have much to offer the common man materially. The regime was asking the population for understanding over the need to tighten up. But many people felt that all they were getting in return were promises of an indefinitely deferred, more abundant, more just future.

Popular opinion had become increasingly critical of the real or feared dislocations produced by the new leadership's economic policies. The specifics of change were coming home and hitting some household budgets and ways of life. The sharp cutbacks in the sale of alcoholic beverages were bitterly resented by moderate imbibers forced to wait for hours in unruly lines for a lowly bottle of white wine. Inflationary price hikes on particular cuts of sausage were quickly interpreted as the beginning of across-the-board food price rises aimed at trimming the enormous government subsidy of the agricultural sector. Reductions in the bloated staffs and proliferating numbers of unproductive research institutes were forcing some white-collar workers to face the prospect of blue-collar work in factories. All the talk of the need for greater pay differentials in order to stimulate worker productivity was causing concern among many over ending up relatively worse off in a future of widening class differences.

Gorbachev in particular had developed a peculiar public image problem reflecting the innate conservatism of a wide stratum of at least the Russian population. Many found Raisa Gorbacheva's high media profile offensively imperial and condescending; when she handed out candy to children, some complained, it reminded them of Csarinas in ages past handing out rubles notes to poor subjects.[54] Rumors and jokes of marital infidelity between the Gorbachevs circulated, and stories spread of an assassination attempt on either Raisa or Mikhail during their summer vacation.

Multiple catastrophes seemed to mark Gorbachev's tenure as an unlucky one: Chernobyl in April; the *Admiral Nakhimov* sinking in the Black Sea with 269 drowned, three years to the day after the Korean Airlines shootdown and with exactly the same number of casualties;[55] a fire at the Zagorsk monastery, center of the Russian Orthodox Church;[56] and the fire and then scuttling of a Soviet missile-carrying nuclear submarine off Bermuda.[57] Churchgoing, peasant *babushki* had even atheistic, sophisticated city dwellers searching for the ominous biblical prophecy concerning the reign of a great prince Michael: "And there shall be a time of trouble, such as never has been since there was a nation till that time."[58] Even the disaster of Chernobyl, which in Russian means wormwood, was seen by some as foretold in Revelations 8:10–11: "The third angel blew his trumpet, and a great star fell from heaven, blazing like a torch, and it fell on a third of the rivers and on the fountains of water. The name of the star is Wormwood. A third of the waters became wormwood, and many men died of the water, because it was made bitter." The port wine stain on Gorbachev's forehead was seen by others as the "mark of the beast" of those who worshiped not God but the "image of the beast," as described in Revelations 16:2 and 19:20.[59]

Meanwhile, *glasnost* was provoking not only excitement but also malaise and unease. Publicity was crucial to Gorbachev's evolving reform platform because it shed light on the real conditions in the country. But while inspiring some to attack the problems, it was demoralizing others by leading them to view the nation's ills as insuperable and perhaps best swept under the rug, as during Brezhnev's time.

THROWING DOWN THE GAUNTLET ON STALIN

Against this background, Burlatskiy's "dialogue" in *Literary Gazette* at the beginning of October was remarkable for its portrayal of the historic dimension of the issues and the struggle going on. The piece constituted a virtual declaration of war by the Gorbachev leadership on apparatchiks unwilling to adapt to the new order. It was time, according to Burlatskiy, to get away from the command economy prevalent since Peter the Great. It was true that after Stalin's death and then again after 1965, economic reforms and hopes for democracy and social self-management had disappeared, "as if swallowed by quicksand." But this did not mean that such reforms contradicted the whole system. Rather, the repeated attempts at reform meant that they were inevitable, and now the current leadership had the "political will" and the "courage" to push the matter through.[60]

Given what was going on at home, one wonders how Gorbachev could simultaneously prepare for his upcoming summit with Reagan in Reykjavik. When Gorbachev, Ligachev, and Yakovlev had met with the writers in June, Gorbachev had been unwilling to take up the Stalin issue for fear that it would be more divisive than productive. Now Gorbachev and his colleagues evidently reached the conclusion that without confronting Stalin's legacy and its continued hold on the way the country was governed, their reform efforts would inevitably be frustrated. The same day Burlatskiy's "dialogue" appeared, nearly the entire Politburo and Secretariat showed up at a national social science conference to hear Gorbachev and Ligachev announce the need for new textbooks, including one on the history of the CPSU.[61]

NOTES

1. Moscow Television Service, February 25, 1986 (FBIS-SOV, February 26, 1986, Supplement no. 041, O 25 and 9).

2. *Le Monde*, July 16, 1986 (FBIS-SOV, July 30, 1986, R 27).

3. The decree releasing him from his position was signed April 21, 1986. See *Sobraniye Postanovleniy Pravitelstva SSSR*, no. 22, (1986).

4. *Die Zeit*, May 9, 1986 (FBIS-SOV, May 8, 1986, G 6).

5. *Pravda*, November 23, 1985.

6. *Pravda*, June 17, 1986 (FBIS-SOV, June 17, 1986, R 1).

7. Moscow Television Service, June 18, 1986 (FBIS-SOV, June 18, 1986, R 33–34).

8. TASS, July 14, 1987 (FBIS-SOV, July 14, 1987, R 1).

9. TASS, August 16, 1986 (FBIS-SOV, August 18, 1986, R 4).

10. *Pravda*, July 9, 1986 (FBIS-SOV, July 25, 1986, R 9–10); and TASS, July 14, 1986 (FBIS-SOV, July 15, R 1).

11. Moscow Domestic Service, August 18, 1986 (FBIS-SOV, August 19, 1986, R 1).

12. TASS, June 20, 1986 (FBIS-SOV, June 20, 1986, G 1).

13. For the official report on the plenum, see *Pravda*, June 17, 1986 (FBIS-SOV, June 17, 1986, R 1). For Gorbachev's speech at the plenum, see ibid., (R 1–31). For Ryzhkov's speech at the Supreme Soviet, see *Pravda*, June 19, 1986 (FBIS-SOV, June 20, 1986, R 3–39).

14. *Pravda*, May 10, 1986 (FBIS-SOV, May 22, 1986, R 16–20).

15. *Izvestiya*, April 18, 1986 (FBIS-SOV, May 13, 1986, S 5–7).

16. *Pravda*, June 22, 1986 (FBIS-SOV, June 22, 1986, R 21–23).

17. *Detente*, No. 8, Winter 1986–87.

18. Ibid.

19. Ibid.

20. Ibid.

21. *Pravda*, July 10, 1986 (FBIS-SOV, July 15, 1986, R 6).

22. Ibid.

23. *Pravda*, July 22, 1986 (FBIS-SOV, July 24, 1986, R 1–2).

24. Ibid., R 1.

25. *Sovetskaya Rossiya*, December 16, 1983 (FBIS-SOV, December 16, 1983, R 14).

26. Moscow Domestic Service, July 31, 1986 (FBIS-SOV, August 4, 1986, R 1–15).

27. In Stavropol, per Moscow Domestic Service, September 19, 1986 (FBIS-SOV, September 22, 1986, R 6). For his speech in Krasnodar, see Moscow Television Service, September 18, 1986 (FBIS-SOV, September 19, 1986, R 5–21).

28. Moscow Domestic Service, August 15, 1986 (FBIS-SOV, August 16, 1986, R 1); and Moscow Domestic Service, September 26, 1986 (FBIS-SOV, September 29, 1986, R 1).

29. *Pravda*, October 1, 1986 (FBIS-SOV, October 3, 1986, R 12–14).

30. *Pravda*, October 2, 1986 (FBIS-SOV, October 7, 1986, R 1–3).

31. See, in particular, the speeches by Moscow raykom first secretaries A. N. Nikolayev and V. V. Vinogradov in *Pravda*, November 13, 1987 (FBIS-SOV,

November 13, 1987, 65–66 and 70–71). Nikolayev, for example, said, "It may be said that Boris Nikolayevich visited dozens of enterprises and organizations in the city. Yes, these meetings did take place but they were purely excursions. They were limited to producing an ostentatious effect and were no more than walks through shops, laboratories, and so forth."

32. *Asahi Shimbun,* August 6, 1986.

33. Georgiy Smirnov had also served there at the same time and should be added to Yakovlev's "tail." Smirnov was director of the Institute of Philosophy from 1983 to 1986; was briefly identified as an assistant to Gorbachev in the stenographic report of the 27th Party Congress; and was then identified in *Pravda,* February 5, 1987, as the new director of the Institute of Marxism-Leninism.

34. *Vedomosti Verkhovnogo Soveta RSFSR,* no. 37, September 10, 1986 (FBIS-SOV, October 31, 1986, R 7–14).

35. *Asahi Shimbun,* September 27, 1986.

36. First announced by Ligachev in his speech on November 6. This would be the third-largest grain harvest in Soviet history and the largest since the record harvest in 1978 of 238 million tons. For the yearly figures, see Tsentralnoye Statisticheskoye Upravleniye SSSR, *Narodnoye Khozyaystvo SSSR v 1980 g.* and . . . *v 1985 g.* (Moscow: Finansy i Statistika, 1981 and 1986), 202 and 180, respectively.

37. *Pravda,* January 18, 1987 (FBIS-SOV, January 27, 1987, S 1–13).

38. Moscow Domestic Service, June 9, 1986 (FBIS-SOV, June 10, 1986, F 1).

39. *Teatr,* no. 8 (August 1986), signed to press June 5.

40. Moscow Domestic Service, July 31, 1986 (FBIS-SOV, August 4, 1986, R 2).

41. Moscow Domestic Service, July 31, 1986 (FBIS-SOV, August 4, 1986, R 4 and 11).

42. Moscow Television Service, February 25, 1986 (FBIS-SOV, February 26, 1986, Supplement no. 41, O 21).

43. *Pravda,* May 28, 1986 (FBIS-SOV, June 5, 1986, S 2–4).

44. *Izvestiya,* June 2, 1986.

45. *Pravda,* November 21, 1986 (FBIS-SOV, November 26, 1986, R 1–8).

46. *Pravda,* June 17, 1986 (FBIS-SOV, June 18, 1986, R 26).

47. *Literary Gazette,* October 1, 1986 (FBIS-SOV, October 8, 1986, R 6–19). The newspaper dialogue was drawn from Burlatskiy's play, *Two Views of One Office,* which opened in December. In June 1987 in a television discussion, Burlatskiy said that he had written the play from July to October 1986 (Moscow Television Service, June 10, 1987 [FBIS-SOV, June 15, 1987, R 4]).

48. *Novyy Mir,* no. 6 (June 1987) signed to press April 28.

49. *Pravda,* July 2, 1986.

50. *Pravda,* November 16, 1986 (FBIS-SOV, November 17, 1986, R 6–11; and December 5, 1986, R 5–12).

51. *Pravda,* April 23, 1987 (FBIS-SOV, April 24, 1987, R 6).

52. *Novyy Mir,* no. 6 (June 1987), signed to press April 28.

53. The impressions that follow are based on my personal observations.

54. For a later wrapup of public opinion on Raisa Gorbacheva, see *Washington Post*, November 28, 1987.

55. Moscow Domestic Service, September 1, 1986 (FBIS-SOV, September 2, 1986, R 1); see *Pravda Ukrainy*, April 1, 1987 (FBIS-SOV, April 16, 1987, R 14–16) for the outcome of the trial of the skippers of the ships involved in the disaster; and *Izvestiya*, May 8, 1990, for an account of later efforts by divers to remove 600 tons of fuel oil from the *Admiral Nakhimov*. This last source puts the number of casualties at 423, of which 65 remained entombed in the ship.

56. *Izvestiya*, September 30, 1986 (FBIS-SOV, September 30, 1986, R 17).

57. TASS, October 4 and 6, 1986 (FBIS-SOV, October 6 and 7, V 1).

58. Daniel 12:1. Given Gorbachev's reformist, anti-Stalinist platform, the passage is even more intriguing for the "good triumphs over evil" optimism that follows in the subsequent verses: "But at that time your people shall be delivered, every one whose name shall be found written in the book. And many of those who sleep in the dust of the earth shall awake, some to everlasting life, and some to shame and everlasting contempt. And those who are wise shall shine like the brightness of the firmament; and those who turn many to righteousness, like the stars for ever and ever."

59. Some American fundamentalists also saw in Gorbachev's birthmark, and other circumstances, evidence that the general secretary was the Antichrist. See *Washington Post*, June 5, 1988.

60. *Literary Gazette*, October 1, 1986.

61. *Pravda*, October 2, 1986 (FBIS-SOV, October 8 and 21, 1986, R 1–6 and R 1–14, respectively).

Chapter 8 ───────────────────────────────

The Road to Reykjavik, and Back

───

*E*ven as Gorbachev battled on several fronts at home, he prepared for an astounding go-for-broke performance in Reykjavik.
After Geneva he clearly concluded that he had the best chance of dealing
productively with Reagan one on one. Besides, attempts to pressure
Reagan indirectly through the Europeans had proved unproductive.
Despite numerous warnings, the United Kingdom and the Federal
Republic of Germany had agreed to cooperate in SDI research with
the United States. In West Germany, moreover, the CDU had scored
a victory in state elections in Lower Saxony in early June, and Kohl's
prospects for victory in federal elections in January 1987 seemed to be
reviving.

Gorbachev reportedly expressed his frustration with the dominant
European attitude on security in a long conversation with Spain's Felipe
Gonzalez on May 20. "Is the idea that the USSR will send tanks into
Europe in the event of a hypothetical conflict so deeply rooted in the
European population and among the politicians of the new generation?"
he was said to have quizzed his Spanish guest. According to the
press account of their conversation, Gonzalez confirmed that this was
"undoubtedly" the case, whereupon Gorbachev responded, "I believe
that they will not allow Reagan to carry out disarmament."[1]

Nevertheless, the general secretary was intent on giving it a spectacular try. Even in failure Reykjavik would shatter European confidence
in the steadfastness of the U.S. commitment to protect Western Europe
with the American nuclear umbrella. But it would also leave European
leaders even more distrustful of Gorbachev's intentions for the security
of the "European home" they shared with him.

RECONSIDERING A WASHINGTON SUMMIT

In Geneva in November 1985, Gorbachev had accepted Reagan's
invitation that they meet next in Washington. He had done so immediately and had attached no conditions.[2] Back in Moscow, however, either
Gorbachev developed second thoughts on his own about the alacrity
with which he had taken up Reagan's suggestion for a follow-up
meeting, or he had the view imposed on him that U.S. movement

on concrete issues would have to be forthcoming for there to be a summit in Washington.

By the time of his report to the 27th Party Congress, in any event, the general secretary had begun to develop just such preconditions. The next summit should provide "practical results" in arms control and should not be a forum for "idle conversation." There were at least two areas in which agreements could be reached: a nuclear test ban and an accord on zero INF in Europe. If the U.S. displayed "readiness to seek agreement," there would be no problem in settling on dates for a summit.[3]

Gorbachev's backtracking at the congress was a forewarning of the protracted back-and-forthing between Moscow and Washington over the conditions and location of the next meeting between the U.S. and Soviet leaders. In March Gorbachev proposed a summit in Europe to sign a test ban agreement.[4] In April, more seriously, it was decided that Shevardnadze and Shultz would meet in Washington on May 14–16. Within a week, however, Moscow canceled the scheduled ministerials, citing the April 15 U.S. bombing raid on Libya.[5] Gorbachev then stated that a summit in 1986 was still possible if the United States altered its foreign policy course of "poisoning the international atmosphere," or if it showed promise of "real progress in disarmament."[6]

Gorbachev and Shevardnadze made it clear that Soviet diplomacy was still operating along two tracks. In his Lenin Day speech in April Shevardnadze said, "We will . . . conduct a direct and honest dialogue with our partners in the quest for mutually acceptable results. This is one orientation of our party's foreign policy activities. Another is that of open dialogue with the world public."[7] Gorbachev put it even more pithily shortly before his foreign minister spoke. Asked about preparations for a second summit with Reagan, Gorbachev told workers in Tolyatti that "We have to put pressure on them, and hard!"[8]

Notably, however, it was during this very period of talking tough and playing hard to get that Gorbachev admonished Soviet diplomats that they not maneuver Soviet policy into dead-end positions. Even while publicly calling on the United States to change its stance, Gorbachev was secretly preparing significant alterations in Soviet positions. It was a pattern that would be repeated time and time again. As soon as Gorbachev would appear to have painted himself into a corner, he would stride right out.

PREPARING FOR ICELAND

Before long the diplomatic minuet resumed. In early June Reagan reportedly sent Gorbachev a letter asking him to reschedule the postponed Shultz-Shevardnadze ministerials so as to work out summit arrangements. In a speech in Glassboro several weeks later, Reagan—evidently commenting on the package of proposals put forward by the Soviets in Geneva on June 11—acknowledged that the Soviet Union had begun to make a "serious effort" toward arms control which could represent a turning point in relations. In his first meeting with Reagan on June 23, Yuriy Dubinin, the new Soviet ambassador in Washington, handed over Gorbachev's reply to Reagan's letter. In it Gorbachev reportedly took the position that a summit in 1986 would make no sense without "concrete achievements," but he avoided making this a precondition for a meeting.[9]

In a speech in Warsaw at the beginning of July, Gorbachev said his letter to Reagan contained "specific proposals on how to bring things out of a blind alley" on arms control.[10] Reagan's answer of July 25 reportedly offered a seven-and-one-half-year nonwithdrawal period from the ABM Treaty, with the right to deploy an ABM system after that. Though not publicized at the time, it also required that either side intending to deploy such a system offer a plan for the elimination of all offensive ballistic missiles, it attached no timetable to this.[11]

The exchange of letters between the two leaders set the stage in late July for agreement on rescheduling the Shultz-Shevardnadze ministerials, now set for September 19–20.[12] U.S. and Soviet officials met for talks on regional and other issues several times in August.[13] Meanwhile, Gorbachev continued his effort to exert public pressure on the United States to come to terms on a nuclear test ban, extending the Soviet moratorium for the fourth and last time (until January 1, 1987) and suggesting that a test ban could be the "main result" of a summit in 1986.[14]

When Shevardnadze finally arrived in Washington the letter he handed to Reagan from Gorbachev suggested a get-together on short notice in Iceland. It is uncertain, however, exactly when the idea of inviting Reagan to Iceland was conceived. But whatever the state of play in Moscow in late summer concerning another meeting with Reagan, the August 23 arrest in New York of Soviet UN employee Gennadiy Zakharov threw relations with Washington into turmoil. On August 30 Soviet authorities in Moscow responded by arresting American reporter Nicholas Daniloff on spy charges. The affair dominated not only the headlines but diplomats' time for a month and seemed to diminish drastically the prospects for a summit anytime soon.

It is tempting to speculate that Daniloff's arrest was a provocation from hard-line elements in Moscow bent on scuttling Gorbachev's developing diplomacy toward Washington. If so, however, the timing of the affair was inadvertently set by the U.S. side rather than by skeptics of Gorbachev's policy in the USSR. Zakharov did not have diplomatic status yet behaved as if he did. His transgressions were so blatant that American officials felt they had no choice but to arrest him. The extent to which the timing and wider impact of the move were considered is not clear, but the arrest of Daniloff reportedly came as a surprise to Washington.[15]

Nonetheless, an article in *Pravda* immediately after Daniloff's arrest contained a strong hint that Gorbachev was engaged in an "abrupt turning point" in foreign affairs and was indeed encountering opposition from the "left." "Contradictions in the world arena do not rule out political agreements and compromises," wrote Prof. Yu. Pankov. "Attacks on Lenin's peaceful coexistence ideas have been made by our ideological opponents at various times and on various 'fronts' of the ideological and political struggle. Even now such attacks are not infrequent."[16] Pankov's polemic seemed to draw from Gorbachev's then-still secret speech at the Foreign Ministry. "Lenin paid exceedingly close attention to arranging peaceful relations between the young Soviet republic and the capitalist countries. He saw them as an essential prerequisite for the successful fulfillment of the creative tasks of the socialist revolution."[17]

There were several issues other than a possible second meeting with Reagan, however, which could easily have stirred up the leftists in Moscow at about this time. One was nuclear testing. As already noted, in August Gorbachev had announced the fourth extension of the Soviet moratorium. Chief of the General Staff Akhromeyev conceded at a press conference several days later that the move involved "a certain degree of detriment" in military terms. Nevertheless, Akhromeyev defended it as "tolerable" when assessed "comprehensively" within the context of the overall "correlation of forces." Soviet defenses were still "being maintained at an appropriate level."[18]

Concessions at the CDE talks may also have aroused the leftists. Here again Akhromeyev was designated the point man for the leadership as it moved to deliver on Gorbachev's promise of a more forthcoming stance on verification in his statement of January 15. In late August Akhromeyev personally addressed the conference in Stockholm to announce Soviet agreement to permit "a quota of one or two inspections a year on its territory" to verify compliance with the confidence-building measures being negotiated.[19] It was the first time Moscow had accepted the principle of on-site, on-demand inspection of military exercises. Several days later, however, in nailing down the details, Akhromeyev defended Moscow's insistence that any inspections from the air "be carried out by groups from the other side in aircraft of the side that is being inspected."[20] Nevertheless, on September 21 an accord was reached in Stockholm—the first East-West arms accord concluded since 1979.[21]

Rather than any specific issue, however, it was probably the Gorbachev leadership's inclination to compromise rather than stonewall that was provoking a reaction in some circles. While still calling for movement from the United States toward "resolving at least one or two significant problems of international security," none other than Gorbachev personally identified himself during this period with the need for "compromise."[22] There was an interim solution to the Zakharov-Daniloff problem on September 12, when both men were released from detention but forbidden to return to their home countries.[23] Gorbachev, to be sure, offended many in the West when he referred to Daniloff as "a spy who has been caught red-handed." But the more important point the general secretary went on to make was that his leadership would not yield to this foreign provocation and would continue "to be strong and resolutely pursue its peace-loving policy."[24]

When Shultz and Shevardnadze at last met in Washington on September 19–20, Shevardnadze delivered a letter to Reagan from Gorbachev, said to be in reply to a Reagan letter of July 25. Only later, however, was it disclosed that Gorbachev had proposed a meeting in a third country to review the agenda for a Washington summit. Reagan had reacted positively to the idea, but he countered that nothing could be done until the Zakharov-Daniloff affair was resolved.[25] This was not, however, the only dispute that monopolized the attention of the foreign ministers and left little time for discussion of arms control issues. There was also a serious controversy over the number of diplomats the United States would permit to remain at the Soviet Mission to the UN (SMUN) in New York, and over a related State Department order expelling 25 of them, all said to be KGB spies.

Nevertheless, at a press conference following their two days of talks in Washington, Shultz and Shevardnadze agreed that the conditions now existed for a productive summit—if the Daniloff-Zakharov matter and SMUN controversy could be resolved.[26] The two foreign ministers talked again in New York on September 28 on the margins of the UN General Assembly and agreed temporarily to postpone final resolution of the SMUN dispute.[27] Regarding Zakharov and Daniloff, they were finally able to announce that the two detainees were headed home.

Having thus cleared the decks, the two sides announced that Reagan and Gorbachev would meet in less than two weeks in Reykjavik. Technically it was not to be a summit but, rather, the highest-level round of consultations to prepare for a summit in Washington, as agreed in Geneva in November 1985.[28] Although Shevardnadze made no mention of this factor, it could not have been lost on the Soviet side that the meeting would be held on the eve of mid-term congressional elections in the United States, in which Reagan was investing much time and energy seeking to prevent the loss of a Republican majority in the Senate.

REYKJAVIK ROLLER COASTER

Some American officials later expressed great surprise over the wide-ranging proposals Gorbachev presented in Reykjavik. The expectation had been that the talks would center on INF, on which the two sides were closer than ever to an agreement sharply reducing but not totally eliminating the number of INF missiles deployed in Europe, as well as cutting Soviet deployments in Asia. In September, during the ministerial talks in Washington, the Soviets had informally suggested an accord limiting LRINF warheads in Europe to 100 on each side and completely eliminating all Pershing IIs; outside Europe Soviet SS-20s in Asia would be frozen and the United States would have the right to match them with comparable numbers of systems deployed in the United States. The United States in response had proposed an "interim" agreement limiting INF globally to 200 warheads: 100 in Europe, including some Pershing IIs; and 100 in Asia/United States.[29] After his talks in Washington with Shultz, Shevardnadze revealed that the USSR had dropped its demand for a freeze on British and French nuclear forces as part of an INF deal.[30]

But beyond INF, the notion of a "grand compromise" involving START and SDI was still in the air, encouraged in large part by movement over the summer in Soviet positions in Geneva. Moscow's initiatives were reported to have stirred debate within the Reagan administration over whether to accept limits on SDI research in exchange for sharp cuts in strategic weapons.[31] Gorbachev, furthermore, had made clear after the Geneva summit that he would continue to try to convince Reagan that SDI was a dangerous program. Even as the Soviet leader asserted in September 1986 that the USSR would not yield to "provocation" by breaking the "threads of contacts" with the United States, he insisted that the "value of contacts lies not in contacts themselves, but in their results." If Reagan really desired to move toward a nuclear-free world and agreed that a nuclear war would be "intolerable," then there should be no "fundamental obstacles" toward reaching disarmament agreements.[32]

With the benefit of hindsight, a close reading of Shevardnadze's press conference in New York on September 30 could divine some hints of what was in store. The world would be condemned to a chronic "fever" if the "temperature" of U.S.-Soviet relations remained "for a long time at a critically dangerous level," asserted the foreign minister. This could be averted only if the arms race were stopped, including its spread to outer space. In the view of the Soviet leadership, what was required were "extra-powerful stimuli, a start on the most direct and the shortest road leading to results." Gorbachev had therefore proposed, and Reagan had accepted, an "urgent meeting" on October 11–12.

The objective of the talks in Iceland, according to Shevardnadze, would be "to make a direct assessment of the situation and work out some clear instructions designed to achieve progress in some questions relating to nuclear arms—progress sufficient for attaining substantial results." It was the Soviet side's view that "various options exist for a solution to the question of medium-range missiles . . . —this is perhaps the most promising direction—and on strategic, offensive, and space weapons." The problem of banning nuclear tests would also figure prominently in the talks. "I would not like to say that the US proposals contain not a grain of rationality," stated Shevardnadze. But "the moment has now come when it is necessary to adopt a fundamental political decision, determine on which questions there is mutual understanding, and draw up corresponding draft agreements."[33]

Indeed, this was what the Soviet delegation arrived in Reykjavik professing it was prepared to do. Early in his talks with Reagan Gorbachev tabled a draft "directive" from the two leaders to their foreign ministers calling on them to prepare agreements or treaties based on agreed "principles." The Soviet proposal covered all the areas under discussion in Geneva, as well as nuclear testing:

- In START it called for 50-percent reductions from present levels in each leg of each side's strategic triad.
- In INF it reiterated Moscow's agreement to eliminate all Soviet and American LRINF in Europe without taking British and French nuclear systems into account. It proposed that LRINF in Asia be dealt with in separate negotiations. In addition, it called for negotiations on SRINF missiles in Europe with ranges under 1000 km.
- On defense and space issues, it called for a ten-year commitment not to withdraw from the ABM Treaty. All testing of space-based elements of a ballistic missile defense, furthermore, would be prohibited except research and testing in laboratories.
- Finally, it stated that bilateral negotiations on a comprehensive test ban (CTB) should be resumed as soon as possible.[34]

The Soviet package implied that offensive cuts would depend on defensive limits. Nevertheless, the components were at first discussed separately rather than as a package. The United States dropped the notion of an "interim" INF agreement that would have left each side with 100 LRINF warheads in Europe, but it continued to press the Soviet side to reduce its warheads in the Far East to 100 if not to zero. During a long night of bargaining at the experts level, the Soviet side agreed to an initial freeze on SRINF. In START the USSR rejected U.S. proposals for three sublimits on ballistic missile warheads while agreeing to reduce its heavy missiles by 50 percent as long as the United States did not deploy any missiles in this category. At the beginning of the second day Gorbachev dramatically agreed to limit Soviet LRINF in Asia to 100 warheads, the equivalent of only 33 SS-20s. In this connection Gorbachev later stated that the USSR was prepared for the most stringent verification measures necessary to monitor such an agreement, including the right to on-site inspection.

After this, however, the two sides reached an impasse in the defense and space area. Gorbachev continued to insist on a pledge not to withdraw from the ABM Treaty for ten years and on restricting SDI testing and research to laboratories. Reagan responded by proposing to tie a nonwithdrawal commitment to the elimination of all offensive ballistic missiles in ten years, thus adding a specific timetable to the proposal he first made in his July 25 letter to Gorbachev. Gorbachev countered with a call for the elimination of all offensive strategic arms. Both leaders reaffirmed their desire to eliminate all nuclear weapons of any type. The talks ended with Reagan refusing to agree with Gorbachev that SDI research and testing be restricted to laboratories while offensive weapons were being reduced. Gorbachev's high-risk gamble to draw Reagan into a "grand compromise" had failed.[35]

RECRIMINATIONS

The meeting in Iceland broke up with mutual recriminations over who had said exactly what and in what context. Both sides sought to blame the other for the lack of any concrete agreement while nevertheless seeking to present the overall meeting in a positive light. In Europe especially there was undisguised shock over the extent to which Reagan had seemed prepared to bargain away the U.S. intercontinental nuclear umbrella without consulting his NATO partners. Washington quickly abandoned all talk of dismantling all strategic missiles within ten years.

Before long Reagan became embroiled in yet another controversy. In early November not only did his Republican party lose its majority in the Senate, but the first reports of secret U.S. arms sales to Iran began to surface. Before November was over, Attorney General Edwin Meese disclosed that members of Reagan's own National Security Council staff had diverted some of the profits to the Nicaraguan contras to help finance their efforts against the Sandinista regime.

The Politburo, meanwhile, tempered its praise of Gorbachev's conduct in Reykjavik, downgrading it from the "fully approved" expressed after Geneva to an unadorned "approved."[36] Furthermore, the general secretary's press conference and two speeches detailing his conversations with Reagan suggested unusual sensitivity over his performance in Iceland and a strong desire to shape public perceptions of it.[37] Reykjavik was not a "no-lose" proposition for Gorbachev. He had put his personal prestige on the line in favor of the grand gamble to restrain SDI. When the gamble failed, Gorbachev had to scramble to defend it as having been worth the risk.

At about this time, moreover (as we shall see later in greater detail), Ogarkov seemed to register his opposition to the evolution in declaratory military doctrine under his successor, Akhromeyev.[38] Ogarkov's main focus continued to be the maintenance of a war-fighting capability, whereas Akhromeyev was stressing war prevention and parity at progressively lower levels in both nuclear and conventional armaments. In October 1983 Ogarkov had drawn the line (or had it imposed on him) at 120 SS-20s in Europe, at most a freeze in the Far East, and all of this only if there were no U.S. deployments; at Reykjavik Akhromeyev had gone along with a zero INF option in Europe and only 100 SS-20 warheads in the Far East. Whatever support Ogarkov had in what appeared to be his dissent, however, the political status of the professional military would be further dramatically reduced at the Revolution Anniversary parade on November 7, when its representation on the Lenin Mausoleum was drastically cut back.

Equally interesting and even more important was the swing in the attitude of Yegor Ligachev. Before Reykjavik, as we have seen, Ligachev joined Gorbachev in what could be interpreted as an attack on Gromyko. Several days after Reykjavik, however, Gorbachev's deputy sounded very much like Gromyko, pessimistically declaring that the meeting had "clarified beyond doubt that the Washington administration does not desire genuine accords, that it is seeking to achieve military superiority over the USSR."[39] When Ligachev delivered his major speech on November 6, he was still accusing the United States of striving for superiority. But he now tempered this charge with the judgment that Reykjavik had been a "major event" that had proved "the need to persistently search for untraditional approaches to pressing problems"—perhaps intended by Ligachev as another implicit swipe at Gromyko's brand of diplomacy. Moreover, Ligachev now optimistically declared that the meeting had showed that "Accords leading to nuclear disarmament are possible."[40]

After Reykjavik, nonetheless, U.S.-Soviet disarmament negotiations appeared completely deadlocked. Delegations led by Shultz and Shevardnadze met in Austria on November 5–6, on the margins of the opening session of the Vienna CSCE follow-up conference. The Soviet position had definitely reverted to an insistent demand for tight linkage among INF, START, defense and space, and nuclear testing issues.

Shevardnadze gave Shultz a draft "key provisions" of agreements in each of these areas. It reflected Moscow's positions in light of the bargaining at Reykjavik.[41] According to press reports, the talks were completely unproductive, degenerating at times into screaming matches. Seasoned negotiators such as Karpov and Nitze were said to have called each other "liar."[42]

The American side concluded that serious negotiations were not likely until the early spring.[43] On the Soviet side, Soviet television reflected the chill in relations when it refused to broadcast a New Year's Day greeting to the Soviet people from President Reagan. "We have no basis for the exchange of such New Year's messages," asserted Foreign Ministry spokesman Geradiy Gerasimov. "Why should we create any illusions about our relations?" A year earlier, in contrast, after the first Reagan-Gorbachev meeting in Geneva, Soviet television had carried such a message—the first by a U.S. President since 1972. And a year later it would do so again after the more productive and upbeat third summit in Washington.[44]

In part Moscow was probably waiting to take a better reading of the fallout from Reykjavik in Europe and Washington. In part the Soviet leadership simply needed time to sort itself out and settle on its approach to the United States in the coming year. But through it all the possibility of working toward an INF agreement delinked from the other Geneva issues probably remained a live option waiting simply for the right context in which to be announced. Immediately after Reykjavik Karpov said as much in London and Bonn—only to be undercut immediately as the Soviet position firmed up in Moscow.[45] In the end, however, it turned out that Karpov was premature rather than wrong.

Gorbachev for one was certainly not about to abandon "new thinking." In fact, during this period Gorbachev for the first time pushed at the very highest level Yuriy Krasin's thesis of December 1985 of the priority of "all-human values" over class struggle. In an October 20 meeting with a delegation of international cultural figures, Gorbachev cited Lenin to support the view that "general human values took priority over the tasks of this or that class. The significance of this thought is felt especially keenly today." Gorbachev continued, "It is very desired that in the other part of the world they too understand and accept the thesis about the priority of general human values over all others to which some or other people are committed."[46]

An essay in *Pravda* in mid-November by historian Ye. Plimak developed this line in striking fashion. Plimak argued the need to update Marx's notion that a "united mankind" would be possible only after the triumph of communism. In the nuclear era, pleaded Plimak, it was necessary to work toward "the establishment of an integrated, interdependent mankind living a peaceful life even in conditions of a socially heterogeneous world." Going even further than Gorbachev had in his November 1985 Supreme Soviet speech, Plimak called for great caution by revolutionaries in the Third World, warning that "any local conflict has a tendency to expand into a regional, even world conflict." In the nuclear age, wrote Plimak, "violence can easily change from the 'midwife' of history into its 'gravedigger.'" Finally, "our times teach us to develop compromise forms of the struggle too, and practice them widely."[47]

Soviet spokesmen nevertheless expressed the expected outrage over Reagan's call on November 18 for support of those "who would take arms against the sea of darkness" and for what they called his distortions of what had actually happened at Reykjavik.[48] They also predictably criticized Washington's announcement on November 26 that the United States would break through the weapons limits of the unratified SALT II Treaty two days later when the one hundred and thirty-first B-52 bomber armed with ALCMs became operational. But Moscow generally struck a pose of restraint, announcing that it would refrain from abandoning SALT limits for the time being.[49]

The year ended with a surprisingly candid admission by Deputy Foreign Minister Aleksandr Bessmertnykh of Moscow's weak leverage against SDI. On a nationally televised roundtable discussion devoted entirely to SDI, the veteran diplomat, who had several years of experience in the United States, refused to mince words. "It must be admitted that the current US President—and until recently he has been fairly popular—has nevertheless managed to secure a situation in which the broad public supports this program," said Bessmertnykh. "As far as Congress is concerned, there is some stratification taking place. . . . The majority of them believe and say that they are against the SDI but are in favor of carrying out the research part all the same. The whole problem of American liberalism lies in this vagueness."[50] It was an analysis of U.S. "liberals" reminiscent of that of the SPD after its loss to Kohl in 1983.

NOTES

1. *Cambio 16*, December 15, 1986.
2. *New York Times*, November 21–22, 1985.
3. Moscow Television Service, February 25, 1986 (FBIS-SOV, February 26, 1986, Supplement no. 41, O 31).
4. *Pravda*, March 30, 1986 (FBIS-SOV, March 31, 1986, AA 1).
5. *New York Times*, April 12 and 16, 1986.
6. *New York Times*, April 21 and 22, 1986.
7. *Pravda*, April 23, 1986 (FBIS-SOV, April 23, 1986, R 7).

8. Moscow Television Service, April 8, 1986 (FBIS-SOV, April 9, 1986, R 3).

9. *New York Times*, June 16, 20, 24, and 25, 1986.

10. Moscow Television Service, July 1, 1986 (FBIS-SOV, July 2, 1986, F 6).

11. *Washington Post*, February 16, 1987.

12. *New York Times*, July 30 and August 5, 1986.

13. *New York Times*, August 12 and 27, 1986.

14. *Pravda*, August 19, 1986 (FBIS-SOV, August 19, AA 1–7). The first extension, for three months, came in Gorbachev's statement of January 15, 1986. Replying to a message from the Delhi Six (the leaders of Argentina, India, Mexico, Tanzania, Sweden, and Greece), on March 14, 1986, Gorbachev extended the moratorium for the second time until the next U.S. nuclear blast. Gorbachev announced the third extension, to last until August 6, in his May 14, 1986, TV report on the Chernobyl disaster. In December 1986 a "Soviet Government Statement" would reaffirm the intention to resume testing in 1987 after the first U.S. explosion (*Izvestiya*, December 19, 1986 [FBIS-SOV, December 18, 1986, AA 8–9]).

15. *New York Times*, September 13, 1986.

16. *Pravda*, September 1, 1986 (FBIS-SOV, September 5, 1986, CC 2–3).

17. Ibid., CC 2.

18. Moscow Television Service, August 25, 1986 (FBIS-SOV, August 26, 1986, AA 4).

19. *Red Star*, August 30, 1986 (FBIS-SOV, September 2, 1986, AA 2).

20. TASS, September 4, 1986 (FBIS-SOV, September 5, 1986, AA 1).

21. For a description of its main provisions, see *Washington Post*, September 21, 1986, and *New York Times*, September 22, 1986. In August 1987 Soviet officials fully cooperated in facilitating the first U.S. request to inspect a military exercise on Soviet territory (*New York Times*, September 22, 1987).

22. *Izvestiya*, September 9, 1986 (FBIS-SOV, September 9, 1986, AA 10–11).

23. TASS, September 12, 1986 (FBIS-SOV, September 15, 1986, A 1).

24. Moscow Domestic Service, September 18, 1986 (FBIS-SOV, September 19, 1986, R 3–4).

25. Paul H. Nitze, "The Nuclear and Space Negotiations: Translating Promise to Progress," speech to the World Affairs Council, Boston, Massachusetts, January 14, 1987; text in U.S. Department of State, Bureau of Public Affairs, Current Policy No. 910, February 1987.

26. *Washington Post*, September 21, 1986.

27. On October 22, 1986, Foreign Ministry spokesman Gerasimov announced the expulsion of five more American diplomats from Moscow, as well as the pulling out of all Soviets working for the American embassy and the U.S. consulate in Leningrad. TASS, furthermore, announced the same day that Adolf Tolkachev, said to have been a spy for the United States, had been executed. See *Washington Post*, October 23, 1986.

28. TASS, September 30, 1986 (FBIS-SOV, October 1, 1986, A 1).

29. *New York Times*, October 8 and 10, 1986; Secretary George Shultz, "The INF Treaty: Strengthening U.S. Security," statement before the Senate Foreign

Relations Committee, January 25, 1988 (Washington, DC: U.S. Department of State, Bureau of Public Affairs, Current Policy No. 1038, February 1988), 7; and Strobe Talbott, "The Road to Zero," *Time*, December 14, 1987, 29.

30. *Washington Post*, September 21, 1986.

31. See, for example, *New York Times*, July 3, 1986, and *Washington Post*, June 29, 1986.

32. *Izvestiya*, September 9, 1986 (FBIS-SOV, September 9, 1986, AA 4 and 10–11).

33. TASS, September 30, 1986 (FBIS-SOV, October 1, 1986, A 2–3, 6–7).

34. What is described as the text of Gorbachev's draft "directive" can be found in the *Washington Post*, February 16, 1987. For Gorbachev's three accounts of the Reykjavik negotiations, see Moscow Television Service, October 12, 1986 (FBIS-SOV, October 14, 1986, DD 26–57); Moscow Television Service, October 14, 1986 (FBIS-SOV, October 15, 1986, DD 1–11); and idem, October 22, 1986 (FBIS-SOV, October 23, 1986, AA 1–10).

Secretary Shultz's account of Reykjavik can be found in his November 17, 1986, speech at the University of Chicago, "Nuclear Weapons, Arms Control, and the Future of Deterrence" (reprinted in *Department of State Bulletin* 87, no. 2118 [January 1987]: 33–34). Ambassador Nitze's account is in his address in Boston on January 14, 1987, "The Nuclear and Space Negotiations".

35. *Washington Post*, October 19, 1986 and February 16, 1987, and the Shultz and Nitze accounts cited in note 33.

36. *Pravda*, October 15, 1986 (FBIS-SOV, October 15, 1986, DD 11).

37. Moscow Television Service, October 12, 1986 (FBIS-SOV, October 14, 1986, DD 26–57); Moscow Television Service, October 14, 1986 (FBIS-SOV, October 15, 1986, DD 1–11); and Moscow Television Service, October 22, 1986 (FBIS-SOV, October 23, 1986, AA 1–10).

38. APN Military Bulletin, no. 2 (October 1986): 5–6. The article was released in Moscow on October 27 (*Washington Post*, October 28, 1986).

39. *Pravda*, October 17, 1986 (FBIS-SOV, October 24, 1986, R 9).

40. Moscow Television Service, November 6, 1986 (FBIS-SOV, November 7, 1986, O 16–17).

41. TASS, November 10, 1986 (FBIS-SOV, November 13, 1986, AA 1–6).

42. *Washington Post*, November 11, 1986.

43. Ibid.

44. *Washington Post*, January 1 and 2, 1988.

45. Press Association, October 14, 1986 (FBIS-SOV, October 16, 1986, DD 1–2); and DPA, October 15, 1986 (FBIS-SOV, October 16, 1986, DD 3).

46. *Literary Gazette*, October 22, 1986 (FBIS-SOV, October 22, 1986, CC 1).

47. *Pravda*, November 14, 1986. For Plimak's identification with the Institute of the International Workers Movement, see the roundtable discussion on "More Socialism!" in *Ogonek*, no. 12 (March 1988). For a historical survey of the ebb and flow of Soviet thinking on the dangers of regional escalation in the nuclear age, see Fukuyama, "Soviet Civil-Military Relations."

48. See Arbatov in particular, in *Pravda*, November 21, 1986.

49. *Pravda*, December 7, 1986 (FBIS-SOV, December 8, 1986, AA 1–3).

50. Moscow Television Service, December 22, 1986 (FBIS-SOV, December 23, 1986, AA 17–18).

Chapter 9

The January Plenum: Political Reform

A decade and a half earlier, two years before he was exiled to Ottawa, Aleksandr Yakovlev had spelled out what amounted to the guiding precepts of a policy of utilitarian *glasnost*. "Information, apart from its direct propagandistic value, is of even greater practical assistance to the leading organs in the scientific control and study of public opinion," he had written in the party's premier ideological journal. Information made "the masses more competent to observe, react, and criticize—one of the conditions for the effective participation of millions of Soviet citizens in the government of the country. It would otherwise be impossible to have a normally functioning socialist system or a growth of consciousness and social participation on the part of the workers."[1]

It was a social engineering, narrowly utilitarian approach to information—and certainly not an appreciation for a Western-style bill of rights—that the Gorbachev leadership sought to use, through the transmission belt of public and informed opinion, to pressure the party and other bureaucracies to respond to the calls for change. In order to control its own bureaucracies more effectively, the central leadership had to encourage a certain degree of freedom at the grass-roots level to criticize its own ruling structures. Only by encouraging the media, the intelligentsia, rank-and-file party members, and the public to speak out on sanctioned topics could Moscow hope to get more realistic feedback on the actual state of affairs in the country and to gain greater leverage on its own lower-level representatives.

In this highly charged and tricky political atmosphere, rumors persisted that Second Secretary Ligachev was a pole of attraction for Central Committee members and other notables threatened by and upset over the pace and scope of Gorbachev's intended reforms, to say nothing of their direction. The plenum on cadre policy in particular, which Gorbachev had announced in late July 1986 in Khabarovsk, seemed to have run into problems. Clearly the party leadership's pressure for change had provoked a negative reaction from many of its own representatives at lower levels. But despite the rumors, it was not clear that Gorbachev's reformist impulses were being resisted at the very top among his colleagues. Ligachev, to be sure, had on occasion made remarks suggesting

opposition to various aspects of the reform measures under consideration and would be increasingly caustic regarding some trends in the
arts and the media. Yet at the same time, even Ligachev underwent
a demonstrable "radicalization" on some of these same issues. Rather
than a brake on reform, Ligachev appeared at this juncture to be one of
its prime generators as the party prepared for what would be its landmark
January 1987 plenum on cadres and democratization.

The unofficial second secretary was in fact very active throughout this
crucial period. Contrary to the speculation concerning his allegedly more
conservative outlook, Ligachev in early November lent his authority to
the notion of holding a plenum on cadre policy. He also continued to
appear to be a strong supporter of the wave of politically useful liberality
in the arts already evident even before the 27th Party Congress. In
addition, Ligachev publicly sponsored some concrete measures to bring
fresh blood into the Academy of Sciences. Finally, and most interesting,
Ligachev appeared to spearhead criticism of Gromyko, Shcherbitskiy,
and Kunayev—strange behavior were Ligachev really intent on slowing
the momentum of the unfolding agenda for reform.

LIGACHEV CENTER STAGE

In May 1986 in a speech to oil workers in the Tatar autonomous
republic, Ligachev had ridiculed proposals put forward during the
precongress discussion of the draft Party Program and Rules strictly
to limit the tenure of leading workers. "Our party has taken this
approach to the problem," he had said. "We should be looking not
at the calendar, but the true results of the work of directors." A
critical assessment of performance, and not age or time in place,
should be the guide to how long a leading worker should occupy his
post.[2] Ligachev thus seemed to oppose what would be Gorbachev's
rumored desire to impose strict retirement regulations on the regime's
officials.

Ligachev, however, either had a change of heart or was capable of
applying his views selectively. This became apparent in mid-October
1986 when he sponsored and presided over the installation of Guriy
Marchuk as new president of the Academy of Sciences, replacing the
ancient A. P. Aleksandrov. "As secretary of the party's Tomsk and
Novosibirsk obkoms," Ligachev told the meeting in endorsing Marchuk,
"and engaging in the organization and development of major scientific
centers in Novosibirsk and Tomsk, I dealt constantly with G. I. Marchuk
and other eminent scientists."[3] Based on his observations, Ligachev
said that Soviet science and the academy in particular needed "serious
restructuring," not just "small, partial improvements, but . . . a radical

turning point in the way it operates." It was "urgent," he emphasized, to reinforce the academy with "fresh young scientific forces."[4]

A month later, after calling Ligachev's earlier remarks "fair," Marchuk reminded an Academy Presidium meeting that "on May 12, 1962 the CC CPSU and the USSR Council of Ministers adopted a resolution according to which scientific leadership posts can be occupied by individuals no older than 65. . . . I think that in Academy organizations this age norm, which in its time was recognized as optimal, should be resurrected."[5] It would be the only move in any Soviet institution until well after the January plenum toward imposing any limits on tenure, and Ligachev—rumors of his conservatism to the contrary—was intimately associated with it.

None other than Ligachev was selected to give the Revolution anniversary speech in early November.[6] This seemed to confirm the centrality of his role in the preparations not only for the cadre plenum but also for the economic plenum that would follow it. Ligachev quickly verified that cadre policy would indeed be the focus of the next plenum, thus dampening increasing speculation as to whether the plenum would be held after all. The second secretary also used the occasion to endorse and characterize restructuring as the "transformation of deep-rooted structures in the economy and in the political and social spheres." A "struggle is under way," Ligachev said on November 6, "between the forces of renewal and those who would wish to derail restructuring and push us into a mire of economic stagnation and social apathy. There can be no concessions to the obsolete." Ligachev even called for the "purification" of Soviet society of everything "alien" to it; this, of course, had been the title of T. Samolis's controversial precongress article, for which Ligachev had criticized *Pravda*, a point *Pravda* editor Viktor Afanasyev would later be quick to point out.[7]

From the leadership down through the ranks, affirmed Ligachev, all in the party had to "learn to work and live in conditions of expanding democracy." It was not time "to place one's trust in strictly administrative methods." Nevertheless, Ligachev set out a basically conservative view of the cohesion of Soviet society. On the issue of what "guaranteed" success, he put great faith in popular support, but it was an ideological formulation that imposed an identity of views between the people and the party:

> The CPSU does not doubt victory in achieving the goals set: A guarantee of this is the support of the Soviet people, who are wholeheartedly in favor of changes for the better. A further guarantee of this is the inviolable social and international unity of our society, the strengthening alliance of the working class, the collective farm peasantry and the people's intelligentsia. This alliance, this unity, proceeding from the events of October 1917, has

been and remains the most reliable guarantee of the success of revolutionary transformation work.[8]

At this point, however, Ligachev was not necessarily out of step with the consensus in the Politburo or with Gorbachev. In his Khabarovsk speech in late July, for example, the general secretary had not shied away from mixing calls for greater democracy with descriptions of the USSR as "a country where the party is the ruler."[9]

Despite his earlier widely noted warnings against imposing a market economy on the Soviet Union, Ligachev outlined and endorsed the agenda of what would be the June 1987 plenum on economic reform. "The transition from partial improvements and transformations to an integral radical reform of the administration and of economic management is being put onto a practical plane," he assured his listeners. "It should embrace planning, financing, price-setting and supplies, and it should embrace all cross-sections of management of public-sector production, of the national economy, and of branch and territorial programs. It should embrace all stages of the reproduction cycle and all factors of economic growth." And lest anyone still have doubts about where Ligachev stood, he added that "the party deems it to be a matter of crucial importance to speed up the creation of this new, flexible system."[10]

With these words Ligachev in effect sanctioned a key economic conference organized by the lifelong reformist and fellow "Siberian" Aganbegyan. It would meet November 13–15 to elaborate what would be the outlines of the economic reform measures eventually approved by the June 1987 plenum. It was agreed, according to Aganbegyan, that "the main content of the reform of management, conceived as the transition from predominantly administrative to predominantly economic regulators, comprises fundamental restructuring of price formation, the financial and credit machinery, and material and technical supplies, and broad development of horizontal economic ties between enterprises."[11]

In January 1987 Ligachev would cite Aganbegyan's partner in reform, sociologist Tatyana Zaslavskaya, for having "convincingly shown" that it was necessary to draw workers into the management of production and that "using purely administrative methods, you will actually go backward."[12] In April visiting U.S. Congressman Jim Moody described Ligachev as having outdone even Gorbachev "in talking about low productivity, weak economic incentives, poor quality products and the seriousness of drug and alcohol abuse in the Soviet Union."[13] On one particular issue, however, Ligachev opposed the agenda of some economic reformers. Despite the "radical" adjustments he was willing to endorse, Ligachev assured the nation in his November 6 speech that the principle of guaranteed employment was off-limits to change and "sacred."

THE VOROSHILOVGRAD SCANDAL

In May 1986 at the Foreign Ministry Gorbachev had called for a bold new approach to human rights at the upcoming CSCE review conference in Vienna. As that conference was opening in November, it soon became clear that Gorbachev had more in mind than a one-time media blitz designed simply to score diplomatic points abroad but do absolutely nothing to improve life back home. And one of the first indications of the seriousness of the new approach was Ligachev's call on November 6 for strengthening socialist legality. "Our party regards strengthening law and order, ensuring constitutional guarantees for the inviolability of the individual, and preserving the rights and legitimate interests of the Soviet people as an important political task."[14]

Ligachev's comment foreshadowed *Pravda's* announcement at the end of the month of a Central Committee resolution entitled "On Further Reinforcing Socialist Legality and Law and Order and Strengthening the Protection of Citizens' Rights and Legitimate Interests." The Andropov and Chernenko leaderships had tightened the legal screws on already circumscribed civic liberties; the Gorbachev leadership was now in the process of loosening them as part of its courtship of the intelligentsia for support against the party and state bureaucracies. The new resolution called the "strict observance of socialist legality and citizens' rights . . . one of the most important, inalienable aspects of the restructuring process." Henceforth, it demanded, "cases of unsubstantiated detentions and arrests and of citizens being unlawfully charged must be completely eradicated from the work practice of law enforcement organs."[15] Coincidentally, arrests for serious political offenses dropped dramatically, at least in large cities, beginning in September 1986.[16] In addition, in February 1987, political prisoners began to be released before the end of their terms. By the end of 1988 more than 600 political prisoners would be released from detention.[17]

Coincidentally, there appeared the first media salvo in what would develop into the Voroshilovgrad scandal. One of Ukrainian leader Shcherbitskiy's regional fiefdoms evidently was to be made an object lesson of the new legal requirements. According to *Pravda*, Voroshilovgrad judicial and security officials had conspired in June 1986 to prevent journalist Viktor Berkhin from pursuing his investigation of "shortcomings in the work of law enforcement organs." Berkhin had been detained on charges of "hooliganism" and only released following the intervention of the USSR Prosecutor's Office in Moscow.[18] Berkhin, it later became known, had been subjected to prolonged questioning and what amounted to medical torture by repeated injection of drugs into his body; he never recovered his health and died in July 1987.[19]

In June 1988 at the 19th Party Conference, Gorbachev would praise the KGB for working "in accord with the spirit of the times" and not "fighting tooth and nail" to maintain the old order.[20] Indeed, in early January 1987 KGB Chief Chebrikov published an open letter in *Pravda* reporting that he had fired the KGB head in Voroshilovgrad oblast and ordered the chairman of the Ukrainian republic KGB to "institute disciplinary proceedings against other staffers . . . guilty of illegal actions." The KGB, wrote Chebrikov, was "taking additional measures to ensure rigorous adherence to legislation in the activity of State Security organs."[21] At the end of January MVD Chief Vlasov sent the newspaper a letter acknowledging similar failures on the part of MVD personnel in Voroshilovgrad and at republic headquarters in Kiev. Mirroring Chebrikov's action, Vlasov said that instructions had been issued to MVD personnel nationwide "to stamp out any display of prejudice or bias when conducting inquiries or preliminary investigations, as well as instances of unjustified detention or arrest, the illegal institution of criminal proceedings against citizens, bureaucracy, callousness, and indifference to people's fate or to the defense of the working people's legitimate rights and interests."[22]

By mid-February Shcherbitskiy was compelled to write to *Pravda* acknowledging criticism of the affair as "valid and fair" and informing readers that the Ukrainian Central Committee had fired B. T. Goncharenko, first secretary of the Voroshilovgrad oblast party organization.[23] Viktor Boyko, party boss in Dnepropetrovsk (where Shcherbitskiy and Brezhnev had served in earlier years) and V. F. Dobrik of Lvov both lost their jobs for "serious" shortcomings in their work.[24] Several days after this, Shcherbitskiy was personally criticized at a Ukrainian party plenum.[25] Shcherbitskiy nevertheless survived the Voroshilovgrad scandal. But two months later, republic KGB Chairman S. N. Mukha was replaced by Nikolay Golushko. Judging from the short published biography, Golushko spent an important part of his earlier career in Tomsk—precisely during Ligachev's tenure as local party chief.[26]

Golushko's replacement of Mukha was reminiscent of the 1970 ouster of republic KGB Chief V. F. Nikitchenko by Vitaliy Fedorchuk. Like Golushko, Fedorchuk was a Ukrainian who had been working at KGB headquarters in Moscow. Fedorchuk's assignment to Kiev had been a key early move in Brezhnev's campaign against Petr Shelest, whom Vladimir Shcherbitskiy eventually replaced in May 1972. Now Shcherbitskiy was under attack from Moscow and, like Shelest before him, had lost his hand-picked KGB chief. Mukha had worked under Shcherbitskiy in Dnepropetrovsk in the 1950s, had been appointed deputy chairman of the Ukrainian KGB in 1973, and was then made chairman in 1982 when Fedorchuk moved back to Moscow to replace Andropov as head of the national KGB.

RIOTS IN ALMA-ATA

In the midst of the campaign against Shcherbitskiy, Moscow finally succeeded in toppling Kunayev from his entrenched position as head of the Kazakhstan republic party organization. Kunayev had survived pressure earlier in the year to leave office. Before the 27th Party Congress Pravda had criticized him by name for turning a blind eye to widespread corruption and mismanagement, something rarely done to incumbent Politburo members.[27] Soon after, in his report to the congress, Gorbachev had twice criticized Kazakhstan. In late August Kunayev's detractors in Moscow turned the heat back on with a Central Committee decree attacking his republic's leadership for agricultural failures.[28]

Kunayev finally succumbed in mid-December, when at a republic party plenum and at his own "request" he retired "on pension."[29] The replacement of Kunayev by the Russian Gennadiy Kolbin sparked violent riots spearheaded by Kazakh students in Alma Ata. Kazakhstan's population of 16 million was 40.8 percent Russian and 36.0 percent Kazakh.[30] In the Ukraine, with a population of over 50 million, of which roughly three-quarters were ethnic Ukrainian, the specter of even greater violence may have helped stave off Shcherbitskiy's ouster, but not his humbling. Kunayev, meanwhile, who had been allowed to retire from his post in Alma-Ata in December, was dropped from the Politburo with a similar explanation at the January plenum. By March, however, Kunayev found himself facing "party proceedings . . . for crude violations of the norms of party life, the creation of his personality cult, the distortion of cadres policy, and the manifestations of total license."[31] The June 1987 plenum then ousted him from the Central Committee for "serious shortcomings."[32]

Ligachev seemed to go out of his way to associate with the pressure against Shcherbitskiy and Kunayev (as well as Gromyko, as discussed elsewhere). The second secretary repeatedly criticized agricultural shortcomings in the Ukraine and Kazakhstan.[33] On ever-sensitive nationality issues, Ligachev had taken the lead in endorsing a merit-based policy of circulating cadres between republics rather than letting local clans develop by permitting untrammeled promotions from within, as far back as the 27th Party Congress.[34] Six months after the Alma-Ata riots Ligachev would tell an educational conference in Georgia that there was a dangerous parallel between the favoritism shown Georgian applicants to Tbilisi University (94 percent of the students were Georgian) and the situation that had prevailed in Kazakhstan.[35] "The purposeful development of bilingualism," Ligachev stressed to Georgian party activists, "has been and remains a key component of the work in the sphere of nationality relations."[36]

Finally, it was Ligachev who appeared to be the most likely sponsor of the highest-level beneficiaries of the personnel changes in Kazakhstan and the Ukraine. Kolbin had been near the top of the honor role featured in the *Pravda* "First Secretary" editorial of July 22, 1986, which was devoted to themes sounded shortly before by Ligachev in Voronezh, and none other than Ligachev had presided over Kolbin's installation as party leader in Ulyanovsk in December 1983. In the Ukraine, as we have seen, new KGB Chief Nikolay Golushko had worked in Tomsk during Ligachev's days there as regional party chief.

SAKHAROV, AND MAZUROV, RETURN

The last half of 1986 saw the recall from political oblivion of Kirill Mazurov, ousted from the Politburo by Brezhnev and his partisans in November 1978 on flimsy grounds of "health." Mazurov, as was pointed out in Volume I, had played a prominent role at the funeral of Fedor Kulakov, whose suicide paved the way for Gorbachev's promotion to the Central Committee Secretariat in 1978, and everything suggested that Mazurov had been close to Brezhnev's rivals, Aleksey Kosygin and Andrey Kirilenko. Now this same Mazurov suddenly reappeared in a new role on behalf of veterans, and was even interviewed on the main evening TV news show, *Vremya* on September 25—a rare apparition of a virtual nonperson from the past.[37] In general Mazurov's near-unique return to grace seemed another instance of the Gorbachev leadership courting former associates of Kosygin and Kirilenko and victims of Brezhnev; in the next few years these would include Gennadiy Voronov and even Shcherbitskiy's predecessor, Petr Shelest.[38] More specifically, Mazurov's reappearance was perhaps another demonstration of what seemed to be Ligachev's high regard for the Belorussian party organization, as well as Ryzhkov's past ties to republic First Secretary Nikolay Slyunkov, who would soon be promoted to Moscow.

Nothing so dramatized Gorbachev's break with the Brezhnev legacy, however, as the recall to Moscow of Academician Andrey Sakharov in December 1986 to do "patriotic work."[39] When the Academician was bundled off to internal exile in Gorkiy on January 22, 1980, the action had shocked the nation's intelligentsia far more than had the invasion of Afghanistan. Now, as the CSCE review conference began to deliberate in Vienna and Gorbachev prepared for the January plenum, his phone call to Sakharov on December 16 was in marked contrast to Chernenko's phone call to Stalin's henchman Molotov in May 1984 readmitting him to the party in the midst of Moscow's diplomatic "deep freeze."[40]

Upon his arrival in Moscow, Sakharov immediately called for the release of all political prisoners, mourned the death of dissident Anatoliy

Marchenko several weeks before in Chistopol prison, and criticized the Soviet military presence in Afghanistan.[41] Symbolically, on the day the Sakharov decision was announced at a press conference, a *Pravda* article commemorating the eightieth anniversary of Brezhnev's birth contained the first *ad hominem* criticism of the former leader. But it was far from a totally black assessment of the Brezhnev regime, combining instead an appreciation for the "appreciable advances" in domestic and foreign policies under Brezhnev with condemnation of the "mood of self-satisfaction and total license" which Leonid Ilyich had allowed in his "latter years" in power.[42]

Coincidentally, there was a new wave of permissiveness in the arts, and Ligachev as secretary in charge of ideology seemed to have sanctioned much of the ferment.[43] Much of it, to be sure, was politically motivated against the old guard and designed to underscore the depths of the social and moral rot that had been permitted.[44] And it frequently took on anti-Stalinist overtones, as with release of the Georgian-produced and Shevardnadze-sponsored movie *Repentance*, featuring a Beria-like central character.[45] Ligachev, however, was not an avant gardist when it came to the arts. Earlier in 1986 he had asked leading figures in the theater world, "Why does the stage not have striking and profound images of communists—the people constituting our main political force—the party—directing the development of society?"[46] Nevertheless, Ligachev in 1985 had been credited with giving final approval for the staging of *Silver Wedding Bells*, a tale of local corruption and the imprisonment of a journalist who digs too deeply—strikingly prescient of the Berkhin-Voroshilovgrad scandal.[47] And again it was Ligachev, according to rumors circulating in film circles, who had given the final go-ahead for showing *Repentance*.[48]

A TROIKA OF POSTPONEMENTS

All of these developments appeared designed to create a political-moral atmosphere inimical to opponents of political reform as preparations for the plenum on cadre policy proceeded backstage. In addition to fictional anti-Stalinist pieces, Yegor Yakovlev, editor of the newly audacious *Moscow News*, wrote of Lenin's "Last Testament" and of his proposal to remove Stalin from the leadership.[49] Gorbachev and his supporters appeared determined to push forward. The audaciousness of moves such as the recall of Sakharov suggested not only that Gorbachev's support in the inner circles of power must have been formidable, but that the resistance to reform on the peripheries was so tenacious that Gorbachev felt the need for political moves that might temporarily stun it.

In late July in Khabarovsk Gorbachev had first declared his intention to hold the cadre plenum. In late August Valentin Falin had said the plenum would take place in October or November. Gorbachev's meeting with Reagan in Reykjavik in mid-October, however, presumably ruled out the earlier variant of Falin's forecast. But a few days after Reykjavik however the plenum seemed back on track for November when a Supreme Soviet session was scheduled to open on November 17.[50] The plenum presumably would be held just before the parliamentary session. Gorbachev, furthermore, seemed to be lobbying his agenda for the plenum when he met with a "large group" of republic and regional party first secretaries in the Central Committee on October 22. "Of the highest importance is the party's policy of continuing to develop democracy, criticism and self-criticism, and openness on a broad scale," read the media report on the meeting. It was imperative "to make the system of Soviet democracy more dynamic and effective."[51] In addition, as we have seen, on November 6 Ligachev authoritatively confirmed that the plenum would be held.

Yet the timing of the plenum was soon up in the air. The campaigns against Kunayev and Shcherbitskiy were intended to diminish the remaining opposition at the top. Pressure against Kunayev had been revived in late August and against Shcherbitskiy in late November. Gorbachev propagandized the themes of the day in a meeting with theater notables in early December.[52] Democracy "does not mean that anything goes," he warned. It was instead necessary "to strengthen the country, impart dynamism to it and prevent blunders in politics and in our practical activities." As on other such occasions, Ligachev and Yakovlev accompanied Gorbachev, and Gorbachev's celebrated phone call to Academician Sakharov soon followed. But if Gorbachev and his supporters had hopes of holding the plenum in December after Kunayev's ouster, the riots in Alma-Ata soon made that impossible.

Clearly, and well beyond the troubles in Kazakhstan, the issues that Gorbachev had proposed be discussed at the plenum were provoking prolonged contention behind the scenes. By Gorbachev's own admission, the plenum went through three postponements before it finally opened on January 27, 1987.[53] "Some comrades," he conceded, had questioned whether "we are not manoeuvering too sharp a turn." But in "many meetings and conversations with members of the Central Committee" and others, Gorbachev asserted, he and his Politburo and Secretariat colleagues had been told unambiguously that they should not only "firmly" pursue their policy line but "redouble" their efforts in every area.[54] Before the plenum Gorbachev was said "to want to introduce new laws governing Communist party officials," which "could include a mandatory retirement age, rotation of jobs and competition for party positions."[55] Seeming to confirm that someone at the top favored such measures, not long before the plenum *Izvestiya* publicized Chinese cadre reforms. These reportedly called for the qualifications of party and administrative workers at the district level and higher to "be determined by their direct subordinates, and also by leaders of subordinate organizations, through a secret ballot every year."[56] According to one account, though, it took a threat by Gorbachev to resign to get the Politburo finally to approve the speech he was to deliver at the plenum.[57]

THE JANUARY PLENUM

In Zaykov's later recollection, Gorbachev "delivered his 3-hour report as if in one breath, with fervor. There was a tense silence in the hall. Everyone realized the responsibility of the moment."[58] Gorbachev went out of his way to characterize his speech to the Central Committee on January 27 as representing the Politburo's views and not merely his own.[59] Its focus was on how "to raise the level and effectiveness of control 'from below' so that each executive and each official constantly feel their responsibility to and dependence on the electorate, on the work collectives, public organizations, on the party and the people as a whole." On the key question of "broadening inner-party democracy," Gorbachev said that "comrades" had suggested that there be secret balloting on lists of multiple candidates for secretaries, "including first ones," from the district level up through the republic. Ligachev's late 1985 apparent preference for open balloting was no longer the order of the day.[60]

"Of course," Gorbachev reminded his audience, it would still remain an "unshakable" principle that the decisions of higher party bodies would be "compulsory for all lower party committees, including those on personnel matters." Nonetheless, it was the Politburo's opinion that "further democratization should also apply to the formation of the central leading bodies of the party." In addition, it was necessary to get away from the "brief and formal" nature of Central Committee plenums which had come to prevail. "Each Central Committee member," he said, "should be guaranteed the right to raise questions and participate in their collective constructive discussion. . . . There can be no persons outside criticism or people with no right to criticize."[61]

In the course of his long speech, Gorbachev touched on most of the various themes emphasized in the media in the months leading up to the plenum. Alluding to the distortions flowing from the Stalin period, for example, he said, "The causes of the situation go back far into the past and are rooted in that specific historical situation in which by virtue of well-known circumstances vigorous debates and creative ideas disappeared from theory and social sciences while authoritarian evaluations and opinions became unquestionable truths that could only be commented upon." Picking up the anti-Brezhnev theme, he asserted that the Politburo was compelled "with the utmost frankness" to state that the "leadership of the country had failed, primarily for subjective reasons, to see in time and in full the need for change and the danger of the intensification of crisis phenomena in society and to formulate a clear policy for overcoming them and making better use of the opportunities intrinsic to the socialist system." Obviously in reference to the Voroshilovgrad scandal, he said that "materials from the central press for January" showed that "persecution of people for criticism is far from being a rare thing."

Toward the end of the report, Gorbachev announced the agenda for the subsequent plenum. Drafting of the Thirteenth Five-Year Plan (1991–95), he said, would begin "shortly." It would be based on a new system of "radical reform of economic management" affecting not only "fundamental questions of the functioning of the socialist system of economy" but also "many aspects of political and social life, the style and methods of work." It would therefore "be expedient to study the entire range of these problems at the Central Committee's next plenary meeting."

Finally, in what seemed almost a personal postscript, Gorbachev told the plenum that he "would like to take counsel" on the possibility and advisability of convening a party conference in 1988 "on the eve of the report-and-election campaign within the party." The conference could review implementation of the decisions of the 27th Party Congress, evaluate the results of the first half of the current five-year plan, and discuss "further democratization" of the party and society. "The discussion started at this Conference could be continued at report-and-election party meetings and conferences," Gorbachev said, "at which the results of the restructuring work of each party organization should be analyzed in an exacting way."[62]

The resolution issued by the Central Committee at the conclusion of the plenum, however, did not explicitly endorse many of the specific details of the proposals put forward by Gorbachev in his report, which the resolution described as representing the "political and practical conclusions" of the Politburo. The Central Committee appeared estranged not only from Gorbachev personally but from the Politburo collectively. The Central Committee resolution evaded, sidestepped, or blurred some of the central thrusts in Gorbachev's keynote speech.

On the question of what could guarantee the forward progress of *perestroika*, for example, an issue that would acquire increasing importance as the year wore on, Gorbachev touched all bases. "Yes, we have such guarantees," he said. Sounding much like Ligachev in

November, Gorbachev stated that "these are the single will, the joint actions of the party and people united by past experience, by awareness of responsibility for the present and the future of the socialist homeland." But he then went on to enumerate the "all-around development of the democratism of the socialist system" and the "healthy development of the party itself" as "guarantees." By summing up this passage with the statement that it was "the deepening of socialist democratism, the creative endeavor of Soviet people, [and] the vanguard role of Communists in practical deeds that will ensure both the success and the irreversibility of the revolutionary transformations mapped out by the 27th Congress," Gorbachev evidently satisfied his own, Ligachev's, and any other sentiments in the Politburo on this score.

Gorbachev's own tilt toward "democratization," however, was obvious in his description of the agenda for a party conference as being the "questions of further democratizing the life of the party and society as a whole." The resolution of the plenum, however, spoke only vaguely of "effective, conscientious work by all" as the guarantee of restructuring. More important, it said nothing at all about a party conference, charging the Politburo instead with the general responsibility "to carry out, with due account for proposals advanced by Central Committee members, specific measures to perfect the organization of personnel work in the apparatus of the CPSU Central Committee and local party bodies."[63]

Gorbachev nevertheless naturally sought to put a positive spin in his remarks summing up the plenum. "The subject of serious, in-depth democratization of Soviet society has been put to the fore as the major one in the report of the Political Bureau," he said in his concluding speech. This, he emphasized, was "the lever which will make it possible to draw into the reorganization its decisive force—the people," thereby creating "the most reliable guarantees to prevent a repetition of the errors of the past. . . . We need," he said, "democracy like air."[64]

Thirty-four Central Committee members, reported Gorbachev, had managed to comment on his report during the two-day session; seventy seven had been moved to sign up to speak. What was of "paramount importance" was the plenum's "political conclusion that the party and all healthy forces of society stand for change." This, Gorbachev said, "should mark an end to the debates on whether we need change or not." And on the question of a party conference, Gorbachev asserted that those who had spoken at the plenum had been in favor of the idea and that he understood that those who had not spoken were also favorably disposed toward "this proposal which the Political Bureau put forward at the plenum." The Politburo would therefore go ahead and prepare proposals for the date and on how to organize the party conference. These would be presented at "one of the nearest" Central Committee plenums.[65]

YAKOVLEV, SLYUNKOV, AND LUKYANOV MOVE UP

Outside commentary, while focusing on the plenum resolution's failure to support the party conference Gorbachev had proposed, underestimated the importance to Gorbachev and his leading allies of the cadre changes the Central Committee did approve: Gorbachev confidant Aleksandr Yakovlev, elected to the Secretariat at the 27th Congress a year earlier, now also entered the Politburo as a candidate member; Nikolay Slyunkov, a Politburo candidate member since the 27th Congress, was elected to the Secretariat as well, entailing a move from Minsk, where he had been republic party first secretary, to Moscow; and Anatoliy Lukyanov, chief of the Central Committee's General Department since late 1985, was appointed to the Secretariat. In addition, Kunayev, as expected, was retired from the Politburo, and Zimyanin finally left the Secretariat, where he had served since 1976, because of "health."[66]

Yakovlev appeared to be one of Gorbachev's closest advisers ever since returning to Moscow from Ottawa in 1983. In addition, he may have known Ligachev since the early 1960s, when they were both involved in propaganda work in the Central Committee apparatus. Yakovlev's ideas had been evident not only in Soviet "new thinking" on international affairs but also in the ideological and utilitarian rationalization for *glasnost*. At the June 1987 plenum Yakovlev would rise the final notch to become a full member of the Politburo.

Slyunkov appeared closest to Premier Ryzhkov, whose stint as Gosplan deputy chairman from 1979 to 1982 had overlapped with Slyunkov's at the same level from 1974 to 1983. The ties evidently remained strong. Slyunkov now took over the Economic Department in the Central Committee, which Ryzhkov had occupied from November 1982 to August 1985 but which had remained vacant since Gostev's brief tenure from August to December 1985. In this capacity Slyunkov appeared to have been put in charge of orchestrating the operational details of the economic reform program to be unveiled at the June 1987 plenum. At that time he would also be elected a full member of the Politburo. Meanwhile, Yefrem Sokolov replaced Slyunkov as party first secretary in Belorussia.[67] This was the same Sokolov who had been featured along with Gennadiy Kolbin in the July 1986 *Pravda* lead editorial, "First Secretary", which had borne Ligachev's imprint.

Lukyanov's promotion to the Secretariat was perhaps the most interesting and analytically unappreciated. Lukyanov had attended law school at Moscow University at about the same time as Gorbachev. In November 1985 Lukyanov had been put in charge of the Central Committee's General Department, thus managing the paper flow to the Politburo leadership. He now retained this important function while in addition assuming general supervision of the Administrative Organs Department. This department kept track of key cadre appointments in the military, security, and judicial sectors, and had been headed since 1968 by Nikolay Savinkin. Wearing his new hat, as we shall see in the next chapter, Lukyanov began to play a key role in the revving up of the restructuring campaign in the military. Lukyanov, furthermore, appeared to supervise the formulation and implementation of the new legal measures intended to define and guarantee the rights of citizens under *glasnost*.[68]

In short, the personnel changes at the plenum seemed to reflect a joint advance for Gorbachev, Ligachev, and Ryzhkov rather than a zero-sum game. The appointment of Sergey Manyakin a month after the plenum as chairman of the People's Control Committee reinforced this impression. Manyakin was a native of Gorbachev's Stavropol but had served since 1961 as party first secretary of Omsk oblast next to Ligachev's Tomsk.[69] The perception that Gorbachev's grand coalition was still holding together seemed to be confirmed by other diverse events after the plenum.[70] Brezhnev's son-in-law, Yuriy Churbanov, for example, was finally arrested on charges of "graft and corruption," and it was rumored that he would figure in a spectacular trial to underscore the leadership's determination to root out and punish corrupt officials.[71]

NOTES

1. Interestingly, this passage from *Kommunist*, no. 10 (1971): 53, was quoted by Roy A. Medvedev in his book *On Socialist Democracy*, 208–9.

2. Soviet Television, May 21, 1986, in BBC Summary of World Broadcasts, May 26, 1986. This passage, however, was omitted in *Pravda's* May 22, 1986, account of Ligachev's speech (FBIS-SOV, May 28, 1986, R 7–12).

3. *Vestnik Akademii Nauk SSSR*, no. 11 (November 1986), signed to press November 5.

4. *Pravda*, October 17, 1986 (FBIS-SOV, October 24, 1986, R 7–9).

5. *Vestnik Akademii Nauk SSSR*, no. 1 (January 1987), signed to press January 6, 1987.

6. Moscow Television Service, November 6, 1986, (FBIS-SOV, November 7, 1986, O 2–20).

7. *La Stampa*, February 24, 1987.

8. Moscow Television Service, November 6, 1986, (FBIS-SOV, November 7, 1986, O 14).

9. Moscow Domestic Service, July 31, 1986 (FBIS-SOV, August 4, 1986, R 4).

10. Moscow Television Service, November 6, 1986 (FBIS-SOV, November 7, 1986, O 6).

11. For Aganbegyan's comments on the conference, see *Ekonomicheskaya Gazeta*, no. 48, November 20, 1986 (FBIS-SOV, December 4, 1986, S 1–3). See

also his interviews in *Nedelya*, no. 1, January 8, 1987 (FBIS-SOV, January 22, 1987, S 7–16), and *Literary Gazette*, February 18, 1987 (FBIS-SOV, February 25, 1987, S 6–13), for wide-ranging previews of the upcoming economic reforms. A year later the conference proceedings were published in book form; for the announcement of *The Reform of Economic Management: Problems and Quest*, see *Ekonomicheskaya Gazeta*, no. 45 (November 1987; FBIS-SOV, November 12, 1987, 75).

12. *Pravda*, January 25, 1987 (FBIS-SOV, February 2, 1987, R 10).

13. *Washington Post*, April 26, 1987.

14. Moscow Television Service, November 6, 1986 (FBIS-SOV, November 7, 1986, O 9).

15. *Pravda*, November 30, 1986 (FBIS-SOV, December 8, 1986, R 8–12).

16. The U.S. Helsinki Watch noted a year later that "since September 1986, there have been no Art. 70 or Art. 190–1 (two commonly used political offenses) arrests in Moscow or Leningrad, and only one in Kiev. . . . It appears that there has been a decision to cease these trials, at least in the large cities, while the review process is under way. But new arrests under *other* articles have been reported for provincial areas, where conditions are harsher" (*News from Helsinki Watch*, no. 3 [September 1987]: 2). Article 70 involves anti-Soviet agitation and propaganda; Article 190–1 covers slander against the Soviet state and social system.

17. George Shultz, "Vienna Meeting: Commitment, Cooperation, and the Challenge of Compliance," address at the closing session of the Conference on Security and Cooperation in Europe (CSCE), Vienna, January 17, 1989, (Washington, DC: United States Department of State, Bureau of Public Affairs, Current Policy No. 1145, January 1985), 1.

18. *Pravda*, November 29, 1986 (FBIS-SOV, December 5, 1986, R 4); and *Pravda*, January 4, 1987 (FBIS-SOV, January 9, 1987, R 1–6).

19. AFP, October 21, 1987, citing *Meditsinskaya Gazeta* (FBIS-SOV, October 22, 1987, 52).

20. *Pravda*, June 29, 1988.

21. *Pravda*, January 8, 1987 (FBIS-SOV, January 9, 1987, R 1).

22. *Pravda*, January 30, 1987 (FBIS-SOV, February 6, 1987, R 2–3).

23. *Pravda*, February 15, 1987 (FBIS-SOV, February 18, 1987, R 13–14). See also *Pravda Ukrainy*, January 8 and March 3, 1987 (FBIS-SOV, January 13, 1987, R 24, and March 13, 1987, R 8–11, respectively).

24. *Pravda*, March 18, 1987 (FBIS-SOV, March 23, 1987, R 1); and Moscow Television Service, March 20, 1987 (FBIS-SOV, March 23, 1987, R 1).

25. *Pravda*, March 28, 1987 (FBIS-SOV, March 30, 1987, R 7).

26. *Pravda Ukrainy*, May 26, 1987 (FBIS-SOV, June 4, 1987, R 1). Golushko, a Ukrainian by nationality, graduated from Tomsk State University in 1959 and then worked in "prosecution organs." He was said to have joined the KGB in 1963 and in "recent years" to have held "responsible posts in the USSR KGB apparatus." Ligachev was the party oblast first secretary in Tomsk from 1965 to 1983.

27. *Pravda*, February 9, 1986 (FBIS-SOV, February 12, 1986, O 1–3).

28. *Pravda*, August 28, 1986 (FBIS-SOV, September 5, 1986, T 1–4).

29. TASS, December 16, 1986 (FBIS-SOV, December 17, 1986, R 1).

30. On the riots, see TASS, December 18, 1986 (FBIS-SOV, December 19, 1986, R 1); *New York Times*, December 19, 1986; *Washington Post*, December 19 and 23, 1986; and *The Guardian*, December 30, 1986. Eventually one of the student leaders of the protest was sentenced to death (Alma-Ata Domestic Service, June 16, 1987 [FBIS-SOV, June 17, 1987, R 10–11]).

31. *Pravda*, March 16, 1987 (FBIS-SOV, March 19, 1987, R 15).

32. TASS, June 26, 1987 (FBIS-SOV, June 26, 1987, R 47). See also the CPSU CC resolution, "On Serious Shortcomings in the Tashkent Oblast Party Organization's Work on Party Admissions and Strengthening the Party's Ranks" (*Pravda*, June 18, 1987 [FBIS-SOV, June 25, 1987, R 5–8]).

33. *Pravda*, January 25, 1987 (FBIS-SOV, February 2, 1987, R 10); and *Kommunist*, no. 4 (March 1987), signed to press February 23, 1987.

34. *Pravda*, February 28, 1986 (FBIS-SOV, February 28, 1986, Supplement 043, O 21). See also Ligachev's article in *Kommunist*, no. 12 (1985).

35. *Zarya Vostoka*, June 3, 1987 (FBIS-SOV, June 24, 1987, R 8).

36. *Pravda*, June 4, 1987 (FBIS-SOV, June 9, 1987, R 8). For a survey of the nationality scene during this period, see Paul A. Goble, "The Nationality Problem," in Maurice Friedberg and Heyward Isham, eds., *Soviet Society under Gorbachev* (Armonk, NY: M. E. Sharpe, 1987), 76–100.

37. I am indebted to Werner Hahn for the date of Mazurov's TV reappearance. At the end of the year Mazurov was elected first chairman of the newly organized All-Union War and Labor Veterans Organization (*Red Star*, December 18, 1986 [FBIS-SOV, December 31, 1986, V 1–6]). The Politburo had earlier endorsed establishment of the organization at the same session at which it approved Gorbachev's remarks in Stavropol and Krasnodar (Moscow Domestic Service, September 26, 1986 [FBIS-SOV, September 29, 1986, R 2]).

38. See the interview with Voronov in *Izvestiya*, November 18, 1988, and with Shelest in *Argumenty i Fakty*, no. 2, January 14–20, 1989 (FBIS-SOV, January 13, 1989, 58–61).

39. *Washington Post*, December 16, 1986.

40. Molotov, incidentally, died at age 96 not long before Gorbachev's call to Sakharov (*Izvestiya*, November 11, 1986 [FBIS-SOV, November 12, 1986, R 1]).

41. *Washington Post*, December 24, 1986.

42. *Pravda*, December 19, 1986 (FBIS-SOV, December 19, 1986, R 3–4).

43. *Washington Post*, October 30 and December 1, 1986. On April 19, 1986, Ligachev had told a meeting of theater workers: "'Silver Wedding,' 'Dictatorship of the Conscience,' 'Ivan,' 'From Today's News,' 'Rank and File'—I am listing the works I have seen or read—this is just the start of that to which the 27th party congress summoned figures of literature and art. We hope that the efforts of the playwrights and theaters in this direction will grow" (*Teatr*, no. 8 [August 1986], signed to press June 5, 1986).

44. For surveys, see Roy A. Medvedev, "From Thaw to the Breakup of the Ice," *Dagens Nyheter*, March 8, 1987 (FBIS-SOV, March 23, 1987, R 16–21); and Anthony Olcott, "Glasnost' and Soviet Culture," in Maurice Friedberg and Heyward Isham, eds., *Soviet Society under Gorbachev* (Armonk, NY: M. E. Sharpe, 1987), 101–130.

45. Shevardnadze later claimed that as Georgian party leader in 1982 he had urged his "friend" and director Tengiz Abuladze to "film 'Repentance' at any cost." See Shevardnadze's interview in *Le Nouvel Observateur*, October 14–20, 1988.

46. *Teatr*, no. 8 (August 1988), signed to press June 5, 1986.

47. *New York Times*, January 8, 1986.

48. *Washington Post*, October 30, 1986.

49. *Moscow News*, no. 3, January 18, 1987 (FBIS-SOV, January 21, 1987, R 1–5).

50. Moscow Domestic Service, October 17, 1986 (FBIS-SOV, October 23, 1986, R 11).

51. *Red Star*, October 24, 1986 (FBIS-SOV, October 24, 1986, R 1–2).

52. *Red Star*, December 5, 1986 (FBIS-SOV, December 8, 1986, R 1–2).

53. Moscow Television Service, February 25, 1987 (FBIS-SOV, February 27, 1987, R 4). For other official accounts of how the plenum was prepared and conducted, see the report on Vadim Medvedev's briefing in *Rude Pravo*, February 19, 1987 (FBIS-SOV, February 25, 1987, F 1–3); and Lev Zaykov's speech in Prague (Bratislava *Pravda*, March 5, 1987 [FBIS-SOV, March 11, 1987, F 3–4]).

54. TASS, January 27, 1987 (FBIS-SOV, January 28, 1987, R 3).

55. *The Sunday Times* (London), January 18, 1987.

56. *Izvestiya*, January 9, 1987 (FBIS-SOV, January 20, 1987, B 2).

57. *The Guardian*, May 11, 1988.

58. Bratislava *Pravda*, March 5, 1987 (FBIS-SOV, March 11, 1987, F 3).

59. For the text, see TASS, January 27, 1987 (FBIS-SOV, January 28, 1987, R 2–48).

60. Ligachev and others would later say that electoral practices in Hungary and Poland had been examined in fashioning the January plenum initiatives. See Werner Hahn, "Electoral Choice in the Soviet Bloc," *Problems of Communism* (March–April 1987): 29–39, for an examination of the Polish and Hungarian experience, as well as of the new Soviet measures.

61. TASS, January 27, 1987 (FBIS-SOV, January 28, 1987, R 30).

62. TASS, January 27, 1987 (FBIS-SOV, January 28, 1987, R 2–48).

63. *Pravda*, January 29, 1987 (FBIS-SOV, January 30, 1987, R 1–12).

64. *Pravda*, January 30, 1987 (FBIS-SOV, January 30, 1987, R 16).

65. Ibid., R 18

66. *Pravda*, January 29, 1987 (FBIS-SOV, January 30, 1987, R 12–13).

67. TASS, February 6, 1987 (FBIS-SOV, February 9, 1987, R 7).

68. Lukyanov's conversations in April with visiting Hungarian Party Secretary I. Horvath would include "activities in improving socialist democracy" (*Pravda*, April 18, 1987 [FBIS-SOV, April 23, 1987, R 10]).

69. *Izvestiya*, March 1, 1987 (FBIS-SOV, March 4, 1987, R 3).

70. At about this time Roy Medvedev described the differences between Gorbachev and Ligachev as "mostly psychological." Ligachev was an ascetic. Nevertheless, according to Medvedev, "his relations with Gorbachev are excellent: They could be said to belong to the same faction" (*Corriere Della Sera*, January 30, 1987).

71. *The Sunday Times*, February 1, 1987; and TASS, February 3, 1987 (FBIS-SOV, February 4, 1987, R 10).

Chapter 10 ————————————————————

Perestroika and the Military

---

*A*fter the 27th Party Congress, the regime's efforts to cool the external environment and reallocate resources at home continued to be both reflected in and advanced by its treatment of military doctrine. The latter consisted mostly of old lines polished up but with some interesting and potentially significant new twists and changed accents introduced by Gorbachev and Akhromeyev as they sought to revise Ogarkov's legacy. Gorbachev, to be sure, used the new rhetoric to assault the legitimacy of NATO's nuclear deterrence and flexible response doctrines and to reassure Western publics that Soviet intentions were peaceful. As far as the outside observer could see, however, it all remained on the political-declaratory level, with little if any clear impact as yet on the military-operational side.

Nevertheless, at home Gorbachev appeared to use the refurbished doctrinal framework to argue for restraint on military spending and for greater defense sector assistance to the civilian economy. All the key political indicators pointed in this direction. The number of military representatives on the Lenin Mausoleum was more than halved beginning with the Red Square parade on November 7, 1986. A year later the regime pledged to publish defense budgets that could be realistically compared with those of other nations. It would be years before there could be independent outside confirmation of any reduction in the defense burden on the Soviet economy. Nevertheless, Gorbachev's announcement in December 1988 of a reduction in Soviet troop strength of a half-million soldiers (to be dealt with in the last chapter of this book) gave substance to the impression that this was his leadership's intention all along.

Meanwhile, General Dmitriy Yazov's appointment to succeed Sokolov as defense minister in May 1987 came as close to a total surprise to outsiders as any of Gorbachev's major personnel moves. Yazov's rise, however, had been a year in the making, and its inception coincided with the beginning of the leadership's radicalized domestic offensive in summer 1986. In foreign affairs, furthermore, Sokolov's abrupt dismissal after West German teenager Mathias Rust landed his Cessna in the heart of Moscow would result in simplified endgames in the negotiations both on INF and Afghanistan (both also the subject of later chapters).

AKHROMEYEV REVISES OGARKOV

Within the military establishment itself, and paralleling Gorbachev's "new thinking," quite early Akhromeyev began to put his own professional stamp on military doctrine with a revision of the one-volume *Military Encyclopedic Dictionary*. The original edition had appeared in 1983 under the editorial direction of Ogarkov and presumably had been intended to have a long shelf life.[1] By August 6, 1985, however, a second, revised edition had been sent to the typesetters under the authority of Akhromeyev, who as chief of the General Staff was now listed as head of the editorial commission.[2] Work on the revision had obviously been under way when Gorbachev and Akhromeyev had polemicized with Ogarkov in April-May 1985 over how dangerous to characterize international tensions. Presumably the changes incorporated into the new reference work were reflected in Gorbachev's speech in July 1985 in Minsk. The volume was finally sent to the printers on April 21, 1986, apparently held back for any updating made necessary by the 27th Party Congress.

Politically, of course, the new volume was fascinating for the retrospective glimmers of light it shed on Andropov's early troubled tenure and on Akhromeyev's political partisanship. This was the same volume, as we have seen, which suggested that the early seven-month vacancy in the presidency under Andropov involved the question of the chairmanship of the Defense Council as well. In addition, the Akhromeyev-edited dictionary curiously omitted any mention of Chernenko having headed the Defense Council. This slighting of Chernenko's offices seemed conclusive evidence that Akhromeyev and Ogarkov early on had committed themselves to rival groupings in the civilian leadership. For it was Ogarkov, it will be remembered, who, shortly after Andropov's death, advertised to the world that Chernenko was the new head of the Defense Council.

Marshal Viktor Kulikov, who had been displaced at the General Staff by Ogarkov in 1977, wrote the first major review of the revised dictionary in *Pravda* in December 1986. He noted that its authors collective had been "guided in their work by new theoretical provisions put forward at the 27th CPSU Congress, and have revised and enlarged the content of a number of articles." It was also time, Kulikov suggested, to revise the eight-volume *Soviet Military Encyclopedia*, published in 1976–79 and edited by Ogarkov, to take into account "all the new trends in the military-political situation, the state of military matters, and the prospects of their development."[3] Whatever Kulikov actually thought of the volumes under discussion, he certainly appeared to be relishing the thought of revising his old nemesis.

Indeed, the entry in the Akhromeyev-revised dictionary under "Military Doctrine" reads almost word for word the same as in the

Ogarkov-authorized original—with one notable exception. The old version had stated that the main direction of Soviet military doctrine was "ensuring the defense of the socialist Fatherland." This was now expanded to read "ensuring the defense of the socialist Fatherland, preventing world war." Similarly, the entry under "Military Strategy" in the new edition was for the most part unchanged, except for the addition of a key sentence at the end: "The most important task for Soviet military strategy in contemporary conditions is working out the problems of preventing war."[4] Akhromeyev drew on this new formula in his speech to the Supreme Soviet in late November 1985, commenting on Gorbachev's first meeting with Reagan in Geneva.[5] In fact, the joint statement at the summit had underscored "the importance of preventing any war" between the United States and USSR, "whether nuclear or conventional."[6]

The new stress in Akhromeyev's comments on the primacy of preventing a world war, rather than preparing to counter aggression and in the process perhaps deterring it, clearly reflected the accents of Gorbachev's diplomacy toward the United States and Europe, as well as a new or rediscovered appreciation (as we shall see) of the dangers of conventional war. It went beyond the standard concern for preventing a conventional conflict from escalating into a nuclear one, to a new urgency that a major war be prevented altogether. As such, it seemed to reflect a profoundly greater pessimism over the probability of achieving anything approaching a meaningful victory against NATO even in a conventional conflict. Indeed, Soviet projections of a possibly prolonged conventional exchange in a future war seemed based as much on an improved NATO capability to engage in conventional war, without a desperate early resort to nuclear weapons, as on an increased Soviet ability to keep such a conflict from going nuclear. Furthermore, the Gorbachev leadership had probably reached a consensus early on that the costs of engaging in a high-tech arms race, such as recommended by Ogarkov, to improve the odds of prevailing in such a war would be ruinously expensive as well as ultimately in vain.

The new accent on war prevention, however, did not begin to find resonance within the military establishment beyond Akhromeyev until early 1987. Sokolov first approached it in an article for Le Monde in which he wrote that weapons were now so destructive that they could no longer be utilized.[7] But only in his Armed Forces Day article in late February 1987 did the defense minister for the first time state that war prevention was now the "main proposition" of Soviet military doctrine.[8] By late May a major declaration on military doctrine issued by the Warsaw Pact summit in Warsaw—which Sokolov attended—stated categorically that "the use of military means for resolving any disputed question is intolerable in the present conditions." It also posed and elaborated on as an ultimate goal the "reduction of the armed forces and conventional armaments in Europe down to the level when neither side, in ensuring its defense, would have means for a sudden attack on the other side, for starting offensive operations in general."[9]

The lag between Akhromeyev's initial sponsorship and his high command colleagues' later endorsement presumably denoted resistance to the new line. Indeed, right after Reykjavik, Ogarkov particularly appeared to register his dissent, emphasizing the need for war preparation instead of taking up the new line of war prevention.

> The most important tenets advocated by the Soviet military doctrine are to maintain the Soviet Armed Forces in high combat readiness, ensure their quick deployment in the event of a surprise attack by the enemy, strike at the enemy with a series of devastating retaliatory blows and by so doing face the tasks ensuing from the need to defend the Socialist Fatherland. Hence Soviet military doctrine says the Armed Forces must be able not only to defend the country against a potential aggressor by countering it with passive means and defensive tactics but also to deliver crushing counter-attacks at the enemy so as to overwhelm it under whatever circumstances.[10]

In arguing along old lines on military doctrine, Ogarkov probably also intended to signal his opposition to the radically new proposals Gorbachev and Akhromeyev took with them to Reykjavik.

NEW LINE ON CONVENTIONAL WAR

Gorbachev also unveiled another new doctrinal twist in 1986: the idea that even a conventional war in Europe could have catastrophic consequences for the entire world. As with "reasonable sufficiency," Gorbachev first tried his new reasoning on French leader François Mitterrand, this time during the latter's visit to Moscow in July 1986. "It is not only nuclear war that is of mortal danger to [Europe]," said Gorbachev in a dinner speech. "There are more than 150 atomic reactors, hundreds of chemical plants on European territory. Just a few conventional artillery shells are enough to destroy a reactor and take the toll of many lives. Whatever the variant, conventional or nonconventional, an armed conflict would trigger off a world catastrophe."[11]

At the very least, this assertion was meant to boost the proposals for deep reductions in conventional weapons on the continent put forward in the Budapest Appeal. At the same time, it sought to build on that element of anti nuclear sentiment which Gorbachev had sought to capitalize on in the wake of the Chernobyl disaster.[12] It was also consistent with the new assertion that preventing all war—both nuclear and conventional—was now the primary task of Soviet military doctrine. But perhaps most important, though not spelled out, Gorbachev's statement may actually have reflected an increasingly pessimistic assessment by the Soviet high command of the chances for victory against NATO in the European theater. Soviet worst-case scenarios no doubt gave more credit than in the West to a NATO armed with the latest in high-tech weapons and pursuing AirLand Battle and follow-on force attack (FOFA) tactics. After careful study of local wars employing the latest exotic technology—particularly in the Middle East—Soviet military writers concluded that "losses in modern combat, even in combat employing only conventional weapons, increase significantly, for the effectiveness of weapons has sharply risen."[13]

Ogarkov, of course, had urged that the USSR rise to the military challenge and allocate ever-greater funds to the development of exotic new military systems. But Gorbachev and Akhromeyev may have concluded that following Ogarkov's recommendations could not guarantee that the Soviet Union would wind up in any comparatively better or more secure position. Given the destructive nature of new conventional systems, their argument may have run, any hypothetical advantage in being able to prevent a conflict from going nuclear was becoming meaningless. The nature of the European battlefield, furthermore, was now such that it would be impossible not to set off a nuclear conflagration—both in the European theater and the Soviet homeland—when conventional arms struck nuclear power stations.

After this first tryout, however, the new line disappeared until April 1987, when it was revived to support Moscow's proposal for an INF double-zero in Europe. The first hint of its comeback appeared in the report on Dobrynin's meeting with a delegation from the WEU Assembly.[14] Gorbachev then gave it wider circulation when he included it in a speech in Prague. "Given the high density of the population and the degree of urbanization," the Soviet leader explained, "Europe is oversaturated with weapons. Three-million strong armies confront each other in it. Even a 'conventional war' would be ruinous here, and not only due to the fact that 'conventional' weapons are now exceeding many times over in destructive force the weapons used in World War II, but also because there are about 200 power sets of nuclear power stations on its territory, a ramified network of large chemical factories which, if hit, would make the continent unsuitable for life."[15]

A month later Akhromeyev turned this into an even more general proposition, going well beyond the boundaries of Europe. "Nuclear war can only lead to mankind's destruction," wrote the marshal in his VE Day article in *Red Star*. "A world war involving the use of conventional means will, if it is launched by an aggressor, also bring mankind incalculable and even unpredictable disasters and suffering."[16] In September Gorbachev reached the ultimate conclusion, when he asserted to several hundred French representatives in the Kremlin that "any war today would turn into a nuclear war with the obvious consequences."[17] In his book *Perestroika*, finished at about this time, Gorbachev wrote in the same spirit that "military technology has developed to such an extent that even a non-nuclear war would now be comparable with a nuclear war in its destructive effect."[18]

It was Akhromeyev who gave the most extensive reasoning behind what was asserted to be Moscow's new view on the danger of war in the contemporary world. Answering a question from Senator Alan Cranston on a live U.S.-Soviet "telebridge" in September 1987, Akhromeyev gave his "professional" assessment of the likelihood of a conventional war not remaining conventional. Akhromeyev's remarks were noteworthy on two counts: first, his recognition of the fragility of the "firebreak" between conventional and nuclear conflict—the conventional phase would be intensely nuclear oriented given that one of the primary missions of each side would be to knock out the other's nuclear weapons; and, second, his implicit admission—much like that of Khrushchev on at least one occasion—that no-first-use pledges do not count for much once war starts.

On the first point, Akhromeyev told his listeners, "Imagine: Both sides already have hundreds of nuclear power stations which in a conventional war can be destroyed by conventional weapons—but what will the consequences of this be? Secondly, imagine a war in progress even with the use of conventional weapons, but each side's nuclear warheads are in the area of combat operations; they are situated in the area of the theater of military operations, they can be destroyed by conventional weapons." On the second point, the chief of the General Staff matter-of-factly pointed out that "in the case when war is in progress they [nuclear weapons] can be used without sanction. You and we must ponder the fact that a conventional war under present conditions—the probability that it will remain within the conventional framework is getting lower and lower if nuclear weapons are not destroyed."[19]

To a certain extent, the new assertions were beginning to resemble the nuclear "paradox" arguments that had justified the Soviet entrance into negotiations on strategic weapons some 15 years earlier. In retrospect they foreshadowed far more than an inclination to engage in conventional negotiations less sterile than MBFR, and they were probably the forerunners of an internal Soviet debate on the pros and cons of a unilateral reduction of troops and conventional weaponry—even dearer to the professional soldier than strategic delivery vehicles.

THE MILITARY AND ARMS CONTROL

Even so, the spur-of-the moment proposal by Gorbachev in Reykjavik to reduce SS-20 warheads in Asia to 100 must have provoked grave misgivings among many in the military. On the earlier, less critical issue of the Soviet Union's unilateral nuclear test moratorium, Gorbachev had emphasized in 1986 that the decision to extend it had not been an "easy" one for the country's leadership.[20] Presumably, if the military had a choice, on purely technical and professional grounds they would have continued testing.

Nevertheless, there was no shortage of military spokesmen with an appreciation for the moratorium's political considerations and who were ready creditably to defend the decision in public. Akhromeyev in particular told reporters in Moscow a year after the moratorium had been in effect, "We had to take a certain damage to ourselves, but we took into account that this damage was tolerable." The East-West balance, he asserted, had been "maintained."[21]

Akhromeyev played a similar role in INF. Institutionally the military's basic acquiescence to "zero-zero" LRINF in Europe—however grudging—had come before the talks in Iceland. In Reykjavik Akhromeyev had been put in charge of the group of Soviet experts dealing with disarmament issues; Nitze had found him "tough, intelligent, forceful, and practical."[22] The selection of the chief of the General Staff may have been designed to forestall or discourage opposition elsewhere in the military to Gorbachev's far-reaching proposals. After Reykjavik Ogarkov, as we have seen, seemed by implication to register his dissent to the direction the bargaining had taken in Iceland.

Afterwards Gorbachev made clear that the military was only one of a number of institutional players that had contributed to the package put forward in Reykjavik. "In addition to the Politburo and Secretariat of the Central Committee, the Ministries of Foreign Affairs and Defense," Gorbachev said on television after Reykjavik, "other departments, scientific representatives, military experts and specialists from various branches of industry took part in the work."[23]

In May 1986 Dobrynin had praised the rise of a "modern Soviet school of foreign policy and military-political studies." With no mention of the military per se, he had called on Soviet scientists to go further and engage in "new, even more profound studies on international and military-political problems," including "the question of what constitutes reasonable sufficiency."[24] The following April Aleksandr Yakovlev called on civilian and military specialists to work together. The concept of "sufficiency," he said, "needs to be revealed and filled with substance."[25]

With Dobrynin's arrival in the Central Committee and Shevardnadze's restructuring of the MFA, there was by this time the beginning of a potentially significant process of civilian-military cross-fertilization. At the very top Akhromeyev was intimately involved with Gorbachev and other members of the civilian leadership in fashioning new Soviet arms control and military doctrine positions. At a lower level a number of officer veterans of Nikolay Chervov's arms negotiations directorate in the General Staff had moved out to work in the Central Committee's International (Viktor Starodubov) and Propaganda (Geliy Batenin) departments and the MFA's Arms Control Administration (Konstantin Mikhaylov).[26]

Gorbachev's subsequent statement on February 28 again delinking the INF negotiations from the other two sets of talks in Geneva was remarkable for his self-identification as head of the Defense Council, the first time any Soviet leader had done so since Brezhnev in East Berlin in October 1979. Gorbachev also made a point of underscoring the Politburo's collective approval of the INF initiative, stating that he was announcing it "on behalf of the Soviet leadership." If there had been misgivings within the military, then Gorbachev's declaration served as another demonstration of the civilian leadership's determination to demonstrate the military's subordinate role in the elaboration of Soviet national security policy, including INF. A week later commentator Aleksandr Bovin publicly asked for "competent answers" to why the SS-20s had been built and deployed in the first place.[27]

RESTRUCTURING AND THE RISE OF YAZOV

Whether or not Gorbachev actually met Yazov for the first time in July 1986 during his trip to the Far East, Yazov, as commander of the Far East military district, evidently made a strong impression on Gorbachev at that time.[28] Half a year later, not long before Yazov was promoted to Moscow, *Red Star* would inform readers that Gorbachev had asked Yazov about discipline when he met in Khabarovsk with the command personnel of Yazov's district. In reply Yazov had "confessed . . . that discipline in the district had not improved recently and had even worsened in individual units and subunits. He presented accurate figures. Hundreds of officers and dozens of generals attended this talk. Now this talk is called in the district nothing other than a lesson of truth."[29]

Yazov was born in 1923 in the Siberian village of Yazovo in the Omsk region. He joined the army in 1941, and was commissioned the next year at age 19, was wounded but returned to active combat during World War II. Twenty years after the war Yazov graduated from the

Voroshilov General Staff Academy in 1967. From 1980 to 1984 Yazov was commander of the Central Asian military district but probably played only a secondary role in Afghanistan, the main responsibility of the adjoining Turkestan military district. He arrived in Khabarovsk at about July 1984, presumably charged with reorganizing the district in light of the shortcomings shown up by the KAL fiasco the previous September.

Before his assignment to the Far East military district, Yazov had had a number of opportunities to make some important connections. At the General Staff Academy he had studied with Akhromeyev as well as V. I. Varennikov, who would later rise to first deputy chief of the Main Political Administration. From 1974 to 1975 Yazov worked in the Main Personnel Directorate of the Defense Ministry. Both his predecessor and successor as commander of the Central Asian military district—P. G. Lushev and V. N. Lobov, respectively—had been promoted to high posts in 1986–87. Lushev replaced Petrov as first deputy defense minister in July 1986; Lobov was appointed first deputy chief of the General Staff by early May 1987.[30] Ivan Tretyak, whom Yazov would bring out of semiretirement to replace fired Air Defense Chief Aleksandr Koldunov in the wake of the Cessna incident, had been Yazov's boss in 1977–79, when Yazov was first deputy to Tretyak, at the time commander of the Far Eastern military district. "My new appointment [as air defense chief] was a bolt out of the blue for me," Tretyak recounted in 1988. "The defense minister phoned first."[31]

Even before the meeting with Gorbachev in Khabarovsk in July 1986, Yazov was developing a national profile and emerging as a champion of restructuring. Only a month after Gorbachev came to power, Yazov had been the subject of a major biographical essay in *Red Star* in which a former subordinate described him as "demanding" and "even harsh" but nevertheless businesslike and to the point.[32] A year later, in what was perhaps a dress rehearsal for the Gorbachev trip, Defense Minister Sokolov chaired a meeting in Khabarovsk with the party aktiv of the Far East military district. Yazov was the main speaker at the event, which was said to be dedicated to the tasks of restructuring the work of party organizations in light of the June plenum. *Red Star* reported that Yazov had analyzed the activity of commanders, political organs, and party organizations in the district and called on them to approach all questions with the "highest exactingness and efficiency."[33] In October, after his encounter with Gorbachev, Yazov again gained favorable mention in the newspaper when the cadre chief of the Main Political Administration praised him and several others for their work with the Komsomol.[34]

Yazov's arrival in Moscow coincided with the January 1987 plenum. One of the most interesting personnel moves approved by that plenum had been the appointment to the Secretariat of Anatoliy Lukyanov, who may have had ties with Gorbachev dating from Moscow State University in the early 1950s. Given Lukyanov's legal background and writings and long years of work in the apparatus of the Supreme Soviet, it appeared that he would probably be closely involved in implementing the "democratization" measures endorsed by the Central Committee. Indeed, that eventually proved to be the case. Lukyanov's more immediate impact, however, was on military cadres. Only days after the January plenum ended, it became clear that Lukyanov had begun to supervise the work of Nikolay Savinkin, since 1968 head of the Central Committee's Administrative Organs. Judging from his public appearances, Lukyanov's wide-ranging and critical prerogatives included the defense sector and law enforcement organs.

In his role as overseer of military cadres, one of Lukyanov's first moves was probably Yazov's promotion to deputy defense minister in charge of personnel. The officer Yazov displaced, significantly, was none other than Ivan Shkadov, who in the wake of the KAL shootdown in September 1983 had pressed for greater authority for commanders and more resources for the military. More recently Shkadov had left the impression that his attitude toward Gorbachev's perestroika was lukewarm at best.[35]

RESTRUCTURING IN, SOKOLOV OUT

With Lukyanov and Yazov now in place, restructuring finally began to hit the military establishment with more noticeable force. To outsiders, one of the first inklings was a *mea culpa* in *Red Star* on February 19. The unattributed report dealt with the case of some officers censured for suppressing criticism. The article admitted that its previous reports on the matter, on April 13 and July 23, 1986, had been tendentious.[36] Several days later Akhromeyev called for "an influx of fresh forces into leadership posts" in his article for Armed Forces Day.[37]

By mid-March, there had been a major meeting of the party aktiv in the Defense Ministry devoted to restructuring. Sokolov delivered the main report, placing the meeting within the context of Gorbachev's address to the high command in Minsk nearly two years before. "The implementation and deepening of restructuring should lead us gradually to a new standard of Army and Navy combat readiness," Sokolov said. "This is especially relevant because the aggressive tendencies in the policy of the United States and the other NATO countries are persisting and there is an evident striving to change the military-strategic parity of forces in their own favor and force the USSR to submit to their diktat." Sokolov repeated Akhromeyev's call for an "influx of fresh forces" but combined it with a demand for "ensuring continuity in leadership." According to *Red Star's* write-up, few sectors of the military establishment escaped being criticized in the speeches that followed Sokolov's presentation.[38] In addition, several days later *Pravda* reported on corruption in the Kaliningrad Higher Engineering Troops Academy, returning to the same case again in late April.[39]

If Sokolov was under pressure, he was moving with the flow while seeking to slow its advance. The aging defense minister seemed to have recuperated from whatever had caused him to miss the November 7 parade on Red Square the previous fall. His new first deputy minister, P. G. Lushev, had stood in for him, but the military as an institution had suffered another striking snub. Compared with the eleven uniformed representatives on May Day 1986, only four officers—Akhromeyev, Kulikov, Lushev, and Lizichev—reviewed the anniversary parade from the Lenin Mausoleum on November 7, 1986, and to add insult to injury, they had been made to stand beneath the lowest ranking of the civilian leadership.[40] May Day 1987 would see a repeat performance, except that with Sokolov back on the reviewing stand the military representation would rise to five.

Nevertheless, Sokolov, was quite active during the first half of 1987 and accompanied Gorbachev to the Warsaw Pact summit in East Berlin at the end of May. But there had been some anomalies. In March *Red Star* carried a report on a meeting of the party aktiv of the Group of Soviet Forces in Germany (GSFG) addressed by Sokolov, with Ogarkov in attendance.[41] Excluding obituaries, it was perhaps the first and only time since Ogarkov's ouster from the General Staff and Sokolov's appointment as defense minister that the two had been linked in print this way. The reader was left to ponder whether the "subtext" of the report was that the two were now making public their alliance on some important issue. Then in May, however, an anonymous Soviet official told a Western correspondent that Sokolov was seriously ill with heart disease. Despite strong resistance from the military establishment, the story went, the chances were 80 percent that Sokolov would be replaced by a civilian—perhaps, it was claimed, Boris Yeltsin. Other officials told the same correspondent that Gorbachev had had to postpone his trip to Prague in April because of resistance in the military to his proposal for zero SRINF in Europe.[42]

Even with the titillating rumors out in the open, the end came with surprising suddenness when nineteen-year-old West German citizen Mathias Rust buzzed the Lenin Mausoleum and landed his Cessna on the edge of Red Square in the heart of Moscow the evening of May 28—Border Guards Day, no less. Gorbachev, Gromyko, Ryzhkov, Shevardnadze, Sokolov, and Medvedev were all in East Berlin winding up the first day of the pact summit, but they left the following day. Within 24 hours of their return to Moscow, TASS moved the first of several reports on the Politburo meeting and subsequent Supreme Soviet Presidium decree that retired Sokolov, fired Air Defense Chief Koldunov, and appointed Yazov defense minister.[43] A month later at the June plenum of the Central Committee, Yazov replaced Sokolov as a candidate member on the Politburo. Reflecting the intensity of the animosity of Gorbachev and his supporters toward Sokolov, dating at least from the infighting over the succession to Ustinov, Sokolov was apparently not even given an office in the Defense Ministry's Inspectorate General, the usual practice for retired marshals.

The account of the Politburo meeting on May 30 was scathing in its indictment of shortcomings in the air defense forces and the Defense Ministry in general. "The Politburo pointed out that the Air Defense Forces' command displayed impermissible lack of concern and resolve to intercept the intruding aircraft, in not resorting to combat means," stated the press report. "This fact points to serious shortcomings in the organization and conduct of combat readiness for defending the country's airspace, and to a lack of due vigilance and discipline, and to major omissions in the management of troops on the part of the USSR Ministry of Defense."[44] The Soviet press even replayed comments by *bête noire* Zbigniew Brzezinski: "The Russians have done what the US military and political leadership has not had the courage to do, namely: Punish military leaders when there is a significant setback. . . . The Russians have set us an example of how to assume responsibility and how to be accountable for such things."[45]

"You have to show people the truth, albeit two years late," Yeltsin told a meeting of the party aktiv of the Moscow air defense district in mid-June. "The party had the courage to tell the whole world about the crisis within society but in the district, apparently, 'all was well.'" Referring to the Cessna incident Yeltsin said: "In labor collectives people are saying: We would like the commanders of the Soviet Army to look workers in the face and explain how such a thing could happen."[46] According to new air defense chief Ivan Tretyak's revelations the following February, his predecessor Koldunov had gone home the night Rust landed "knowing nothing at all about the incident. There were no reports."[47] In a twist of fate, Tretyak had been commander of the Far East military district at the time of the KAL 007 shootdown, for which Koldunov—but not Tretyak—appeared to have taken some heat.

FROM "STRENGTHENING" TO "MAINTAINING" DEFENSE

In his Order of the Day on Armed Forces Day in February 1986, Sokolov had called only for "maintaining" defense capabilities and combat might "at the requisite level," rather than the usual appeal for "strengthening" them. By Victory Day in May, however, Sokolov had gone back to the more familiar "strengthening." Nevertheless, in commenting on resource allocations in 1986, other officials seemed more in tune with Sokolov's earlier and milder call for "maintaining" the country's defenses than with his more demanding "strengthening" formulation.

Gorbachev, for example, in explaining his economic priorities to Spain's Felipe Gonzalez during a long conversation on May 20 in the Kremlin, reportedly said, "So far, we have been applying intellectual resources to defense; now we are going to devote them to technological renewal and industrial development."[48] Not long after, the Defense Ministry's peripatetic General Nikolay Chervov told a Western interviewer that Soviet military leaders realized "more than you think" what a burden the military-industrial complex put on the Soviet economy. "It is in the interests of the country's security and stability to have a lull in the arms race that will permit us to construct new and better cities and to give the people more consumer goods. But believe me: Our people are fully aware of security requirements and will understand us."[49]

There were several unusual leadership statements in public along the same lines. Premier Nikolay Ryzhkov told the Supreme Soviet in June that the leadership intended to involve all machine-building industries, "including the defense ministries, in producing the most modern equipment for light industry."[50] In much the same vein, Zaykov told an audience in Irkutsk later in the month that the defense sector was being asked to do more than just produce civilian output and consumer goods. It was also necessary, he said, "to involve them in the retooling of light industry, the food industry, public catering, and trade."[51]

Even as Gorbachev was moving Lukyanov and Yazov into place at the January 1987 plenum, though, his rhetoric and that of the Central Committee resolution adopted at the plenum unexpectedly spoke again in terms of the need for strengthening the country's defenses.[52] That, however, was perhaps a reflection of the post-Reykjavik temporary cooling of U.S.-Soviet relations. In any event, the key phrases in defense minister Sokolov's two most important remaining ceremonial orders of the day—Armed Forces Day (February 23) and Victory Day (May 9)—soon reverted to consistent moderation. Instead of the call for strengthening the nation's defense might, they both now spoke only of "maintaining" it at the appropriate level.[53] The Victory Day statement was particularly significant, for it was the first revision of the stock phrasing on that day since Ustinov had dropped it entirely on May 9, 1976—and that omission, as we have seen, coincided with the slowdown in defense spending growth which was probably still in force.

Meanwhile, after the January plenum's rhetorical hiccup, the civilian leadership continued to reinforce the new line on aiding the civilian sector in 1987, as restructuring began to gain greater currency in the defense establishment. In early February a congress of trade union workers in the defense industry reportedly drew up "ways to radically increase labor, productivity, improve the quality of consumer goods, and save resources."[54] Several weeks later Gorbachev told citizens in Tallinn, Estonia, "We have now in fact even requested the defense industry to manufacture equipment for the light and food industry."[55] Subsequently Gorbachev argued that the concept of defense sufficiency would prevent the West from imposing on the USSR an all-out arms race, which could bankrupt the country and frustrate economic reform. "But we shall not make a single step in excess of the demands and requirements of sensible, sufficient defense," he told the national trade union congress."[56] His presentation again suggested that his economic priorities were incompatible with giving the military everything it wanted.

Throughout 1987 Gorbachev and other civilian spokesmen gave clear notice of an intention to continue to pressure the military establishment to restrain its spending by pledging to make public its real scope. In an August speech to the UN-sponsored conference on disarmament and development, Deputy Foreign Minister Vladimir Petrovskiy for the first time publicly admitted that the published defense budget did not include, of all things, weapons. Instead, it only "reflects what the USSR Ministry of Defense spends on personnel of the Armed Forces, logistics, military construction, pension funds, and a number of other expenditures. Scientific research, design and testing work, and armament and military technology purchases are accounted for in other articles of the USSR state budget." After price reform, suggested the Soviet representative, it would be possible to engage in a "realistic" comparison of military budgets.[57] A month later Gorbachev stated that the necessary figures might be ready for public release within two to three years.[58] Not long after, the slogans for the seventieth anniversary of the October Revolution were missing the usual call for "Glory to the valiant Armed Forces of the USSR!"[59]

NEW DIRECTIONS?

Two years after Minsk, Gorbachev finally had a defense minister of his own choosing and a restructuring program moving into high gear in the military establishment. In terms of the intended public profile, the new line clearly meant renewed and revived emphasis on the "human factor," including a less forgiving attitude toward corruption within the military, the quality of the officer corps, and the widespread and sometimes brutal hazing of enlisted men; more efficient use of resources; greater aid to the civilian sector; and some restraint on defense spending increases. But there was no way the outside world could assess how these rhetorical and programmatic flourishes actually translated into the real world of rubles and kopecks and force posture.

Neither of the defense establishment's two top professionals were yet able to spell out the operational implications of the current line with the detail offered by Ustinov in July 1982 in the wake of Brezhnev's nuclear no-first-use pledge. The more forward-leaning Akhromeyev stated in May 1987, "Defensive counteroperations to repulse enemy aggression form the main element in training our troops and naval forces."[60] But even after the late May 1987 Warsaw Pact summit statement on military doctrine, which called for reductions that would leave both sides in Europe unable to mount a surprise attack, Yazov's late July 1987 *Pravda* article sounded strikingly rigid and pugnacious. The Soviet and Warsaw Pact arsenal, in Yazov's depiction, would be "rigorously" defined in response to the threat faced from "imperialist military preparations." At the strategic nuclear level, "reasonable sufficiency" meant that the Soviet force structure would be "determined by the need to prevent anyone getting away with impunity with a nuclear attack in any, even the most unfavorable circumstances." On the conventional level, it meant fielding "a quantity and quality of armed forces and armaments capable of reliably ensuring the collective defense of the socialist community." Overall it meant being able to give a "crushing rebuff" to any aggressor.[61]

To the extent military commanders began to highlight the importance of defensive operations, they were simply giving greater publicity to a trend that dated from the late 1970s, years before Gorbachev came to power.[62] As such, the military's growing attention to defensive operations was simply a prudent military response to a perceived military problem—that is, to NATO's increased potential capabilities for prolonged conventional warfare on Warsaw Pact territory. By 1987 an estimated 30 percent of Soviet military exercises during the year were said by Pentagon sources to have been "defensive in nature," up from only 10 to 20 percent.[63] And even this was not the optimal mix for at least two *Red Star* officer-correspondents. Given the need to be able "to confront an active, technically well-equipped enemy—and we cannot count on a weak enemy," they called for the percentage of defensive exercises and drills to "be far higher than it is now. Fifty-fifty—this is probably the most expedient and fair ratio of the time allocated for training operations in attack and in defense."[64]

But the political leadership's declarative statements were already providing room for maneuvering by some civilian and military analysts to call on the military establishment not simply to beef up its defensive capabilities but to work with the political leadership toward a new East-West military equation. In September 1987 Gorbachev reiterated the bottom-line appeal of the Warsaw Pact's statement in May on military doctrine. The restructured armed forces on both sides, Gorbachev wrote in his article pegged to the opening of the UN General Assembly, should be "sufficient to repulse a possible aggression but would not be sufficient for the conduct of offensive actions."[65] In the meantime, USA Institute Deputy Director Andrey Kokoshin and Major General Valentin Larionov of the General Staff Academy, in an article reexamining the 1943 defensive operation at Kursk, wrote that the Warsaw Pact's formulation on military doctrine meant eventual reductions "to a level necessary for meeting only defensive missions." Larionov, who had collaborated with Marshal Vasiliy Sokolovskiy in the 1960s on *Military Strategy*, now joined Kokoshin in declaring that "the conviction that has existed until now that only a 'decisive offensive leads to victory' no longer applies to nuclear war."[66]

Kokoshin and Larionov were not voices in the wilderness crying for changes in Soviet operational practice going beyond new formulations in declaratory doctrine. They were also not merely simple propagandists appealing to the sentiments of the left wing of the West German SPD. By the end of 1987 close readers of Soviet military writings began to detect a significant turnaround. In January the book *Tactics* had stated that "the offense is the main form of battle." By October, the first book Yazov produced as defense minister stated, "Soviet military doctrine considers the defense as the main form of military operations."[67] The following March, when Yazov met with U.S. Defense Secretary Frank Carlucci in Bern, and in July, when Akhromeyev toured the United States as guest of the chairman of the Joint Chiefs of Staff, both Soviet officers assured their American interlocutors that Soviet exercises and training manuals would soon be changed to reflect a more defensive character.[68]

NOTES

1. Ogarkov, *Voyenniy Entsiklopedicheskiy Slovar*.
2. Akhromeyev, *Voyenniy Entsiklopedicheskiy Slovar*.
3. *Pravda*, December 20, 1986 (FBIS-SOV, January 8, 1987, V 1–2).
4. Ogarkov and Akhromeyev, *Voyenniy Entsiklopedicheskiy Slovar*, 1983 and 1986, 240 and 712, respectively.
5. *Izvestiya*, November 28, 1985 (FBIS-SOV, December 2, 1985, R 13).
6. *Pravda*, November 22, 1985 (FBIS-SOV, November 22, 1985, Supplement, 1).
7. *Red Star*, January 23, 1987 (FBIS-SOV, January 23, 1987, AA 4).
8. *Pravda*, February 23, 1987 (FBIS-SOV, February 24, 1987, V 2).
9. *Pravda*, May 31, 1987 (FBIS-SOV, June 1, 1987, BB 19 and 21).

10. APN Military Bulletin, no. 2 (October 1986): 5–6. According to the *Washington Post*, October 28, 1986, Ogarkov's remarks were released on October 27, 1986.

11. TASS, July 7, 1986 (FBIS-SOV, July 8, 1986, G 4).

12. In his first post-Chernobyl speech, however, a televised address to the nation, Gorbachev had not yet arrived at the new argument on the danger of conventional war. Instead, he put forward the rather orthodox warning that "the accident at Chernobyl showed again what an abyss will open if nuclear war befalls mankind. For inherent in the nuclear arsenals stockpiled are thousands upon thousands of disasters far more horrible than the Chernobyl one" (*Pravda*, May 15, 1986 [FBIS-SOV, May 15, 1986, L 4]).

13. M. A. Gareyev, *M. V. Frunze—Voyenniy Teoretik* (Moscow: Voyenizdat, 1985, signed to press October 17, 1984), 243–44.

14. TASS, April 8, 1987 (FBIS-SOV, April 28, 1987, G 2).

15. *Pravda*, April 11, 1987 (FBIS-SOV, April 14, 1987, F 17). See similar remarks attributed to Marshal Akhromeyev by Sergey Plekhanov on April 17, 1987 on the radio show "Top Priority" beamed in English to North America (FBIS-SOV, April 22, 1987, CC 4).

16. *Red Star*, May 9, 1987 (FBIS-SOV, May 15, 1987, V 3).

17. Moscow Television Service, September 29, 1987 (FBIS-SOV, September 30, 1987, 28).

18. Gorbachev, *Perestroika*, 127.

19. Moscow Television Service, September 23, 1987 (FBIS-SOV, September 24, 1987, 20–21).

20. See Gorbachev's television addresses on March 29, May 14, and August 18, 1986.

21. *Washington Post*, August 31, 1986.

22. Nitze, "The Nuclear and Space Negotiations."

23. Moscow Television Service, October 14, 1986 (FBIS-SOV, October 15, 1986, DD 2).

24. *Kommunist*, no. 9 (June 1986), signed to press June 11, 1986, and said to be based on Dobrynin's report on May 27, 1986, to the Second All-Union Conference of Scientists on Problems of Peace and the Prevention of Nuclear War.

25. *Kommunist*, no. 8 (May 1987), signed to press May 12, 1987.

26. Raymond L. Garthoff, "New Thinking in Soviet Military Doctrine," *Washington Quarterly* 11, no. 3 (Summer 1988): 150.

27. *Moscow News*, no. 10, March 8, 1987 (FBIS-SOV, March 13, 1987, AA 1).

28. *Red Star*, July 31, 1986 (FBIS-SOV, July 31, 1986, R 8).

29. *Red Star*, January 16, 1987.

30. He was first identified in this position in *Red Star*, May 8, 1987 (FBIS-SOV, May 11, 1987, G 1).

31. *Moscow News*, no. 8, February 21, 1988 (FBIS-SOV, February 24, 1988, 74). For more on Yazov's career and changes in the high command under Gorbachev, see Dale R. Herspring, "On Perestroyka: Gorbachev, Yazov, and the Military," *Problems of Communism* (July-August 1987): 99–107; and Alexander Rahr, "Further Changes in the Military," Radio Liberty Research, RL 276/87, July 15, 1987.

32. *Red Star*, April 13, 1985.

33. *Red Star*, July 10, 1986.

34. *Red Star*, October 31, 1986.

35. See Herspring, "On Perestroyka," 102.

36. *Red Star*, February 19, 1987 (FBIS-SOV, March 4, 1987, V 1–3).

37. *Sovetskaya Rossiya*, February 21, 1987 (FBIS-SOV, February 27, 1987, V 3).

38. *Red Star*, March 18, 1987 (FBIS-SOV, March 20, 1987, V 1).

39. *Pravda*, March 21 and April 25, 1987 (FBIS-SOV, April 1 and May 5, 1987, V 1–4 and V 1, respectively).

40. *Pravda*, November 8, 1986.

41. *Red Star*, March 7, 1987 (FBIS-SOV, March 10, 1987, V 1–2).

42. *The Sunday Times*, May 10, 1987.

43. TASS, 1657 GMT, May 30, 1987 (FBIS-SOV, June 1, 1987, R 1).

44. *Pravda*, May 31, 1987 (FBIS-SOV, June 1, 1987, R 2).

45. *Izvestiya*, June 1, 1987 (FBIS-SOV, June 1, 1987, R 1).

46. *Red Star*, June 17, 1987 (FBIS-SOV, June 17, 1987, V 1–5).

47. *Moscow News*, no. 8, February 21, 1988 (FBIS-SOV, February 24, 1988, 74).

48. *Cambio 16*, December 15, 1986.

49. *La Repubblica*, June 17, 1986 (FBIS-SOV, June 20, 1986, AA 5).

50. *Pravda*, June 19, 1986 (FBIS-SOV, June 20, 1986, R 22).

51. *Pravda*, June 29, 1986 (FBIS-SOV, July 8, 1986, R 9). The extent to which this is happening, or which Zaykov envisioned, has not been disclosed.

52. TASS, January 27, 1987 (FBIS-SOV, January 28, 1987, R 45–46); and *Pravda*, January 29, 1987 (FBIS-SOV, January 30, 1987, R 10).

53. See *Red Star*, February 22 and May 9, 1987 (FBIS-SOV, February 26, 1987, V 1, and May 12, 1987, V 1, respectively).

54. *Vremya*, Moscow Television Service, February 3, 1987 (FBIS-SOV, February 5, 1987, S 1).

55. Moscow Domestic Service, February 19, 1987 (FBIS-SOV, February 25, 1987, R 28).

56. Moscow Television Service, February 25, 1987 (FBIS-SOV, February 27, 1987, R 14).

57. TASS, August 25, 1987 (FBIS-SOV, August 26, 1987, CC 8). See also Gorbachev's message to the conference in *Pravda*, August 26, 1987 (FBIS-SOV, August 26, 1987, CC 6).

58. *Pravda*, September 17, 1987 (FBIS-SOV, September 17, 1987, 24).

59. *Pravda*, October 11, 1987 (FBIS-SOV, October 13, 1987, pp. 71–72).

60. *Red Star*, May 9, 1987 (FBIS-SOV, May 15, 1987, V 6).

61. *Pravda*, July 27, 1987 (FBIS-SOV, July 27, 1987, BB 3–4).

62. For a survey of this evolution, see Stephen M. Meyer, "The Sources and Prospects of Gorbachev's New Political Thinking on Security," *International Security* 13, no. 2 (Fall 1988), 152–53.

63. *Washington Times*, March 10, 1988.

64. *Red Star*, December 9, 1987 (FBIS-SOV, December 16, 1987, 84).

65. *Pravda*, September 17, 1987 (FBIS-SOV, September 17, 1987, 24).

66. *Mirovaya Ekonomika i Mezhdunarodnyye Otnosheniya*, no. 8 (August 1987). See also the subsequent article by Kokoshin and Larionov in the same journal, no. 6 (June 1988). For a detailed survey and analysis of the major works on military doctrine during this period, see Garthoff, "New Thinking in Soviet Military Doctrine."

67. *New York Times*, March 7, 1988.

68. *Washington Post*, March 18 and July 13, 1988; and *Christian Science Monitor*, March 18, 1988.

Chapter 11

The June Plenum: Economic Reform

*U*ntil it began to prepare for what would turn out to be the June 1987 plenum, the leadership had not really had to sort itself out on the details of economic reform. Since coming to power Gorbachev and his coalition had agreed in principle on the need to move away from an administrative-command economy toward one more reliant on economic relationships. But there was presumably a wide range of diverse viewpoints on how much to loosen the bonds of central planning and give vent to market-type relationships of supply and demand.

The impending plenum alone would have guaranteed tensions and disputes as the leadership went beyond exhortation to developing a concrete plan and program for economic reform. But to these was added renewed conflict over what had been agreed at the January plenum on political reform. Gorbachev and his closest supporters obviously did not consider the matter decided once and for all. That, after all, had been the point of Gorbachev's demand for a follow-up party conference at which democratization could be discussed further. Moreover, beginning with his closing speech at the January plenum, Gorbachev and his supporters sought to give a radical interpretation to the plenum's uneasy consensus on political democratization.

Hints began to appear of Ligachev's reservations over the direction in which the more radical wing of the leadership was attempting to push both political and economic reform. Overloading and speeding up the reform agenda and indiscriminate criticism of the past, Ligachev seemed to argue, was creating more confusion and opposition than understanding and support. Furthermore, once controls were lifted, it would be difficult to reassert them, should it be necessary to do so. Ligachev, until then the leadership's hatchet man on cadres, shifted gears and began to tout the advantages of patience and reeducation over indiscriminate firings and forced retirements. To his earlier profile as protector of party privilege but not corruption, he now began to add a populist tinge as defender of the "social contract" against those radical economists who would countenance the sacrificing of guaranteed employment on the altar of economic efficiency.

189

In fairness to Ligachev's political acumen, it was true that nothing like the specter of unemployment could be counted on to put the working class, both blue- and white-collar, on guard against *perestroika* and economic change. And it was no accident that on this point specifically Gorbachev chose to advertise his differences with the economist Shmelev shortly before the June 1987 plenum. The population at large was probably too cynical and apathetic to pay attention to Ligachev or any other member of the leadership on this or any other issue. But by the same token, despite repeated assertions to the contrary, there was never any compelling evidence that Gorbachev was able to generate substantial support from the grass roots for his more radical economic program either.

As had been the case in January on political reform, the outcome of the June plenum on economic reform was the result of compromise, though clearly not so difficult to reach as had been the case earlier. In both instances the cause of reform had advanced on the strength of a solid centrist consensus on the need for change. But at the top there remained an uneasy tension between those wanting to push matters even further and those wanting at least a tactical pause to consolidate progress and clear up confusion. Below, meanwhile, the apparatus took advantage of the situation to move as little as possible.

"NO FORGOTTEN NAMES"

As fundamental as it was to the politics of reform, after the January plenum the crucial evolution of the nuances over democratization vis-à-vis the party's leading role did not capture the attention of the world press. Instead, most attention was riveted on a series of remarkable historical commentaries as the leadership began to lay down the guidelines for treatment of the seventieth anniversary of the 1917 Revolution in November.

Reformers, many of whom had lived through the missteps of Khrushchev a quarter of a century before, sought to push forward in large part simply to avoid being pulled backward again. But as could be expected in the Soviet context, they alarmed their detractors as much as they gained the applause of their supporters. In December *Literary Gazette* had interviewed Academician Sakharov but then failed to publish the interview, reportedly scheduled for early February. According to one Western press report, the planned publication of the interview had come to be "regarded as a casus belli and the last straw by some senior CPSU officials."[1] Nevertheless, despite rumored differences between Gorbachev and Ligachev over the limits of *glasnost* and the process of historical rediscovery, there seemed to be remarkable consensus over the need to press forward.

In early February, soon after the January plenum, Aleksandr Bovin wrote a striking article with some of the same themes of Burlatskiy's remarkable "dialogue" the previous October. "In Moscow a new note is struck, but in the localities things go on in the old way. . . . I cannot help thinking that we are underestimating the scale and the strength of the resistance to the strategy of . . . revolutionary rebuilding of the whole of our way of life," warned Bovin. It was not enough that "key positions are in reliable, energetic hands. . . . Because in my lifetime THEY have twice thrown US back, succeeded twice in barring the way to long overdue and urgently needed changes." The main enemy could be described as "homegrown bureaucratic Soviet socialist conservatism."[2]

Accompanied by Ligachev and Yakovlev, Gorbachev in mid-February delivered his first public speech instructing media representatives on how to handle the seventieth anniversary of the Bolshevik Revolution, which would be celebrated in November. "There must be no forgotten names, no blank spaces, either in history or in literature," Gorbachev said. "We should not relegate to the shadows those who made the revolution." In the same vein, the general secretary declared, "We must value every year of our 70 years of Soviet history. . . . Both things happened—the joyous and the bitter. Whatever happened to us, we marched forward." Moreover, "We have to see history as it is," Gorbachev stated. "It all happened. There were mistakes, and grave ones; but the country was moving forward. Take the years of industrialization or collectivization: that was life, reality; it was the destiny of the people with all its contradictions—with both its achievements and its mistakes." Finally, alluding again to the Stalin period, Gorbachev said, "The party has already given its assessment of the mistakes and miscalculations of our errors; but even then, at that most difficult time, the party lived and fought. To our lot has fallen the role of trailblazers."[3]

This was basically the same balanced approach to history authorized by the Central Committee in its "appeal" a month later in which it outlined what should be the dominant tone in celebrating the upcoming "jubilee."[4] It was also the line that would dominate Gorbachev's speech on November 2. Nevertheless, Gorbachev's balance was quickly forgotten by outside observers, who, when Ligachev said much the same thing throughout the year, treated it as evidence of the second secretary's more "conservative" outlook.

On March 23, for example, Ligachev told a conference at the State Committee for Television and Radio Broadcasting that it was "no secret" that the country had "passed through both unfading achievements and the bitterness of temporary defeats, difficult and complex stages."

Nevertheless, he asserted, "Nobody can erase the indisputable fact that it was in the years of Soviet power and thanks to Soviet power that the country became a world leader." It was therefore "necessary to ensure really full and impressive propaganda of the achievements of Soviet power." Ligachev emphasized that "we are in favor of an honest and candid view, but we are resolutely opposed to the falsification of our glorious past, against the depiction of our history as a string of errors and disappointments."[5]

On March 23 Ligachev boasted that "never before has the party . . . displayed such tangible and constant support for bold, controversial, and constructive contributions by the press." There therefore seemed to be ample leadership support for the fundamental critiques of the Stalinist period, which soon resumed in the mass media. Some were in response to the leadership's endorsement of no "blank pages" in history.[6] A landmark of the period was the long-postponed publication of Anatoliy Rybakov's novel *Children of the Arbat*, written many years earlier and featuring a psychological study of Stalin on the eve of the great purges.[7] With the approach of the plenum on economic reform, other works were more specifically aimed at bolstering the case that the centralized management system devised under Stalin, while perhaps appropriate for the 1930s and 1940s, was long overdue for drastic revision.[8] Some writers went beyond this to damn the system as a pernicious deformation of Leninism from the very beginning.[9] Khrushchev and Brezhnev were also assessed, the former generally more favorably than the latter, though Khrushchev was criticized for squeezing the peasantry, an aspect of Stalinism he had at first condemned.[10]

The leadership itself, however, continued to treat both Stalin and Khrushchev with circumlocutions. Since Gorbachev's praise in May 1985 of Stalin's wartime leadership, the dead dictator's name had not been pronounced in public by any member of the Politburo or Secretariat. On June 15, however, Lukyanov broke the silence. Soviet history, he said, "has contained mistakes and distortions of the Leninist line, the repressions of the time of Stalin's personality cult, violations of socialist legality, and voluntarist zigzags."[11] It suggested that Lukyanov's anti-Stalinist article in *Pravda* in 1979 on the eve of the Stalin centenary had not been a fluke.

WHAT IS PERESTROIKA'S "GUARANTEE"?

At the 27th Congress Gorbachev had routinely stated that it was the party that acted as the "guiding force and the main guarantor for the development of socialist self-government." But he had also asserted that Lenin had seen "the main force for the development of the new order in democratization and the living creativity of the working people."[12] Given seven decades of contrary practice, however, Gorbachev's nod toward democratization could easily be dismissed as the hypocritical fluff routinely served up on such occasions. Indeed, in Voronezh on July 9, 1986, Ligachev had stated that it was the party's revitalized leading role in Soviet society which was the "guarantee" of progress, and in Khabarovsk at the end of the month Gorbachev had not hesitated to describe the USSR as a country in which "the party is the ruler."

The January plenum, however, showed that Gorbachev had more than fluff in mind, but it was unclear exactly what kind and how much democratization he intended, and what impact this would have on the party's traditional ways of doing business. In his opening speech at the January plenum Gorbachev had hewed to what must have been the Politburo consensus to satisfy all poles of opinion by including among the "guarantees" of restructuring "the deepening of socialist democratism, the creative endeavor of Soviet people, [and] the vanguard role of Communists in practical deeds."[13] Gorbachev's concluding speech and the agenda he set out for a forthcoming party conference, however, made clear that he placed the "serious, in-depth democratization of Soviet society" above the other "guarantees." In contrast, the Central Committee betrayed its uneasiness by evading the issue of guarantees in its plenum resolution and by saying nothing at all about a party conference.[14]

In February *Pravda* reported on the election of the party first secretary in the Izhmorskiy district of Kemerovo oblast. Picking up Gorbachev's key suggestion at the January plenum, there had been two candidates in the secret balloting.[15] Gorbachev commented favorably on the event soon after in a speech in Riga, and *Pravda* subsequently outlined an upcoming experiment in multicandidate elections for Supreme Soviet seats as well.[16] In Riga Gorbachev again stated that an upcoming plenum would decide the matter of a party conference, which should "discuss everything concerned with improving internal party activity and the life of the CPSU, including the very nature of elections and the formation of elective party organs."[17] In early March Zaykov stated in Prague, "We cannot conceive of a situation in which the senior officials in state agencies, enterprises, institutions, and social organizations are elected in a democratic way, but in the party apparatus everything remains unchanged. . . . Further democratization must also affect the formation of leading central party agencies."[18]

Even Ligachev sounded much like Gorbachev during this period. In a major article in *Kommunist* signed to press on February 23, the second secretary wrote that the plenum had "expressed very strongly the idea that restructuring cannot be carried out in isolation from the expansion of *glasnost*, from the deepening democratization of inner party, state, and social life, from the refinement of socialist self-government and of the electoral system, and from the development of democracy in the production sphere, the decisive sphere of human activity." Ligachev believed that "democracy and glasnost are both the condition for and the result of restructuring."[19] Several weeks later in Saratov in early March, the second secretary praised the "creative intelligentsia" for being the "party's closest assistant in the cause of people's psychological restructuring."[20]

But Ligachev was also beginning to spell out more clearly the limits—in his view—of reform. In Saratov he repeated earlier complaints that "in some places the names of artists at the peak of the Russian and our own Soviet classics are pushed into the background in publications." (Less than two weeks later, author Yuriy Bondarev bitterly complained that the state of Russian literature could be compared with that in July 1941, "when progressive forces, displaying uncoordinated resistance, retreated under pressure from the ramming assaults of civilized barbarians.")[21] More fundamentally, perhaps indicating his concern over the direction other members of the leadership were seeking to push democratization, Ligachev warned that any hopes of "weakening our system from within on the path of democratization, and of turning it into a channel of political pluralism," were "just pipe dreams. Profound restructuring in no way signifies the break-up of our political system."[22] The second secretary then repeated many of these same warnings—even while seconding Gorbachev's call for no more "blank pages" in the treatment of history—in his March 23 remarks to television and radio officials on how to treat the upcoming major anniversary of the revolution. "The class adversary," he claimed, was trying to discredit *perestroika* by asserting that the reforms of the Gorbachev era did not go far enough. "They try in vain to make out that only the notorious 'market economy,' political 'pluralism,' and the creation of a political opposition within the party and country are capable of resolving the problems facing the Soviet Union."[23]

Other leaders, meanwhile, were parroting Gorbachev's emphasis on expanding democratization as the key to success. In Prague Zaykov called it "the core of restructuring, its load-bearing structure." Elaborating on the conclusions of the January plenum, Zaykov seconded Gorbachev when he stated, "We see in the steady development of socialist democracy the main guarantee of the irreversibility of the restructuring process, a guarantee that the errors of the past will not be repeated and that the people's creative potential will be revealed."[24] Several days later, on a visit to his hometown of Sverdlovsk, Ryzhkov asserted that "broad democratization" was the "one path" to restructuring and the "main guarantee" of its success.[25] And the

Central Committee's "appeal" on celebrating the 70th anniversary of the Bolshevik Revolution stated that "The comprehensive development of the democratism of the socialist system—this is the guarantee that the strategic task of bringing society into a qualitatively new state will be solved."[26]

Gorbachev's supporters evidently had high hopes for effecting a significant turnover in the membership of the Central Committee at the party conference—even though it was still unscheduled and even though the Party Statutes approved at the 27th Congress left it to the Central Committee to decide ad hoc what rules should apply at a party conference.[27] Their hopes were transparently signaled by Prof. Yu. A. Bondar, who in *Sovetskaya Rossiya* recounted that the last party conference, held in February 1941, had been empowered to remove and replace up to 20 percent of Central Committee full members elected by the previous party congress with candidate members promoted to full membership.[28] Given *Sovetskaya Rossiya's* closeness to Ligachev a year later in the Nina Andreyeva "letter" affair, it appeared that as late as March 1987 even Ligachev must have supported what seemed to be Gorbachev's intention to purge further the membership of the Central Committee at the party conference.

By April when Gorbachev traveled to Czechoslovakia, he was able to claim that the USSR had succeeded in defining the "basic paths" of movement to "new boundaries of social, economic and scientific-technical progress." These were, he said, "the development of all forms of representative and direct democracy; the expansion everywhere of self-management; increasing the role of labor collectives, local soviet, and public organizations; the strengthening of the legal and economic guarantees of the individual's rights; the role of law; and openness and control by the people." Much of this was still in the realm of hopes, intentions, and self-promotion. Nevertheless, Gorbachev's confident assertion was in striking contrast to his admission in Hungary the previous summer of still not having found the right recipes.[29]

YAKOVLEV-LIGACHEV: PUSH-PULL

In early April Yakovlev began to espouse an explicitly more radical view unlike anything heard publicly from a Soviet leader until then. In a speech in the Central Asian capital of Dushanbe, little of which was reported in the central press, Gorbachev's closest associate went beyond calling "socialist democracy" an "effective accelerator" of revolutionary change. Democracy, according to Yakovlev, meant "struggle, competition, and rivalry. . . . The search for the way to build socialism more effectively, with minimum outlay, is inseparable from clashes of opinions, assessments, and interests. It is possible, even inevitable, some people will lose out in the clashes of attitudes, standpoints, and interests."[30]

The tenor and thrust of Yakovlev's remarks seemed to contradict Ligachev's condemnation in Saratov of "political pluralism," and they evidently precipitated a reaction in Moscow. Little more than a week later, Gorbachev for the first time acknowledged publicly that there were "specific carriers" of the "braking mechanism" at the top, "both at the level of the Central Committee and the government, and of ministers." The general secretary, however, assured his Komsomol Congress audience that there was no political opposition to restructuring per se.[31] Nevertheless, the two-part formula with which the leadership had started the democratization campaign in July 1986 briefly flashed back into view. In his Lenin Day speech Ryzhkov reaffirmed his earlier belief that "radical democratization" was the "main lever" of restructuring. But he then went on to list the party's "own healthy development" as well as the "expansion and deepening of socialist democracy" as guarantees that restructuring would be irreversible.[32] Ligachev, presumably the most authoritative source of resistance against revising the January compromise, told a press conference in Budapest several days later that the January plenum had drawn up "the conditions for making restructuring irreversible—the extension of the democratization of Soviet society and the perfection of cadre policy."[33]

Almost at the same time, however, Vadim Medvedev, who had worked for Yakovlev in the Propaganda Department in the early 1970s, delivered a speech in Baku on the same critical wavelength as that of Yakovlev in Dushanbe earlier in April. If there had been any doubts as to Medvedev's political profile and policy predilections, he put them to rest with his reference to the "slime" that had accumulated in the party and society in the decades preceding the April 1985 plenum. When it came to enumerating what would guarantee *perestroika*, furthermore, Medvedev mentioned only democratization. And he seemed to defend Yakovlev's call in Dushanbe for political "struggle, competition, and rivalry" when he dismissed those who felt "the call for discussions and polemics is capable of making restructuring uncontrollable and of shaking loose the foundations of socialism."[34]

On May Day Gorbachev and his closest supporters were strong enough to break the mold of the traditional photograph of the leadership standing on the Lenin Mausoleum. Instead of the usual full-frontal treatment, *Pravda* featured a sharply angled shot taken from below—a startling departure from precedent sure to shake up political "old believers." In terms of the leadership rankings, moreover, Zaykov's new prominence was most notable. On November 7, 1986, Zaykov had stood below Ligachev and Chebrikov. Now he stood ahead of Chebrikov and equidistant with Ligachev from Gorbachev. The photograph and standings seemed designed to drive home the message that the January plenum had ushered in a new era of politics, and that supporters of the view that democratization above all guaranteed the irreversibility of *perestroika*—such as Zaykov—were on the rise.

Gorbachev's determined campaign for democratization, however, had the effect of stiffening the opposition to it within the leadership and galvanizing it into action, even if that meant going against the dominant consensus. These cross-currents of opinion were soon reflected in the unusual report on the May 8 meeting of the Politburo, which was said to have discussed letters from working people. These were reported as unanimously supportive of restructuring. "At the same time, there are letters that report existing shortcomings and instances of infringement of discipline and order, suppression of criticism, and opposition to the current reforms."[35] Subsequent developments suggested it was most likely Ligachev who insisted on the Politburo's public acknowledgment of these critical sentiments. The very diversity of the concerns stated in the letters, however—coming as they did from the left, the right, and the middle of the political spectrum—hinted that their sponsor's immediate concern was more how best to steer and pace *perestroika* so as not to alienate public support, rather than the ultimate aims of *perestroika* itself.

Within a month Ligachev took advantage of a tour of Shevardnadze's home republic of Georgia to insist again on the two-part formula the leadership had agreed on prior to the January plenum. In a major speech in Tbilisi he maintained, "The growth of the CPSU's leading role and the strengthening of its ties with the masses is a key condition of the successful implementation of the 27th Congress' political course."[36] On cadres, Ligachev devoted much time to what in retrospect must be considered criticisms of Yeltsin's personnel policies and political style in Moscow. A "modern cadre corps" had been developed across the country, intoned Ligachev, and now it was "very important" to address the need for its continuing training and education. Unfortunately, Ligachev said, "this has been somewhat neglected" and "replacement has become almost the sole method of work with cadres." Patience was needed, he stressed, to spend time with cadres, "to turn them into genuine leaders, and to give them an opportunity to prove themselves." It was "necessary to spend more time on the spot, not to travel on junkets but to spend as much time with the collective as may be necessary to do the job and to give real assistance."[37]

The speech underscored the remarkable transformation of Ligachev's public profile from supporter of the general secretary to apprehensive skeptic. The fact that it was delivered in the home base of Gorbachev's

long-time acquaintance Shevardnadze, furthermore, seemed to underscore a cooling of relations between Ligachev and Gorbachev. He did
not back away from his emphasis on the need to purify the ranks of the
party, and he supported elections and *glasnost* as means of avoiding
mistakes and phenomena such as "protectionism and the selection of
cadres according to family ties, personal loyalty, servility, and toadyism."
Nevertheless, he called for patience in dealing with cadres and warned
against indiscriminately abandoning some of the party's traditional
economic functions (on which more in the next section), all of which
must have been comforting to old-style leaders. Moreover, his caution
against the dangers from "irresponsible demagogues" who would use
democratization and *glasnost* to kindle "nationalist and religious ideas"
would appear prophetic much sooner than probably even Ligachev
expected.[38] This no doubt boosted his appeal to conservatives within
the party and state apparatuses and nudged Ligachev closer to them.
Now more than ever conservatives had reason to look to Ligachev—if
not as their savior—-then certainly as the lesser and far preferable of
two evils.

Several weeks later Ligachev followed up his Tbilisi speech with a
major article that again suggested a degree of estrangement from the
Politburo consensus on democratization. Writing on the issue of what
"guaranteed" the "irreversibility" of restructuring, Ligachev reiterated,
"These guarantees lie in the strengthening unity of the will and actions
of the party and the people. They lie in the healthy development of the
party itself." The positive developments under way within the party
were "associated with the development of its ties with the nonparty
multitude, and an increase in the ideological-moral conditioning of Communists." For Ligachev the expansion of socialist democracy beyond
intraparty relations represented a guarantee not of all-encompassing
perestroika but of a more narrow and yet still immensely important
guarantee against the return of Stalinism—or, in Ligachev's words,
"that the errors of the past, which were connected with breaches of
legality and collective leadership, will not be repeated."[39]

CONSENSUS AND DEBATE OVER ECONOMIC REFORM

After the January plenum Roy Medvedev asserted that Ligachev
had turned over the ideology portfolio to Aleksandr Yakovlev, newly
promoted to candidate member of the Politburo, and exchanged it for
agriculture.[40] Medvedev's assertion was a year and a half premature,
though it may have been an indication that Gorbachev and his closest
supporters would have liked to sidetrack Ligachev into agriculture. As
it turned out, for the time being Ligachev picked up the one without

giving up the other, and, rather than a trimming of his powers, an expansion occurred.

In any event, contrary to his conservative reputation, Ligachev in his new capacity soon struck progressive notes on all counts in a *Kommunist* article devoted to restructuring in the "agro-industrial complex." He repeated his earlier criticisms of the farm situation in the Ukraine and Kazakhstan. He registered his opposition to the policies of Brezhnev and Chernenko, which had favored massive investments in land reclamation and gigantic complexes, by calling for strict accounting of expenditures on agriculture. He joined Gorbachev in calling for an NEP-like "bold turn" (the acronym for Lenin's early 1920s New Economic Policy), and stressed the need for regulation by economic methods. He even signaled his approval for earning lots of money, though he warned that individuals should not be ruled by financial considerations alone.[41] Several weeks later Ligachev expressed his impatience over shortcomings during his early March visit to Saratov. "The pace and depth of changes in the country are not in accord with the plans we have outlined," he complained. "The changes for the better, as you know, are moving slowly."[42]

In general there seemed to be harmony in the leadership at least on the agenda for the upcoming plenum. Ligachev had outlined in general terms the economic reform measures under consideration in his speech on November 6, 1986. At the January plenum Slyunkov had been promoted to the Secretariat and made chief of the Central Committee Economic Department, from which he began to coordinate planning for the plenum. One by one the senior leadership spoke in favor of management reform. And week after week the Politburo considered and approved various components of the package.

A week and a half after the January plenum, *Pravda* published the draft Law on State Enterprises.[43] It included provisions for elections of production leaders, something Gorbachev had suggested in his speech to the 27th Party Congress a year earlier, and for greater independence of plants and associations from Gosplan and central ministries in Moscow. The existing outdated law had been adopted in 1966, in connection with the then already outdated Kosygin reforms. In February the Council of Ministers also adopted a resolution on consumer services cooperatives, and the first cooperative cafe opened in Moscow a month later.[44]

The leadership was evidently determined to push ahead and work out the details of a reform program, no matter how imperfect or messy the initial cut. Ryzhkov was an appropriate choice for leadership speaker on Lenin Day. To applause from his audience he declared, "The Soviet communists see their main contribution to the common cause of the entire movement as being to build up the strength of example of socialism. . . . Revolutionary restructuring today is our main national and internationalist duty."[45] The day after Ryzhkov spoke, Ligachev, speaking in Budapest, offered further upbeat comments on the changes in store. "We describe the transformations in the country. . . as revolutionary, and not just for effect, because they are indeed revolutionary. . . . This means we wish to break away from the well-known gradual nature of our development. We are making a leap toward a new and high quality condition in Soviet society."[46] The management reform plenum would take place "shortly," he said, but he "deliberately" declined to say precisely when. "If it turns out that the plenum has to be somewhat postponed because the topics and materials to be debated must be well prepared, then it is going to be rumored there is once again a schism in the CPSU Politburo."[47]

At about the same time, and with the evident endorsement of the absent Ligachev, the Politburo began systematically to examine the various facets of the upcoming economic reform: the financing, credit, and pricing mechanisms;[48] and central planning (Gosplan), material and technical supply (Gossnab), and science and technology.[49] By mid-May Gorbachev at the Baykonur cosmodrome was advertising the upcoming plenum as sure to be "momentous and very important for the country," and the Politburo was discussing preparation of Gorbachev's report and other key materials.[50] By May 20 the next Supreme Soviet session was scheduled for June 29. The expectation had to be that the Central Committee would meet the week before; the first item on the agenda for the parliamentary session, after all, was announced as "the restructuring of the management of the national economy at the present stage of the country's economic development."[51] On May 22 the Politburo approved proposals "for improving the forms and methods of work of the USSR Council of Ministers apparatus."[52]

Optimistic talk and Politburo approval notwithstanding, commentary in the media was already suggesting that in their specifics the measures under consideration were often half-baked and contradictory, and in their fundamental premises they were torn between the failed but familiar old and the promising but untested new. Reformist Tatyana Zaslavskaya complained of the draft Enterprise Law, for example: "The rehabilitation of the old economic mechanism in the draft law's third section practically cancels out the self-management of labor collectives proclaimed in the second section."[53] L. Popkova sparked a spirited debate over "Where Are the Pies Bigger and Better?" with her argument in *Novyy Mir* that the market and socialism were "incompatible" and that the "pure market economy" still had a "bright future ahead."[54] V. Liptiskiy countered in *Pravda* that "the desire to go beyond the bounds of socialism could lead to 'bigger and better pies' with an inedible filling."[55]

Far and away the biggest splash was made by reformist economist Nikolay Shmelev with publication of his article "Advances and Debts" in *Novyy Mir*.[56] It was a trenchant and unsparing examination of the distortions, imbalances, and paradoxes of the national economy, whose origins Shmelev saw in Stalin's dismantling of Lenin's NEP. "Today we have a shortage economy, unbalanced in virtually every point, in many respects uncontrollable, and if we are totally honest, scarcely susceptible to planning, an economy which still does not accept scientific and technical progress." It would take "years, perhaps even generations" to set it straight. Shmelev even went so far as to question the principle of guaranteed employment. "Let us not close our eyes to the economic harm done by our parasitical confidence in guaranteed work," he suggested. He even recommended that "a very good cure for laziness, drunkenness, and irresponsibility" would be "a real danger of losing your job and going onto a temporary allowance or being obliged to work wherever you are sent."

In his speeches and articles Ligachev had repeatedly stressed the inviolable nature of the state's guarantee of full employment. Very likely with this issue uppermost in mind, Ligachev reportedly admonished Shmelev, phoning him to say that the article was "harmful."[57] Ligachev's reprimand was probably also aimed well beyond Shmelev; Shmelev had worked in Aleksandr Yakovlev's Propaganda Department in the Central Committee from 1968 to 1970, and had then been a researcher and department chief in Oleg Bogomolov's Institute of Economics of the World Socialist System from 1970 to 1983. In any event, it was an extremely sensitive issue, and Gorbachev soon felt compelled to go on record endorsing Shmelev's overall analysis but also firmly rejecting ("that will not do") his suggestion that "unemployment is a suitable thing for us." Despite all the problems, Gorbachev asserted that what distinguished Soviet society was that it was "stable. . . . People are protected, today and for the future."[58] In July Burlatskiy clearly had Shmelev in mind when he wrote of "facile opinions about the need for, and even usefulness of, unemployment as a lever for promoting the growth of labor productivity."[59] By fall even Shmelev claimed to have been "somewhat carried away and in the heat of polemics" to have used "words which have basically been compromised, for instance the word 'unemployment.'" He was "convinced as a professional that unemployment as such is not a problem for our society."[60]

SPARRING BEFORE THE PLENUM

On balance Shmelev's blunt comments on unemployment were probably a grievous tactical error for his cause, for in raising the issue

Shmelev immediately made the entire reformist agenda all the more suspect to opponents and skeptics. On unemployment, the radical reformers had to back off quickly. Though they may have had the upper hand going into the plenum, it was far from a free upper hand. Ligachev may have been in a minority among his Politburo colleagues, but he nevertheless must have retained acknowledged leverage stemming from widespread support for his less radical stance from regime elements at lower levels. The dynamics at work already called into question whether Gorbachev was ahead in his gamble on a party conference. Still an open question was the extent to which there was a grass-roots party audience waiting to be stirred into action and join him against resistance in the middle levels of the party and state bureaucracies.

At the top, however, Ligachev's support probably eroded in May, when Geydar Aliyev dropped out of sight. Especially in retrospect, Aliyev's defense of the life style of party leaders at a press conference shortly after Yeltsin's speech at the 27th Party Congress had marked him as a likely ally of Ligachev. Though the rumored victim of a heart attack,[61] Aliyev was probably also hurt politically by a Party Control Committee report "On Serious Shortcomings in Implementing the 27th CPSU Congress Decisions on Improving the Training of Skilled Worker Cadres and Carrying Out the Reform of Vocation Education in the Azerbaidjan SSR."[62] If Aliyev had been among those braking the process of economic reform, then his sudden indisposition—whether politically motivated or, indeed, the result of a heart attack—should have improved the prospects for a reformist outcome from the upcoming plenum.

Nevertheless, Ligachev went on the offensive and in early June in Tbilisi called openly for greater regime control of the reform process. At the January plenum Gorbachev had criticized party leaders who found it hard to give up "dispatcher functions" and wanted to "keep a tight grip on things."[63] Now, in contrast, Ligachev asserted that "economic life under socialism, in all its forms, must be open to planning, monitoring, and regulation. For this reason the republic party, soviet, and economic organs must keep a firm grip on the levers of economic management." The second secretary warned, "It is easier to lose that grip than to regain it later. This must be constantly kept in mind." And with the June plenum just around the corner, he warned that "the party line of developing individual labor activity has nothing to do with unbridled privately owned enterprise."[64]

On June 8–9 the leadership staged a conference in the Central Committee which amounted to a dress rehearsal for the upcoming plenum. Gorbachev asked the many assembled notables to comment on the progress of restructuring and give their opinions on the draft Enterprise Law and the proper role of central management organs under the foreseen new order. Slyunkov led with a report on the various measures under consideration, after which the floor was opened for discussion.

From the comments it was obvious that there remained many disagreements on the basics, loose ends on the specifics, and unexplored areas in the package being readied for the plenum. Great as were the disruptions which the economic reform would bring to established practices, however, it was not a frontal assault on central planning or a sharp veering toward market relationships. Bogomolov pointed out that there was "one crucial question which I think we are avoiding somewhat coyly. This is the matter of the market under socialism, the regulated market of course. . . . The word market is used mostly in a pejorative sense. The word marketeer is usually a term of abuse."

In summing up at the end of the meeting, Gorbachev observed that the discussion had been "honest" though at times "polemical," with "different approaches and different viewpoints" being put forward. Restructuring was "progressing with difficulty, complexity, and contradictions, but it is progressing." What were needed were "new fillips to ensure that this process is accelerated and gathers strength." It was "impossible," he said, to "expect we will produce the ideal Law on the State Enterprise in one attempt, with a single sweep, at a single sitting." The draft was not "ideal," but "we must pass the law, start working according to its provisions, reveal its strong and weak aspects, and improve it if necessary." The new system needed to be in place by 1991 when the thirteenth Five-Year Plan would begin, but even then "we will still be learning."

That the regime was still trying to square the circle, however, was made clear by Gorbachev's statement: "The question is, how to combine centralism with initiative. Here we need the mechanism and the system of indicators. It is here that we are searching." Under the envisioned reforms, he said, the "center" would retain the "main proportions, the main balances, defense questions, questions concerning the development of republics, and so on. Only on the basis of social ownership is it possible to create an opportunity to have such a center," he boasted, "capable of forecasting, estimating, setting goals, and achieving them. This is where our advantage lies." He concluded with the warning that "we must rebuff those who want to offer us antisocialist alternatives."[65]

Meanwhile, as the conferees met, Ligachev signed to press his major article "On the Revolutionary Essence of Restructuring in the USSR," already mentioned earlier in this chapter. In terms of specifics, Ligachev appeared to endorse the entire reform program—in industry as well as in agriculture—already drawn up by the Politburo leadership. There was, however, one curious formulaic twist that reinforced the impression Ligachev had left in Tbilisi: that he ascribed less urgency to management reform than did not only Gorbachev but the decisive majority in the Politburo. According to Ligachev, the socioeconomic development of Soviet society would be accelerated "on the basis of scientific-technological progress and of the activation of the human factor." Only after highlighting these two factors did Ligachev go on to assert that production needed to be stimulated "not by general appeals and instructions, but by economic management methods and the democratization of production life."[66]

In contrast, the main point of Gorbachev's Politburo-approved report to the June plenum would be that "radical reform of economic management is the most important element of restructuring." The divergence in general approach between Gorbachev and Ligachev would become even more apparent in late July, when the general secretary would tell a Central Committee conference on machine-building that "the fulfillment of everything that has been mapped out [by the June plenum] will be determined by the resolution of two key issues: the broad introduction of the new economic mechanism and the acceleration of scientific and technical progress." Only after underscoring these two factors did Gorbachev add, almost as if to draw attention to the difference between his formula and that of Ligachev, that "understandably, the use of these main levers for lifting the economy must be combined with an enhancement of the role of the human factor."[67]

THE JUNE PLENUM

When the Central Committee finally met on June 25–26, 1987, Gorbachev offered an analysis of the stagnant Soviet economy which confirmed what objective observers had been saying for several decades.[68] The economy was in a "precrisis situation," Gorbachev warned, and the gap between the USSR and capitalist countries had begun to widen even in the field of science and technology. Any attempt simply to muddle through with "a little pressure from above and . . . a few more partial measures" would "entail extraordinarily grave consequences."[69]

The general secretary alluded to the reforms sponsored by Khrushchev, Kosygin, and Kirilenko in the 1950s, 1960s, and late 1970s, respectively. But these, he said, had been "incomplete and inconsistent" and at best had produced only "a short-term benefit." To avoid the same fate, it was now imperative not to let the new Enterprise Law "be encircled by a palisade of numerous instructions which could emasculate its essence and apply the brakes to restructuring." The planned "package" of nearly a dozen specific measures had to be adopted by the end of the year, and this constituted "the most far-reaching and most extensive restructuring in all the years of socialist building."

The basic premise of the planned restructuring of the economy was "the need to step up real competition among enterprises and organizations" and to ensure that "the winners of this competition . . . receive a tangible economic advantage." "Commodity-money relations," Gorbachev told the plenum, were an "organic part" of the socialist economic system. "Their skillful utilization regarding prices and financial and credit levels, their planned assimilation, the running of the market in accordance with their laws, and the strengthening and boosting of the prestige of the ruble promote the creation of an effective, cost-conscious mechanism and the strengthening of socialism in practice." But the general secretary conceded that synchronizing central planning with freer play for "commodity-money relations" would be much harder than "issuing commands and directives."[70]

Gorbachev asserted "a unity of views on the fundamental questions of restructuring and of domestic and foreign policy" within the leadership. But it was plain that many thorny details of the plenum's central issue of management reform were far from being resolved even on the conceptual level, to say nothing of the practical implementation and testing that still lay ahead. But Gorbachev insisted in his closing speech that problems had to be faced rather than allowed to accumulate, and that the "especially pernicious" fear of making mistakes had to be overcome.[71]

Besides economic questions, Gorbachev revisited what was obviously the still troublesome subject of democratization. The Politburo, according to Gorbachev, considered the "extensive development of democracy" the "most effective means" of resolving the "contradiction" between the "masses' growing activeness" and the "bureaucratic style of activity still alive in various spheres and the attempts to freeze restructuring." But "press materials, familiarization with the state of affairs locally, and information coming in attest that the development of openness and democratism is proceeding with difficulty and, in some places, even painfully." "Certain comrades have shown a lack of understanding and fear of democratic changes," charged the general secretary. "This question is so important that the plenum will, I think, discuss it and take a clear, firm stand."[72] At the Supreme Soviet session that followed the plenum, Premier Ryzhkov again demonstrated his closeness to Gorbachev on this issue when he called "resolute democratization" the "most effective restructuring weapon."[73]

Accordingly, the resolution on management restructuring adopted by the Central Committee in fact stated, "The plenum deems it necessary to pursue with ever greater vigor and consistency the course toward democratizing Soviet society, regarding this as the principal condition for direct involvement of broad masses of working people in restructuring, as a guarantee of the irreversibility of the process of renewal." But elsewhere in the resolution it was also asserted that "it is now especially important and necessary to strengthen party influence in all directions of the restructuring drive, guarantee skillful guidance over public processes and elaboration of new creative approaches to party work. . . . Party organizations are called upon to be the vanguard of the transformation work."[74]

Aganbegyan later said that at the Central Committee plenum, "some very emotionally charged speeches were made, people expressed their criticism of the proposed legislation (on state enterprises) and made it clear on which points they dissociated themselves from it. Everyone really voiced their innermost views." Nevertheless, if one were to compare the plenum with a "conflict . . . in the Japanese parliament, then everything passed off very calmly," stated the economist.[75] In fact, the Central Committee did give its stamp of approval to the various measures already systematically examined and formulated (however imperfectly) by the party and state leadership in the months leading up to the plenum.[76]

Despite its reluctance to address the issue of a party conference directly in its resolution at the January plenum, the Central Committee now set June 28, 1988, as the date on which the 19th Party Conference would open.[77] Delegates would be elected in April-May 1988. The agenda would be much as Gorbachev proposed: "1. On the course of the fulfillment of the decisions of the 27th CPSU Congress, the main results of the first half of the 12th Five-Year Plan period and the tasks of party organizations in deepening the process of restructuring. 2. On measures to further democratize the life of the party and society." On one crucial matter of detail, however, the Central Committee clearly demurred: the resolution was silent on the possibility of electing new full members of the Central Committee at the party conference. For the time being, at least, Gorbachev had to settle for less than a full loaf in his attempt to pressure the Central Committee from below.

On leadership cadres, however, Gorbachev did extremely well. The plenum promoted Central Committee secretaries Slyunkov and Yakovlev from candidate to full members of the Politburo; appointed Central Committee Secretary Nikonov directly to full membership in the Politburo without his having first to serve as a candidate member; elected new Defense Minister Yazov a candidate member of the Politburo, and released the retired Sokolov; and expelled ousted Kazakhstan party leader Kunayev from the Central Committee for "serious shortcomings."[78] At the Supreme Soviet meeting that followed, moreover, Grishin resigned even his seat as a deputy,[79] although it is unknown whether he was also forced to give up his sinecure of "state counselor" in President Gromyko's secretariat.

NOTES

1. *Le Matin*, February 16, 1987 (FBIS-SOV, February 19, 1987, R 13).

2. *New Times*, no. 5, February 9, 1987 (FBIS-SOV, February 20, 1987, R 21–25).

3. *Pravda*, February 15, 1987 (FBIS-SOV, February 17, 1987, R 1–8).

4. *Pravda*, March 14, 1987 (FBIS-SOV, March 18, 1987, R 3–4).

5. *Zhurnalist*, no. 5 (May 1987), signed to press April 8, 1987. A shorter account of Ligachev's remarks appeared in *Pravda*, March 25, 1987 (FBIS-SOV, March 26, 1987, R 9–11).

A number of Gorbachev's other comments in mid-February continued to have much in common with Ligachev's outlook. Criticism and self-criticism were to be encouraged, Gorbachev said in his meeting with media leaders, but it was "intolerable when a particular publicist does not criticize, but humiliates a person." Some media criticism was beside the point. "A *kolkhoz* chairman was criticized on a television program," Gorbachev recounted. "Instead of showing what was really important—farm losses and incompetent management—the camera was aimed at the roof of this house: You see, his roof's been repaired: Well, is the chairman supposed to live without a roof?"

6. Prof. Yu. Afanasyev, for example, chancellor of the State Historical-Archives Institute, called for more facts on Stalin and Khrushchev to be published (*Sovetskaya Kultura*, March 21, 1987 [FBIS-SOV, April 30, 1987, R 1–10]). Historian A. Samsonov was particularly active in denigrating Stalin's wartime record (Moscow Television Service, April 24, 1987 [FBIS-SOV, April 30, 1987, R 10–11]; and *Sotsialisticheskaya Industriya*, May 24, 1987 [FBIS-SOV, June 8, 1987, R 18–24]).

7. *Druzhba Narodov*, no. 4–6 (1987). Anatoli Rybakov, *Children of the Arbat*, Harold Shukman, trans. (Boston and Toronto: Little, Brown, 1988).

8. See the interview with Oleg Bogomolov in *Izvestiya*, May 14, 1987 (FBIS-SOV, May 27, 1987, S 1–5).

9. See the interview with Anatoliy Butenko in *Moskovskaya Pravda*, May 7, 1987 (FBIS-SOV, May 26, 1987, R 3–8) and Nikolay Shmelev, *Novyy Mir*, no. 6 (June 1987), signed to press April 28.

10. Boris Mozhayev, *Literary Gazette*, February 11, 1987 (FBIS-SOV, February 20, 1987, R 20).

11. *Pravda*, June 16, 1987 (FBIS-SOV, June 19, 1987, CC 3).

12. Moscow Television Service, February 25, 1986 (FBIS-SOV, February 26, 1986, Supplement no. 41, 0 24–25).

13. TASS, January 27, 1987 (FBIS-SOV, January 28, 1987, R 16).

14. *Pravda*, January 29, 1987 (FBIS-SOV, January 30, 1987, R 1–12).

15. *Pravda*, February 10, 1987 (FBIS-SOV, February 12, 1987, R 2–4).

16. *Pravda*, March 29, 1987 (FBIS-SOV, March 31, 1987, R 1–2).

17. Riga Domestic Service, February 19, 1987 (FBIS-SOV, February 25, 1987, R 12–13).

18. Bratislava *Pravda*, March 5, 1987 (FBIS-SOV, March 11, 1987, F 7).

19. *Kommunist*, no. 4 (March 1987), signed to press February 23, 1987.

20. *Vremya*, March 5, 1987 (FBIS-SOV, March 10, 1987, R 8–9); and *Pravda*, March 6, 1987 (FBIS-SOV, March 10, 1987, R 5–6).

21. See the account of Bondarev's remarks at the March 17 meeting of the secretariat of the RSFSR Union of Writers in *Literaturnaya Rossiya*, March 27, 1987.

22. *Vremya*, March 5, 1987 (FBIS-SOV, March 10, 1987, R 8–9); and *Pravda*, March 6, 1987 (FBIS-SOV, March 10, 1987, R 5–6).

23. *Zhurnalist*, no. 5 (May 1987), signed to press April 8, 1987.

24. *Pravda*, March 6, 1987 (FBIS-SOV, March 10, 1987, F 6).

25. *Pravda*, March 11, 1987 (FBIS-SOV, March 18, 1987, R 13).

26. *Pravda*, March 14, 1987 (FBIS-SOV, March 18, 1987, R 5).

27. See Section IV, Article 40 of the Party Statutes (*Pravda*, March 7, 1986 (FBIS-SOV, March 11, 1986, Supplement 52, 0 6)).

28. *Sovetskaya Rossiya*, March 27, 1987 (FBIS-SOV, April 7, 1987, R 7).

29. *Pravda*, April 11, 1987 (FBIS-SOV, April 14, 1987, F 8).

30. *Kommunist Tadzhikistana*, April 12, 1987 (FBIS-SOV, May 7, 1987, R 7–8). Yakovlev had been in Tadzhikistan on April 6–9.

31. Moscow Television Service, April 16, 1987 (FBIS-SOV, April 17, 1987, R 5).

32. *Pravda*, April 23, 1987 (FBIS-SOV, April 24, 1987, R 9–10).

33. TASS, April 25, 1987 (FBIS-SOV, April 27, 1987, F 5).

34. *Bakinskiy Rabochiy*, April 28, 1987 (FBIS-SOV, May 22, 1987, R 4–5).

35. Moscow Domestic Service, May 8, 1987 (FBIS-SOV, May 11, 1987, R 1).

36. For Ligachev's June 3, 1987, speech to the Georgian party aktiv in Tbilisi, see *Pravda*, June 4, 1987 (FBIS-SOV, June 9, 1987, R 3–9) and the lengthier account in *Zarya Vostoka*, June 4, 1987 (FBIS-SOV, June 18, 1987, R 1–14).

37. *Zarya Vostoka*, June 4, 1987 (FBIS-SOV, June 18, 1987, R 14).

38. *Pravda*, June 4, 1987 (FBIS-SOV, June 9, 1987, R 8).

39. *Problemy mira i sotsializma*, no. 7 (July 1987), signed to press June 9, 1987 (FBIS-SOV, August 6, 1987, R 1–11).

40. *Corriere della Sera*, January 30, 1987.

41. *Kommunist*, no. 4 (March 1987), signed to press February 23, 1987.

42. *Vremya*, March 5, 1987 (FBIS-SOV, March 10, 1987, R 8–9); and *Pravda*, March 6, 1987 (FBIS-SOV, March 10, 1987, R 5–6).

43. *Pravda*, February 8, 1987 (FBIS-SOV, February 18, 1987, S 1–27).

44. *Izvestiya*, February 13, 1987 (FBIS-SOV, February 26, 1987, S 1–3); and TASS, March 12, 1987 (FBIS-SOV, March 20, 1987, S 3); and *Washington Post*, March 14, 1987.

45. *Pravda*, April 23, 1987 (FBIS-SOV, April 24, 1987, R 2–17).

46. Moscow Domestic Service, April 23, 1987 (FBIS-SOV, April 27, 1987, F 1).

47. Budapest Television Service, April 26, 1987 (FBIS-SOV, April 27, 1987, F 6).

48. *Pravda*, April 24, 1987 (FBIS-SOV, April 27, 1984, R 1).

49. Moscow Domestic Service, April 30, 1987 (FBIS-SOV, May 1, 1987, R 1).

50. *Pravda*, May 14, 1987 (FBIS-SOV, May 14, 1987, R 5); and Moscow Domestic Service, May 14, 1987 (FBIS-SOV, May 15, 1987, R 1).

51. *Izvestiya*, May 24, 1987 (FBIS-SOV, May 26, 1987, R 1).

52. *Pravda*, May 23, 1987 (FBIS-SOV, May 27, 1987, R 1).

53. *Sovetskaya Rossiya*, March 24, 1987 (FBIS-SOV, April 2, 1987, S 1).

54. *Novyy Mir*, no. 5 (May 1987), signed to press March 31, 1987.

55. *Pravda*, June 7, 1987 (FBIS-SOV, June 10, 1987, S 1–2).

56. *Novyy Mir*, no. 6 (June 1987), signed to press April 28, 1987.

57. *The Guardian*, June 24, 1987. The numerous stories of Ligachev's interventions on editorial matters reflected at least in part his responsibilities in the ideological sphere. But Ligachev was not alone in this. Writer and *Novyy Mir* editorial board member Anatoliy Strelyaniy tells of Gorbachev criticizing him for his journal (no. 2, 1987) having printed the article "Devious Numbers," whose basic message was that Soviet statistics were not to be trusted (*Washington Post*, October 4, 1987).

58. Moscow Television Service, June 21, 1987 (FBIS-SOV, June 22, 1987, R 3–6).

59. *Pravda*, July 18, 1987 (FBIS-SOV, July 23, 1987, R 23).

60. *Sovetskaya Kultura*, October 17, 1987 (FBIS-SOV, October 23, 1987, 61).

61. AFP, May 30, 1987 (FBIS-SOV, June 1, 1987, R 2).

62. *Izvestiya*, May 14, 1987 (FBIS-SOV, May 27, 1987, R 5–8).

63. TASS, January 27, 1987 (FBIS-SOV, January 28, 1987, R 37).

64. *Zarya Vostoka*, June 4, 1987 (FBIS-SOV, June 18, 1987, R 8).

65. *Pravda*, June 13, 1987 (FBIS-SOV, June 16, 1987, R 1–24).

66. *Problemy mira i sotsializma*, no. 7 (July 1987), signed to press June 9, 1987 (FBIS-SOV, August 6, 1987, R 1–11).

67. *Pravda*, July 26, 1987 (FBIS-SOV, July 27, 1987, R 1).

68. *Pravda*, June 26, 1987 (FBIS-SOV, June 26, 1987, R 1–46).

69. Ibid., R 25–26.

70. Ibid., R 29.

71. *Pravda*, June 27, 1987 (FBIS-SOV, June 29, 1987, R 14).

72. *Pravda*, June 26, 1987 (FBIS-SOV, June 26, 1987, R 20).

73. *Pravda*, June 30, 1987 (FBIS-SOV, July 1, 1987, R 32).

74. *Pravda*, June 27, 1987 (FBIS-SOV, June 29, 1987, R 1–46).

75. *Dagens Nyheter*, June 28, 1987 (FBIS-SOV, July 13, 1987, R 15).

76. See "On the Party's Tasks in the Fundamental Restructuring of the Economy's Management," *Pravda*, June 27, 1987 (FBIS-SOV, June 29, 1987, R 16–18); and "Basic Provisions for Radical Restructuring of Economic Management," *Pravda*, June 27, 1987 (FBIS-SOV, June 30, 1987, R 1–22).

77. *Pravda*, June 27, 1987 (FBIS-SOV, June 29, 1987, R 18–19).

78. TASS, June 26, 1987 (FBIS-SOV, June 26, 1987, R 47).

79. TASS, July 14, 1987 (FBIS-SOV, July 14, 1987, R 1).

Chapter 12

Ligachev, Chebrikov, and the Yeltsin Affair

With the June plenum on economic reform out of the way but the seventieth anniversary of the Bolshevik Revolution fast approaching, the unresolved tensions over democratization and cadre policy quickly spilled into the open with renewed prominence and urgency. At the June plenum Gorbachev had underscored that democratization was still a contentious issue, and he had demanded that the Central Committee endorse his position. But the Crimean Tatar and Baltic demonstrations that followed the plenum almost immediately challenged Gorbachev's program and set the stage for a public assault by Ligachev. Actually, the evidence suggested that Ligachev's hand on cadre policy had already been strengthened at the plenum, even though he was in the minority in the Politburo on democratization. Yeltsin, Gorbachev later revealed, had delivered unreported but critical remarks on the course of *perestroika* at the June plenum but found no support. Subsequently Ligachev apparently received a mandate to discipline Yeltsin using the issue of excessive cadre turnover in Moscow, and even Gorbachev seemed to support it.

The fundamental issue in summer 1987 was increasingly neither the limits of *glasnost* nor how to evaluate the Stalin and Brezhnev periods, but the extent to which democratization should be allowed to redefine and even erode the party's "vanguard" role and accumulated prerogatives in Soviet politics. As nationality and regional tensions burst into the open, Ligachev tried to build on the support for his stance against Yeltsin regarding cadres to challenge Gorbachev on the democratization issue. However, even though Yeltsin complicated Gorbachev's position with his second surprise outburst at the October 21 plenum, Ligachev was not able to crack Gorbachev's majority in the Politburo on democratization. Even as Yeltsin was being railroaded out of the leadership in November 1987, Gorbachev's call on November 2 for a revitalized Supreme Soviet was ironically and most likely unintentionally laying the basis for Yeltsin's remarkable resurrection as a populist, anti-apparatchiks' privileges politician in March 1989.

When the Yeltsin affair exploded into the open in November, Gorbachev revealed that the Politburo had rebuked the Moscow party leader as far back as January for his callousness toward cadres. Apparently Gorbachev had sought to distance himself from Yeltsin's intemperateness, even while loath to see him forced out of the leadership. Yeltsin's reported failure to appeal to Gorbachev to intercede on his behalf until August 1987 certainly suggested less of an affinity between the two leaders than commonly presumed. Nevertheless, the tension Yeltsin created may have been useful to Gorbachev in giving him greater room to maneuver—as long as Yeltsin exercised some discipline. In October-November 1987 Yeltsin did not, and Gorbachev was forced to resort to traditionally harsh methods running counter to *glasnost* and democratization in order to control the damage and put even greater distance between himself and Yeltsin.

The general secretary's revelations in November served to underscore the paradox that Yeltsin's decline had occurred precisely during the period in which the leadership had managed to forge a working if unstable consensus on the core of its reform platform. The personalities and public profiles of both Ligachev and Yeltsin, however, muddied the analysis of the conflict between them. When all was said and done, beyond his assaults on cadres corruption and privileges, Yeltsin was not a consistent radical on either political or economic reform. Ligachev, on the other hand, had to be considered a key player in putting together the 1987 reforms—less radical than some other leaders, to be sure, but not the widely depicted throwback to an earlier era.

On the issues of *glasnost* and treatment of the past, Ligachev obviously stood for a more disciplined and utilitarian— rather than permissive and libertarian—attitude toward media disclosures. But despite widespread impressions to the contrary, it was easy to find cautionary injunctions from Gorbachev paralleling every dark warning from Ligachev. Indeed, even as Ligachev pressed his case for conserving the unassailable primacy of the party, the boundaries of *glasnost* continued to expand. New revelations on the Stalin and Brezhnev periods continued to spill forth in the media, and the process of rehabilitating the leading victims of Stalin moved into high gear.

TATARS ON RED SQUARE

On June 23, two days before the start of the June plenum, a delegation of Crimean Tatars met with First Deputy Premier Petr Demichev and sought to press their demand for the reconstitution of the Crimean Autonomous Republic. which had been disbanded by Stalin in 1944 on the charge that Crimean Tatars had collaborated with the Germans. The mass deportation of 238,000 Tatars to Central Asia and the Urals had ensued, during which an estimated one-quarter to one-half perished.[1]

After a decree in 1967 restored their constitutional rights, some Tatars had managed to trickle back into the Crimea, but only against great resistance from the authorities and the new, non-Tatar local populations. Now Demichev, without satisfying them, reportedly promised the Tatar representatives that a state committee would be set up to examine their claims.

Two weeks later, on July 6, the Tatars held the first of several widely publicized protests in and on the edge of Red Square and near the headquarters of the Central Committee, where they demanded a meeting with Gorbachev.[2] Perhaps as a result, a State Committee chaired by Gromyko was set up on July 9. From July 23 to 27, nevertheless, the Tatars held an unprecedented four-day sitdown demonstration just off Red Square. After first refusing to meet with Gromyko, they finally sent a small delegation to confer with the Soviet president as well as with Demichev and MVD Chief Vlasov.[3] The Tatars again emerged unsatisfied ("We didn't hear what we wanted to hear," said one activist[4]), and on July 30 some "extremists," as described by TASS, staged another demonstration near Pushkin Square.[5] This time the authorities broke up the demonstration and expelled Tatar leaders from Moscow.[6] By September 1 the Moscow Soviet issued regulations banning such gatherings in Red Square, around the Kremlin, and in other major downtown squares.[7]

In the meantime, protests sprung up in the Baltics. On June 14 thousands demonstrated in Riga against the 1940 annexation of the three Baltic republics. On August 23, the anniversary of the 1939 Molotov-Ribbentrop pact, protests took place in the capitals of Estonia, Latvia, and Lithuania. Seeking to impede them, the authorities issued new laws requiring the submission of permits ten days before a planned demonstration.[8] With memories of the riots in Alma-Ata still strong, the specter of representatives of various nationalities using *glasnost* to press their demands must have unsettled many in the leadership. Even a reactionary segment of Russian nationalism had pushed itself forward earlier in the year under the banner of an unofficial organization called *Pamyat*, or "Memory."[9]

LIGACHEV ON "CONSTRUCTIVE OPENNESS"

In light of his earlier warnings of potential ethnic extremism, Ligachev no doubt felt vindicated by the public venting of long-repressed nationality tensions. In any event, he seemed to be feeling his oats as early as July 1, and again on July 3, when he visited the editorial office of *Sovetskaya Kultura*, one of the leading press organs of radical reform. There Ligachev made remarks that must have pleased more conservatively inclined functionaries, propagandists, and political activists looking for a possible lifesaver in the stormy seas of *perestroika*. In contrast to the "slime" Vadim Medvedev in April had said developed in the decades before the Gorbachev leadership's rise to power, Ligachev spoke of "some scum and debris" that had been washed up more recently by restructuring and renewal.

Some "'energetic' people", according to Ligachev, were trying to "supplant our spiritual values with their own dubious ideas and intentions." He recounted that the Siberian "village" writer Valentin Rasputin, widely admired by the intelligentsia during the Brezhnev years for his civic courage and literary honesty, had complained to him of the rising "aggressiveness of so-called mass culture and the flood of shallow musical compositions." Ligachev agreed that democratization was "a most important lever of restructuring," but he warned, "we will not depart from the principles of the class and realistic nature of art." As he had over a year earlier, he complained that "in certain works the word 'communist' is nowhere to be found" and that socialist realism and the positive hero appeared out of fashion. Ligachev derided a documentary on the Leningrad *Popmekhanika* group as "an ideological and artistic jumble!" He called on the media and the arts not to push Russian and Soviet classics into the background, and exhorted the press to carry more articles by party and state officials. What was needed, stressed the second secretary, was "constructive openness" and a tactful and respectful attitude toward the opinions of others by all engaged in the new *glasnost*.[10]

Gorbachev soon sought to redress Ligachev's injunctions, but the general secretary's remarks in a meeting on July 14 with executives of the mass media and creative unions constituted a complex, multidirectional shuffle. Gorbachev's speech was designed to challenge Ligachev's remarks at *Sovetskaya Kultura* and to defend his own, more radical inclinations while nevertheless retreating toward more centrist, less exposed positions. The general secretary complained that Soviet political culture and standards of debate were "inadequate." But in contrast to Ligachev, Gorbachev stated that he had "no reason to make any great political reproaches" over the contribution of the creative intelligentsia to *perestroika*, and he used the formula "socialist pluralism" for the first time. This phrase, however, did not yet have the politically more permissive connotations it would acquire in only a few months; Gorbachev now used it only to appeal against the cliquishness in some editorial boards of cultural publications, of which Ligachev had also complained. As had Ligachev, Gorbachev also warned that the Central Committee would not tolerate the rejection of values "beyond the limits of socialism," but he then quickly added that no one should construe his remarks as the signal for criticism to stop.

On other issues Gorbachev elaborated on his mid-February instructions regarding preparations for the seventieth anniversary of the Bolshevik Revolution, in the process dramatically sharpening his criticism of Stalin's excesses while calling for a balanced appraisal of that era. "I think that we never will be able to forgive or justify what happened in 1937–38, and never should," he said. "Never! Those who were in power at that time are responsible for that, and comrades, that does not detract from all we have today, what the party and people did in coming through those trials. There were great and serious losses. We know what came of 1937 and 1938, and how this hit the party cadres, the intelligentsia, and the military cadres." As he had in February, and as had and would Ligachev, Gorbachev presented a far from negative summing up of Soviet history. "We are bound to see what enormous strength is to be found in socialism and in our system, which withstood that, entered the fight against nazism, and was victorious. . . . We take pride in each day we live through, and each day is precious to us, even when it has been most difficult because it has been our school of history, our history lessons."[11]

The more radical Yakovlev, meanwhile, did not seem prepared to cede any ground on democratization and *glasnost*. In a speech in Kaluga, he rejected any suggestion that "it would do no harm to set some kind of limits on *glasnost*. Clearly, when people begin to speak of such limits it means that openness is hampering some people. But this," he explained, "is the very purpose of openness and democracy: To prevent people from living outside morality and the law and to refer to public judgment those who ignore the collective's interests and give their own personal considerations priority over everything."[12] Yakovlev's remarks were reprinted most extensively in *Sovetskaya Kultura*, the same liberal publication Ligachev had visited to press his more conservative views. As he had in April in Dushanbe, therefore, Yakovlev again positioned himself on the more radical end of the spectrum of leadership opinion, creating room between himself and Ligachev for Gorbachev to bob and weave in.

LIGACHEV CONTRADICTS GORBACHEV

According to Yeltsin's friend and booster, Mikhail Poltoranin, editor of *Moskovskaya Pravda* during Yeltsin's tenure in Moscow, it was in July 1987 that Ligachev's backstage efforts against Yeltsin took an ominous turn. Although the outside world would be ignorant of the campaign until November, it had built a head of steam sufficient to proceed even in the absence of the vacationing Ligachev. After his two visits to the *Sovetskaya Kultura* offices, Ligachev traveled to Hungary for what appeared to be a working vacation from July 4 to 10, and then made no more public appearances until August 14. Coincidentally, Yeltsin also took a month off, dropping out of the limelight from July 4 to August 1. During this period when Yeltsin was vacationing on the Black Sea, Moscow party Second Secretary Yuriy Belyakov, until then considered Yeltsin's right-hand man, confronted Poltoranin on the need "to choose which side [he] was on."[13]

The campaign against Yeltsin appeared to have some degree of approval even from Gorbachev. At the June plenum Yeltsin apparently criticized the achievements of *perestroika* as well as the work of the Secretariat. At the October plenum later in the year, according to a transcript released in early 1989, Yeltsin referred to remarks at the June plenum (presumably his own) calling for *perestroika* to start with a restructuring of the work of "party committees, the party as a whole, beginning with the CPSU Secretariat." According to the same document, Gorbachev charged in October that in June Yeltsin had "wanted that they [Central Committee members] should support him, but he remained alone."[14] In any event, during the meeting on July 14 with mass media and creative union leaders, Gorbachev seemed to come down fully on the side of Ligachev on the treatment of cadres, as set forth in the latter's early June speech in Tbilisi. "Social demagogues have found their way into some editorial offices of newspapers and magazines," stated Gorbachev. "They are being particularly vicious in their attacks on the cadres. But we should understand very well that the cadres corps carries the vast load of restructuring." Although the malfeasance of some had to be exposed and "dragged out into the daylight," the general secretary cautioned that "there must be no disrespectful attitude toward cadres in general."[15] His choice of words suggested, in retrospect, a deliberate effort to distance himself from Yeltsin. For as Poltoranin later explained, the term "social demagoguery" was Ligachev's own shorthand for Yeltsin's efforts to curb the privileges of party officials, such as access to special stores and special schools for their children.

On July 14 Gorbachev certainly appeared highly sensitive to the issue of the role of the party, presumably reacting—as it would become clearer in August—to pressure from Ligachev. But the general secretary responded in a way that sought to put the ball back in the court of the party firsters. The party was the "genuine organizer" of Soviet society and its "political vanguard," affirmed Gorbachev, and "I do not think that now anyone will have the conception, the idea that it is possible to get by without the party." Yet only if the party itself lived "a full-blooded existence," he said, could it "fulfill its organizing and leading role." There was still "one deciding force: the people," and "everything must be put in its place through the democratic process."[16]

In several more outings before going on vacation in August, Gorbachev appeared to signal a new drive to cut the bureaucracies, but then he seemed to back off. In Zelenograd on July 29, he drew attention to "our enormous management apparatus. Some 18 million in management! An apparatus like that is not necessary."[17] A week later, visiting an agroindustrial combine in the Moscow oblast town of Ramenskoye, Gorbachev warned that restructuring was not some flighty "reorganizing itch." But he then assured his listeners, "we do not intend to break our cadres, our people." There would be "an influx of fresh forces," to be sure, "but on the whole these are the cadres with whom we must accomplish the task of restructuring." Nevertheless, Gorbachev reiterated that "the basis of restructuring is democratization." He conceded, "Some people have been frightened, some people have started to say: Where are we going, how will it end?" But these people, said the general secretary, "are forgetting the most important thing, that people always have common sense."[18]

After Ramenskoye, Gorbachev met with a group of American teachers of Russian on August 7, but then he disappeared from public view until September 28, telling a French delegation the next day that he had been officially on vacation from August 24 to September 24.[19] According to Gorbachev, during his time off he had finished working on a book—obviously a reference to *Perestroika*—and had been absorbed with thinking through the speech he would deliver for the seventieth anniversary of the revolution.[20] *Perestroika* would be released in early November, to coincide with Gorbachev's major speech on November 2 (to be dealt with later).[21] The manuscript, however, must have been completed by September 18; in the final text Gorbachev wrote that the draft was already with the publisher by the time Shultz and Shevardnadze agreed in Washington that an INF treaty should be concluded by the end of the year.

Aimed as it was largely at foreign audiences, *Perestroika* contained Gorbachev's most detailed and explicit treatment to date of the priority of human values over class struggle in foreign policy (on which more will be said in the next chapter). On domestic matters, Gorbachev reiterated that "democratization is . . . the main guarantee that the current processes are irreversible" and that "*perestroika* itself can only come through democracy." Institutionally this meant "revolutionary transformations" of the "status and activity" of the Soviets as "bodies of political power and as the foundation of socialist democracy." Gorbachev noted criticism of the Soviet leadership from the "left" for being too slow and from the "right" for excessive haste, but be declared that all agreed he and his colleagues were "implementing reforms in earnest."[22]

Meanwhile, on the first day of Gorbachev's absence Yeltsin spoke at a plenum of the Moscow city party committee.[23] Whatever actually transpired, a *Kommunist* analysis of the plenum publicly pinpointed—without naming Yeltsin—what were later explicitly identified as the weaknesses in Yeltsin's management style. "The more complicated the tasks being carried out by the city party organizations, the more primitive and essentially directive the assignments that raykom [district party committee] functionaries must fulfill," wrote *Kommunist* staffers S. V. Kolesnikov and N. G. Tyurin.[24] "One sometimes gets the impression that the gorkom is still trying to solve many of the capital's undoubtedly difficult problems by strengthening organizational pressure, by concentrating on the 'apparatus' side of matters, and by 'accelerating' the rearrangement of cadres at both city and rayon level," continued the two reporters. "It is, of course, understandable that there is an aspiration to overcome political indolence and chronic apathy and break down the habitual slowness, sluggishness, and inertia of a number of functionaries, and to do this as rapidly as possible. However," they warned, "it is precisely here that careful, thoughtful, and practical work in party organizations and labor collectives is particularly necessary."[25]

According to Gorbachev's account on November 11, while on vacation he had received a letter from Yeltsin tendering his resignation from the leadership. It is fair to speculate that it was the *Kommunist* write-up—or, more precisely, the backstage pressure against Yeltsin which the article now publicly epitomized—which pushed Yeltsin over the edge after his failure to find support at the June plenum. Although the report did not name Yeltsin, its criticism of the management style said to be prevalent in the Moscow gorkom was at the core of what even some of Yeltsin's supporters would later identify as his main failing and real vulnerability.

In any event, no sooner had the damning issue of *Kommunist* been signed to press on August 25 than Ligachev spoke at a teachers' conference outside Moscow in Elektrostal and most clearly laid out his fundamental difference with Gorbachev. The "primary guarantee" that reforms would be fully implemented, Ligachev told the conference, "is the Communist Party's leading role in restructuring and the improvement of the style and methods of its activity." Ligachev's statement was a critical turning point in the leadership's own intramural commentary on the reformist course it had set for itself, and it directly contradicted Gorbachev on the importance of democratization. It was the first time since the January plenum that any leader had called the party's leading role, rather than democratization, the "primary guarantee" that the January and June plenum reforms would succeed. To be sure, Ligachev went on to tell the teachers that the "deepening of democracy and self-management" were also "reliable guarantees." But he reinforced his message of the party's primacy by reiterating that "the people led by the party—this is the decisive force of acceleration."[26]

On historical issues, Ligachev reaffirmed his own past radical statements and endorsed Gorbachev's indictment a month before of the illegalities of the 1930s. On Stalin, for example, he said that it was "very important to responsibly analyze the causes" of the "personality cult," and "to create conditions whereby anything like that would be impossible." "This," he asserted, "is our sacred duty, our obligation." Much as he had done in his article in the July issue of *Problemy mira i sotsializma*, he stated that the "linchpin" of this process was the democratization of Soviet society.

Nevertheless, Ligachev appeared to soften somewhat his earlier portrayal of Stalin's crimes, as well as to speak in relatively satisfied terms of the party's past de-Stalinization efforts. As he had in March, he condemned attempts to characterize Soviet history as an "unbroken chain of errors"—a phrase to be reiterated by Nina Andreyeva in her letter to *Sovetskaya Rossiya* in March 1988. But at one point, in referring only to "instances of groundless repressions," he seemed to go beyond this to minimize Stalin's lawlessness. The 20th Party Congress had condemned Stalin's "personality cult," emphasized Ligachev, had rehabilitated "many thousands of honest Soviet people," and had "restored socialist legality." Furthermore, it was "highly significant," said Ligachev, that the "overwhelming majority" of party members repressed by Stalin had remained loyal to socialism until death—perhaps an implicit rebuke of Gorbachev's policies, which were provoking resentment and doubts on fundamental issues among long-time party members still wedded to the system and to the beliefs forged by Stalin.[27]

CHEBRIKOV LEANS TOWARD LIGACHEV

With the general secretary still on vacation, Chebrikov raised eyebrows next with his September 10 speech on the one hundred and tenth anniversary of the birth of KGB founder Feliks Dzerzhinskiy. Chebrikov avoided any formulation as to what "guaranteed" the success of *perestroika*. But the KGB chief's comments nevertheless appeared drafted to signal his sympathy with Ligachev's emphasis on the need for the party to control the process of democratization, and a parallel tendency toward distrust of the intelligentsia.

While praising the success of Soviet diplomacy in advancing "new political thinking," Chebrikov warned that "Western reaction" and "imperialism's special services" were trying to take advantage of expanding Soviet democracy to remove "the process of increasing the working people's sociopolitical activeness from the party's influence, splitting the monolithic unity of party and people, and installing political and ideological pluralism." The creative intelligentsia, he said, were prime targets of the subversive efforts of Western reactionary forces "to push individual representatives . . . into positions of carping, demagogy, nihilism, the blackening of certain stages of our society's historical development, and the abandonment of the main purpose of socialist culture—the spiritual elevation of the working people." Expanding democracy and *glasnost* presupposed "debates and the clash of opinions and positions," Chebrikov conceded. But the "organic combination of socialist democracy and discipline, autonomy and responsibility, citizens' rights and duties" must not be forgotten. "A clear awareness is needed," warned Chebrikov, "that restructuring is taking place in our state and society under the leadership of the Communist Party, within the framework of socialism, and in the interests of socialism."

Chebrikov also recalled the events in Alma-Ata, Moscow, and the Baltics and, as had Ligachev, warned of the efforts of "imperialist reaction" to play on the "virus of nationalism." But along with these warnings Chebrikov again endorsed the basic reform policies of the Gorbachev leadership—and implicitly cautioned critics of the evolving INF treaty not to break party discipline (as we shall see in the next chapter). "Even today," the KGB chief asserted, much of what Dzerzhinskiy stood for in the 1920s was "topical" as the CPSU resolved "at a new qualitative level questions of developing heavy industry, primarily machine building, transport, increasing labor productivity, widely introducing the latest scientific and technical achievements into production, improving economic management, combating red tape, and extending democracy and *glasnost*." Implicitly reflecting on the Voroshilovgrad scandal, Chebrikov said that work aimed at "strengthening legality and law and order" was "still not being carried out efficiently enough."[28]

In the same vein, an unsigned commemorative piece in *Pravda* asserted that Dzerzhinskiy "constantly reminded Cheka staffers . . . that power in its entirety is vested in the soviets and not in the provincial Cheka organs." Dzerzhinskiy, it went on, "never forgot to repeat: Not a single person should be illegally arrested or subjected to criminal proceedings. He demanded tactful treatment of people and respect for their dignity and honor, and emphasized the importance of educational measures for casual offenders."[29] While this benign view of Dzerzhinskiy was laughable, the message was meant to reinforce the current policy of greater regime respect for legality.

It was thus the role of the party which set Ligachev, and to some extent Chebrikov, fundamentally at odds with Gorbachev. On the pace and scope of economic restructuring, Ligachev was still on board—as long as it was understood that the "profound changes" he favored were to be within the "framework of developing socialism." Thus in Elektrostal Ligachev excoriated "those steeped in bureaucratism" who were "prepared to reduce everything to partial changes." But as he had on numerous occasions before this, he also underscored the limits of the changes he supported. "Among the class opponents," he said, "there are also those who praise us for our restructuring, investing it with a distorted content that is convenient for them, and who entertain hopes that the Soviet Union will deviate from socialism in the direction of a market economy, ideological pluralism, and Western democracy. Vain hopes."[30]

LIGACHEV'S SELF-ADVERTISEMENT

The speeches by Ligachev and Chebrikov were widely interpreted as scarcely veiled public expressions of dissent from Gorbachev's policies of *glasnost* and historical rediscovery. To be sure, Ligachev again struck out against the "craze for primitive music which grips children," long a pet peeve of his. Chebrikov's casting of aspersions on the cultural intelligentsia, furthermore, was ominous. But by and large both speeches were not entirely out of line with the more cautious leadership stance that had been in effect since July. Ligachev asserted that "genuine *glasnost* has nothing to do with demagoguery and a disrespectful attitude toward our present, toward the history of socialist building," and he criticized those using *glasnost* to "settle personal scores" and to "indulge in left-wing phrasemongering."[31] But in this respect Gorbachev and most of his closest publicists had already sounded the same line at least six weeks earlier.

Burlatskiy, for example, had lamented in July in *Pravda* that "much time will elapse before we all really master the art of conducting honest and conscientious polemics, hearing out one's opponent and even adversary, and overcoming in oneself the atavistic urge to 'crush' or 'liquidate' at any cost an opinion which does not coincide with our own opinion." With the demonstrations by the Russian nationalist Pamyat organization and Crimean Tatars clearly uppermost in mind, Burlatskiy had rhetorically asked, "Who among us favors the unlimited 'right to demonstrate?'" To which he had answered, "Local nationalists, extremists from 'Pamyat' and from other kindred groups, people pursuing selfish interests, so-called 'refuseniks' who want to emigrate, and so forth. Each of these groups opposes the other and if they are given a free rein you see if they do not start engaging in fisticuffs."[32]

Nonetheless, Ligachev was promptly branded by many as a defender of stagnation for asserting that there had been impressive accomplishments during the 1960s and 1970s. Actually what Ligachev had in mind was probably far more promoting himself than defending Brezhnev. The second secretary gave as examples of notable accomplishments the establishment of Akademgorodok in Novosibirsk and of a gigantic oil and gas complex in Tomsk. In both instances, Ligachev had been in charge of the region at the time. In retrospect, there was a resemblance between Ligachev's burnishing of his resumé as a dynamic regional apparatchik and Kirilenko's remarks on his seventieth birthday in October 1976. On that occasion Kirilenko, I have speculated, had sought to thrust himself forward as an alternative to the ailing Brezhnev. Eleven years later, Ligachev in Elektrostal seemed to be engaged in a similar operation—under drastically different circumstances, of course—of advertising himself to party functionaries increasingly uneasy over Gorbachev's democratization campaign. Even if this was not a case of self-promotion, Ligachev's stress on good party members doing good things even under Brezhnev supported his assertion that it was a revitalized party, rather than a more democratic society, that was the main "guarantee" of *perestroika*. There had been healthy forces in the party all along, according to Ligachev, and his tacit message was that it was imperative to rely on these party-based elements to bring the country out of its crisis rather than gambling on a diffusion of politics to wider, more public arenas.

Ligachev's otherwise extremely critical remarks on the Brezhnev period went generally unrecognized, with the result that his reformist streak continued to be underappreciated. "As well as the positive changes in the country there developed negative phenomena," Ligachev stated in Elektrostal. "The development rate of the extensive economy slowed down, abuses of power became widespread, discipline became lax, and the USSR's international prestige declined. Moreover, there was unbridled eulogizing of the country's former leadership. Danger loomed over the party." The party was ready to "ruthlessly reveal mistakes and talk openly about them," said Ligachev, "and, most importantly of all, actively and vigorously set about eliminating them."[33] Ligachev's assessment of the Brezhnev era was not very different from that of Gorbachev, who since February had portrayed the Soviet past as a combination of triumphs and tragedies. And both were in line with *Pravda's* commemorative article on Brezhnev in December 1986, which had exressed similarly mixed positive and negative assessments.

Three weeks later, however, with Gorbachev still on vacation, Ligachev sounded a more clearly intimidating note on history and *glasnost* when he convened a meeting of media leaders on September 16 and invoked the pressure of what he alleged was critical public opinion in an effort to rein in more radical media outlets. "Certain publications," he warned, "as is noted by the public, have not been able to orient themselves correctly, to organically unite a true interpretation of our history with the solving of present-day problems of restructuring. Moreover,

individual periods of history are at times interpreted one-sidedly."
Returning to familiar themes, he again asserted that "one cannot permit
a disrespectful attitude to our people, to those generations who built
socialism and stood up for it in the mortal combat with fascism," and
he cautioned that "our opponents abroad" were counting on "reviving
nationalistic sentiments."[34]

Though unreported by *Pravda*, this meeting was said to have
witnessed a clash between *Moscow News* editor Yegor Yakovlev and
Ligachev. Prior to it, according to a Western dispatch, Ligachev had
privately upbraided the editor for publishing a laudatory obituary of the
dissident author Viktor Nekrasov, who had died in exile in Paris. On
September 16 Ligachev criticized Yegor Yakovlev for allegedly not having
followed the leadership's instructions on the matter from Politburo
member and Central Committee Secretary Aleksandr Yakovlev. The
editor reportedly responded by denying that such instructions existed,
and subsequently wrote to Gorbachev offering to resign from *Moscow
News*. Gorbachev, on vacation, telephoned the editor and asked him to
stay on.[35]

There were parallels between this conflict and that between Yeltsin
and Ligachev. Yeltsin and Yegor Yakovlev both contacted the vacationing
Gorbachev with word that they were under pressure from Ligachev and
wanted the issue resolved; in both instances Gorbachev asked them
to stay on. Nevertheless, opponents of Gorbachev's *glasnost* policies
were now apparently bolstered by Ligachev's remarks. In May 1988,
after the Nina Andreyeva episode, it would be revealed that on
September 17, 1987—in other words, the day after Ligachev's meeting
with the media chieftains and his clash with Yegor Yakovlev—work
on the almost finished anti-Stalin TV documentary *The Process* was
suspended and its director taken off the project. Instead of being
shown that fall in connection with the seventieth anniversary of
the revolution, it would not appear until the following spring.[36]

In the meantime, as Yeltsin and Yegor Yakovlev were under pressure to leave the scene, Geydar Aliyev returned. Aliyev, who had
dropped out of sight in May—the rumored victim of a heart attack
but also the obvious target of a Party Control Committee report critical
of his home base of Azerbaidzhan—finally resurfaced on September
8, when he showed up at the International Book Fair in Moscow.[37]
Aliyev had probably been Brezhnev's last appointment to the Politburo
in November 1982. His graceful exit from active political life now
suggested that he had skillfully maneuvered during the successions
to Andropov and Chernenko and had not tied himself too closely to
the Chernenko camp.

At the upcoming plenum on October 21, Aliyev would retire from
the Politburo "because of his state of health," and several days later

he relinquished his post of first deputy premier.[38] Aliyev's retirement, though, was not total; the following spring he would be observed attending a meeting of the Council of Ministers in the capacity of state counselor, along with Nikolay Baybakov, Veniamin Dymshits, Ziya Nuriyev, and Boris Yeltsin, by then deprived of his Moscow leadership post but attending in his new status of minister.[39] Aliyev's soft landing at a time when Ligachev was riding high may have reflected an alliance of convenience on the part of both. A year later, however, as Gorbachev worked to diminish Ligachev's authority, an exposé in the central press would link Aliyev to corruption in Azerbaidzhan.[40]

GORBACHEV: WHAT KIND OF REVOLUTION?

The general secretary finally returned from vacation and made his first appearance in public on September 29, when he met with a delegation from the USSR-France Society in the Kremlin. On this occasion he announced that he had been working on his book *Perestroika* and again used the term "socialist pluralism," only this time attracting far more notice than he had during the summer. Nevertheless, the general secretary showed continuing sensitivity on the issue of the party, but, as he had done before going on vacation, he sought to turn this pressure back on the "party vanguardists" by insisting that a leading party had to reform itself or be left behind. "We have begun the initiative to restructure the party; we feel the party should lead these processes because it formulated the policy of restructuring."[41]

Gorbachev then immediately set off for a tour of Murmansk and Leningrad. In Murmansk he revealed that the Politburo had met the Monday after his return from vacation and concluded "that we have entered the critical stage of restructuring." It was, he said, "a revolution—without shots—but . . . a deep and serious one."[42] In Leningrad he continued to insist that if the party was to lead society, it had to shape itself up first. "You have probably already noticed that my entire speech is permeated essentially with a single theme," he told a meeting of the city's party aktiv. "The party has to step up in all its sections, in all its echelons, at all levels, step up its work, not tolerate lagging behind in restructuring, and lead restructuring at the new and exceedingly important stage." The general secretary told the activists that restructuring needed "talented, highly moral cadres which are seized completely by the idea of the revolutionary renewal of society and which are close to the people."

Most revealing in Leningrad was Gorbachev's assertion, "I do not at all want it to be understood as an appeal—as was once the case during the years of the Cultural Revolution in China—to open fire on the functionaries. No, no, comrades. It would be a mistake." Restructuring could not be managed without cadres, said Gorbachev, but there was still a problem with those who were incapable of restructuring themselves. The reference to Mao's Cultural Revolution was subsequently dropped from the press accounts of the speech. But it was clear that however intent Gorbachev was on pushing on with cadre reform, he was running into considerable resistance.[43]

YELTSIN SPOILS THE ANNIVERSARY

This, then, was the backdrop for the Central Committee plenum that met on October 21 to approve the draft text of Gorbachev's November 2 speech commemorating the seventieth anniversary of the Bolshevik Revolution. Two days after the plenum, Gorbachev met with Secretary Shultz and unpredictably backed away from setting the dates for a summit in Washington. The next week, however, the Soviet side relented, and Shevardnadze flew off to Washington to settle the matter. Soon a cacophony of leaks from Soviet sources alleged various combinations of assaults by Yeltsin at the plenum not only on Ligachev but also on Gorbachev—all of which intensified speculation about a split in the Politburo.[44]

The uproar that Yeltsin, by all accounts, caused on October 21 understandably must have left even the feisty Gorbachev in an unsettled, perhaps distracted, and certainly somewhat cautious mood. But despite widespread speculation to the contrary, it was not clear that the foreign policy zigzag was a direct consequence of internal leadership politics. To the contrary, as will be discussed in the next chapter, there was much to suggest that it represented a tactical—but not wholly unproductive blunder—over how the new Soviet positions presented to Shultz would be perceived by Western publics and in turn pressure the United States. If anything, the new stance on START sublimits which the Soviet side unveiled during the Moscow ministerial, and the speed with which it corrected its tactical miscalculation, seemed to point to leadership consensus rather than disarray, at least on policy toward Washington.

Morover, Yeltsin, did not appear to have criticized any aspect of Soviet foreign policy on October 21—an impression that would be confirmed in 1989 when what was asserted to be a full transcript of the plenum was published in a new Central Committee journal. In fact, the transcript showed that aside from Gorbachev's own remarks on "new thinking" in his opening speech, foreign policy was mentioned by discussants at the plenum rarely, and then only to praise it.[45] Indeed, by the time Gorbachev met with Secretary Shultz, Yeltsin's fate was probably settled. It would later be revealed that the plenum had judged Yeltsin's speech "erroneous" and instructed the Politburo and the Moscow party committee to consider his request to quit. Furthermore, as we shall see in the next chapter, Gorbachev's speech on November 2 would mark a further advance for "new thinking" on foreign affairs, going even beyond the detailed discussion of peaceful coexistence, class struggle, and the priority of human values set forth in *Perestroika*, finished in mid-September.

On domestic issues, however, it was harder to argue against the widespread perception that Yeltsin's ouster was a loss for reformist positions associated with Gorbachev, and a gain for conservatives led by Ligachev and Chebrikov. Gorbachev's bitterly denunciatory speech against Yeltsin on November 11, the accusations of Yeltsin by his former subordinates in the Moscow city party organization, and the unwillingness (until March 1989) of the leadership to publish Yeltsin's October 21 remarks all left the impression of an atavistic reversion to the politics of old and of a serious blow to radical reform. Moreover, on November 2—and repeatedly thereafter—Gorbachev would caution not only against conservative resistance to reform but also against pressure from the "excessively zealous and impatient," who would skip stages on the path toward restructuring and "attempt to do everything in one stroke." In doing so, he appeared to some observers to be bending to conservative pressure to rein in Yeltsin-like radicals. Perhaps alluding to Gorbachev's seventieth anniversary speech, Shevardnadze would recall in early 1990 how roughly two years earlier the question of whether to include the phrase "political pluralism" in a "very serious document" had been discussed "in a narrow circle." A majority had objected, and the phrase had been struck.[46]

A number of circumstances, however, suggested the need to revise the simplistic portrayal of the Yeltsin affair as a straightforward clash between reformers and conservatives, and as a defeat for Gorbachev and a triumph for Ligachev and Chebrikov. The conflict had long been brewing, and though it reinforced the emerging estrangement between Ligachev and Gorbachev over democratization, the issues at stake and the shifting coalitions behind them were not identical. Yeltsin himself would repeatedly ascribe his differences with Ligachev to disagreements over tactics rather than ultimate goals. Moreover, Yeltsin's relations with Gorbachev had apparently deteriorated after Yeltsin's arrival in Moscow. Several years later, when questioned about Gorbachev's support for him, Yeltsin explained, "At the start a very good relationship developed between the two of us. Afterward, however—in my opinion Ligachev had a hand in this too—this relationship soured."[47] Finally, while repeatedly calling for Ligachev's resignation after the 19th Party Conference, on at least one occasion Yeltsin said that Chebrikov should stay on. "Comrade Chebrikov knows the system well and should be part of it," Yeltsin told a Komsomol audience in late 1988.[48]

In retrospect, it seems probable that relations between Yeltsin and Gorbachev had long had their ups and downs. As early as the 27th Congress, as we have seen, Volgograd First Secretary Vladimir Kalashnikov, who had worked with Gorbachev in Stavropol in the 1970s, had taken explicit exception to Yeltsin's caustic remarks about entrenched officialdom. In October 1986, early in the democratization and cadre reform drive, a key *Pravda* editorial may have put Yeltsin on notice that his style of flashy populism was not what the senior leadership had in mind. At the January 1987 plenum, moreover, and perhaps even before that, Gorbachev had balanced his attacks against conservatism with cautions against ultraliberalism. "It is necessary at the same time to warn comrades against artificially speeding up events and putting the cart before the horse," Gorbachev had told the January plenum.[49] On the eve of the June plenum Ligachev was able to cite such warnings from Gorbachev. "The rapidity of transformations is not an end in itself for us. Clear definition of the rates of restructuring is a paramount task, both politically and in practice. While procrastination and indecision are destructive, M. S. Gorbachev has observed, haste, impatience, and unjustified rushing ahead can do great damage."[50] And even more recently, Gorbachev in *Perestroika* had again mentioned criticism from both the left and the right.

A postmortem of the Yeltsin incident also served to raise long-overdue questions as to the nature of Yeltsin's radicalism. In 1987 the leadership had unveiled its "radical" political and economic reform programs at the January and June plenums—even as Yeltsin had sunk further and further into trouble. To be sure, there were numerous expressions of fears for the future of *perestroika* and of public sympathy for Yeltsin after his ouster.[51] But some insiders cautioned that it was not a case of a liberal falling victim to conservatives: "The word is not liberal but populist."[52] According to Dimitri Simes, who visited Moscow before the affair was revealed, Yeltsin had become "quite unpopular, not just among party traditionalists, but among communist yuppies as well. Privately they accuse him of 'playing on democracy,' being 'insensitive' to people—read to bureaucrats—and, worst of all, allegedly threatening to close down the hard-currency Beryozka stores where my hosts and their friends are loyal customers." Simes concluded that "with this group, at least, the Yeltsin ouster would play well. It would reassure the new elite that Gorbachev is a no-nonsense chief executive not about to tolerate populist fantasies."[53]

Yeltsin had gone on record with some strikingly radical utterances since his attacks on cadre inertia, elite corruption, and party privileges at the 27th Congress. On economic reform, for example, Yeltsin told

Yugoslav interviewers in October 1986 that history had taught that "an economic reform does not yield benefits if it stops halfway, if it comes down to a compromise, to an attempt to paint the car instead of replacing the worn-out engine." According to Yeltsin, "We have attempted in the past to introduce economic methods into the purely command method of managing the economy, and then, as in the case of the transplants, the incompatibility of the tissue became evident, and the new tissue was rejected. Now we intend to follow through to the end, although we realize that this will not be so simple."[54]

After the firing of Sokolov in the wake of the Rust-Cessna incident, Yeltsin even commented on incompetence in the armed forces. "In labor collectives people are saying: We would like the commanders of the Soviet Army to look workers in the face and explain how such a thing could happen."[55] As much as this dovetailed with the efforts of Gorbachev—and even of Sokolov's replacement, Yazov—to bring *perestroika* more forcefully to the armed forces, the scathing tone of Yeltsin's indictment went far beyond that of other critics of life in the military and must surely have earned Yeltsin an extra measure of resentment from military professionals.

Yeltsin's attacks on corruption and elite privileges had sparked a furious reaction. A *Moskovskaya Pravda* reporter interviewing Yeltsin in April 1987 recounted that the paper's mail reflected "the political clash that is taking place between healthy and degenerate forces. . . . 'Don't snipe at us, surely it's clear that this is futile,' an elderly Muscovite, the wife of a nomenklatura official, writes maliciously. 'We are the elite, and you cannot halt the stratification of society. You are not strong enough. We will rip up the puny sails of your restructuring and you will be unable to reach your destination. So moderate your ardor.'"[56]

According to *Moskovskaya Pravda* editor Poltoranin, Yeltsin and Ligachev had different notions of "social justice." Ligachev felt that "existing privileges must not be touched, but the conditions of those who, as yet, do not enjoy certain opportunities must be improved." Yeltsin, in contrast, wanted to close the special stores for officials and to lessen the exclusivity of special schools attended by many children of high officials. The fundamental difference between Ligachev and Yeltsin, in Poltoranin's view, was that Ligachev believed the party apparatus "can constitute the motive force behind *perestroika*," while Yeltsin was of the opinion that "the party apparatus—and not just in Moscow—is too compromised . . . and must be removed, just as you do with topsoil contaminated by radiation." The apparatus, in turn, once it sensed the disagreements between the two leaders, did all it could to poison further their relationship by feeding "distorted information" about Yeltsin to Ligachev.[57]

In general, as a radical reformer Yeltsin achieved greatest consistency in his almost wholesale firings of cadres in leading Moscow posts and in his trimming of their perquisites—the very areas in which Gorbachev seemed to be backtracking in the face of strong resistance from Ligachev. According to Western scholar Timothy Colton, Yeltsin conducted the most extensive purge of the Moscow apparatus since Khrushchev was city boss in 1949–50. All told, Yeltsin replaced two-thirds of the city's 33 party district leaders. On the soviet side, not only did Yeltsin quickly fire long-time "mayor" Promyslov and replace him with Valeriy Saikin, as we have seen, but he also replaced Promyslov's eleven deputies and 17 of 19 heads of major city administration directorates who had served under Promyslov. Many of these dismissals, furthermore, were accompanied by harsh public criticism. But otherwise, according to Colton, Yeltsin's "vision of reform was riddled with inconsistencies and . . ., on some key economic and political issues, was far from the cutting edge of change." Indeed, as Colton points out, very little was said of Yeltsin's radicalism by any of the speakers at the Moscow gorkom session of November 11 which formally removed him and replaced him with Zaykov.[58] And in numerous statements after his firing, Yeltsin for his part never sought to develop the notion that he and Ligachev differed over the "strategic" aims of *perestroika*.[59]

Instead, the main charges aired against Yeltsin on November 11 concerned his personality and his treatment of cadres.[60] Gorbachev pictured Yeltsin's intervention on October 21 as a surprise, violating "party and purely human ethics" and "by-passing the Politburo." The general secretary accused Yeltsin of "political immaturity" and "personal ambitions," which, according to Gorbachev, had developed into a troublesome issue at about the beginning of the year. "On the eve of the January plenum and at the Central Committee plenum itself we tried firmly to set you straight," Gorbachev told Yeltsin at the November 11 meeting of the Moscow party committee. Even before January, said the general secretary, the Politburo had warned Yeltsin that his plans for a further "cadre shakeup" in Moscow were "impermissible," and there had been another discussion with Yeltsin before the June plenum. By late summer Yeltsin had raised the possibility of resigning in a letter to the vacationing Gorbachev, but he had agreed not to press the issue until after the seventieth anniversary celebrations. Yet Yeltsin then precipitated the final sequence of events which led to his ouster by unexpectedly delivering a four-minute outburst at the October 21 plenum.[61]

In his published *mea culpa* in November, Yeltsin insisted that there had been no "ulterior motives" or "political orientation" in his action at the October 21 Central Committee plenum. Although his short speech at the October plenum was not published until 1989, Gorbachev and other speakers on November 11 gave some indications of its general thrust—though often putting an unfair and inaccurate spin on it. Yeltsin, according to Gorbachev, had accused the "Politburo, the Secretariat, and individual comrades" of lacking "revolutionary vigor" in implementing restructuring. Indeed, though Gorbachev did not name Yeltsin's specific targets, according to the transcript published in 1989 Yeltsin in fact directly attacked Ligachev and criticized unnamed "several members of the Politburo" for lavishing praise on Gorbachev.[62] However, while the speakers on November 11 repeatedly attacked Yeltsin for allegedly attempting to pit the Moscow party organization against the Central Committee and the Politburo, this was not the obvious thrust of his October 21 remarks, though it may have been of his unpublished statement at the June plenum.

In any event, the numerous mentions of Yeltsin's "ambition" suggested he found it extremely frustrating to languish at the Politburo candidate member status. Yeltsin had never been promoted to full membership, though demonstrable confidants of the general secretary, such as Aleksandr Yakovlev, had. Nevertheless, in May Yeltsin had been rumored as a possible replacement for Sokolov—even before the Cessna landing in Red Square.[63] And in June a Western dispatch reported the rumor that Gorbachev wanted to replace Geydar Aliyev with Yeltsin as first deputy premier.[64] However, there are grounds for suspecting that these rumors reflected more the hopes of Yeltsin, born of frustration, than reality or the intentions of Gorbachev. And in general some of the accusations against Yeltsin on November 11, though obviously meant to sully Yeltsin's reputation, begged the question of the extent to which Yeltsin and his aides, through their contacts with the Western media and diplomatic corps, had managed to put their own pro-Yeltsin and anti-Ligachev spin on Western reporting out of Moscow for the previous two years. The chief of the Moscow gorkom Party Organizational Work Department, for example, complained that it had been "essentially transformed into an administration for serving the 'diplomatic corps.'" And at the party conference the next summer, Ligachev would criticize Yeltsin for his numerous interviews with the "bourgeois press" and tauntingly ask, "Do you like having all the foreigners attend you, Boris?"[65]

If Gorbachev's account of Yeltsin's behavior was correct, it was not surprising that Yeltsin was disciplined. Indeed, given the nature of Yeltsin's outburst, the Politburo must have felt it incumbent to come down hard on him in order to drive home the message that such undiscipline would not be tolerated. Yeltsin's punishment, however, was relatively lenient but not unusual: demotion to first deputy chairman of the State Construction Committee, or Gosstroy, with the rank of minister. In this respect the affair had some interesting parallels to that of N. G. Yegorychev, Grishin's predecessor in the 1960s as Moscow city party boss. Yegorychev abruptly lost his position in June 1967, shortly after apparently criticizing Soviet policy in the Arab-Israeli war at a Central Committee plenum. Unlike Yeltsin, however, Yegorychev was not in the Politburo, but like Yeltsin, Yegorychev was made a deputy minister for the automobile and tractor industry. In late 1987 the leadership may have intended eventually to switch Yeltsin to diplomatic work. Yegorychev, after all, had been sent abroad in 1970 as ambassador to Denmark, returning to Moscow only in 1984 under Chernenko, as already noted. But three years later Yegorychev was posted to Kabul, as we shall see in a subsequent chapter on the Soviet withdrawal from Afghanistan.

POLITBURO CONSENSUS STILL BACKS GORBACHEV

Despite Ligachev's triumph over Yeltsin, Gorbachev still appeared to retain majority support in the Politburo on the key issue of democratization, though not on all the details. In fact, this support seemed solid enough even to permit Gorbachev to shift the formulaic terms of reference on the issue of *perestroika*'s "guarantees." The shift came in his November 2 speech when Gorbachev declared, "Two key problems in the development of society determine the destiny of restructuring. These are the democratization of all public life and the radical economic reform." Of these two, Gorbachev stated, "democratization" was "the soul of restructuring" and the "firmest guarantee of the transformation of policy and of the economy."[66] Coming on top of similar statements in his book *Perestroika*, this was another assertive counterpoint by Gorbachev to Ligachev's statement in Elektrostal that "the Communist Party's leading role in restructuring and the improvement of the style and methods of its activity" was the "primary guarantee" that reforms would be fully implemented.[67]

There apparently were limits, however, to how far Gorbachev's majority was willing to go on the issue of democratization. In neither his book nor his speech did Gorbachev explicitly endorse "pluralism"—socialist, political, or otherwise—a point of contention since the January plenum. Nevertheless, while Ligachev's viewpoint, to be sure, was reflected in Gorbachev's November 2 speech, it was not in the context of the overarching "guarantee" formula. "The success of restructuring depends primarily on the energy, purposefulness, and force of example of the party and each Communist," said Gorbachev. And again, while paying obeisance to the party's vanguard role, Gorbachev insisted that the party had to become more active if it was to lead the restructuring process. "Without a sharp stepping up of activity by all party organizations, we shall not accomplish restructuring," he insisted. "Where party leaders, Communists, have awakened the initiative and spontaneous action of the masses, have boldly embarked on the path of democratization, *glasnost*, introduction of financial autonomy, collective contracting, have given scope to new forms of labor organization and incentive, satisfaction of people's requirements, the matter has gone forward, and decisively at that."[68]

In his treatment of Soviet history, Gorbachev paused at each of its major stages to underscore the prodemocratization moral. On the Stalin era, Gorbachev asserted, "It is perfectly obvious that the lack of the proper level of democratization of Soviet society was precisely what made possible both the cult of personality and the violations of the law, arbitrariness, and repressions of the thirties—to be blunt, real crimes based on the abuse of power." On the Khrushchev years, Gorbachev said that despite its accomplishments "no few subjectivist errors" and "not infrequent" resort to "voluntarist methods, with the aid of the old political and economic mechanism," had led to errors. "However, the main reason for the failure of the reforms that were undertaken in this period," stated Gorbachev, "was the fact that they were not based on the broad spread of the processes of democratization."[69]

For the future, all but unnoticed Gorbachev signaled his intention to revitalize the Supreme Soviet and the soviet structure in general, which—understandably unfathomed at the time—would create within a year and a half the arena for Yeltsin's reincarnation as a populist parliamentarian. "The development of self-government will proceed above all through the soviets," said Gorbachev, "which must, in accordance with the party's designs, fully justify their role as plenipotentiary organs of decision." The new political processes raised the question of what Gorbachev called the "culture of socialist democratism"—the lack of which he said was largely responsible for many defects. "The true culture of socialist democracy will never accept either a command-pressure style nor organizational woolliness. . . . There is no doubt either about something else: the broader and deeper that democracy is, the more attention is required by socialist legality and law and order, and the more we need organization and conscious discipline. . . . There is an enormous range of opinions, convictions, and assessments," said Gorbachev, "which naturally require careful considerations and comparison. We are in favor of a diversity of public opinion and of richness of intellectual life."[70]

BUKHARIN'S REVENGE

It was easy, however, to be distracted and overlook these crucial statements by Gorbachev on democratization—as well as on "new thinking," as we shall see in the next chapter. Most observers focused instead on what the general secretary said or did not say about Stalin, his crimes, and his victims.[71] Gorbachev's treatment of Nikolay Bukharin in particular was closely examined for indications of which way the wind was blowing in the leadership. Bukharin had been one of Lenin's favorites, but he later led the opposition to Stalin's forced collectivization of the countryside and overturning of NEP in favor of rapid industrialization and the first five-year plan. After a spectacular show trial, Bukharin was executed in 1938. His young wife, Anna Larina, was jailed, sent to the camps, and exiled from Moscow until Khrushchev's Secret Speech in 1956. Bukharin's rehabilitation had been debated behind closed doors under Khrushchev but decided against for fear of the impact such a move would have on the party faithful, especially abroad.[72] Now, in the weeks preceding Gorbachev's speech, there were expectations in some quarters that Bukharin would finally be officially exonerated.

When Gorbachev failed to do this and instead defended many of the basic lines of development of Soviet history, much commentary asserted that the speech was more conservative than would have been the case had Ligachev not been able to take advantage of Yeltsin's misstep at the October 21 plenum. While critical of the excesses of collectivization and pointing out that Soviet diplomacy could have been more effective, Gorbachev in principle approved of Stalin's agrarian policies, industrialization, and Soviet foreign policy before and after World War II. Furthermore, Gorbachev spoke only of "many thousands" of victims of Stalin instead of the more factual millions. Finally, Gorbachev warned against "pressure from the excessively zealous and impatient," which it was widely assumed referred to Yeltsin.

But as early as the January plenum, as we have seen, Gorbachev had issued a similar warning. Furthermore, in its balanced treatment of history, the speech Gorbachev delivered reflected guidelines he had spelled out as early as mid-February. Though lacking the many detailed case histories of Stalin's repressions which Khrushchev had revealed in his Secret Speech of 1956, Gorbachev nevertheless succeeded in presenting his indictment of Stalin in public rather than in secret. On the number of Stalin's victims, moreover, Gorbachev perhaps deliberately stayed within the order of magnitude used by Khrushchev, who in his Secret Speech never went beyond "many thousands" and "tens of thousands."[73] Finally, a comparison of the transcript of Gorbachev's October 21 preview at the plenum of the speech he intended to deliver and the speech he actually gave on November 2 reveals no glaring retreats.

Gorbachev's ally Aleksandr Yakovlev, however, reacted testily when pressed on the number of purge victims at a press conference on November 3, suggesting that estimates in the millions were mere "rumor."[74] Yakovlev's sensitivity possibly reflected heated inner-party debates on how far Gorbachev could go in the speech, and resistance from the likes of Ligachev and Chebrikov to going any further. Nonetheless, Gorbachev, as had Khrushchev, deprived admirers of Stalin of one of their basic lines of defense: that Stalin had been ignorant of the crimes being committed all around him. "Documents in our possession say that this is not so," stated the general secretary. Going well beyond even his sharp condemnation in July, Gorbachev now stated unequivocally and with at last explicit reference to the dead dictator by name, "The guilt of Stalin and those closest to him before the party and the people for the mass repressions and lawlessness that were permitted are immense and unpardonable."[75]

Rather than questioning the de-Stalinization that had occurred under Khrushchev, Gorbachev implicitly criticized the Brezhnev leadership for allowing it to founder. Under Khrushchev "thousands of innocent people who suffered were completely rehabilitated. But the process of restoration of justice was not seen through, and it effectively stopped in the mid-sixties." Gorbachev in effect underscored the fact that on this issue at least, the 1960s generation—the *shestidesyatniki*, those who cut their teeth politically on the 20th and 22nd Party Congresses—were now back and ready to pick up on the anti-Stalinist cause where Khrushchev had been forced to break it off, and that they had the support of the very same Central Committee that had just witnessed Yeltsin's political demise. "Now, in accordance with the decisions of the October 1987 plenum of the Central Committee," announced Gorbachev, "we have to go back to this again."[76]

The Politburo, Gorbachev said in his speech, had set up a commission to review all the known documents relating to cases of repression under Stalin and to adopt the "relevant decisions." In addition, a Central Committee "special commission" would be organized to prepare a new outline of the history of the party.[77] Even though Gorbachev's treatment of Bukharin on November 2 was mixed, a major interview with Bukharin's widow recounting his life and repression by Stalin appeared within weeks in *Ogonek*.[78] In early February 1988 Bukharin's juridical rehabilitation would be announced to the world—the first step toward his political rehabilitation in June. Even before Gorbachev's November 2 speech, on October 26 Soviet television had screened an eye-opening documentary on the development of Soviet missiles, *Risk*. Anti-Stalinist and sympathetic to Khrushchev, it was reportedly shown at Gorbachev's personal request.[79] If Ligachev's remarks on September 16 had indeed—however indirectly—stopped work on the anti-Stalin TV documentary *The Process*, Soviet citizens were nevertheless not deprived of rich historical fare. Besides *Risk*, a documentary headed for movie theaters, *More Light*, premiered on November 3 and featured in its opening sequences film clips from 1917 showing Bukharin.[80]

LIGACHEV'S VOCAL MINORITY

Pravda's lead editorial on November 7 reiterated, "The democratization of society is the strongest guarantee of transformations in politics and economics, ruling out any backward movement."[81] *Pravda's* major editorial on November 11, however—the day the Moscow gorkom met and Gorbachev disowned Yeltsin—omitted the "guarantee" formula and instead emphasized those portions of Gorbachev's November 2 speech which had accented the role of the party. The editorial thus appeared to have Ligachev's tracks all over it and suggested that Ligachev was still trying to pull Gorbachev back to the understanding of July 1986 on the party-dominated, utilitarian purposes of the democratization campaign. "As the Soviet land enters the decisive stage of restructuring in greater depth and on a larger scale, so the more the success of the revolutionary renewal of all spheres of our life depends and will continue to depend on the energy, purposefulness, and strength of example set by the Leninist party."[82]

The November 11 editorial served notice that the "radical improvement" of party work was the "paramount task" of the day. As had Gorbachev on November 2, it stated, "Life demonstrates that where . . . party leaders and Communists have aroused the masses' initiative and independent action, where they are taking the path of democratization and *glasnost*, where scope is being given to the new forms of labor organization and incentive, and where there is concern for the satisfaction of people's needs, it is there that things are going well." Which party organizations provided good examples? Why, none other than those of Belorussia and Kazakhstan.[83]

'The editorial thus implicitly praised the efforts of republic party leaders Sokolov and Kolbin. In so doing it must have reminded attentive readers of the paper's July 22, 1986, editorial, "First Secretary," which placed Sokolov and Kolbin at the top of its honor roll when they were both still regional party leaders. That column, as we have seen, had paraphrased Ligachev's call several weeks before in Voronezh "to bring people into closer contact with party work, carry it out in an atmosphere of broad democracy." Ligachev's speech and the *Pravda* editorial had then been as much heralds of the leadership's growing radicalization as had been Gorbachev's subsequent speech at the end of July 1986 in Khabarovsk.

The account of the Politburo meeting on November 12, however, made clear that Ligachev was still in a minority position despite Yeltsin's exit from the leadership. "The Politburo pointed out that the attention of the party, local soviet and economic bodies, and of trade union and Komsomol organizations should be centered [on] the key problems determining the fate of restructuring—the democratization of public life and radical economic reform."[84] This was the formula Gorbachev had used on November 2, and the media report of the Politburo's deliberations seemed intended to set Ligachev straight.

ZAYKOV ASCENDANT

Finally, Lev Zaykov's appointment to replace Yeltsin seemed to give Gorbachev—rather than Ligachev—a more reliable hand in charge of the Moscow party organization. Zaykov, moreover, as a full member of the Politburo and a Central Committee secretary, came to the job with greater clout than Yeltsin ever had, and would unexpectedly retain rather than give up his Secretariat position long after becoming Moscow party boss. Zaykov's track record suggested he had served Gorbachev well in battles against Romanov, in efforts to restrain the defense budget, and in the democratization drive earlier in 1987. For the future, reform seemed not to have been derailed but simply deprived of Yeltsin's populist fireworks. Zaykov appeared ready to continue to pressure the capital's apparatchiks to change their ways, but in a manner calculated not to demoralize them as a class—unlike Yeltsin. For as much as the Gorbachev leadership tried to pressure the apparats both from above and below, for now it was still compelled to work through them.

When asked whether Zaykov got along well with Ligachev, Yeltsin's friend Mikhail Poltoranin remarked six months later, "It would seem so. They are always together. . . . They are like Siamese twins."[85] It was true that Ligachev and Zaykov made frequent public appearances in each other's company during the winter of 1987–88. However, the longer-term record suggested that Zaykov actually displaced Ligachev as the second-ranking member of the Secretariat rather than supported Ligachev's efforts against Gorbachev. On May Day 1987, as we have seen, Zaykov moved past Chebrikov in the lineup atop the Lenin Mausoleum and stood equidistant with Ligachev from Gorbachev. On November 7, with Ligachev strengthened by Yeltsin's impending exit from the leadership, Zaykov dropped back to his old position below Chebrikov. In 1988, however, Zaykov would once again pass Chebrikov and pull even with Ligachev on May Day in the wake of the latter's failed Nina Andreyeva challenge. In fall 1988, after Ligachev's authority was substantially undermined at the September 30 plenum, Zaykov at the Supreme Soviet would nominate Gorbachev for "president"—by precedent normally a sure sign that Zaykov and not Ligachev was the second-ranking member of the leadership. Then on November 7, Zaykov would stand right next to Gorbachev on the mausoleum parade review stand, clearly outranking Ligachev.[86] The overall record thus suggested that if Zaykov occupied a centrist, swing position in the spectrum of Politburo opinion, he more often than not leaned toward Gorbachev rather than Ligachev—including in November 1987.

NOTES

1. Alan W. Fisher, *The Crimean Tatars* (Stanford: Hoover Institution Press, 1978), 170.

2. For accounts of the early demonstrations, see AFP, July 23, 1987 (FBIS-SOV, July 24, 1987, R 1); AFP, July 24–26, 1987 (FBIS-SOV, July 27, 1987, R 9–12). For the "TASS Announcement" setting forth the official view on the merits of the Crimean Tatar demands and announcing formation of the Gromyko committee, see TASS, July 23, 1987 (FBIS-SOV, July 24, 1987, R 1–3).

3. TASS, July 27, 1987 (FBIS-SOV, July 28, 1987, R 1).

4. AFP, July 27, 1987 (FBIS-SOV, July 28, 1987, R 1).

5. TASS, July 30, 1987 (FBIS-SOV, July 30, 1987, R 7).

6. AFP, July 31, 1987 (FBIS-SOV, August 3, 1987, R 10).

7. TASS, September 1, 1987 (FBIS-SOV, September 2, 1987, 31–32); and AFP, September 1, 1987 (FBIS-SOV, September 2, 1987, 32).

8. *Dagens Nyheter*, August 24, 1987 (FBIS-SOV, September 1, 1987, 30).

9. See *Washington Post*, August 9, 1987, for a midsummer survey.

10. *Sovetskaya Kultura*, July 7, 1987 (FBIS-SOV, July 10, 1987, R 13–16).

11. *Pravda*, July 15, 1987 (FBIS-SOV, July 15, 1987, R 1–14).

12. *Sovetskaya Kultura*, July 21, 1987 (FBIS-SOV, July 22, 1987, R 10).

13. *Corriere Della Sera*, May 12, 1988.

14. *Izvestiya TsK KPSS*, no. 2 (1989), 239 and 284.

15. *Pravda*, July 15, 1987 (FBIS-SOV, July 15, 1987, R 10).

16. Ibid., R 8–9.

17. *Pravda*, July 30, 1987 (FBIS-SOV, July 31, 1987, R 3).

18. Gorbachev also announced that there would be a plenum on agriculture (*Pravda*, August 6, 1987 [FBIS-SOV, August 10, 1987, R 7–9]). But despite his assertion that the Politburo had agreed to this, he would not be able to schedule a date for it (February 1989) for over a year, until after clipping Ligachev's wings in late September 1988.

19. *Pravda*, September 30, 1987 (FBIS-SOV, September 30, 1987, 33).

20. Moscow Television Service, September 29, 1987 (FBIS-SOV, September 30, 1987, 25–31).

21. On the release of *Perestroika* in Moscow and Washington, see the *New York Times*, November 2 and 3, 1987.

22. Gorbachev, *Perestroika*, 18 on democratization; 96–99 on the Soviets; 111 on criticism from the "left" and "right"; 129–36 on peaceful coexistence and class struggle; and 228 on delivery of manuscript to publisher.

23. For Yeltsin's speech, see *Moskovskaya Pravda*, August 9, 1987 (FBIS-SOV, September 17, 1987, 28–40).

24. *Kommunist*, no. 13 (September 1987), signed to press August 25, 1987.

25. Ibid.

26. *Uchitelskaya Gazeta*, August 27, 1987 (FBIS-SOV, August 28, 1987, 18–20).

27. Ibid.

28. *Pravda*, September 11, 1987 (FBIS-SOV, September 15, 1987, 29–34). In April 1987 in Moscow, correspondent Don Oberdorfer asked a high-ranking KGB officer what Gorbachev was all about. "Finally the Lord has turned his face to us, after years when we were heading toward the brink," the officer replied, with what Oberdorfer describes as an intensity of feeling that startled him (*Washington Post*, April 26, 1987).

29. *Pravda*, September 10, 1987 (FBIS-SOV, September 15, 1987, 35).

30. *Uchitelskaya Gazeta*, August 27, 1987 (FBIS-SOV, August 28, 1987, 23).

31. Ibid., 22.

32. *Pravda*, July 18, 1987 (FBIS-SOV, July 23, 1987, R 24–25).

33. *Uchitelskaya Gazeta*, August 27, 1987 (FBIS-SOV, August 28, 1987, 18–23).

34. *Pravda*, September 17, 1987 (FBIS-SOV, September 18, 1987, 33–34).

35. *El Pais*, September 24, 1987. At the 19th Party Conference the following summer Ligachev would specifically criticize *Moscow News* for its "ersatz" news.

36. *Pravda*, May 17, 1988 (FBIS-SOV, May 26, 1988, 67–68).

37. Moscow Domestic Service, September 8, 1987 (FBIS-SOV, September 8, 1987, 30).

38. Moscow Domestic Service, October 21, 1987 (FBIS-SOV, October 22, 1987, 42); and TASS, October 23, 1987 (FBIS-SOV, October 26, 1987, 30).

39. *Izvestiya*, May 15, 1988 (FBIS-SOV, May 20, 1988, 34–39).

40. *Literary Gazette*, September 21, 1988 (FBIS-SOV, October 5, 1988, 57).

41. *Pravda*, September 30, 1987 (FBIS-SOV, September 30, 1987, 28 and 35).

42. *Vremya*, Moscow Television Service, September 30, 1987 (FBIS-SOV, October 1, 1987, 53 and 57).

43. Moscow Television Service, October 13, 1987 (FBIS-SOV, October 14, 1987, 65–66).

44. *Christian Science Monitor*, October 29, 1987; *New York Times*, October 30, 1987; and *Washington Post*, October 31, 1987.

45. *Izvestiya TsK KPSS*, no. 2 (1989): 209–87.

46. *Izvestiya*, February 19, 1990.

47. Budapest Television Service, February 20, 1989 (FBIS-SOV, February 21, 1989, 78).

48. For the transcript of what Yeltsin reportedly told students at the Higher Komsomol School on November 20, 1988, see *Russkaya Mysl*, January 6, 1989.

49. Moscow Domestic Service, January 27, 1987 (FBIS-SOV, January 28, 1987, R 37).

50. *Problemy Mira i Sotsializma*, no. 7 (July 1987), signed to press June 9, 1987 (FBIS-SOV, August 6, 1987, R 5).

51. *Washington Post*, November 18, 1987.

52. *Washington Post*, November 15, 1987.

53. *Washington Post*, November 22, 1987.

54. *Nin*, October 26, 1986 (FBIS-SOV, January 21, 1987, R 14).

55. *Red Star*, June 17, 1987 (FBIS-SOV, June 17, 1987, V 3).

56. *Moskovskaya Pravda*, April 14, 1987 (FBIS-SOV, April 22, 1987, R 9).

57. *Corriere della Sera*, May 12, 1988.

58. Timothy J. Colton, "Moscow Politics and the El'tsin Affair," The Harriman Institute *Forum* 1, no. 6 (June 1988): 4 and 7.

59. According to correspondent David Remnick, in November 1988 Yeltsin told a Komsomol audience in the Urals city of Perm that "[Ligachev and I] don't disagree on the strategic direction of *perestroika*. But we differ on many questions of tactics."

According to the Perm journal *Young Guard*, which reported the remarks by Yeltsin cited by Remnick, Yeltsin remained "a shining representative of the command-administrative elite—the apparat." The personal and political complexity of Yeltsin's character comes through in Remnick's report on an election campaign appearance by Yeltsin in February 1989 in which he sought to be nominated to run for deputy to the new Supreme Soviet. Remnick described Yeltsin as a "professional Soviet pol, a ward heeler writ large. . . . In Boris Yeltsin there is certainly more than an ounce of Huey Long. . . . Yeltsin, somehow, is capable of being, at once, honest and demagogic, generous and vain" (*Washington Post*, February 18, 1989).

60. The speeches by Gorbachev and others at the November 11 plenum of the Moscow city party committee were published in *Pravda*, November 13, 1987 (FBIS-SOV, November 13, 1987, 59–73).

61. Rowland Evans and Robert Novak, in *Washington Post*, December 7, 1987.

62. *Izvestiya TsK KPSS*, no. 2 (1989): 239–41.

63. *The Sunday Times*, May 10, 1987.

64. *The Observer*, June 9, 1987.

65. Moscow Television Service, July 1, 1988 (FBIS-SOV, July 5, 1988, Supplement, 104).

66. Moscow Television Service, November 2, 1987 (FBIS-SOV, November 3, 1987, 49).

67. *Uchitelskaya Gazeta*, August 27, 1987 (FBIS-SOV, August 28, 1987, 18–19).

68. Moscow Television Service, November 2, 1987 (FBIS-SOV, November 3, 1987, 53–54).

69. Ibid., 45, 48.

70. Ibid., 50.

71. The *New York Times'* report on Gorbachev's speech, for example, mentioned only in passing one passage on democratization, whereas the reports in the *Washington Post* and the *Christian Science Monitor* ignored the subject entirely.

72. Roy A. Medvedev, *Nikolai Bukharin* (New York: W. W. Norton, 1980), 164–65).

73. Khrushchev, *The Crimes of the Stalin Era*, S 15, S 32, and S 54. The same year, however, Khrushchev reportedly told an Italian CP delegation that eight

million had died in Stalin's purges (Robert Conquest, *The Great Terror*, rev. ed. [New York: Collier Books, 1973], 713).

Gorbachev nevertheless went beyond *Pravda's* article on the centenary of Stalin's birth (December 21, 1979), which referred to "mass repressions" that brought grief to "many eminent party and state figures, great military commanders, honest communists and non-party soviet people." And *Pravda's* article on Stalin's ninetieth birthday (December 21, 1969) had spoken only of "facts" of illegality which affected in the main only "cadres."

74. *New York Times*, November 4, 1987.

75. Moscow Television Service, November 2, 1987 [FBIS-SOV, November 3, 1987, pp. 45].

76. Ibid.

77. Ibid.

78. *Ogonek*, no. 48 (November 1987), signed to press November 24, 1987.

79. DPA, October 21, 1987 (FBIS-SOV, October 22, 1987, 52); and Moscow Television Service, October 26, 1987 (FBIS-SOV, October 27, 1987, 59–60).

80. TASS, November 3, 1987 (FBIS-SOV, November 4, 1987, 76).

81. *Pravda*, November 7, 1987 (FBIS-SOV, November 10, 1987, 65–66).

82. *Pravda*, November 11, 1987 (FBIS-SOV, November 12, 1987, 61–62).

83. Ibid. The same day, *Sovetskaya Rossiya* reported on a Central Committee resolution "On Glasnost in the Work of Party and Trade Union Organizations and Soviet Organs in Vladimir Oblast," which sounded many of the same themes (FBIS-SOV, November 12, 1987, 58–60).

84. Moscow Domestic Service, November 12, 1987 (FBIS-SOV, November 13, 1987, 58).

85. *Corriere della Sera*, May 12, 1988.

86. For Moscow Television Service's coverage of the respective parades, including the leadership lineups, see the Editorial Reports in FBIS-SOV, November 9, 1987, 32–34; May 2, 1988, 56–57; and November 8, 1988, 73–75.

Chapter 13

INF: Stutter-Step to Washington

───

After Gorbachev's go-for-broke performance in Reykjavik, Moscow recast its disarmament tactics for 1987 even while continuing to pursue a U.S. commitment to the ABM Treaty which would constrain SDI within commonly accepted testing limits. This more sober stage of foreign policy under Gorbachev was framed by what seemed to be the perceived need to conclude at least an INF agreement with the United States before the start of the 1988 presidential election campaign, and the hope that Soviet concessions on INF, START, and defense and space issues would elicit U.S. movement toward a compromise with Moscow on the ABM Treaty. Gorbachev apparently did not want to begin formulating the next Five-Year Plan (1991–95) while only marking uncertain time with the outgoing Reagan administration and facing potentially even greater uncertainties on arms control and defense programs with the next, as yet unknown, United States president.

Partly as a pressure tactic and partly in recognition of the realities of the American political calendar, Soviet spokesmen would later openly suggest that an INF agreement had to be ready by fall or early winter 1987. A signed treaty could then be submitted to the Senate for ratification hearings early in 1988, lessening the chances that it would be turned into a political football after the start of the presidential primaries in February. There were to be many cliff-hangers along the way. Many were contrived by Moscow to heighten the suspense and thus to increase the pressure on Washington to make concessions. Others appeared to be occasioned by what seemed to be Gorbachev's frustration over U.S. reluctance to compromise on the ABM Treaty. But by the time it was all over, the Soviet leadership itself made the crucial concessions necessary to adhere to the timetable it appeared to have set at the beginning of 1987.

Given Gorbachev's strong showing at the January and June 1987 plenums, however, and despite the break with Ligachev over democratization, he was not under make-or-break political pressure at home to achieve a breakthrough in U.S.-Soviet relations in order to consolidate his leadership role. Rather, Gorbachev and most of his colleagues collectively appeared to see an INF treaty and a summit with President Reagan as useful for promoting stability and continuity abroad in order better to pursue reforms at home and to justify restraining growth in defense spending. Under the best of circumstances, the uncertainties over the success of *perestroika* were enormous, and therefore a predictable and less threatening external environment was absolutely essential.

In 1981 the INF zero option had been scored by its critics as nonnegotiable with Moscow. Those critics were now proven wrong. Even with the impact of the Iran-contra affair on Reagan's capacity to govern still highly uncertain, in early 1987 Gorbachev announced the first of several Soviet retreats toward long-held U.S. positions on INF. Soviet strategy appeared to be to work for early agreement not only on INF but on several other limited yet tangible accords with the Reagan administration, and then to press the United States for dramatic movement on START and defense and space issues. The end result, if this step-by-step approach succeeded, would amount to a toned-down version of Moscow's original Reykjavik package.

It was the American reluctance to go along with Gorbachev on the second phase of this game plan, and not the Yeltsin affair, which seemed to provoke the Soviet flip-flop in September-October on the conditions for a Washington summit. In the end Moscow settled for a commitment by Washington to use the summit to draft instructions to the two sides' delegations in Geneva on further negotiations on START and defense and space issues. Finally, in Washington at the White House on December 8, 1987, the U.S. and Soviet leaders signed a global double-zero INF agreement far more stringent than that first proposed by Reagan six years before. In addition, on the basis of an ambiguous political commitment to the ABM Treaty, which failed to resolve the two sides' differing interpretations over what it did or did not allow in regard to SDI, they set their sights on a START treaty and return summit in Moscow by May-June 1988.

SOBER NEW YEAR: PREPARING TO DELINK

Burlatskiy opened 1987 with an impassioned plea for "tremendous efforts" to combat American stereotypes of the Soviet Union as "enemy number one." A breakthrough in public perceptions would probably require "important and radical agreements" between the two countries.[1] Establishment observers, however, argued among themselves whether it would be possible to reach significant agreements with Reagan. Bovin, for example, saw the predominant "wave of neoconservatism" making Western foreign policy "harder, less flexible." Zorin countered that Reagan's performance in Reykjavik, "objective factors" influencing the president, and "a certain new distribution of forces in Washington" gave grounds for optimism over what might be achieved in the coming year.[2]

For its part, the Soviet leadership appeared ready to do business with the United States even in the waning months of the Reagan administration rather than lose several years waiting for a successor. In January First Deputy Foreign Minister Yuliy Vorontsov replaced Viktor Karpov as chief negotiator in Geneva.[3] Karpov would now spend full-time in Moscow as head of the Foreign Ministry's arms control directorate, established in mid-1986 with Karpov as its first chief. Deputy negotiator Aleksey Obukhov explained that the appointment of a personality with Vorontsov's stature as formal head of the Soviet delegation was designed to accelerate the negotiations and set the stage for a breakthrough in the round then opening.[4]

Moscow's assessment of the Iran-contra affair from the very beginning was that the president would not be irretrievably damaged by it.[5] Thus the decision to delink INF from the Reykjavik package was certainly made even before the release of the Tower Commission report in late February. Well into February, nevertheless, Soviet public insistence on INF linkage to the Reykjavik package remained adamant. Shevardnadze, for example, declared that the very notion of breaking up the Reykjavik package was "irresponsible" and even "immoral."[6] The foreign minister's comments were evidently designed to screen the discussions taking place behind the scenes, for within weeks Gorbachev announced Moscow's readiness to conclude just such a delinked INF Treaty.

Gorbachev's proposal on February 28 called for an agreement on long-range INF missiles based on the Reykjavik understanding—eliminating these systems in Europe and allowing each side to retain 100 warheads in Soviet Asia and on U.S. territory. On SRINF, he said the SS-12s forward-deployed in the German Democratic Republic and Czechoslovakia as counterdeployments to the Pershing II and GLCM would be withdrawn as soon as an agreement on the elimination of LRINF in Europe was signed. The Soviet Union was prepared, he said, to begin talks immediately on other "operational-tactical" missiles in Europe with the goal of their complete elimination.[7]

SHIFT ON SRINF

The development of the Soviet position on INF in 1987 was not without what appeared from the outside to be tactical digressions, deliberate pauses, and perhaps unintended delays. Some appeared designed to build public pressure on Washington and NATO capitals. Others may have been attributable to internal difficulties. The precise nature of the latter, however, was well hidden from public view. *Glasnost* still had its limits, especially regarding foreign policy. Whatever the options under consideration, debate over foreign policy was still screened from external scrutiny. The new line, once decided, was imposed from the center—just as in the pre-Gorbachev era. The announcement of the very decision to delink may have itself been delayed. It had been widely expected that Gorbachev would unveil a surprise initiative in his speech to the peace forum in Moscow on February 16, but he chose instead to dwell on the evils of nuclear deterrence, his most intense attack ever.[8]

If there was a hitch over delinking, it may have arisen from differences or uncertainty over how to handle shorter-range INF missiles (SRINF) with ranges under 1000 km. The evolving new position presumably reflected a combination of perceived military requirements, calculations of optimal negotiating strategy, and public presentational advantages. But it was not arrived at overnight and presumably was the result of a series of compromises within the national security bureaucracies in Moscow and between the USSR and its allies in Eastern Europe. East Germany and Czechoslovakia would be the two Soviet allies most affected by the February 28 initiative. The Warsaw Pact position from the beginning had been that as soon as all NATO LRINF were removed from Europe, the 900-km SS-12s could be pulled back to Soviet territory. Gorbachev's February 28 proposal simply reiterated this understanding. Nevertheless, the timing of trips by Shevardnadze and Defense Minister Sokolov to East Berlin and Prague earlier in February added to the appearance of a last-minute need for further consultations with the allies—and a resultant delay in the unveiling of the eventual INF delink initiative.[9]

Beyond the 900-km SS-12s, however, over the years the United States had also demanded constraints on the 500-km SS-23, even in the "old" INF negotiations. Part of the July 1982 "walk in the woods" package had been a freeze on existing levels of U.S. and Soviet SRINF. The preferred Soviet position had been to postpone resolution of the issue of SRINF missiles, though it had agreed in principle to quantitative limits on missiles with ranges between 500 and 1000 km. But Soviet negotiators had never formally tabled any concrete provisions by the time the talks broke up in late 1983, arguing that SRINF was a peripheral question to be addressed after the central issues of the INF negotiations had been resolved.[10]

Under Gorbachev there was at first a pullback even from a tentative willingness to address SRINF in Europe in the INF context. The Budapest Appeal of June 1986, as pointed out in an earlier chapter, had proposed that "operational-tactical nuclear arms with a range up to 1000 km" be reduced in a new multilateral negotiation on conventional forces and tactical aircraft from the Atlantic to the Urals. Since Reykjavik, however, Moscow's position had gone back to favoring a "freeze" and negotiations in some vague INF context on SRINF missiles in Europe with a range below 1000 km. Thus when Gorbachev issued his statement on February 28, he formalized the move away from the Budapest Appeal framework for negotiations when he called for beginning talks "immediately with a view to reducing and fully eliminating" these other SRINF missiles. But he still did not specify what range below 1000 km he had in mind or, alternatively, which specific missile systems or how negotiations on SRINF would be connected to those on LRINF.

SHULTZ IN MOSCOW

Shortly after its move to delink INF, Moscow agreed to receive Shultz in Moscow for another round of ministerial talks. The focus of the discussions would be on SRINF, as the American side sought to nail down Soviet agreement to specific global constraints on SRINF within an INF treaty, and the Soviet side in turn sought to trump the American demand by calling for the elimination of all U.S. and Soviet SRINF, specifically in Europe.

Curiously, it was now Gromyko—rather than any figure in the military—who seemed publicly to express reservations over giving up any more negotiating capital in dealing with the Reagan administration. "We have done everything possible for normal relations between the Soviet Union and the United States," the former foreign minister declared when receiving new U.S. Ambassador Jack Matlock in the Kremlin in early April. "We made our concrete proposals on this score but in reply all sorts of maneuvers are being undertaken with the aim of sidestepping the solution of burning issues. All this shows that at present the American Administration apparently does not have serious intentions to search for accords."[11] Coming as it did in the midst of what must have been the leadership's deliberations over proposing a double zero in Europe during the impending visit to Moscow by Shultz, Gromyko's negative and very public assessment of the likely U.S. response bordered on political provocation.

Gorbachev nevertheless set the stage for Shultz's visit with a speech in Prague on April 10 in which he reiterated Soviet willingness to enter negotiations aimed at the elimination of all U.S. and Soviet SRINF missiles in Europe. He finally defined the systems to be dealt with as those with ranges between 500 and 1000 km, in effect reaffirming a position the Soviet Union had acceded to in the "old" INF talks. The SRINF negotiations, however, would be separate but parallel to those on LRINF, so as not to complicate the latter. There would be a numerical freeze on SRINF missile deployments for the period of the talks.[12]

During his meeting with Secretary Shultz in the Kremlin on April 14, Gorbachev stated that the USSR was now willing to consider including the obligation to eliminate all SRINF in Europe within an agreement on LRINF. Shultz responded that any limits on SRINF had to be global, given the high mobility of these systems. Gorbachev accepted this point and then expressed his willingness to agree to a global zero on SRINF. Shultz welcomed Gorbachev's espousal of a global agreement, but reflecting sensitivity to European complaints that the United States had acted unilaterally in Reykjavik, he added that the United States would have to consult with its NATO allies over whether zero was the proper limit.[13] Gorbachev immediately took Shultz to task for not agreeing on the spot to zero SRINF.[14]

There would be subsequent statements by Gorbachev suggesting separate negotiations on SRINF systems in Asia.[15] Nevertheless, the Soviet position was in effect that SRINF would be treated globally, with a zero-zero outcome in Europe and matching levels in Soviet Asia and the United States. Because America had no SRINF in the 500-1000 km-range category, however, and because the Soviets consistently rejected buildup or conversion by the United States to match Soviet systems, it followed that what Gorbachev was proposing was a global negotiation on SRINF with a zero global outcome.

Gorbachev made clear to Shultz in Moscow that there could be no summit without an INF treaty. In addition, he proposed that his next meeting with Reagan approve an understanding on "key provisions" to guide future negotiations on START, defense and space, and nuclear testing. The first such "key provisions" paper had been handed over by Shevardnadze to Shultz at their talks in early November in Vienna shortly after Reykjavik. The outline of Moscow's new iteration was basically unchanged since Vienna, except for the dropping of the INF portion, as this was now being handled separately. In START, the Soviet side continued to reject separate sublimits on ICBMs, SLBMs, and bombers while still proposing a 50-percent reduction in its heavy ICBMs and in each leg of the triad.

On nuclear testing issues, Moscow started to soften its insistence on an up-front agreement on a comprehensive test ban (CTB), and at last began to show a more forthcoming attitude on verification. Since 1983 the United States had been seeking verification improvements to the Threshold Test Ban Treaty (TTBT) and the Peaceful Nuclear Explosions Treaty (PNET)—signed in 1974 and 1976, respectively, but never ratified—before discussing any further limits on nuclear testing. After repeated Soviet turndowns of U.S. proposals, in this meeting with Shultz Gorbachev finally stated that "to get matters off the ground" the

USSR was "prepared to work out jointly a formula that would make it possible to ratify the 1974 and 1976 agreements, to come to terms on a considerable lessening of the yield and number of explosions."[16]

On space issues, the Soviets continued to call for strict adherence to and "strengthening" of the ABM Treaty and for ABM research to be restricted to laboratories. Gorbachev, however, now explained that this included any activity "in institutes, at proving grounds, and at plants" as long as they were on earth. Moreover, the Soviets proposed for the first time agreement on a list of devices not to be put into space during a ten-year nonwithdrawal period, though they still did not contemplate permitting any testing whatsoever in space. The "key provisions" also linked the proposed 50-percent reductions in START over five years to agreement on the proposed ten-year nonwithdrawal from ABM.[17]

THE PERSHING Ia WARHEAD ISSUE

Only in Geneva on April 27 did the Soviets clarify which systems they wanted included in an SRINF negotiation. On one hand, they accepted the U.S. demand that both the SS-23 and the SS-12 be limited. But they also called for the destruction of all 72 U.S.-controlled nuclear warheads for the FRG's Pershing Ia missiles, in effect equating these warheads to the roughly equal number of Soviet SS-12s and SS-23s in Europe.[18]

The Soviets probably calculated that their demand could lead to one of several alternative outcomes. Even after Gorbachev proposed zero SRINF on April 14, Moscow made clear its preference for follow-up talks on SRINF rather than settlement of the issue in an overall treaty on INF. Moscow may have judged that the Pershing Ia demand would prove to be such anathema in Bonn that Washington would settle for a treaty on LRINF only. This would leave Soviet SRINF in the field and subject to negotiated reductions only sometime in the distant future, if ever. The Soviets may have been simultaneously attempting to use the Pershing warhead issue to extract additional concessions. In addition, pressing the Pershing issue provided Moscow with a device to use either as an excuse for backing away from reaching an INF accord or as a last-minute "concession" that would demonstrate its statesmanship in the interest of European security.

In any event, Moscow probably wanted at least to test how much support it could muster for its demand in West Germany. Moscow may have also calculated that the issue could serve as a useful device for influencing coalition politics in Bonn, as well as FRG relations with the United States, East Germany, and the USSR. Should Bonn and Washington yield on the issue, Moscow would wind up with gains it had probably previously not counted on: not simply the premature retirement of

72 U.S.-FRG systems but also the perception in Europe, and especially Germany, that the United States had succumbed to Soviet designs that would eventually lead to the denuclearization of Europe and which were already undermining NATO's flexible response strategy.

Moscow was also using other approaches to the FRG, not only sticks but also carrots. In tandem with its own decision to move toward rapprochement with Bonn after Kohl's victory in the January 25, 1987, elections—and even as it prepared to unveil its demand for the destruction of the U.S.-controlled warheads for West Germany's Pershing Ia's—Moscow evidently gave its go-ahead to Honecker to visit Bonn. After repeated postponements, most notably in September 1984, the East German leader would at last be permitted to travel to the FRG. As early as April 1, 1987, it would later be reported, FRG and GDR representatives had agreed on the dates for Honecker's "working visit."[19] In early May, furthermore, it was announced that Bulgarian leader Todor Zhivkov, who in September 1984 had also been forced to cancel his visit to Bonn, would pay an "official visit" to the FRG in June.[20] Finally, and despite the continued insistence by Bonn's ruling coalition and NATO on excluding the Pershing Ia missiles from a global double-zero accord on INF, East Berlin announced on July 15 that Honecker would visit the FRG on September 7–11.[21]

GLOBAL DOUBLE ZERO

Gorbachev's May 19 toast to the Vietnamese asserted that it should be possible to negotiate SS-20s down to zero in the Far East. But in exchange, the United States would have to agree to eliminate its nuclear weapons in the Philippines, Japan, and South Korea; withdraw its aircraft carrier flotilla beyond agreed lines; and eliminate medium-range missiles on U.S. territory.[22] The proposed trade was patently absurd. Gorbachev was offering to exchange 100 SS-20 warheads for the U.S. nuclear presence in Asia. The USSR would not have to give up any of its ICBMs, ships, and aircraft targeted on the region.

In early May there had been reports of military resistance to Gorbachev's willingness to eliminate SRINF missiles from Europe. The leaks did not directly link Sokolov to this resistance but nevertheless suggested that he would soon be replaced—perhaps even by a civilian—because of illness. The sources of the information were said to be highly placed: a Central Committee member and another "top official."[23] Whatever the calculations and intentions behind the leaks, however, Gorbachev's changing relations with the military appeared to be giving him expanding rather than contracting room to maneuver. Since January, as we have seen, the promotions of Lukyanov to the

Secretariat and Yazov to deputy defense minister for personnel had suggested that Gorbachev's grip on the military establishment was tightening. And in any event, Sokolov's ouster at the end of May certainly simplified Gorbachev's handling of INF endgame details.

The first public hints that cardinal decisions on INF were in the making, however, began a full week before Mathias Rust landed his Cessna just off Red Square—and in so doing provided the excuse for summarily retiring Sokolov. Even before this, the atmospherics were improving as commentators hailed the agreement early in the month on nuclear risk reduction centers. These were seen as politically significant, even if only of secondary military importance.[24] The contrast with the cool treatment accorded the Hot Line Upgrade agreement of 1984 was a sign of the times. Following this, starting shortly after mid-May, there were numerous Soviet expressions of optimism over the prospects for a treaty and a fall summit. Burlatskiy wrote, "we are on the threshold of a breakthrough in public opinion abroad which could be compared only with the moods of the World War II years, when the words 'Russian' and 'Soviet' generated a wave of profound affection throughout the world."[25] Volkogonov of the Main Political Administration argued the need for "compromises, mutual concessions, and steps toward each other."[26] Foreign Ministry spokesman Gerasimov and Geneva negotiator Obukhov talked up the idea of an INF treaty and a summit in the fall.[27] Bovin extolled compromise, explaining, "To ensure that both partners can make headway, each must retreat, that is sacrifice part of his preliminary demands for the sake of concord"; he did not interject his earlier view that the outlook for any significant agreements with Reagan was dim.[28] Meanwhile, Soviet jamming of Voice of America broadcasts ceased for the first time since the beginning of the Polish crisis in 1980, though jamming of Radio Free Europe and Radio Liberty continued.[29]

These were the atmospherics in Moscow as the Defense Ministry's General Chervov prepared to visit Geneva in mid-June for talks with U.S. negotiators. According to press reports, Chervov explored what the impact might be on U.S. positions of a Soviet move to global zero LRINF; American negotiators reportedly suggested that in return the United States might not press for the right to convert GLCMs to SLCMs, or to convert Pershing IIs into shorter-range Pershing Ib's, which it might then make available to West Germany.[30] The two sides seemed to be moving toward agreement on the next ministerial meeting between Shultz and Shevardnadze, which might then set a date for a summit.

On June 18, however, Shevardnadze told a Hungarian television interviewer that his meeting with Secretary Shultz "can only take place after the conclusion of the current round of the Geneva talks."[31] It was a puzzling comment, as no date had been set and neither side seemed to be pushing for a break in the negotiations. The earlier optimism over early closure on INF was pushed aside by Soviet insistence that destruction of the P-Ia warheads was an issue on which there could be no compromise.

Not for the first time, though, just as Moscow was striking a tough public pose, it was privately preparing a major step forward. Ironically, the movement in Geneva that Shevardnadze had in mind would turn out to be Soviet and not American. This became clear with the surprise release on July 22 of Gorbachev's interview with the editor of the Indonesian newspaper *Merdeka*. Gorbachev now stated that the USSR was "prepared to remove the issue of retaining the 100 warheads on medium-range missiles that are being discussed at the Geneva talks with the Americans, provided, of course, the United States does the same thing. Operational-tactical missiles will also be eliminated." But he did not link the initiative with removal of the U.S. nuclear presence in Asia.[32]

The move to zero lessened many of the remaining differences over verification and the phasing of reductions. In the end the INF Treaty would incorporate the most intrusive verification measures ever agreed to in any disarmament agreement, and it gave substance to Gorbachev's assertion in his January 15, 1986, statement on disarmament that the USSR was prepared to come to terms on whatever might be necessary in the way of verification. Moscow kept the issue of U.S. warheads for the West German P-Ia's alive, however, and sought to put further pressure on the United States and Bonn to back down. Nevertheless, on July 30 it was announced that Shevardnadze would meet with Shultz in Washington on September 15–17.[33] At the same time, Soviet negotiators at last submitted draft defense and space and START treaties in Geneva. The latter now formally combined the concept of 50-percent reductions, including on heavy missiles, with an overall limit, as proposed by the United States, of 1600 delivery vehicles and 6,000 warheads. It continued to reject the U.S. proposals for ballistic missile warhead sublimits, however, defending the right of each side to structure its forces as it saw fit within the overall established framework.[34] Subsequently, however, during Shevardnadze's talks in Washington, the Soviet side reintroduced its own notion of a 60-percent sublimit on the proportion of the 6000 warheads that could be deployed in any one component of the strategic triad.[35]

Curiously, Gorbachev's own public silence on the P-Ia issue was lost in the din of the demands by other Soviet spokesmen and negotiators for the elimination of the warheads. On August 7, in his last public appearance before going on vacation until late September, the general secretary sounded surprisingly upbeat when he met with a group of American teachers of Russian in the Kremlin. "Notwithstanding all the difficulties, I think that I and the President have a serious dialogue going," he told them. Appraising the upcoming Shultz-Shevardnadze talks in Washington, Gorbachev said that he hoped there would be "a very serious discussion. We hope that all the same it will be possible to reach accords on medium and operational-tactical missiles as a minimum."[36] Two weeks later, Dobrynin and other Soviet officials gave Senator Alan Cranston the "clear impression" that a compromise on the Pershing Ia's was possible.[37]

The general secretary did not commit himself publicly and personally on the Pershing Ia warhead issue until August 25. Even then, Gorbachev's reference was oblique, he went no further than to state that a treaty could be signed "tomorrow" if the United States and the FRG "removed the obstacle that everyone knows about."[38] The following day, Chancellor Kohl made his surprise announcement that the FRG would forego modernization of the Pershing Ia and would eliminate the missiles in the context of a signed and fulfilled INF Treaty.[39] The sequence raised the possibility that Gorbachev had obtained advance notice of the impending Kohl statement and had made his own first comments on the issue only with the secure knowledge that Kohl was about to provide a face-saving solution.

SEPTEMBER MINISTERIAL

Given what seemed Gorbachev's intention to clear the way to a summit, it can be argued that the Soviet side would have worked itself out of its uncompromising position on the Pershing Ia issue on its own—even without Kohl's statement or the follow-up State Department press response in Washington stating that the United States would withdraw the Pershing Ia warheads once the FRG retired the missiles.[40] On September 6 Soviet commentators were reassuring the public that not only the USSR but also the United States had had to make compromises to bring an INF Treaty so close to fruition, and they were reminding listeners of the "enormous threat" posed by the Pershing II, which would now be eliminated.[41]

On September 10, in his widely noted speech devoted to the one hundred and tenth anniversary of the birth of Dzerzhinskiy, KGB Chief Viktor Chebrikov issued what may have been a veiled warning to skeptics of the evolving INF deal to hold their tongues. Dzerzhinskiy, Chebrikov recalled, "sometimes made mistakes, but he always perceived party decisions as a directive, as an order, and rigorously implemented them." This had happened in the debate over the 1918 Brest Peace with Germany, with which Dzerzhinskiy disagreed. Nevertheless, he had "decisively dissociated himself from the tactic of the 'left communists,' which was threatening to split the party."[42] Chebrikov's remarks recalled the warning by Pankov a year earlier, pre-Reykjavik, against any "leftists" who might be thinking of emulating the Trotskyite opposition to Lenin with the slogan "No compromise!"[43]

At the same time, Moscow put on an impressive show of *glasnost* and accommodation on a number of security issues other than INF. In late July publication at last of excerpts of Gorbachev's May 1986 speech at the Foreign Ministry set the stage. Then in late August the USSR made its admission that the public Soviet defense budget did not include weapons or research and development. Elsewhere, also in late August, the USSR earned praise for its handling of the first on-site, on-demand inspection by the United States, under the CDE agreement concluded in Stockholm less than a year earlier, of a military exercise on Soviet territory.[44]

In early September Moscow opened the controversial Krasnoyarsk radar site for a four-hour inspection by a U.S. congressional delegation.[45] Akhromeyev, it will be recalled, had mentioned the issue for the first time in the Soviet media only two years before. In October, Western experts were shown the chemical weapons facility at Shikhany.[46] Only in March had the Soviet representative to the 40-nation Conference on Disarmament in Geneva even acknowledged that the USSR produced and stockpiled chemical weapons.[47] Then in April Gorbachev had announced the end of Soviet production of chemical weapons (not independently confirmed) and the start of construction of a special chemical weapons destruction facility.[48] Here again, although the Soviet tour was highly controlled, Moscow's position had taken great strides in a short time.

During Shevardnadze's three days of talks with Shultz in Washington in mid-September, the Soviet position on SDI and the ABM Treaty underwent the most significant retreat to date. As long ago as at Reykjavik, Gorbachev had declared that "SDI does not scare us."[49] Only now, however, was Gorbachev's declaration beginning to be reflected in Moscow's negotiating position on defense and space issues. Shevardnadze offered a choice of two approaches which went beyond that proposed by Gorbachev in April. The first called for "strict" adherence to the ABM Treaty but conceded that both sides could pursue research consistent with the treaty "as it was signed and ratified in 1972." The alternative approach proposed negotiations on a "labs-list" regime of thresholds explicitly defining what could or could not be tested in space. The Soviet side, moreover, handed over a draft of such a list, which amounted at last to acceptance by Moscow of the principle that some SDI testing could be carried out in space rather than confined to laboratories on earth.[50] Meanwhile, in a major article in *Pravda* addressed to the UN General Assembly, Gorbachev asserted that a

START agreement on 50-percent reductions would be possible in the "first half" of 1988 given the "strict observance" of the ABM Treaty.[51]

After Shevardnadze's three days of talks with Shultz, the two sides announced on September 18 agreement "in principle" to conclude an INF treaty. Furthermore, Moscow agreed to cooperate with the United States in designing and conducting a Joint Verification Experiment (JVE) at test sites in the United States and USSR in order to elaborate improved verification measures for the TTBT and the PNET. This would be the first task of "full-scale stage-by-stage negotiations" on nuclear testing which would get under way by the end of November. The USSR thus conclusively dropped its insistance that nuclear testing talks be aimed exclusively and from the start at a comprehensive test ban. In their joint statement, Shultz and Shevardnadze announced that they would meet again in Moscow in the last half of October. At that time, said the statement, they would settle on the exact dates for the "fall of 1987" summit at which Reagan and Gorbachev would sign an INF treaty "and cover the full range of issues in the relationship between the two countries."[52]

OCTOBER FLIP-FLOP

During his press conference at the conclusion of the Washington ministerial, however, Shevardnadze cautioned, "Unfortunately, . . . we have not yet been able to bring our positions substantially closer together in the question of the 50-percent reductions of strategic offensive weapons in the context of strict compliance with and strengthening of the regime of the ABM Treaty." This, he warned, was "the root question of Soviet-US relations," and had "to be moved forward in the period remaining before the [October] meeting of the ministers, so that they could prepare productive agreements for approval at the summit." Shevardnadze recognized that it was "evidently impossible to change the mind of the US Administration" on SDI. But the USSR, he stated, still insisted that "at a minimum, it is necessary to ensure that strict observance of the conditions of the ABM Treaty is preserved if only for 10 years."[53]

At about this same time, as we have seen, Gorbachev completed the manuscript of his book *Perestroika*. In it he reiterated that at Reykjavik the "key point proved to be observance of the ABM Treaty." A year after the event he still insisted that "we are not giving the matter up as lost." And despite the delinking of INF from the Reykjavik package, he still warned that "since the Americans want to get rid of the ABM Treaty and pursue SDI—which is an instrument for ensuring domination—then there is need for a package where everything is interconnected."[54] Gorbachev's discussion was entirely consistent with the line he would take with Shultz a month later when the two met in the Kremlin. When Shevardnadze, after visiting the UN, Brazil, Argentina, and Uruguay, finally got back to Moscow and reported on October 15 to the Politburo on his discussions in Washington, the official press release on the session stated that the Politburo had "noted the importance" of successfully concluding an INF treaty for following through on the "accord in principle" which Shevardnadze had reached in the United States. The press report, however, made no mention of a summit or of the Politburo having formally "approved" Shevardnadze's negotiations in Washington—in retrospect another sign of trouble ahead and one that occurred well before the October 21 plenum and the crystallization of the Yeltsin affair.[55]

Thus when Gorbachev, in his meeting with Shultz on October 23, backed away from setting the dates for the Washington summit, there were definite grounds for seeing parallels with Reykjavik. The U.S. side was again unwilling to accept limits on SDI and furthermore was not yet ready fully to engage and respond to the new Soviet proposals presented in Washington in September. But merely signing the INF agreement would not be enough for another summit, Gorbachev insisted to Shultz. It was also necessary to immediately "coordinate positions" on START and defense and space issues. At the Washington summit it should be "possible, along with the signing of a treaty on medium- and shorter-range missiles, to record an accord on the key provisions of future agreements on strategic offensive arms and space, which in their turn, could be signed during Ronald Reagan's reply visit to the Soviet Union." But for now, said Gorbachev, "I am put on my guard by possible results."[56] It clearly appeared to be a last-minute effort by Gorbachev to hold up the almost completed INF treaty and the lure of a summit in order to force U.S. concessions on SDI.

Shultz's talks in Moscow had begun the day after Yeltsin's outburst at the Central Committee plenum. When word of the Yeltsin affair began to leak, it appeared to some that Gorbachev's reluctance to settle on the summit may have resulted from pressure from hard-liners in the leadership. Despite widespread speculation to this effect, however, the more likely explanation was that the Yeltsin affair simply added to Gorbachev's irritation over the failure of the United States to respond to his satisfaction to Soviet movement in START and on the ABM Treaty. Indeed, the new positions presented by the Soviets during the Shultz visit were indicative of consensus rather than disarray on arms control issues and relations with the United States. The Soviet side now offered for the first time to consider—within an overall 6000-warhead ceiling and with both sides pledging not to withdraw from and "strictly" comply with the ABM Treaty for 10 years—sublimits of 3000–3300 warheads on ICBMs, 1800–2000 warheads on SLBMs, and 800–900 warheads on ALCMs. It also introduced a unilateral one-year moratorium on work on the Krasnoyarsk radar, toured in September by a U.S. congressional delegation.[57]

What seemed to be the Soviet game plan to pressure the United States emerged at Shevardnadze's press conference on October 23, after the Shultz-Gorbachev talks. In his opening statement Shevardnadze said that the new Soviet START proposals "will possibly require some time for their specific, in-depth examination by the US Administration" and that Moscow was "prepared to wait." He then agreed with what appeared to be a well-primed questioner's suggestion that the United States sought to undermine the ABM Treaty, and added the prediction that "the world public will react appropriately to this US stance."[58]

Moscow, however, clearly miscalculated both the Western public's ability to appreciate the Soviet movement on sublimits and the extent to which this movement would inspire public opinion to pressure the United States for reciprocal concessions on the ABM Treaty in order to free the way for a summit. Indeed, the subject was much too arcane even for the Western press corps to absorb immediately and report from Moscow. As a result, the Soviet movement on sublimits was totally eclipsed by the uniformly negative reaction in Western Europe and the United States to Gorbachev's sudden reluctance to schedule the summit and his hardened stance on summit conditions.

The impression that differences in the Soviet leadership did not extend to U.S.-Soviet relations and arms control was reinforced by Moscow's ability to recover quickly and decisively to its own fumble. Within a week, on October 30, Shevardnadze met with Shultz and Reagan in Washington, and the summit was finally set to begin on December 7. Gorbachev's display of pique, however, was not in vain. In Washington the United States in fact did agree in part to what Gorbachev had sought in Moscow the week before by way of a commitment to work on a "key provisions" document at the summit. According to the October 30 Joint Statement, Reagan and Gorbachev would "examine in an all-round way the issue of drafting instructions for their delegations regarding a future treaty on a 50 percent reduction in United States and Soviet strategic offensive arms and an accord on observing the treaty on limiting antimissile defense systems and not violating it during an agreed-on period."[59]

The consistency of Gorbachev's treatment of "new thinking" in *Perestroika* in mid-September and in his November 2 speech commemorating the seventieth anniversary of the Bolshevik Revolution, moreover, seemed also to belie the notion that hard-liners had taken advantage of the Yeltsin affair to force Gorbachev into retreat on foreign policy. In both cases, rather than retreating, Gorbachev pushed "new thinking" to new frontiers.

In *Perestroika* Gorbachev explained in explicitly detailed fashion why key passages dealing with class struggle in the 1961 Party Program had been reformulated or excised from the new edition approved by the 27th Congress. Gorbachev repeated that "ideological differences should not be transferred to the sphere of interstate relations." This had been one of the first glimmers of "new thinking" under Andropov, when the notion cropped up in the Warsaw Pact summit's Prague Declaration of January 1983. Two and a half years later, in October 1985, Gorbachev had resurrected the theme in Paris, and it was then included in both the draft and final texts of the new Party Program.

Discussing "new ideas about the correlation between class principles and principles common to humanity," Gorbachev in *Perestroika* again asserted that Lenin had spoken "more than once . . . about the priority of interests common to all humanity over class interests"—a point the general secretary had first made shortly after Reykjavik. Now there was an "objective limit for class confrontation" imposed by weapons of mass destruction and the "common human interest" in saving humanity from the threat of universal disaster. Thus it had been decided not to retain in the new Party Program the definition of peaceful coexistence as a "specific form of class struggle" and to exclude the possibility of a "cause-and-effect relationship between war and revolution."

Besides elaborating on these established themes, Gorbachev used *Perestroika* to begin developing the new notion that the military-industrial complex was not essential to the economic vitality of the United States. Nobel Prize laureate V. Leontyev had proved, wrote Gorbachev, that "the militarists' arguments do not hold water from an economic standpoint."[60] Rather than backtracking in the midst of the Yeltsin affair, on November 2 Gorbachev went even beyond this. "Is the capitalist economy capable of developing without militarization?" he asked rhetorically. After noting the experiences of Japan, West Germany, and Italy, Gorbachev concluded that "a number of countries did go through a period of rapid development of the contemporary capitalist economy with minimal military expenditure, and this experience has remained a part of history." After further discussion, Gorbachev returned to this point. "We are convinced—and science confirms it—that, at the present level of technology and organization of production, putting industry back onto a civilian footing and demilitarization of the economy are possible."[61] Although he made the statement in the context of discussing "monopoly capital," he also likely meant it as a comment on the Soviet Union's own economy and military-industrial complex.

WASHINGTON SUMMIT: "TESTING AS REQUIRED"

In any event, after one more ministerial in Geneva on November 23–24 and down-to-the-wire negotiations on remaining technical details, Reagan and Gorbachev finally signed the INF Treaty in the White House on the afternoon of December 8. Two days later they issued a joint statement reiterating their agreement at the Geneva summit two years earlier that "a nuclear war cannot be won and must never be fought." It also registered impressive progress on a number of Geneva issues, including agreement on a subceiling of 4900 ICBM and SLBM warheads within an overall aggregate of 6000 warheads on 1600 strategic nuclear delivery vehicles; a subceiling of 1540 warheads on 154 heavy missiles; a commitment to establish a ceiling on nuclear-armed SLCMs, not to be included in the overall 1600/6000 START totals; and, perhaps most crucially, the following statement on the START-ABM Treaty relationship:

> Taking into account the preparation of the Treaty on Strategic Offensive Arms, the leaders of the two countries also instructed their delegations in Geneva to work out an agreement that would commit the sides to observe the ABM Treaty, as signed in 1972, while conducting their research, development, and testing as required, which are permitted by the ABM Treaty, and not to withdraw from the ABM Treaty, for a specified period of time.[62]

A number of factors appeared to have taken the edge off near-term Soviet anxieties over SDI, though in the long term they remained considerable. First, there was a greater appreciation in both the United States and USSR of the immense technological hurdles that SDI would have to surmount to achieve anything close to President Reagan's original hope of an impenetrable space "shield." Second, the U.S. Congress was increasingly reluctant to satisfy the Reagan administration's funding requests for SDI. Its disinclination was provoked by doubts as to SDI's feasibility, by the alarming federal budget deficit, and by concerns over the impact of SDI on the ABM Treaty and on the prospects for productive U.S.-Soviet disarmament negotiations in general. Finally, there had been a fundamental reappraisal in Moscow of what it would take to counter SDI. Rather than prescribing an enormously expensive program to match SDI, Soviet specialists now claimed that there were much cheaper ways simply to counter and render SDI useless.[63]

None of these factors, however, lessened Moscow's ultimate concern to preserve the ABM Treaty and constrain SDI within stable limits and fairly predictable outcomes. The United States and USSR would quickly disagree on the interpretation of the Washington summit compromise language on the ABM Treaty—not surprising given that it was essentially a pragmatic agreement to continue to disagree while moving forward on other issues—and there would be no START Treaty concluded during the time in office remaining to the Reagan administration. Nevertheless, what could not be denied was that Soviet positions on the Geneva negotiations and SDI had changed dramatically in less than three years under Gorbachev. In January 1985 Gromyko as foreign minister had sought to kill SDI by linking resolution of INF with START and defense and space issues, and calling for a ban even on "research" or "scientific-research work" on space weapons of any basing mode. Now the Politburo had put its imprimatur on the notion that the ABM Treaty did after all permit some "research, development, and testing"—even of SDI.

NOTES

1. *Literary Gazette*, January 14, 1987 (FBIS-SOV, January 15, 1987, A 5).

2. Moscow Television Service, January 24, 1987 (FBIS-SOV, January 28, 1987, AA 10).

3. *Washington Post*, January 11, 1987.

4. *New York Times*, January 16, 1987.

5. In its analysis of the Tower Commission Report, for example, TASS asserted that "the investigators went out of their way to absolve the administration of the charges that it had deliberately tried to cover the tracks and conceal the truth about the 'Irangate'" (TASS, February 26, 1987 (FBIS-SOV, February 27, 1987, A 1)).

6. *Rude Pravo*, February 6, 1987 (FBIS-SOV, February 12, 1987, F 3).

7. *Pravda*, March 1, 1987 (FBIS-SOV, March 2, 1987, AA 1–3).

8. Moscow Television Service, February 16, 1987 (FBIS-SOV, February 17, 1987, AA 15–26).

9. The foreign minister was in East Berlin on February 2–4 and in Prague on February 4–5; the defense minister was in Czechoslovakia on February 9–13.

10. North Atlantic Treaty Organization, Special Consultative Group, "INF: Progress Report to Ministers (Brussels: NATO Press Service, December 8, 1983), 17 and 42–43.

11. TASS, April 6, 1987 (FBIS-SOV, April 7, 1987, A 2).

12. *Pravda*, April 11, 1987 (FBIS-SOV, April 14, 1987, F 13).

13. The argument that the zero option was prejudicial to NATO's flexible response strategy could be heard again after Reykjavik. The USSR had indeed provisionally agreed to dismantle its SS-20s opposite Europe. But the debate over the adequacy of NATO's available options for flexible response once all Pershing IIs and GLCMs were dismantled sounded remarkably similar to that which had led to NATO's INF deployment decision in the late 1970s in the first place, though the psychological climate was now much different. For

a reflective survey of post-Reykjavik trends in Europe, see *Christian Science Monitor*, July 28–31, 1987.

14. *Pravda*, April 15, 1987 (FBIS-SOV, April 15, 1987, A 7); Secretary Shultz, *The New York Times*, April 16, 1987, and "The INF Treaty," 7.

15. *Pravda*, April 22, 1987 (FBIS-SOV, April 22, 1987, F 5).

16. *Pravda*, April 15 and 22, 1987 (FBIS-SOV, April 15 and 22, 1987, A 6–8 and F 6, respectively). See also Karen Puschel, "Gorbachev and Arms Control: Learning to Live with SDI," *Survival*, 31, no. 1 (January–February 1989): 39.

17. Ibid

18. *New York Times*. April 28, 1987.

19. DPA, July 16, 1987 (FBIS-WE, July 16, 1987, H 1).

20. BTA, May 6, 1987 (FBIS-EE, May 8, 1987, C 8).

21. ADN, July 15, 1987 (FBIS-EE, July 16, 1987, G 1).

22. *Pravda*, May 20, 1987 (FBIS-SOV, May 21, 1987, E 8).

23. *The Sunday Times*, May 10, 1987.

24. Moscow Domestic Service, May 5, 1987 (FBIS-SOV, May 6, 1987, AA 4). The agreement would be signed in Washington by Shultz and Shevardnadze on September 15, 1987, with President Reagan presiding over the Rose Garden ceremony at the White House.

25. *Sovetskaya Kultura*, May 21, 1987 (FBIS-SOV, June 10, 1987, R 11–15). Public opinion polling in Europe was indeed revealing greater trust in Gorbachev as a man of peace than in Reagan (*Washington Post*, May 29, 1987).

26. *Red Star*, May 22, 1987 (FBIS-SOV, June 4, 1987, V 7).

27. Gerasimov in *Rude Pravo*, May 23, 1987 (FBIS-SOV, June 2, 1987, AA 2); Obukhov in *Izvestiya*, May 28, 1987 (FBIS-SOV, June 4, 1987, AA 1).

28. *Izvestiya*, June 4, 1987 (FBIS-SOV, June 15, 1987, AA 1).

29. AFP, May 26, 1987 (FBIS-SOV, May 28, 1987, A 5). Soviet jamming of BBC Russian broadcasts had ceased in January 1987 (Press Association, January 21, 1987 [FBIS-SOV, January 22, 1987, CC 1–2]).

30. *New York Times*, July 1, 1987.

31. Budapest Television Service, June 18, 1987 (FBIS-SOV, June 22, 1987, G 5).

32. *Pravda*, July 23, 1987 (FBIS-SOV, July 23, 1987, CC 1–10).

33. The Soviet announcement, as was customary, did not give precise dates. See TASS, July 30, 1987 (FBIS-SOV, July 31, 1987, CC 1).

34. *Pravda*, July 30, 1987 (FBIS-SOV, July 31, 1987, AA 1–2); and TASS, July 31, 1987 [FBIS-SOV, August 3, 1987, AA 1].

35. TASS, September 22, 1987 (FBIS-SOV, September 23, 1987, 12–13).

36. *Pravda*, August 8, 1987 (FBIS-SOV, August 11, 1987, A 7 and 9).

37. *Washington Post*, August 22, 1987.

38. In his "appeal" to the UN conference on disarmament and development (*Pravda*, August 26, 1987 [FBIS-SOV, August 26, 1987, CC 5]).

39. For the main points from Kohl's statement, see Bonn Federal Press and Information Office, August 26, 1987 (FBIS-WE, August 27, 1987, H 1–2).

40. *Washington Post*, September 3, 1987.

41. *International Observers' Roundtable*, Moscow Domestic Service, September 6, 1987 (FBIS-SOV, September 8, 1987, 8–13).

42. *Pravda*, September 11, 1987 (FBIS-SOV, September 15, 1987, 30).

43. *Pravda*, September 1, 1986 (FBIS-SOV, September 5, 1986, CC 2–4).

44. *New York Times*, September 22, 1987.

45. *New York Times*, September 7, 1987; and *Washington Post*, September 9, 1987.

46. *Washington Post*, October 5, 1987.

47. *New York Times*, March 6, 1987.

48. *Pravda*, April 11, 1987 (FBIS-SOV, April 14, 1987, F 16). On January 8, 1989, at the Paris conference devoted to strengthening compliance with the 1925 Geneva Protocol, Shevardnadze would announce that the USSR would begin later in the year to destroy some of its chemical weapons stockpile.

49. Moscow Television Service, October 12, 1986 (FBIS-SOV, October 14, 1986, DD 35–36).

50. *Washington Post*, September 19, 1987; and *Christian Science Monitor*, September 30, 1987.

51. *Pravda*, September 17, 1987 (FBIS-SOV, September 17, 1987, 24).

52. TASS, September 18, 1987 (FBIS-SOV, September 21, 1987, 15).

53. *Izvestiya*, September 20, 1987 (FBIS-SOV, September 21, 1987, 17–18).

54. Gorbachev, *Perestroika*, 229.

55. Moscow Television Service, October 15, 1987 (FBIS-SOV, October 16, 1987, 49).

56. TASS, October 23, 1987 (FBIS-SOV, October 26, 1987, 3–5). For reports on the dynamics of the talks in Moscow, see *Wall Street Journal*, October 27, 1987; and *Washington Post* and *New York Times*, October 28, 1987.

57. TASS, October 23, 1987 (FBIS-SOV, October 26, 1987, 4).

58. *Pravda*, October 25, 1987 (FBIS-SOV, October 27, 1987, 12, 14).

59. *Pravda*, October 31, 1987 (FBIS-SOV, November 2, 1987, 14).

60. Gorbachev, *Perestroika*, 128–134.

61. Moscow Television Service, November 2, 1987 (FBIS-SOV, November 3, 1987, 56–58). See also Yu. Krasin's elaboration of this theme in *Pravda*, January 27, 1988 (FBIS-SOV, February 4, 1988, 4–6), where Krasin emphasizes that "the military—industrial complex is by no means synonymous with monopoly capitalism."

62. TASS, December 11, 1987 (FBIS-SOV, December 11, 1987, 15–17). For an account of the bargaining at the summit, see *Washington Post*, December 13, 1987.

63. For a fuller examination of the evolution in Soviet thinking, see Puschel, "Gorbachev and Arms Control." 34–51.

Chapter 14 ───────────────────────

Withdrawal from Afghanistan

─────────────────────────────────────

Gorbachev's February 8, 1988 declaration that Soviet troops would leave Afghanistan within ten months of a peace settlement coincided with the beginning of "ratification" hearings on the INF Treaty before a special Supreme Soviet commission on February 9. In retrospect, a strong case could be made that the Soviet leadership had been working the INF and Afghan problems on parallel tracks for at least two years. The difference was that the INF track had been highly visible and more credible, whereas the Afghan track had been for the most part submerged and not very convincing until the very end.

In both instances, INF and Afghanistan, Moscow had started out hoping for a much better deal than it eventually got. On Afghanistan especially, in the end Moscow had to settle for far less than it originally saw as acceptable—or could even have envisioned as remotely possible. The withdrawal from Afghanistan was a painful, protracted decision-making process in which Moscow's bargaining hand steadily deteriorated after summer 1986. It was made all the more agonizing by the revitalized supply of Western arms to the Afghan resistance, most notably Stinger missiles, which suddenly and dramatically devalued Moscow and Kabul's military and political assets.

After years of resisting putting forward a concrete timetable, Moscow went from an initial proposal in 1986 of four years to final agreement in 1988 on nine months. In the end the Gorbachev regime was forced to give up its insistence, inherited from earlier Kremlin leaderships, on the need for an end to "outside" interference before a Soviet troop withdrawal could commence. As the Soviet withdrawal finally began on May 15, 1988, Moscow had no guarantee and probably scant hope that its client regime in Kabul would survive for long after February 15, 1989, and completion of the departure of all Soviet troops.

DOUBLE-TRACKING INF AND AFGHANISTAN

In retrospect, this book has argued, it appears most likely that 1985 saw the beginning of a multifaceted effort by the new Gorbachev leadership to work toward extricating Soviet forces from Afghanistan. This effort started to gather some still easily dismissed momentum in 1986 just as Soviet movement in INF began to attract far greater attention. At the 27th Party Congress in February 1986, Gorbachev's attention-riveting characterization of the Afghan situation as a "running sore" came little more than a month after his January statement on disarmament. This had contained some important concessions on long-standing INF issues and the first Soviet agreement to zero INF in Europe. Gorbachev's congress speech was soon followed by changes in Kabul, where Babrak Karmal's ouster as PDPA leader on May 4 and his replacement by security chief Najib suggested that Moscow realized it needed to have a more trustworthy and more nimble proxy on the spot in the Afghan capital. Three years later General Valentin Varennikov—General Staff supervisor of the war effort from approximately early 1985 until the Soviet withdrawal—would bitterly describe Karmal as "a demagogue of the highest class." According to Varennikov, Karmal "deserved the trust neither of his own colleagues, nor of his people, nor of our advisors."[1]

Coincidentally, Kabul also followed up on Gorbachev's congress promise of a specific troop withdrawal timetable, formally proposing four years to the Pakistanis at the Geneva proximity talks in May. Although there were intimations of negotiating flexibility, a timetable anywhere in the range of four years was ridiculously high. Moreover, it was still premised on the prior ceasing of outside interference and the establishment of a Kabul regime acceptable to Moscow. The offer was predictably rejected by the Pakistanis, who maintained that a Soviet withdrawal could be accomplished in four months or less.[2] But the specific timetable nevertheless indicated movement in Moscow toward a somewhat more defensible position.

Gorbachev's July 1986 call in Vladivostok for Afghan "national reconciliation" came little more than a month after a new Soviet START proposal dropped the attempt to double-count U.S. INF missiles in Europe. Gorbachev's notion of "national reconciliation" envisioned creating a government in Kabul that could include politicians abroad "ready sincerely to participate in the nationwide process of constructing a new Afghanistan" in other words, leaders of the Afghan resistance, or *mujahidin* need not apply. Nevertheless, although "national reconciliation" would later acquire ominous overtones for Moscow's allies in Kabul, for now it seemed simply propaganda aimed at relieving Western pressure to withdraw Soviet troops.

In addition, Gorbachev's appeal for "national reconciliation" appeared to be another instance of Gorbachev coopting the language of a U.S. proposal in order to give it his own interpretation. Although by now mostly forgotten, it had been none other than President Reagan who in October 1985 had called at the United Nations for negotiations of regional conflicts by the warring parties. In the case of Afghanistan, Reagan had specified that this should include the Soviet Union. The negotiating process would be designed to achieve "an end to violence, the withdrawal of foreign troops, and national reconciliation."[3]

The perception that the USSR was approaching Afghanistan basically as a public relations problem in dealing with Europe, the United States, and China was reinforced by the less-than-perfect execution of Gorbachev's announcement in Vladivostok that the USSR would withdraw six regiments from Afghanistan by the end of the year.[4] The pullback began in October[5] but appeared in part a sham and proved in whole a propaganda fiasco.[6] In addition to condemnation from the United States, Beijing dismissed the withdrawal ploy as "an obvious attempt to deceive the world," charging that it actually masked a reinforcement of 15,000 Soviet troops in Afghanistan with updated equipment.[7] Gorbachev's initiative seemed to have fallen victim to poor coordination with the military and to a deteriorating position in the field under the impact, beginning in late summer, of U.S. shipment of heat-seeking Stinger antiaircraft missiles to the Afghan resistance.[8] The Stingers reportedly claimed their first victims—three Soviet Hind Mi24 helicopter gunships trying to land at Jalalabad airport 60 miles east of Kabul—on September 26, 1986.[9] The missiles certainly did not help Southern Theater of Military Operations (TMO) Commander Zaytsev and 40th Army commander Boris Gromov, both appointed under Gorbachev in summer 1985, to improve the situation militarily, and the action may have forced an unanticipated recalculation of the wisdom of the partial withdrawal advertised by Gorbachev in Vladivostok.

The Stingers, however, most likely did not precipitate Moscow's decision to withdraw all its forces from Afghanistan. To the contrary, the Stingers probably sorely tested the existing intention and desire of the Gorbachev leadership to leave. The missiles, after all, arrived on the scene half-a-year after Gorbachev put the problem of Afghanistan firmly on Moscow's diplomatic agenda by referring to it as a "running sore" at the 27th Party Congress, and well after Najib's replacement of Karmal in Kabul. By challenging Soviet air supremacy over Afghanistan, the Stingers bolstered the morale and the battlefield fortunes of the mujahidin, thereby frustrating Soviet efforts to pressure the resistance into sharing power in Kabul on PDPA terms in return for Soviet withdrawal. Even while upsetting the basic premises of this scenario, in the end the Stingers probably sealed the Soviet decision to leave by putting a purely military solution further out of reach. Moreover, even as Moscow grappled for a way to get out, the Stingers devalued potential Soviet assets in any serious future bargaining over the terms of a Soviet departure, and made the likely results of a political solution—if one was to be made all the more painful.

"PLEASE HELP US"

After the mid-October summit in Reykjavik, Moscow struggled to figure out what to do next, not only in regard to INF and the Geneva talks but also on Afghanistan. The delinkage once again of INF from START and defense and space issues would not be announced until the end of February 1987. Meanwhile, and much earlier, a variety of public and private signals indicated that the process of sorting out the substance and timing of the upcoming INF move was not impeding movement on Afghanistan. A senior adviser to Gorbachev reportedly told an American member of the visiting U.S.-Soviet Dartmouth conference in November 1986, "we know we have to get out, but we don't know how to get out. Please help us." Only a month later, however, Gorbachev reportedly told Najib, who was in Moscow on December 11–14 on an "official friendly visit"—the first at such a high level in six years—that Gorbachev and Pakistan's Mohammed Zia would agree on a 12-month troop withdrawal timetable during talks planned for June 1987.[10] Three years later Najib confirmed that Gorbachev had issued what amounted to an ultimatum in December 1986, telling Najib that Soviet troops would be "out of Afghan territory in one and a half to two years."[11]

This private warning from Moscow had an almost immediate public reflection in Kabul. At the turn of the year Najib addressed an extraordinary expanded plenum of the PDPA Central Committee and announced a six-month ceasefire to begin January 15. This would facilitate a "speeding up" of national reconciliation and the active pursuit of "contacts with those taking part in gangs and with neutral forces." Najib declared that his regime had "no wish to exclude from the national reconciliation process the various political groups of a centrist and monarchist persuasion, or the leaders of armed anti-government groups operating abroad—that is, the mujahidin. However, dialogue with the opposition would apparently be only with those who "may accept a compromise with the people's power." Nevertheless, within this context the creation of a coalition government was a "possibility."[12]

Shevardnadze and Dobrynin visited Kabul on January 5–7 to underscore Moscow's sponsorship of Najib's new line. Shevardnadze waxed optimistically about the "real opportunity" for national reconciliation and predicted that the withdrawal of Soviet troops was "not far off." "There is unlikely to be anyone in the world who desires more strongly than we do the success of nationwide reconciliation in Afghanistan," Shevardnadze asserted. That, he said, would bring peace and "the rapid return of Soviet troops to the homeland—all our lads, who are awaited at home with such impatience, anxiety, and hope by mothers, fathers, wives, fiancées, and comrades at work."

Nevertheless, in Kabul Shevardnadze described the discredited and faction-ridden PDPA as the "backbone" of Afghanistan and reiterated Moscow's long standing precondition for withdrawal: "It depends first of all on the cessation of intervention from without and on guarantees that it will not be resumed." The linkage between national reconciliation in Afghanistan and reaching an accord in Geneva, emphasized the foreign minister, was "a very immediate one, very direct and close." Those who maintained that a peace accord depended only on the withdrawal of Soviet troops from Afghanistan "do not speak the truth."[13]

VORONTSOV'S TWIN ASSIGNMENTS

The parallel treatment of the Afghan and INF issues became even more pronounced, yet still hard to appreciate, in early 1987. Abroad Moscow put together its post-Reykjavik diplomatic strategy, while at home Gorbachev scored significant gains at the January plenum on cadre policy and democratization. In January First Deputy Foreign Minister Yuliy Vorontsov was named formal head of the Soviet delegation to the Geneva arms talks in a move meant to impart new momentum to the negotiations. Before long it also became evident that Vorontsov had acquired responsibility for high-level coordination of Soviet policy on Afghanistan; in 1988 he would even be posted to Kabul as Soviet ambassador while continuing to wear the hat of first deputy foreign minister.

At the end of February Gorbachev at long last announced Soviet willingness to reach an INF agreement delinked from START and defense and space issues. By mid-February the first call for the withdrawal of Soviet troops from Afghanistan without any preconditions had appeared in the Soviet press. Significantly, this remarkable though not widely distributed, appeal was signed by the liberal economist Yevgeniy Ambartsumov of Oleg Bogomolov's Institute for the Economics of the World Socialist System.

Bogomolov, as already noted, had worked for Andropov in the Central Committee in the 1960s. Bogomolov's institute, it would later become clear, had been a veritable nest of expert opinion arguing the case—up to now only in private—that the invasion of Afghanistan had been a mistake. Publicly other members of Bogomolov's institute—most memorably Yu. S. Novopashin in 1982—had made the case against military interventions in regional conflicts only obliquely (if still probably unmistakably to insiders) using the "force of example" argument. Now Ambartsumov openly called the continued Soviet military presence in Afghanistan "pernicious" and an obstacle to domestic perestroika.[14]

At about the time Ambartsumov's article appeared, former Secretary of State Henry Kissinger visited Moscow as part of a U.S. delegation that met with Gorbachev and other high officials. Reflecting on his many conversations in the Soviet capital, Kissinger found those on Afghanistan the most interesting. He arrived in Moscow convinced the Soviets would never permit the overthrow of the Kabul PDPA regime; he left "no longer so sure." Kissinger asked a "senior Communist" whether the Soviet leadership could "stand by while a communist government collapsed." His interlocutor pointed out that the government in Kabul "was not communist and technically not even socialist." His hosts "emphasized their desire for total withdrawal," wrote Kissinger. They also affirmed the goal of a government of national reconciliation that would include representatives of the guerrilla groups. They hinted at a short period for withdrawal; they seemed prepared to discuss, though not to be specific about, the evolution of the Kabul government after a withdrawal."[15]

In fact, the proposed Soviet withdrawal timetable soon did get dramatically shorter, yet still far from convincing. On a tour of Southeast Asia, on March 2 in Thailand Shevardnadze reportedly mentioned 22 months. This was reduced almost immediately to 18 months at the ongoing proximity talks in Geneva. Although Pakistan insisted on no more than 7 months, UN mediator Diego Cordovez was able to claim that the difference between the two sides had been reduced to less than one year.[16]

The next clear decision point on the parallel issues of INF and Afghanistan was revealed in Gorbachev's July 22, 1987, interview for *Merdeka*. Don Oberdorfer has concluded that the basic Soviet decision to withdraw from Afghanistan was made in April-July 1987[17]. According to one of his sources, the Politburo engaged in intense debate in spring 1987, and the Central Committee did much the same at its plenum in June. In any event, it was in the *Merdeka* interview that Gorbachev announced Soviet willingness to agree to a global double-zero accord on INF. It was also here, though less appreciated at the time, that Gorbachev stated that the Soviet Union was in favor of compressing the timetable for the withdrawal of its troops from Afghanistan. He announced that "in principle, the question of the withdrawal of Soviet troops from Afghanistan has been decided."[18]

In addition, Gorbachev also claimed to see "some encouraging signs" of progress on Cambodia.[19] In December 1978 200,000 Vietnamese troops had invaded that country and replaced the infamous Pol Pot's Khmer Rouge regime with one led by Heng Samrin. In September 1981, in the first of a series of annual withdrawals timed primarily to influence voting in the UN over Cambodian representation in the General Assembly, Vietnam claimed to have withdrawn some

24,000 troops.[20] But despite subsequent withdrawals and a pledge in 1985 by Hanoi and Phnom Penh to withdraw all Vietnamese troops from Cambodia by 1990,[21] the Vietnamese presence in Cambodia had been reduced to only about 140,000 by 1987.[22]

Now, however, with the Gorbachev regime eager to mend relations with China and with a leadership change in Hanoi, there were fresh diplomatic maneuverings. Shevardnadze had already held talks in Hanoi in March, during a long swing through Southeast Asia, and had discussed both a Cambodian settlement and normalization of Sino-Soviet relations.[23] On July 28 Gorbachev met with the vacationing Heng Samrin in Moscow.[24] In Phnom Penh the Heng Samrin regime would soon issue several policy statements on national reconciliation.[25] The first of these coincided with a meeting in Phnom Penh of representatives of the USSR, Vietnam, Laos, and Cambodia reportedly devoted to finding a political solution to the end of the Cambodian conflict.[26]

YAZOV REPLACES SOKOLOV

Sokolov's firing as defense minister in late May and his removal from the leadership at the June party plenum probably simplified the endgame not only on INF but also on Afghanistan. Sokolov had commanded the Soviet invasion force in late 1979. In an interview a decade later, General Varennikov claimed that the General Staff had opposed the invasion but that its advice had been ignored by Defense Minister Ustinov.[27] Varennikov did not mention what Sokolov's views had been, but it is noteworthy that Sokolov in 1979 was not in the General Staff. Instead, he worked directly for Ustinov as first deputy defense minister for General Matters and most likely, given subsequent developments, heartily endorsed the invasion plan. Sokolov had then apparently remained in charge of the overall Soviet military presence in Afghanistan until his promotion to defense minister in December 1984 after Ustinov's death.[28] In 1987, with not only INF but also Afghanistan on the front burner of Soviet decision making, it was therefore no wonder that Gorbachev and his supporters seized on the Rust-Cessna incident to oust Sokolov. "This is good news for you," a Soviet contact reportedly told UN Afghan mediator Diego Cordovez. A month later, as Yazov replaced Sokolov as a Politburo candidate member and Yakovlev was made a full member, the same Soviet source confided to Cordovez, "This is very important for you."[29]

Indeed, it is worth noting that even before this, and beginning at about the time of the January 1987 Central Committee plenum, the apparently increased resolve of the Soviet leadership to extricate itself from Afghanistan had coincided with the movement of Gorbachev appointees to key control points over military personnel: Lukyanov had become Central Committee secretary supervising the Administrative Organs Department; and Yazov had been promoted from the Far East to Moscow to replace Shkadov as deputy defense minister for personnel. Now in May-June 1987, Yazov made it all the way to the top over Sokolov's suddenly superannuated body.

Whatever Yazov's opinion of the war in Afghanistan, his involvement had clearly been less than central. He was in charge of the Central Group of Forces in Czechoslovakia when Soviet troops entered Afghanistan in 1979. From November 1980 to June 1984, he had commanded the Central Asian military district encompassing the Kazakh, Kirgiz, and Tadzhik republics and headquartered in Alma-Ata, Kazakhstan. In this capacity he had no doubt assisted the neighboring Afghan war effort. But command of the Soviet campaign in Afghanistan was actually located to the west in the Turkestan military district, covering the Uzbek and Turkmen republics. The headquarters of the 40th Army operating in Afghanistan was in Termez on the Uzbek-Afghan border. The 40th Army in turn was subordinate to the Turkestan military district and to the Southern Theater of Military Operations (TMO), both headquartered in Tashkent.[30] The Southern TMO reportedly had been created for the December 1979 invasion, was later disbanded, but then was revived in late 1984. The Central Asian military district at that time fell not within the jurisdiction of the Southern TMO but, rather, that of the Far Eastern TMO—reinforcing the impression that Yazov's involvement in the Afghan operation from late 1980 to mid-1984 had been more peripheral than direct.[31]

The impact of Sokolov's removal on both INF and Afghanistan, though important, should nevertheless not be overestimated. In INF hints of compromise toward global double zero began at least a week before Sokolov's ouster. Similarly, on Afghanistan Gorbachev had used his interview with the Italian Communist party newspaper *L'Unita* in mid-May to give his personal imprimatur to hints that a place might be found for the Afghan monarch Zahir Shah, living in exile in Italy since 1973, in a future government of national reconciliation in Kabul.[32]

Even with Sokolov removed in Moscow, moreover, the PDPA resisted Gorbachev's call for a compressed withdrawal timetable. That public declaration in *Merdeka* came just days after Najib arrived in the Soviet capital on July 19 for a working visit and meeting with Gorbachev.[33] Privately Gorbachev reportedly shocked Najib by bluntly telling him, "No matter what else you may have heard, I hope you are ready in 12 months because we will be leaving whether you are or not."[34] In September, on the eve of Shevardnadze's trip to Washington, a 12-month withdrawal period would be rumored but only a lengthy 16-month timetable actually offered, while the minimum Pakistani demand was for no more than 7 months.[35]

HINTS AT THE SUMMIT

Nevertheless, during the Washington ministerial in September at which the Pershing Ia compromise in INF was wrapped up, Shevardnadze privately told Shultz for the first time that he "would not exclude" that the issue of Soviet troop withdrawal from Afghanistan "could be resolved in the life" of the Reagan administration. Two months later Soviet Deputy Foreign Minister Vorontsov reportedly dropped further "strong hints" to U.S. Under Secretary of State Michael Armacost that the Soviet leadership was moving closer toward a decision on withdrawal. Vorontsov did not consistently repeat that a national reconciliation regime in Kabul acceptable to the Soviets had to be in place before the withdrawal of Soviet troops could begin. He also declared that the next round of proximity talks should take place in February and should be "the final round."[36]

Kabul finally formalized the offer of 12 months on the last day of November, a week before Gorbachev's departure for the Washington summit.[37] As Gorbachev arrived in Washington on December 6, *Moscow News* published Academician Andrey Sakharov's call for the "swift withdrawal of Soviet troops from Afghanistan"—the first time Sakharov's views on the issue were allowed to appear in the Soviet media.[38] Only the day before, Sakharov's signature had appeared alongside those of Gorbachev and other members of the Politburo and Secretariat on the official obituary of Academy of Sciences physicist Yakov Zeldovich.[39]

At the summit, Gorbachev reinforced Vorontsov's hints to Armacost. When he met with the press on December 10, Gorbachev did not reiterate the Soviet demand that agreement on a coalition government in Kabul be part of a withdrawal agreement. Instead, he stated, "Our position is that the beginning of the withdrawal of troops must at the same time become the beginning of the termination of assistance with arms and money to the dushmans [mujahidin]. From the very first day this is declared, our troops will start withdrawing." The Soviet withdrawal could thus precede rather than follow an internal political settlement. But Gorbachev refused to commit himself on when the Soviet withdrawal might begin.[40]

After the summit an unusual Central Committee conference on December 16 seemed a deliberate exercise in high-visibility Soviet hand-holding of a shaky and nervous Kabul regime. It was devoted to the question of "developing direct sponsorship links between Soviet republics and oblasts and Afghanistan's provinces."[41] Shevardnadze and

Ligachev both spoke, and Vorontsov, Slyunkov, Chebrikov, Dobrynin, and Murakhovskiy attended. Despite the VIP attendance, however, this was not a new policy; when in Kabul a year earlier, for example, Shevardnadze and Dobrynin had stressed the importance of trade and aid and Soviet assistance in developing the "social sphere" in Afghanistan.[42]

Shevardnadze, however, made a return visit to Kabul in early January 1988 which was anything but reassuring to the PDPA regime. For the first time he publicly declared that the USSR "would like the new year of 1988 to be the last year of the stay of Soviet troops in your country." The foreign minister stated that though the external and domestic aspects of an Afghan settlement were still "linked," the "main thing" now was to complete the Geneva process. The Soviet withdrawal would begin when the obligation of the US, as a guarantor of a peace accord, to cease aiding the Afghan resistance went into effect. Shevardnadze did not reject the suggestion that armed resistance might continue inside Afghanistan after such an accord went into effect. Instead, he put dissenters within the PDPA on notice against resisting the tide of Soviet policy when he warned that those who might "bring to the fore considerations of an ideological nature . . . risk putting themselves outside the highest moral law."[43]

Meanwhile, however, the U.S. position on the timing of an aid cutoff to the Afghan resistance was in flux. The perceived seriousness of the Soviet intent to withdraw caused a review in Washington of the U.S. agreement in principle in December 1985 to co-guarantee an Afghan accord with the Soviet Union. Up to this point the understanding had been that the United States would cut the flow of aid to the resistance as soon as the Soviet withdrawal began. The Reagan administration now stated that for this to happen, Moscow must also terminate its assistance to Kabul—a formulation that came to be known as "negative symmetry." In addition, the United States demanded that the Soviet pullout be "front-loaded"—in other words, that a major component of the Soviet presence be pulled out early in order to lessen the chances that the withdrawal could be reversed.[44]

GORBACHEV'S ANNOUNCEMENT

Despite this more demanding U.S. position, which Moscow rejected, on February 8 Gorbachev announced that the USSR was willing to pull its forces out in 10 months, beginning May 15, if the Afghan accords were settled by March 15. The Soviet Union, furthermore, was willing to front-load the withdrawal; in the subsequent accord this would be stipulated as the removal of half the Soviet troops in the first 90 days.

Moreover, the withdrawal would not depend on a prior internal political settlement in Afghanistan; Gorbachev accepted the possibility of even greater internal violence following the departure of Soviet troops. Finally, Gorbachev generalized his 27th Congress Afghan metaphor. "Regional conflicts," he stated, "are bleeding wounds which can result in gangrenous growth on the body of mankind." An Afghan accord would be "an important rupture in the chain of regional conflicts."[45]

The next day, as he opened the Supreme Soviet ratification "hearings" on the newly signed INF Treaty, Ligachev praised Gorbachev's Afghan statement as "splendid."[46] Ten days later, speaking to the February plenum of the Central Committee, Gorbachev drew a parallel between an Afghan accord and the INF Treaty, and asserted that the Politburo had begun to grapple with a way out of Afghanistan after the April 1985 plenum.[47] Four days later, in his Armed Forces Day report, Defense Minister Yazov sought to deflate speculation about high command resistance to an Afghan withdrawal when he called Gorbachev's February 8 statement "of immense significance."[48] Several months later, in his Victory Day article, Yazov went even further in his support of Gorbachev's approach to Third World conflicts when he endorsed the view that "the political settlement of the Afghan problem could serve as a model for the elimination of regional conflicts in other parts of the world."[49]

At about this time while the Pakistanis began to cast doubt on whether they would sign a peace accord with the Najib regime, the proximity talks resumed in Geneva on March 2. The only outstanding issue left to resolve with the United States lay outside the scope of the four "instruments" per se—that of aid "symmetry." This was the subject of reportedly intense, lengthy, and repeated representations by Shevardnadze to Shultz in late March in Washington—the same talks that settled the dates for the Moscow summit.[50] Before departing Washington, Shevardnadze told a press conference that "the Afghan question can be resolved without United States guarantees." Asked about the U.S.-suggested option of a joint cutoff of U.S. aid to the mujahidin resistance and Soviet aid to the Afghan government, or "negative symmetry," Shevardnadze replied categorically, "I rule this out."[51] In the meantime, however, the United States suggested the alternative position of "positive symmetry," by which it would continue supplying the mujahidin to the extent that the USSR continued to aid the regime in Kabul.

Despite considerable irritation over Washington's newly articulated insistence on aid symmetry, a Soviet decision to withdraw already seemed irreversible. Several events strongly reinforced the perception that this was the case. Institute director Bogomolov, for instance, was allowed to publish his letter (cited in an earlier chapter) suggesting that the Brezhnev leadership in 1979 had not consulted expert outside opinion on the wisdom of the invasion.[52] Top Soviet officials reinforced this notion by telling Westerners that only a handful of senior leaders had been involved in the decision.[53] Bogomolov's institute subordinate Ambartsumov, who a year earlier had called for an unconditional withdrawal, now reiterated that Afghanistan had been a "mistake" and criticized Gromyko for his role in the blunder.[54] Two months later yet another member of Bogomolov's institute, Vyacheslav Dashichev, would write that the invasion of Afghanistan had been the last straw in a series of "miscalculations" by the "incompetent approach of the Brezhnev leadership toward the resolution of foreign policy tasks."[55]

In addition, on March 16 Moscow announced the appointment of a new ambassador to Kabul, Nikolay Yegorychev. This was none other than the same Yegorychev who in 1967 had been removed as Moscow party chief, much as had Boris Yeltsin 20 years later. After serving three years as deputy minister for the automobile and tractor industry, Yegorychev had been sent in 1970 into diplomatic exile to Denmark and had returned to Moscow only in May 1984, precisely during Chernenko's deep freeze period. Now the Gorbachev regime was in effect sending this two-time political loser to Kabul—not an auspicious sign for the Soviet-dependent PDPA.[56]

Shevardnadze returned to Kabul a third time during the first week of April. While there he reportedly implied in messages to the United States that "positive symmetry" on military assistance was acceptable if the other issues were resolved. By April 5 the mood of negotiators at the proximity talks in Geneva changed from irritation over lack of progress to optimism that a peace accord would be signed shortly.[57] Then on April 7, Gorbachev met with Najib in Tashkent, and the two issued a statement declaring their belief that "the last obstacles to concluding the agreements have now been removed."[58]

Within a week the accords were signed in Geneva. Just before the ceremony Shultz submitted a statement to UN Secretary General Perez de Cuellar setting forth the U.S. view that it retained the right to continue "to provide military assistance to parties in Afghanistan" but would exercise restraint should the USSR also do so. The statement also declared that U.S. agreement to act as guarantor of the accords it was about to sign in no way implied recognition of the regime in Kabul as the "lawful" government of Afghanistan. On these two points Pakistan submitted a similar letter to Perez de Cuellar.[59]

On May 15, 1988, Soviet troops began to leave Afghanistan. Perhaps unintended, it happened to be the thirty-third anniversary of the signing of the State Treaty which ended the post-World War II allied occupation of Austria and led, after a decade of stalling, to the withdrawal of Soviet troops from that country. More to the point, and definitely intended, it was only two weeks before Reagan arrived in Moscow to sign the INF ratification instruments with Gorbachev. On May 25 General Viktor Lizichev, chief of the Main Political Administration, gave the official—and first—figures for the casualties incurred by the Soviet Union while extending "fraternal assistance" to the PDPA regime since the intervention in late 1979 to the start of withdrawal on May 15: 13,310 dead, 35,478 wounded, and 311 missing in action.[60]

NOTES

1. *Washington Post*, March 20, 1989, quoting from the most recent edition of the weekly *Ogonek*.

2. *New York Times*, July 18, 1986.

3. Ronald Reagan, "A Foundation for Enduring Peace," address to the UN General Assembly, October 24, 1985, (Washington, DC: U.S. Department of State, Bureau of Public Affairs, Current Policy No. 756, October 1985), 3. A year later, in his next speech to the UNGA on September 22, 1986, Reagan would repeat the call for "national reconciliation." See idem, "Prospects for World Peace," address to the UN General Assembly, September 22, 1986 (Washington, DC: U.S. Department of State, Bureau of Public Affairs, Current Policy No. 867, September 1986), 3.

4. Moscow Television Service, July 28, 1986 (FBIS-SOV, July 29, 1986, R 18–20).

5. Moscow Television Service, October 17, 1986 (FBIS-SOV, October 20, 1986, D 1–2).

6. Craig Karp, "Afghanistan Resistance and Soviet Occupation." (Washington, DC: U.S. Department of St ate, Bureau of Public Affairs, Special Report No. 118, December 1984), 10–11.

7. *Renmin Ribao*, November 2, 1986.

8. Oberdorfer, "Afghanistan."

9. See David B. Ottaway's report on the background of the decision to provide the Stingers to the mujāhidin in "What Is 'Afghan Lesson' for Superpowers?" *Washington Post*, February 12, 1989.

10. Oberdorfer, "Afghanistan."

11. *Pravda*, November 28, 1989.

12. TASS, January 1, 1987 (FBIS-SOV, January 2, 1987, D 1–4).

13. See Shevardnadze's reception speech (*Pravda*, January 7, 1987 [FBIS-SOV, January 7, 1987, D 1–4]) and interview with BAKHTAR (*Pravda*, January 8, 1987 [FBIS-SOV, January 8, 1987, D 3–4]).

14. *Moscow News*, no. 5, February 8–15, 1987.

15. *Newsweek*, March 2, 1987, 40.

16. Cronin, "Afghanistan Peace Talks," 28–29.

17. Oberdorfer, "Afghanistan."

18. *Pravda*, July 23, 1987 (FBIS-SOV, July 23, 1987, CC 7–8).

19. Ibid.

20. *New York Times*, July 8, 1982.

21. SPK, August 16, 1985 (FBIS-EAS, August 16, 1985, H 1).

22. *New York Times*, July 11, 1987. For Phnom Penh's official chronology of Vietnamese withdrawals, which curiously begins only in 1982, see SPK, May 30, 1988 (FBIS-EAS, May 31, 1988, 34).

23. *Pravda*, March 14, 1987 (FBIS-SOV, March 16, 1987, E 8–9).

24. *Pravda*, July 29, 1987 (FBIS-SOV, July 29, 1987, D 1–2).

25. SPK, August 27, 1987 (FBIS-EAS, August 27, 1987, 16–17); and SPK, October 8, 1987 (FBIS-EAS, October 8, 1987, 17–18).

26. *New York Times*, August 30, 1987.

27. *Washington Post*, March 20, 1989.

28. Scott, "Soviet Defense Minister Sokolov"; and Mark L. Urban, "The Limited Contingent of Soviet Forces in Afghanistan," *Jane's Defence Weekly*, 1985, 3, no. 2 January 12: 71–72. General Valentin Varennikov, a first deputy chief of the General Staff since September 1979, most likely took over Sokolov's supervision of the war effort in Afghanistan about this time.

29. Oberdorfer, "Afghanistan."

30. On the Central Asian and Turkestan military districts, see Akhromeyev, *Voyenniy Entsiklopedicheskiy Slovar*, 701 and 757.

31. Urban, "Limited Contingent," 71–73; and Warner *et al.*, *Key Personnel*, 16, 21, 43, and 53–54.

32. *Pravda*, May 20, 1987 (FBIS-SOV, May 20, 1987, R 14).

33. He departed Moscow on July 21 but was not reported to have returned to Kabul until August 10 (*Pravda*, July 20 and 22 and August 11, 1987).

34. Oberdorfer, "Afghanistan."

35. *Washington Post*, March 11, September 6 and 13, 1987.

36. Oberdorfer, "Afghanistan."

37. *Izvestiya*, December 2, 1987 (FBIS-SOV, December 3, 1987, 37).

38. *Moscow News*, no. 49, December 6, 1987, p. 2 (BIS-SOV, December 15, 1987, 58)

39. *Pravda*, December 5, 1987 (FBIS-SOV, December 8, 1987, p. 82).

40. *Pravda*, December 12, 1987 (FBIS-SOV, December 15, 1987, 21).

41. *Pravda*, December 17, 1987 (FBIS-SOV, December 17, 1987, 35–36).

42. *Pravda*, January 8, 1987 (FBIS-SOV, January 8, 1987, D 5).

43. BAKHTAR interview carried by TASS, January 6, 1988 (FBIS-SOV, January 7, 1988, 23–25).

44. *New York Times*, January 8, 1988.

45. Moscow Domestic Service, February 8, 1988 (FBIS-SOV, February 8, 1988, 34–36).

46. Moscow Television Service, February 9, 1988 (FBIS-SOV, February 9, 1988, 1).

47. *Pravda*, February 19, 1988 (FBIS-SOV, February 19, 1988, 56).

48. *Red Star*, February 23, 1988 (FBIS-SOV, February 23, 1988, 70).

49. *Pravda*, May 9, 1988 (FBIS-SOV, May 10, 1988, 71).

50. *Washington Post*, March 28, 1988.

51. *Pravda*, March 25, 1988 (FBIS-SOV, March 26, 1988, 9).

52. *Literary Gazette*, March 16, 1988 (FBIS-SOV, March 15, 1988, 19).

53. *New York Times*, March 30, 1988.

54. *Asahi Shimbun*, March 12, 1988.

55. *Literary Gazette*, May 18, 1988 (FBIS-SOV, May 20, 1988, 7).

56. By October 1988, with the mujahidin unwilling to negotiate with the increasingly weak Najib regime over sharing power after the completion of the Soviet military withdrawal from Afghanistan, Yegorychev was replaced by the more authoritative Vorontsov in a last-minute effort to strike a deal or at least buy safe conduct for the departing Soviet troops.

Over the years the Central Committee status of the Soviet ambassador proved an interesting barometer of the urgency Moscow attached to its political dealings on the ground in Kabul: F. A. Tabeyev, appointed in November 1979, had been a full member of the Central Committee; P. P. Mozhayev, appointed in August 1986, had been only a candidate member; the hapless Yegorychev had long since lost all Central Committee status by the time he reached Kabul in March 1988; Vorontsov, in contrast, arrived in Kabul in October 1988 with the clout of full membership in the Central Committee, in addition to being first deputy foreign minister.

57. *New York Times*, April 6, 1988.

58. *New York Times*, April 8, 1988.

59. *Washington Post*, April 15, 1988.

60. TASS, May 25, 1988 (FBIS-SOV, May 25, 1988, 27).

Chapter 15 ─────────────────────────

Unilateral Cuts and Further Withdrawals

───────────────────────────────────────

S oon after the November 1988 elections in the United States, Gorbachev proposed to meet both President Reagan and President-Elect George Bush in early December in New York, where Gorbachev had suddenly elected to address the UN General Assembly. The US-Soviet get-together was formally announced on November 15,[1] and took place over lunch on Governor's Island in New York Harbor on December 7.

The meeting was clearly designed by the Soviet side to project continuity in U.S.-Soviet relations and serve as a bridge to the incoming Bush administration, partially short-circuiting the usual lull between presidencies in U.S.-Soviet relations. With decision making on the next five-year plan (1991–95) entering a more intensive phase in 1989, Gorbachev had every reason to work without respite for as much predictability as possible in U.S.-Soviet relations. Besides, Gorbachev had managed to turn every summit with Reagan—with the exception of Reykjavik—to his public relations advantage, not only worldwide but at home as well.

The morning of the scheduled Reagan-Gorbachev farewell, Gorbachev announced at the United Nations a dramatic, unilateral cut in the Soviet army and navy, bringing to a conclusion a debate and decision-making process that probably began in earnest in early fall 1987.

DECEMBER AND JANUARY ANNOUNCEMENTS

By the end of 1990—in other words, before the start of the 13th Five-Year Plan (1991–95)—Soviet forces would be reduced by 500,000 persons, including 50,000 troops and 5,000 tanks from Eastern Europe, and another 5,000 tanks from the European part of the USSR. In addition, a total of 8,500 artillery systems and 800 combat aircraft would be withdrawn from Eastern Europe and the European zone of the Soviet Union, an unspecified number of assault-landing and river-crossing units and armaments would be withdrawn from Eastern Europe, and Soviet divisions in Eastern Europe would be reorganized to give them an "unambiguously defensive" structure. Gorbachev also promised that Soviet armed forces in the Asian part of the USSR would be substantially reduced and that "a considerable part" of Soviet troops would be withdrawn from Mongolia. Finally, he announced that the USSR would be drawing up, as an experiment, plans for converting several defense enterprises to civilian production, and that it would be sharing its experience in shifting personnel and equipment from defense to civilian industry.[2]

Clearly any significant savings, coming early enough to be of any help in the next five-year plan, could be achieved only by a unilateral Soviet reduction of its own defense budget and standing conventional forces as soon as possible. The global elimination of all INF missiles, the impressive reductions envisioned in the START negotiations, and the ongoing withdrawal from Afghanistan had all contributed dramatically to lowering East-West tensions—but at best only marginally to easing the immediate burden of defense spending on the Soviet economy. In the Soviet Union, as in the United States, the lion's share of the defense budget remained devoted to developing and maintaining conventional forces. Any hopes the Gorbachev leadership had of significantly shifting priorities from defense spending to investment and consumption in the end could be realized only by cutting conventional forces.

The prospects for quickly negotiated mutual reductions, however, were slim at best, especially given European and Chinese distrust of Soviet offensively deployed tank divisions in particular. In May 1986 Gorbachev had revealed his exasperation over European perceptions of the Soviet threat to Spain's Felipe Gonzalez. "Is the idea that the USSR will send tanks into Europe in the event of a hypothetical conflict so deeply rooted in the European population and among the politicians of the new generation?" he asked.[3] A year wiser, he had returned to this theme in *Perestroika*, writing that he could understand Europe's fear of the USSR's "immense military might."[4] At about the same time, as we shall see, a debate clearly got under way in Moscow over the need and wisdom of the USSR's large standing forces.

In January 1989, six weeks after his speech at the UN, Gorbachev revealed to a Trilateral Commission delegation visiting Moscow that the military budget would be cut by 14.2 percent and the production of armaments and military technology by 19.5 percent. Furthermore, he stated that the upcoming cut of 500,000 troops would amount to a 12 percent reduction in Soviet armed forces personnel. Given historical precedents and the terms of reference of the debate over a unilateral cut that preceded Gorbachev's December 7, 1988 announcement, it could be speculated that Gorbachev would soon start working toward reductions beyond a half-million. His 12 percent reduction figure implied that the Soviets put their troop strength at about 4,167,000 and that this would drop to about 3,667,000 by the end of 1990—roughly equal to the 3,623,000 claimed by Khrushchev at the beginning of 1960. In light of the fact that Khrushchev had gone on to call for a further demobilization of 1.2 million—and that move had been praised, as we shall see, by some of the leaders in the 1987–88 debate—it all suggested that Gorbachev might have temporarily settled for less than he originally sought.

Gorbachev also told the Trilateral Commission that, of the 500,000 reduction, 240,000 would come from the European part of the USSR, 200,000 from its eastern part, and 60,000 from the south. He also adjusted slightly upward to 5,300 the number of tanks to come out of Eastern Europe, and specified that they would be not obsolete models but the "most modern" types. Furthermore, of the 10,000 tanks being cut in Eastern Europe and the European part of the USSR, 5,000 would be "physically liquidated and the remainder . . . converted into tractors for civilian needs, and training vehicles." Finally, Gorbachev stated that Soviet troops in Mongolia would be cut by 75 percent, and the Soviet aviation "grouping" in that country would be "liquidated."[5]

In January other Warsaw Pact members (except Romania) also announced force and budget reductions of their own. Writing in *Pravda* on February 9, Soviet Defense Minister Yazov stated that the Eastern European reductions would total more than 56,000 troops, more than 1,900 tanks, 130 combat aircraft, and "considerable quantities of other military hardware." He also asserted that their military budgets would be reduced on the average by 13.6 percent.[6]

DEBATE BEGINS

In a sense, as we have seen, the notion of a significant reduction or slowdown of defense spending had been in the air since Gorbachev first used the term "reasonable sufficiency" in Paris in October 1985. Khrushchev had invoked "sufficiency" 25 years earlier in justifying the demobilization of over one million troops and officers. Brezhnev had done likewise in Tula in January 1977—at a time, the West would later find out, when his leadership was cutting the rate of growth of defense spending in half. In 1985, however, Gorbachev had publicly promised not to cut defense spending even while reportedly putting the high command on notice in Minsk that thrift and concern for rebuilding the civilian economy were the priorities of the day.

In July 1988 Deputy Defense Minister for Armaments Vitaliy Shabanov claimed that Soviet military spending had begun to decline during the 12th Five-Year Plan (1986–90)—put more precisely by another senior Soviet official as "'slightly' each of the past two years."[7] But there had been no hard evidence of reduction in the overall rate of increase

of Soviet defense spending in the three years since Minsk, though
cutbacks had been observed in naval deployments.[8] Overall, the trend
in defense spending appeared to have been remarkably stable since
the halving of its rate of growth in the mid-1970s under Brezhnev.
Despite INF, Afghanistan, SDI, three Kremlin successions, and three
years of Gorbachev and "new thinking," the budget for the military
had continued to grow at an estimated steady rate of 2–3 percent per
year since 1976.

Well before Shabanov's statement, however, there had been a
number of indicators that Andropov and then Gorbachev and his allies
were preparing for a significant slowdown—though not necessarily an
absolute cut—in defense spending. These included, as discussed in
previous chapters, the post-Brezhnev moves to rehabilitate Khrushchev
as a historical figure—and the subsequent approving allusions to
Khrushchev's controversial military policies; the many indicators of a
decline in the military's political status, beginning with Ogarkov's ouster
from the General Staff in September 1984; Akhromeyev's new priority in
1985 on war prevention—a significant revision of military doctrine as left
by Ogarkov; and, beginning in mid-1986, the development by Gorbachev
and Akhromeyev of the notion that even conventional war, particularly
in Europe, could have consequences no less catastrophic than those of
nuclear war.

"NEW THINKING" HEATS UP

The incipient debate on a massive reduction in conventional forces
seemed to have entered a much more serious stage by October 1987,
just as negotiations on the INF Treaty were nearing completion. At
the top, Gorbachev was not only beginning to turn his sights to a
START treaty and a compromise on defense and space issues, but
he and Akhromeyev were also more frequently expressing the view
that any sort of meaningful victory in a mass conventional war was
out of the question. In August-September 1987, as we have seen,
Deputy Minister Petrovskiy revealed that the official defense budget
figure made public each year did not cover the cost of weapons or
research and development, and Gorbachev pledged greater *glasnost* on
military expenditures in two to three years as price reforms set the stage
for more valid international comparisons.[9]

In *Perestroika*, the drafting of which was largely finished by mid-
September 1987, Gorbachev wrote that he opposed "major unilateral
steps", begging the question as to what would constitute a "major" cut.[10]
In October, as we have seen, the slogans released for the upcoming
anniversary of the 1917 Revolution omitted the usual call for "Glory to

the valiant Armed Forces of the USSR!" In both *Perestroika* and his major speech on November 2, Gorbachev cautiously broached the possibility of demilitarizing the economy. And though it would not become known until publication of the transcript in early 1989, at the October 21, 1987, plenum Gorbachev gave notice that henceforth priority would be put on quality in the armed forces, thus hinting that perhaps quantity would not be as important as before.[11]

Meanwhile, the troika of Vitaliy Zhurkin, Sergey Karaganov, and Andrey Kortunov in October 1987 coauthored the first of several articles devoted to reasonable sufficiency. They largely discounted the threat of war, questioned the need for a large standing army, praised Khrushchev's unilateral demobilizations, and urged less superpower military competition in the Third World. Zhurkin at the time was a deputy director of the USA Institute, and would soon be tasked with setting up a new Institute for Europe. Karaganov was a section head at the USA Institute and would follow Zhurkin to the new institute. Kortunov was a senior researcher at the USA Institute but would soon move up to head its International Security and Politics section.

Their first article, "Reasonable Sufficiency—Or How to Break the Vicious Circle," was published in the foreign affairs weekly *New Times*.[12] Another Zhurkin-Karaganov-Kortunov article soon followed in the journal of the USA Institute, and before long an even more fundamental treatment of reasonable sufficiency appeared in the CPSU's own leading ideological journal, *Kommunist*. This argued, for example, that "if one uses one's common sense, it is hard to imagine any aims in whose name Western armies could invade the territory of the socialist states." Moreover, "Today and in the long term, the possibility of a premeditated nuclear attack, of a global nuclear aggression, so to speak, is as improbable as the conscious unleashing of a large-scale war in Europe." Furthermore, "If one looks at the issue of large-scale aggression or a major war between two systems, whether on a local or, worse still, global scale, bourgeois democracy does serve as a certain barrier to the unleashing of such a war."[13]

By February 1988, the public debate over a unilateral cut reached a startling level of specificity. In *Literary Gazette* economist V. M. Krivosheyev, yet another member of Bogomolov's Institute of Economics of the World Socialist System, said in an interview that "many socioeconomic problems could be resolved were it not for the forced diversion of resources for the arms race." By way of example, he said that "in the late fifties the Soviet Union unilaterally reduced its Armed Forces by 1.2 million men. This made it possible to build 100 major house building combines. In a comparatively short space of time housing construction was doubled in the country and the old-age pension was doubled."[14] Within weeks, air defense chief Tretyak called Khrushchev's

1.2 million demobilization "rash" and a "terrible blow at our defense capacity, and at our officer personnel." "We shouldn't," he warned, "be lured by apparent benefits."[15] Clearly at issue were not picayune reductions but cuts approaching or exceeding a million troops.

It was evident that a particularly sensitive point in all this was the fear that many officers might be forced to retire early and that the bitter experience of the Khrushchev era, when many lost all pension rights and suffered greatly reduced status, might be repeated. Indeed, in their remarks at the ratification hearings in the Supreme Soviet on the INF Treaty, Yazov and Akhromeyev sought to assure younger officers especially and their families that they would not be prematurely forced out of the armed forces.[16] It was in effect a dress rehearsal for similar assurances that would be given after Gorbachev's announcement at the UN in December. In addition, and also foreshadowing Gorbachev's UN industrial conversion initiative, General Yevgeniy Medvedev stated at the INF hearings that studies to develop a national program for converting defense industries to civilian production were getting under-way.[17]

Meanwhile, almost unnoticed, Defense Minister Yazov's Order of the Day for Armed Forces Day in February 1988 did not call for either "strengthening" or "maintaining" Soviet defense might—a further softening of Sokolov's relatively moderate call a year before for "maintaining" it at the appropriate level.[18] In his speech on the same occasion, furthermore, Yazov joined Gorbachev and Akhromeyev in declaring that a conventional war, given the "destruction of modern chemical enterprises and power facilities, including nuclear ones, would have catastrophic consequences comparable with a nuclear cataclysm." In addition, the defense minister claimed that the USSR had "reduced" the numbers of its ground forces along the Sino-Soviet border—above and beyond the previous year's partial withdrawal from Mongolia. This represented, in effect, unilateral Soviet movement beyond Gorbachev's July 1986 proposal in Vladivostok to discuss a mutual thinning of forces along the border with Beijing. Moreover, Soviet troop exercises in the Far East, Yazov said, were being conducted with "restraint," and the USSR was "not increasing their number and scale."[19] Even before this, Gorbachev's February 8, 1988, statement on Afghanistan had implicitly opened up the possibility of reducing overall Soviet troop strength by some 100,000—that is, by roughly the number that would be withdrawn from Afghanistan.

The INF ratification "hearings" and announcement of the decision to leave Afghanistan also unleashed a number of remarkable treatments in the Soviet media of past foreign policy decisions, not only under Brezhnev but also under Stalin. In his speech on February 22 even Defense Minister Yazov had used the very anti-Stalin formula "period of Stalin's personality cult." In the months that followed journalists and institute experts proceeded to score the decision-making process that had permitted not only the deployment of SS-20s and the invasion of Afghanistan but also the Nazi-Soviet pact and Stalin's postwar policy toward Eastern Europe, especially the 1948 split with Tito. Taken together, they helped the regime to create the appropriate atmospherics in which to forge ahead on further decisions implementing "new thinking."

The piece by Vyacheslav Dashichev of Bogomolov's institute, cited earlier in connection with Afghanistan, was particularly striking.[20] Stalin had transferred his approach to domestic politics to Soviet foreign policy, argued Dashichev, where "the hegemonist, great-power ambitions of Stalinism . . . repeatedly jeopardized political equilibrium between states, especially those East and West." Returning in essence to the theme of Plimak's essay in *Pravda* in November 1986, Dashichev wrote, "In the process the interests of the expansion of social revolution pushed into the background the task of preventing war." Attacking what in effect had been Gromyko's conduct of the Soviet anti-INF campaign but without naming Gromyko, Dashichev derided the approach to external affairs in which "on the one hand we heightened the level of military danger by advancing on the West's positions, and on the other we mounted a broad campaign in defense of peace and spared no resources to organize a mass movement of champions of peace." It was no wonder that "in the eyes of the overwhelming proportion of the Western public the Soviet Union is a dangerous power whose leadership wants to eliminate the bourgeois democracies by military means and to establish a Soviet-type communist system throughout the world."[21]

The Brezhnev-era leadership, charged Dashichev, had wasted the opportunities given it by the détente of the 1970s. Instead of diminishing the external threat "to the minimum level" and devoting attention to domestic reform and development, Soviet actions had led the West to perceive the USSR as "actively exploiting détente to build up its own military forces." The United States, "paralyzed by the Vietnam catastrophe, reacted sensitively to the expansion of Soviet influence in Africa, the Near East, and other regions." This process, which could have been avoided but for the "miscalculations and incompetent approach of the Brezhnev leadership," reached "critical limits" with the Soviet invasion of Afghanistan, provoking opposition from the "major world powers," in which Dashichev included China.[22]

It was now necessary, argued Dashichev, to surmount Stalinism totally in Soviet domestic and foreign policy. Giving absolute priority to "force of example" over "force of arms," Dashichev wrote that "the Soviet Union can and must influence world social progress exclusively via its economic, political, scientific, and cultural successes." And touching on the unilateral reductions debate, Dashichev asserted that it was "striking" that after the civil war and until 1931, the Soviet army had numbered only 560,000 men. "This shows the great services of a brilliant constellation of diplomats—Chicherin, Litvinov, Krasin, Borovskiy, and others—who managed to reduce the external threat to our country to a minimum. The size of our armed forces also indicated that the Soviet Union had no intention of threatening anyone."[23]

AKHROMEYEV AND "QUALITY OVER QUANTITY"

In late May 1988, little more than a week after Dashichev's stunning essay and as foreshadowed by Gorbachev in his as-yet-unpublished speech at the October 1987 plenum, the theses for the upcoming Party Conference announced that henceforth the emphasis in military development would be on quality rather than quantity and held out the hope of a reduction in the burden of defense.[24] In August, elaborating on the theses and Party Conference, Akhromeyev told a meeting in the General Staff that the new emphasis on quality over quantity meant the troops would probably be getting "less."[25]

Akhromeyev's retirement in December from the General Staff, where he would be succeeded by the 49-year-old Far East military district commander and Yazov protégé Mikhail Moiseyev, would coincide with Gorbachev's UN announcement of troop cuts, leading to speculation that Akhromeyev had opposed the move and resigned in protest.[26] More likely, Akhromeyev's retirement had been in the works for some time and simply got caught up in the last-minute planning for Gorbachev's trip and announcement.[27] Akhromeyev would later deny that he had opposed the cuts and would assert that the General Staff had been actively involved in working out their details "right from the start. I mean in summer 1988, not two or three days before Gorbachev's UN speech."[28] Akhromeyev's successor, Moiseyev, would underscore his continuity with Akhromeyev. In February 1989, in his first major public statement, Moiseyev would date the beginning of the "new stage" in organizing the Soviet armed forces, "linked with a defensive military doctrine and a phased arms reduction," to 1985–86—in other words, since Ogarkov's ouster from the General Staff in September 1984 and the rise of Akhromeyev and Gorbachev to power.[29]

Certainly Akhromeyev's yeoman service on behalf of Gorbachev's security and disarmament policies did not suggest a fundamental disagreement with the measures Gorbachev announced. Furthermore, Akhromeyev was the only officer included in the membership of the new Central Committee foreign affairs commission announced in late November 1988—again suggesting a close and mutually supporting relationship with Gorbachev.[30] Moreover, Akhromeyev's retirement proved to be simply a slowdown, and he continued to act as an adviser to Gorbachev on military matters in the latter's new role as chairman of the Presidium of the Supreme Soviet. Finally, the long-standing Gorbachev-Akhromeyev alliance served as a reminder, often ignored, that on this and other security issues there were probably few simple military-civilian splits. Rather, often there was probably a spectrum of opinion in both the civilian leadership and the military high command, with diverse coalitions drawing together members of both.

In any event, the dying down of the debate over reductions after February 1988 may have indicated that it had already been resolved in principle, whatever the eventual details and timing of an announcement. Such a conclusion, moreover, seemed to be reinforced by the new position on future conventional arms negotiations, first broached in Moscow at the end of May during the Reagan-Gorbachev summit[31] and then approved at the Warsaw Pact summit in July. On this latter occasion, although Gorbachev and his Eastern European counterparts meeting in Warsaw failed to announce a much-rumored pullout of Soviet forces from Hungary,[32] they nevertheless did approve a new three-stage framework for upcoming negotiations on conventional force reductions in Europe.

The new position differed significantly from the Budapest Appeal of June 1986. That document had called for first-stage reductions of 100,000–150,000 troops by both NATO and the Warsaw Pact within one or two years of the start of negotiations, followed by further cuts of 350,000–400,000 by each alliance during a subsequent second stage. The new position, in contrast, did not specify any first-stage reductions, calling instead for the first stage of negotiations to be devoted to exchanging and verifying data and to identifying and eliminating imbalances and asymmetries. Only in the second stage would the two sides proceed to mutual reductions of 500,000 on each side.[33] Thus at least theoretically, in not demanding matching Western reductions the new position opened the possibility of highly asymmetrical manpower cuts by the Warsaw Pact during the first stage of negotiations. It could not be precluded, furthermore, that these might even be unilateral. Realistically that made some sense, given that the chance of a negotiated agreement involving 23 countries anytime in the foreseeable future had to be considered close to nil, yet there were plenty of suggestions that the USSR had cuts it wanted to take anyway for economic reasons of its own.

Officially, however, the line as enunciated by both civilian and military leaders continued to be that any significant reductions would have to be on a mutual and negotiated basis. Though no doubt sincerely felt in some cases, in general it was more likely the usual attempt to screen ongoing private discussions from public pressure—and was by no means a principled and final rejection of a dramatically different outcome. In this connection it was instructive to remember that Shevardnadze had denounced as "immoral" the idea of delinking INF from other Geneva issues weeks before Gorbachev did just this in February 1988.

SHEVARDNADZE'S CONFERENCE

At Shevardnadze's late July 1988 conference at the Soviet Foreign Ministry, which Akhromeyev conspicuously attended, a wide range of options was raised on a variety of foreign policy issues, including troop and armament levels in Europe. In the published report on his opening speech, Shevardnadze revealed to the outside world that Gorbachev in May 1986 had called for an end to the military dictum that the USSR had to field as many weapons as all its potential opponents combined. He also expanded on Gorbachev's call at the party conference for an effective parliamentary "mechanism" for the discussion of international issues.[34] It was necessary, said Shevardnadze, "to introduce a legislative procedure in accordance with which all departments concerned with military and military-industrial activity will be under the control of the supreme nationwide bodies." Within their purview should be questions concerning the use of Soviet military power abroad, defense planning, and the military budget.[35]

After Shevardnadze's keynote address, more than 300 experts in eight different sections debated for three days the full range of Soviet national security issues. According to First Deputy Foreign Minister A. G. Kovalev's summary of the discussion on priorities in Soviet foreign policy, "the general view was that it would be unproductive to attempt to uncouple the United States from Western Europe." Opinion was divided on the desirability of a unilateral reduction of Soviet troops in Europe. The need for less secrecy on data about the Soviet armed forces "was expressed with exceptional sharpness." On regional issues, according to the summing up by Deputy Foreign Minister L. F. Ilichev, there was apparent unanimity on the conclusion that "the anticipated class alliance between the working people in the developing countries and the proletariat in the capitalist states did not take place." In his own concluding remarks, Shevardnadze emphasized the importance of "permanent dialogue and permanent contacts" between the United States and USSR.[36]

In the wake of the MFA conference, point men for "new thinking" developed all its themes even further, with Andrey Kozyrev, deputy chief of the Foreign Ministry's International Organizations Administration, going further than the rest. Kozyrev wrote that it was a myth that the class interests of socialist and developing countries coincided. The majority of developing countries, he asserted, leaned toward the Western model of development, and they suffered not so much from an excess of capitalism as from not enough of it. On Soviet security policy, he urged that rational, unilateral steps by the Warsaw Pact not be held up by what he called NATO's irrationality. It was possible, he argued, "to take convincing and major steps in the direction of sufficiency and of eliminating asymmetries in order to set an example."[37]

Kozyrev's advocacy of unilateral reductions, as well as discussions of military restructuring and reform in August by Oleg Bykov in *Pravda* and in November by Lieutenant Colonel Aleksandr Savinkin in *Moscow News*, seemed to confirm that the option of a unilateral reduction was still under consideration.[38] Savinkin went so far as to endorse Khrushchev's early 1960 goal of a 2,423,000-man army. By that time Shevardnadze had told a press conference in Washington in September that in Moscow "we are conducting a colossal amount of work on defining more precisely the basic military-technical parameters of a defensive doctrine, a doctrine of reasonable sufficiency."[39] Then on November 1, at a party meeting in Moscow at the Foreign Ministry, Shevardnadze had stated, "I think that in the very near future we shall be able to show convincingly that our military development . . . is moving ahead strictly in line" with the concept of a defensive military doctrine.[40]

The dramatic leadership changes approved at the September 30, 1988, plenum and the Supreme Soviet session the next day, however, did not suddenly make possible the reductions Gorbachev announced in early December; the evidence suggested these had been in the works for many months. Nevertheless, the announced changes at the top, together with the unannounced but presumed shifts in the composition of the Defense Council, no doubt eased the final stages of working out the details of the reductions announcement by diminishing the strength of conservatives in the leadership. Gromyko surely left the Defense Council on his retirement from the presidency and Politburo; Ligachev, no longer the undisputed second secretary, may have also lost his seat on the Defense Council; and Chebrikov would have had to cede at least the KGB place at the table to Kryuchkov. To whatever extent these changes facilitated the reductions ultimately announced, they served to underscore once again the fact that it was the balance of power in the civilian leadership rather than the views of the high command that in the end was decisive in decision making on this and other major national security decisions.

Symbolically, *Pravda's* photo of the November 7, 1988 leadership lineup on the Lenin Mausoleum not only underscored the Politburo's preeminence over the Secretariat but also completely left out the military. Yazov's Order of the Day for November 7, meanwhile, declared that Soviet diplomacy was "creating more favorable conditions for slackening tension, broadening comprehensive East-West contacts, curbing the arms race, reducing military expenditure, and settling regional conflicts," and the defense minister saluted "new thinking" and "reasonable sufficiency" in his speech on Red Square.[41]

By the time Gorbachev made his dramatic statement in New York, therefore, the idea of a unilateral cut should not have come as a surprise. In fact, the magnitude of the troop reduction Gorbachev announced was only half of what at first seemed to have been under consideration in 1987–88. What caught even careful observers off guard, however, was the quality and location of the armament reductions Gorbachev specified—much of it top-notch offensive equipment in the heart of the Warsaw Pact's forward area in Eastern Europe. Once carried out, the already low ability of the Warsaw Pact to launch a surprise attack on NATO's central front and push across the continent to the English Channel would be further diminished.

Gorbachev was still intent on improving Soviet security by undermining NATO's strategy of nuclear deterrence. But he seemed to have convinced his colleagues in the Politburo and allies in the high command that this could be done more cheaply as well as effectively by reducing the threat to NATO, rather than by trying to overwhelm NATO militarily. Furthermore, if the INF experience had reinforced one lesson for the Soviet leadership, it was that in the end NATO and the West would pull themselves together enough to resist military pressure from the USSR and would often do so in ways compounding rather than easing the threat to Soviet national security.

OTHER BENCHMARKS

As 1988 drew to a close, the Gorbachev leadership could look back on some momentous foreign policy benchmarks. The INF Treaty had been ratified; Yazov and Akhromeyev had met with their U.S. counterparts Frank Carlucci and William Crowe in Bern, Moscow, and Washington;[42] Reagan had toasted Gorbachev in the heart of the "Evil Empire;" Soviet troops had begun to withdraw from Afghanistan; Kohl had met with Gorbachev in the Kremlin in late October; and Gorbachev had announced the first major demobilization since January 1960.

In addition, there had been the signing on December 22 of accords calling for Namibian independence by April 1990 and the phased withdrawal of all Cuban troops from Angola by July 1991. Although the peace process in southern Africa had been mediated by the United States, it had been advanced significantly at the end by Soviet prodding of its clients.[43] According to members of the Soviet Institute for African Studies, since 1983 the USSR had reduced its arms supplies to Africa by 60 percent and cut the number of recipient nations from 22 to seven.[44] On foreign aid in general, Shevardnadze declared in November 1988 that Soviet domestic conditions were placing "rigid" limits, and that the USSR would not be able to increase or even maintain its economic assistance to the Third World at current levels for the next few years.[45]

There had also been progress on Cambodia, the thorniest of the three issues proclaimed by Beijing as obstacles to better Sino-Soviet relations. In May 1988, shortly after Soviet troops began leaving Afghanistan, Phnom Penh and Hanoi announced the withdrawal of an additional 50,000 Vietnamese troops from Cambodia by the end of the year, said the remaining Vietnamese forces would be placed under Cambodian command, and reaffirmed their joint commitment to withdraw all Vietnamese forces by 1990.[46] By late August Deputy Foreign Ministers Tian Zengpei and Igor Rogachev held the first round of Sino-Soviet talks devoted explicitly and exclusively to resolving the Cambodian conflict.[47]

By early December 1988, during Foreign Minister Qian Qichen's talks in Moscow, he and Gorbachev agreed that a Sino-Soviet summit "could probably take place in the first half of the next year."[48] Within days Mikhail Titarenko, director of the Soviet Institute of the Far East, said that normalization of party-to-party relations would be one of the main items of business at the prospective Deng-Gorbachev meeting.[49] Several weeks later Shevardnadze's visit to Tokyo rekindled speculation about a trip by Gorbachev to Japan, by and large treated coolly by Moscow ever since Shevardnadze's first visit in January 1986.[50]

In the Middle East Gorbachev told Palestine Liberation Organization (PLO) leader Yasir Arafat in April 1988 that a solution to the "Middle East problem should be based on negotiations, on an equal and businesslike dialogue and not on armed force and a desire to dictate."[51] An Israeli consular delegation arrived in Moscow on July 28, a first for Israeli diplomats since the Six-Day War.[52] Then at a press conference in Geneva on December 14, Arafat finally used language demanded for years by the United States to express the PLO's recognition of Israel's right to exist, and the following day the United States announced that a U.S.-PLO dialogue would begin through the U.S. ambassador in Tunis. Before long, and taking advantage of the conclusion of the Soviet military withdrawal from Afghanistan, Shevardnadze in February 1989 would make an extensive tour of the Middle East to advance Soviet ideas for an international peace conference.

On Eastern Europe, in March 1988 in Yugoslavia Gorbachev reaffirmed previous Soviet-Yugoslav declarations of universal respect for national sovereignty and the "impermissibility of interference in internal affairs under any pretext whatsoever." This was interpreted by some as nullifying the so-called "Brezhnev doctrine," proclaimed after the Soviet invasion of Czechoslovakia to justify Soviet armed intervention throughout Eastern Europe.[53] Although such interpretations were questionable—and in any event meaningless until put to the test—Soviet rhetoric nevertheless pointed toward more "civilized" Soviet relations not only with the capitalist world but with Warsaw Pact allies and nonaligned socialist countries as well.

The joint declaration Gorbachev signed in Belgrade, for example, also referred to "peaceful coexistence as a universal value in relations among states and peoples," thus blurring the distinction the USSR had long drawn between relations among the socialist countries (except with China since the 1970s), and between them and other states.[54] At the Foreign Ministry, as we have seen, the 1986 reorganization had consolidated Eastern European affairs into one single administration and put a deputy minister in full-time charge of Eastern Europe. This had marked a change from the previous era, when the Bloc Relations Department in the Central Committee presumably ran the show on its own. In October 1988 the Central Committee reorganization went a step further by submerging the Bloc Relations Department within the International Department.[55] Taken together, these moves suggested an intention under Gorbachev to put Soviet–Eastern European relations on more normal state-to-state footings rather than almost exclusively party-to-party ones, as in days gone by.

In any event, the intensity and scope of Moscow's demands on allies paralleled the development of Gorbachev's own domestic reform program: moderate and piecemeal through mid-1986; increasingly more radical thereafter. The early welcoming by Eastern European leaders of Gorbachev's determination to move beyond the tensions and unproductiveness of Moscow's earlier post-INF policy was replaced by disunity over the applicability of *perestroika* to their own particular circumstances. There was some outright resistance, as usual demonstrated most strikingly by Romania.[56] In general Hungary was most supportive of Gorbachev's politics, followed by Poland's Wojciech Jaruzelski; Romania was most resistant, with the GDR not far behind; and Czechoslovakia and Bulgaria were somewhere in between, but most often closest to the East German stance.[57]

On human rights, Soviet release of all known political prisoners convicted under Articles 70 and 190.1,[58] the ceasing of jamming even of Radio Liberty,[59] a dramatic improvement in emigration policy, and an extensive agenda for civic reforms secured the conditional approval of the United States and its allies in January 1989 for a CSCE-sponsored human rights conference in Moscow in 1991. Shevardnadze had set this as a goal at the opening of the Vienna CSCE review conference in Vienna in November 1986—just as in Moscow the Gorbachev regime got set to launch its campaign to improve human rights with the dramatic recall from exile of Andrey Sakharov.

NOTES

1. TASS, November 15, 1988 (FBIS-SOV, November 16, 1988, 4).

2. *Pravda*, December 8, 1988 (FBIS-SOV, December 8, 1988, 17–18).

3. *Cambio 16*, December 15, 1986.

4. Gorbachev, *Perestroika*, 187–88.

5. TASS, January 18, 1989 (FBIS-SOV, January 19, 1989, p. 10).

6. *Pravda*, February 9, 1989 (FBIS-SOV, February 9, 1989, p. 1).

7. *Washington Post*, July 27, 1988.

8. According to Admiral William Studeman, director of U.S. Naval Intelligence, in testimony to the U.S. Congress, Soviet naval deployments declined by 6 percent in 1987, the third year in a row to see a downward trend. Out-of-area ship days for most Soviet ship classes in 1987 were far below 1984 norms (*Jane's Defence Weekly*, March 26, 1988, 600). A year later, Studeman's successor, Rear Admiral Thomas A. Brooks, testified that Soviet submarine production had been scaled back, Pacific fleet operations had been reduced; and some combat ships were being sold as scrap on world markets (*Washington Post*, February 23, 1989).

9. When the regime subsequently backed away from full speed ahead on the always painful process of price reform, it had the effect of also pushing further off into the future the prospects for real *glasnost* on the defense budget.

10. Gorbachev, *Perestroika*, 135.

11. *Izvestiya TsK KPSS*, no. 2 (1989), 222.

12. *New Times*, no. 40, October 12, 1987 (FBIS-SOV, October 14, 1987, 4–7).

13. *SShA: Ekonomika, Politika, Ideologiya*, no. 12 (December 1987), signed to press November 18, 1987; and *Kommunist*, no. 1 (January 1988), signed to press December 25, 1987.

14. *Literary Gazette*, February 3, 1988 (FBIS-SOV, February 3, 1988, 5). Krivosheyev presumably had in mind the 1.2 million demobilization announced by Khrushchev in January 1960, and not the 1955–58 demobilization said by Khrushchev in that same speech to the Supreme Soviet to have totaled 2,140,000.

15. *Moscow News*, no. 8, February 21, 1988 (FBIS-SOV, February 24, 1988, 73).

16. *Red Star*, February 10, 1988 (FBIS-SOV, February 10, 1988, 3); and Moscow Television Service, February 19, 1988 (FBIS-SOV, February 22, 1988, 3).

17. Radio Moscow, February 19, 1988 (FBIS-SOV, Editorial Report, February 22, 1988, 7).

18. *Pravda*, February 23, 1988 (FBIS-SOV, February 24, 1988, 65–66).

19. *Red Star*, February 23, 1988 (FBIS-SOV, February 23, 1988, 70).

20. *Literary Gazette*, May 18, 1988 (FBIS-SOV, May 20, 1988, 4–8).

21. Ibid.

22. Ibid.

23. See also Dashichev's interview in *Der Spiegel*, July 4, 1988 (FBIS-SOV, July 8, 1988, 18–21); the already mentioned article by Oleg Bogomolov in *Literary Gazette*, March 16, 1988 (FBIS-SOV, March 15, 1988, 19); Ernst Genri in *Moskovskaya Pravda*, May 18 and 19, 1988 (FBIS-SOV, June 8 and 9, 1988, 67–70 and 63–65, respectively); the Foreign Ministry's Viktor Karpov and *Izvestiya's* Aleksandr Bovin on "Repercussions," Moscow Television Service, July 7, 1988 (FBIS-SOV, July 11, 1988, 8–15); and Aleksandr Savelyev's description of the defense debate in Moscow in *APN Military Bulletin*, no. 10 (May 1988).

24. *Pravda*, May 27, 1988 (FBIS-SOV, May 27, 1988, 48–49).

25. *Red Star*, August 13, 1988 (FBIS-SOV, August 15, 1988, 72).

26. In answer to a direct question, Foreign Ministry Spokesman Gerasimov first confirmed Akhromeyev's impending retirement for health reasons in an interview on December 7, 1988, with Cable News Network's Steve Hurst in New York. For the official announcement of Akhromeyev's replacement by Mikhail Moiseyev, see *Red Star*, December 15, 1988 (FBIS-SOV, December 15, 1988, 74–75).

27. Meanwhile, Akhromeyev's predecessor, Nikolay Ogarkov, had also gone into semiretirement earlier in the fall, leaving his position as head of the Western TMO for a billet in the Defense Ministry's Group of Inspectors (*Jane's Defence Weekly*, October 15, 1988, 971).

28. See, for example, his interviews in *Moscow News*, no. 5, January 29, 1989 (FBIS-SOV, February 6, 1989, 14–17), and in *La Repubblica*, March 11, 1989 (FBIS-SOV, March 15, 1989, 1–3), from which the quote is drawn.

29. *Red Star*, February 10, 1989 (FBIS-SOV, February 13, 1989, 79).

30. *Pravda*, November 29, 1988 (FBIS-SOV, November 29, 1988, 55).

31. *Izvestiya*, June 1, 1988 (FBIS-SOV, June 3, 1988, 24).

32. *Washington Post*, July 9, 1988.

33. *Pravda*, July 16, 1988 (FBIS-SOV, July 18, 1988, 13–14).

34. *Pravda*, June 29, 1988 (FBIS-SOV, July 1, 1988, Supplement, 13).

35. *Pravda*, July 26, 1988 (FBIS-SOV, July 26, 1988, 30).

36. For all three officials, see their speeches in *International Affairs*, no. 9 (September 1988).

37. *International Affairs*, no. 10 (October 1988), signed to press September 23, 1988. See also Viktor Sheynis's reexamination of the nature of capitalism in *Mirovaya Ekonomika i Mezhdunarodnyye Otnosheniya*, no. 9 (September 1988).

38. *Pravda*, August 11, 1988 (FBIS-SOV, August 19, 1988, 5); and *Moscow News*, no. 45, November 6, 1988 (FBIS-SOV, December 2, 1988, 90–91). See also Vitaliy Zhurkin's comments on *Studio 9*, Moscow Television Service, July 30, 1988 (FBIS-SOV, August 2, 1988, 14).

39. *Pravda*, September 25, 1988 (FBIS-SOV, September 26, 1988, 23).

40. *Vestnik Ministerstva Inostrannykh Del*, no. 22, December 1, 1988, signed to press November 22, 1988.

41. *Pravda*, November 7, 1988 (FBIS-SOV, November 8, 1988, 75); and Moscow Television Service, November 7, 1988 (FBIS-SOV, November 7, 1988, 89).

42. For a useful chronology of U.S.-Soviet military contacts since World War II, see *Red Star*, July 30, 1988 (FBIS-SOV, August 2, 1988, 20–21).

43. Left unresolved, however, was the civil war in Angola. For a retro-spective, see David B. Ottaway, in *Washington Post*, December 23, 1988.

44. *Washington Post*, October 9, 1988. According to one tentative Western estimate, overall Soviet arms transfers to the Third World appeared to have declined some 10–11 percent during the first two years of Gorbachev's leadership but remained the same or increased to besieged Marxist clients such as Nicaragua. See Limberg, "Moscow and Regional Conflicts," 13.

45. *Vestnik Ministerstva Inostrannykh Del*, no. 22, December 1, 1988, signed to press November 22, 1988, 12–17.

46. Hanoi Domestic Service, May 26, 1988; and Phnom Penh Domestic Service, May 27, 1988.

47. *Washington Post*, September 2, 1988.

48. *Pravda*, December 2, 1988 (FBIS-SOV, December 5, 1988, 16).

49. Kyodo, December 6, 1988 (FBIS-SOV, December 6, 1988, 22).

50. Kyodo, December 21, 1988 (FBIS-SOV, December 22, 1988, 12).

51. TASS, April 9, 1988 (FBIS-SOV, April 11, 1988, 26–27).

52. TASS, July 28, 1988, and Jerusalem Television Service, July 28, 1988 (FBIS-SOV, July 29, 1988, 18–19).

53. For a discussion of the "Brezhnev doctrine," see Thomas M. Wolfe, *Soviet Power in Europe 1945–1970* (Baltimore: Johns Hopkins University Press, 1970), 383–85 and 394.

54. "Soviet-Yugoslav Declaration," *Pravda*, March 19, 1988 (FBIS-SOV, March 21, 1988, 35–36). In his November 2, 1987, speech Gorbachev had in a similar manner ambiguously included "the strict observation by all of the principles of peaceful coexistence" as one of the "generally recognized principles" on which the "practice of socialist internationalism rests" (Moscow Television Service, November 2, 1987 [FBIS-SOV, November 3, 1987, 60]. The Party Program approved by the 27th Party Congress, however, had elaborated on peaceful coexistence clearly in the context of discussing relations between capitalism and socialism (*Pravda*, March 7, 1986 [FBIS-SOV, March 10, 1986, Supplement 51, third section, O 4]).

55. *L'Unita*, October 16, 1988 (FBIS-SOV, October 19, 1988, 48–49).

56. Gorbachev paid a visit to Bucharest on May 25–27, 1987, most memorable for his implicit chastisement of the nepotism of Ceausescu's rule (*Pravda*, May 27, 1987 [FBIS-SOV, May 28, 1987, F 1–9]). Evidently relations were already strained even before Gorbachev's arrival: Romania did not send a representative to either the CEMA deputy foreign ministers meeting in Moscow on March 18, 1987 (Moscow Domestic Service, March 18, 1987 [FBIS-SOV, March 20, 1987, BB 4]), or the meeting at the same level of Warsaw Pact representatives on September 7–8, 1987 (TASS, September 8, 1987 [FBIS-SOV, September 9, 1987, 6]).

57. For a review of Soviet–Eastern European relations as of early fall 1987, see Gary Lee and Jackson Diehl, "Moscow and the East Bloc," *Washington Post*, October 12–13, 1987.

58. *Washington Post*, December 13, 1988. This still left over 170 political prisoners incarcerated under various other articles (*Washington Post*, November 19, 1988).

59. *Washington Post*, December 1, 1988. The USSR also ceased jamming KOL Israel and the FRG's Deutsche Welle.

Chapter 16

Toward a New Beginning

*I*n 1988–89, as Gorbachev finished his tenth year in Moscow and fourth year as general secretary, no longer could there be any question that he was different. His leadership was openly intent on debunking the myths of the Brezhnev era and radically changing the system created by Stalin. The question was whether or not Gorbachev had the political skills and stamina to outlast and wear down the resistance his own proposed reforms predictably and unavoidably generated, and how far he intended to go.

Indeed, there were even hints that some highly placed political leaders agreed with Lenin's early mentor and later adversary, Georgiy Plekhanov, that Russia indeed had not been ready for the Bolshevik Revolution and that her current travails stemmed from a political culture that had not been steeped in a long period of learning democratic habits under a bourgeois system.[1] Thus it was not surprising that the tensions between Gorbachev and Ligachev came to a head as Gorbachev maneuvered to forge a more authoritative and democratic Supreme Soviet and to force the party apparatus to concentrate on strategic questions rather than day-to-day management of all facets of Soviet society.

Ligachev, however, was able to challenge Gorbachev at his own game of mobilizing public opinion. Gorbachev hoped to put public pressure on the various apparatuses to reform their ways. To counter Gorbachev, Ligachev could rely on the natural gravitation of the party apparatus to his position, which, while calling for cleaning up the party, also resisted erosion of its leadership role. But even at the grass-roots level Ligachev could appeal to public concern over the potential dislocations—such as unemployment and increasing income disparities—threatened by radical economic reform.

Presumably in an effort to expand his minority support at the top and in search of leverage on his colleagues in the Politburo, Ligachev started pedaling backward even on foreign policy. He did not oppose the Gorbachev regime's specific accomplishments, such as the INF Treaty and the decision to withdraw from Afghanistan. Rather, Ligachev broke at a more basic and therefore ultimately more threatening level: with the regime's new theoretical underpinnings. In criticizing the deemphasis of class struggle, Ligachev even began to sound a bit like Chernenko during the latter's polemics with Andropov in 1982–83. A receptive audience was still out there, and in the increasingly bitter struggle with Gorbachev, Ligachev showed no qualms in appealing to it.

Gorbachev nevertheless managed to outmaneuver Ligachev and to effectively strip him of his second secretary status in September-October 1988, and then to conduct a massive purge of the Central Committee in April 1989. But despite his successful drive for a reformed Supreme Soviet structure and the dramatic results of the March 1989 elections to the new Congress of Peoples Deputies, the general secretary was still left facing an immense and entrenched bureaucracy resistant to change; a populace increasingly disenchanted over the failure of *perestroika* to halt a perceived decline in the standard of living, let alone deliver a higher one; and increasingly bitter ethnic clashes in the Caucasus and in Central Asia and demands for regional autonomy and even independence in the Baltics.

For all his successes, moreover, Gorbachev still seemed fated to be dogged by events that reinforced his image among many as predestined to be unlucky. The past was full of booby traps for Gorbachev, including shoddy apartment buildings constructed over known seismic faults in Armenia, where a disastrous earthquake forced Gorbachev to cut short his December 1988 visit to New York and return home. Then in April 1989, a submarine disaster off Norway and the killing by troops of demonstrators in Tbilisi took the bloom off of Gorbachev's otherwise successful visit to Britain.[2]

Nevertheless, it took an observer's breath away to contemplate the extent to which Gorbachev had managed to push Soviet politics full circle a mere ten years since leaving Stavropol to replace Fedor Kulakov, the man Brezhnev had been grooming as heir. As 1988 turned into 1989, for example, the once outcast Academician Sakharov, just returned from a visit to the United States, toured the Caucasus almost as an official emissary from the Kremlin; a decree stripped the names of Brezhnev and Chernenko even from the buildings where they had last resided; the Central Committee recommended the rehabilitation of the millions of victims of Stalin's infamous troika courts; and Brezhnev's son-in-law Yuriy Churbanov was sentenced to 12 years in prison for corruption.[3] Three months later, moreover, the USSR would hold its first meaningful parliamentary elections since 1917, providing Gorbachev with the most effective leverage yet against recalcitrant apparatchiks.

YAKOVLEV'S WEEDS AND FLOWERS

After the Yeltsin affair, it was Aleksandr Yakovlev who in early December 1987 issued the rallying cry of the radical wing of the leadership as it entered the third phase of the Gorbachev revolution. Yakovlev's formula went beyond a strictly utilitarian notion of democratization and was designed basically as a social engineering instrument to provide the central leadership with greater feedback from below and greater control of its own bureaucracies. Though not totally permissive, the new accent was on greater toleration of diversity and even some encouragement of it. Yakovlev asked at a Central Committee conference of media, science, and cultural workers, "Why does it have to be: 'either—or'? Either the plan, or the market. Either internationalism, or patriotism. Either rock music, or folk poetry. Either democracy, or discipline. Not 'either—or,' but 'both—and,'" he proposed. And then, in a phrase that would be attacked by the likes of cultural conservative Yuriy Bondarev half a year later at the party conference, Yakovlev suggested, "Diversity may include weeds and barren flowers. But they are no reason to restrict diversity itself as a form of life."[4]

At about the same time in Paris, where Ligachev was attending the congress of the French Communist party, he gave an interview to veteran Kremlinologist Michel Tatu of *Le Monde*. Ligachev portrayed himself very much as a team player, not so much bowing to the will of the Politburo majority as a part of it. Gorbachev chaired the Politburo, Ligachev told Tatu, and at the request of the Politburo he, Ligachev, organized and chaired the Secretariat. He and Gorbachev were "on the same wavelength." "Socialist pluralism" in the arts, professions, and society in general was "normal and useful." Furthermore, in Ligachev's most striking display of party discipline, "the key aspect of restructuring is the democratization of society," and "We are convinced that the party must set an example for the democratic running of society as a whole." As to the future decisions of the Politburo commission set up to review the repressions of the Stalin era, "Have a little patience and you will hear them."[5]

Indeed, by this time *Ogonek* had run its interview with Bukharin's widow, Anna Larina. Soon spectacularly revealing essays would appear on major events and personalities of the Stalin era. The first came in mid-January 1988 and dealt with the Leningrad affair and the hounding and execution of N. A. Voznesenskiy.[6] Then a piece appeared on the "monster and thug" Andrey Vishinskiy, prosecutor in the 1936–38 show trials, including that of Bukharin.[7] In early February 1988 Soviet television showed a documentary on Sergey Kirov, the Leningrad party leader whose assassination in 1934 set the stage for Stalin's Great Terror.[8] Two days later the Politburo commission on Stalin's repressions announced the repeal of Bukharin's 1938 conviction but made no mention of his political as opposed to juridical rehabilitation.[9] Exposés on Beria were not far behind, including a three-part series by one of the six officers who had taken him into custody on June 26, 1953.[10]

De-Brezhnevization likewise proceeded on course. In January 1988 the city of Naberezhnyye Chelny, renamed Brezhnev in 1982, regained its original name, as did a district in Moscow and squares in Leningrad and Moscow.[11] Several weeks later an article in *Izvestiya* on the bribe-taking trial of G. D. Brovin, one of Brezhnev's three duty secretaries, also smeared L. Bondarenko, former party boss in Rostov who, it will be recalled, was reportedly one of Gorbachev's rivals to replace Kulakov back in 1978.[12] Meanwhile the investigation of Brezhnev's son-in-law Yuriy Churbanov, charged with abuse of office in accepting over R650,000 in bribes, was formally completed.[13] A month later Fyodor Burlatskiy published the first full-length sympathetic portrait of Khrushchev. This made the point, not merely in passing, that Brezhnev's "negative attitude" to economic reform had "nullified the efforts of the preceding era."[14] By the end of April Khrushchev's son Sergey granted his first interview to a foreign journalist and began telling the inside story of the plotting against his father by Brezhnev and others in 1964.[15]

Against this background, Gorbachev in January 1988 dropped another public hint of an upcoming reform of the soviets. The general Secretary told a Central Committee meeting of cultural, media, and ideological workers, "We will seek new approaches to make better use of the soviets' potential." Party bodies, he said, had too often taken over many of the functions of soviets and had become "overloaded" with functions "uncharacteristic" of them.[16] In February Gorbachev tipped his hand even more clearly. At a Central Committee plenum on education, at which Ligachev gave the main agenda speech, Gorbachev followed with a much wider-ranging address in which he said that the "main problem of the development of our political system" was its "mechanism of authority and management." "Above all what we must be talking about here is radically enhancing the role of the soviets as the pivot of our society's political system and its state embodiment." The party's role as Soviet society's political vanguard was still "essential," but it had to be "completely regenerated" and brought into line with what Lenin originally had in mind.[17]

Gorbachev told the February 1988 plenum that there could be "no half measures" in preparing proposals for political reform to present to the 19th Party Conference, which the June 1987 plenum had scheduled to open June 28, 1988. Nevertheless, at the conference Gorbachev would himself propose just such a "half measure"—combining at each level the posts of party first secretary and chairman of the corresponding soviet—and it would leave many of his own supporters bewildered and critical. At the conference Gorbachev would be partly reacting to pressure from Ligachev and his many partisans in the party apparatus. At the February 1988 plenum the fundamental difference between Gorbachev and Ligachev, papered over by the latter in his December 1987 interview with *Le Monde*, was clearly in evidence once again. Gorbachev told the plenum that "democratization" was the "decisive means of achieving the aims of restructuring," and put into play the phrase "socialist pluralism of opinions." Ligachev, in contrast, emphasized that the "party is the organizer of the policy of restructuring, and its political authority is growing," and he avoided the word "pluralism."

At the February 1988 plenum Ligachev called for inculcating Soviet students with "an understanding of the class nature of the changes taking place in our country," and to reject the "half-baked idea of 'liberalizing Soviet society'" which was "being importunately offered us from outside: liberalism in its Western sense." This was, he said, a "political fraud." Ligachev also began to distance himself from what had been the leadership's presumably agreed line on the need to deideologize Soviet foreign policy. "It is very important," Ligachev said, "that, when assimilating social science subjects, young people learn a class view of the world, an understanding of the link between those interests common to all mankind and class interests."[18] Gorbachev, in contrast, noted at the plenum "our sincere rejection of the ideologization of interstate relations."[19]

Nonetheless, the personnel changes at the February plenum continued to suggest that Gorbachev had survived the Yeltsin affair with his majority intact. Yeltsin was formally dropped as a Politburo candidate member. But none other than Gorbachev-protégé Georgiy Razumovskiy, a Central Committee secretary and head of the Cadres Department, was elected to take Yeltsin's place as a Politburo alternate. In addition, two high-flying defense sector managers were coopted into the leadership—a development especially notable given Gorbachev's accelerated drive to restrain military spending and harness the defense sector to his industrial modernization and consumer goods drive. The plenum appointed Oleg Baklanov, promoted to minister for General Machine Building in 1983 under Andropov, to oversee the military-industrial sector as a Central Committee secretary. It also made Yuriy Maslyukov a candidate member of the Politburo; Maslyukov had been head of the Military-Industrial Commission from 1985 until early February 1988, when he replaced Nikolay Talyzin as Gosplan chairman.[20]

For all the opposition that Gorbachev's ambitious plans for reform was generating, his position at the top continued to appear unassailable. On February 11, however, a week before the plenum, demonstrations began in Armenia over control of the province of Nagorno-Karabakh, populated predominantly by Christian Armenians but lying within the administrative boundaries of Muslim Azerbaidzhan. By February 18, even as Gorbachev in his speech to the Central Committee was calling for a plenum in the future on nationality policy, there were mass demonstrations in the Armenian capital of Yerevan over Nagorno-Karabakh. Ten days later the crisis changed qualitatively as a grisly pogrom in the Azeri town of Sumgait took the lives of at least 32 local Armenian residents. In the Caucasus, at least, political liberalization seemed to be exacerbating rather than helping to bridge old communal hatreds.

NINA ANDREYEVA VERSUS *PRAVDA*

It was in this tense atmosphere that Ligachev made his next move, on the eve of Gorbachev's departure on a five-day visit to Yugoslavia and of a Yakovlev trip to Mongolia. On March 13, 1988, Valentin Chikin's *Sovetskaya Rossiya* published "I Cannot Waive Principles," described as a "letter" from Leningrad technical school lecturer Nina Andreyeva. The very title advertised it as a riposte against Gorbachev, who had long denounced those who saw in his radical approach to *perestroika* "almost a shaking of our foundations, almost a renunciation of our principles."[21] The letter was taken by many as an authoritative signal that the leadership—"afraid that the free creative force which they themselves tried to arouse has now assumed its full proportion"—had done an about-face.[22]

Andreyeva maintained that Stalin's repressions had been blown out of proportion; argued that proponents of the "supposedly democratic slogan of 'anti-Stalinism'" were the "offspring of the classes overthrown by the October Revolution"; paraphrased Ligachev's complaint against those who "try to make us believe that the country's past was nothing but mistakes and crimes"; and denounced the politicization of newly formed "informal" activist groups for going far beyond the bounds of "socialist pluralism." She directly attacked playwright Mikhail Shatrov and novelist Anatoliy Rybakov and implicitly slammed the movie *Repentance* and T. Samolis pre-27th Congress review of readers' letters to *Pravda*, "Purification."[23]

Andreyeva's anti-Semitism and Russian chauvinism were undisguised as she scorned "imaginary relatives . . . in no hurry to invite their fellow-tribesmen to the 'promised land,' turning them into 'refuseniks' of socialism"; lampooned Trotskiy's insistence that he was "not a Jew but an internationalist"; extolled Russian culture and national sacrifice; and excoriated the outrages committed just outside "the Kremlin walls"—a clear reference to the Crimean Tatar demonstrations the summer before. Paralleling Ligachev's discussion of universal versus class interests at the February plenum, she reproached those who now asserted that relations between states should be devoid of class content—in effect attacking Gorbachev's own treatment of the subject at the plenum.

"What is happening today?" Andreyeva asked. "Does the international working class no longer oppose world capital as embodied in its state and political organs?"[24]

Ligachev's sponsorship of the article seemed undeniable.[25] According to Giulietto Chiesa, the well-informed Moscow correspondent for the Italian Communist party newspaper, *L'Unita*, Ligachev was rumored to have told a meeting of newspaper editors that Andreyeva's letter was an "example to be followed."[26] Yet it was unlikely that Ligachev personally shared Andreyeva's most outrageous prejudices or ideological positions. According to Bukharin biographer Stephen Cohen, who was in Moscow at the time, "Ligachev was behind the publishing of the article, but not because he agrees with everything in it. Instead, Ligachev wanted the article printed as an example of the polarization that Gorbachev's brand of reform has created. Ligachev hoped the debate surrounding the article would bring about the removal of *Ogonek's* Korotich and *Moscow News'* Ye. Yakovlev."[27] However, given Ligachev's unusual prominence right after the Andreyeva letter appeared, and the subsequent furious reaction from the Gorbachev wing of the leadership, it seems doubtful that Ligachev's objectives were quite so limited.

Indeed, there was somewhat of a parallel between the Andreyeva episode and the press report ten months earlier of the Politburo meeting of May 8, 1987, which had referred to a variety of concerns and opposition to *perestroika*. In the view of sociologist Yu. Levada, for example, the Andreyeva letter was designed to appeal to three currents of center-right opinion: "Yesterday's supporters of 'moderate' and 'balanced' restructuring which would not affect the deepest foundations of society. . . . Witting and unwitting neo-Stalinists, living in hope of a 'firm hand' supposedly capable of imposing order. And 'fundamentalists' . . . inclined to examine . . . problems from the viewpoint of national exclusiveness and sinister conspiracies." In Levada's opinion, the letter was aimed against "the alliance of the political leadership and the front-ranking section of society," by which Levada presumably meant the Gorbachev-Yakovlev wing of the leadership and liberal progressives among the intelligentsia.[28] Ligachev's highlighting of ultraconservative ideological reservations to *perestroika* seemed designed to slow Gorbachev's radicalization and pull him back to agreed centrist positions. The troglodyte views put forward in the Andreyeva letter certainly suggested that it had become more important to Ligachev to stop Gorbachev's democratization drive than to push his own brand of reformism. Once he succeeded in derailing Gorbachev's campaign, Ligachev may have thought, he could then resume his own push for party-first reformism.

At the very least, Ligachev was not averse to using the many proponents of the views espoused in the Andreyeva letter to bolster his independence from Gorbachev and to limit the general secretary's room to maneuver. The Andreyeva piece seemed meant as a signal from Ligachev to conservative apparatchiks throughout the country that they had a strong protector at the top. More to the point, perhaps, it was meant to tell them that in the upcoming round of elections of delegates to the June-July party conference, they should not hesitate to oppose radicals and deny them representation. Going even further, Ligachev may even have hoped to spark such a groundswell of conservative support that Gorbachev and Yakovlev would have been faced with a *fait accompli* that they would have been too weak to reverse. That outcome would have left Ligachev as the real power behind the facade of Gorbachev's general secretaryship—if Gorbachev managed to hang onto it. Indeed, in press reporting of at least three different events while Gorbachev visited Yugoslavia from March 14 to 18, Ligachev was listed out of alphabetical order and ahead of all other leaders present.[29]

Gorbachev, however, returned to Moscow from Yugoslavia uncowed. Using as a platform his March 22, 1988, meeting with Uruguayan President Julio Maria Sanguinetti, the general secretary declared, "Without imparting a universal nature to democracy, without the development of *glasnost* in every possible way, it is impossible to keep our society constantly active, on the move, and it is impossible to ensure that what has been started will be irreversible." It would be the task of the 19th Party Conference "to engage in profound reconstruction of the political superstructure." "We have given birth to a 'revolution of expectations,'" he said, "and we must ensure a revolutionary turning point in the position of Soviet citizens. . . . Politics has now been opened up to millions of people. In other words, genuine, large-scale politics has begun."[30]

By March 28 Ligachev failed to appear at the commemoration of the one hundred and twentieth anniversary of the birth of writer Maksim Gorkiy.[31] Then on April 2, Irkutsk obkom First Secretary V. I. Sitnikov was fired in the wake of a widely publicized March 8 airplane hijacking which resulted in the deaths of five of the hijackers, a stewardess, and three passengers.[32] Ever quick to take advantage of any opening, it would appear that Gorbachev eagerly moved against Sitnikov because of the latter's closeness to Ligachev. Sitnikov, as we have seen, had been third on the honor roll of local officials praised by the June 1986 editorial in *Pravda* on "First Secretaries," which had paraphrased key passages from a speech earlier that month by Ligachev. More recently, Sitnikov had had the honor of being the first to comment on Ligachev's opening speech at the February plenum.[33]

On April 5 *Pravda* finally published its programmatic retort to the Andreyeva letter. "Principles of Restructuring: Revolutionary Nature of Thinking and Acting" was widely rumored to have been drafted by Aleksandr Yakovlev.[34] Unlike the paper's editorial on November 11, 1987, which in the wake of the Yeltsin affair had included some Ligachev language, this time the editorial exposition of the authoritative line was completely bereft of any specifically Ligachev track marks.[35] The *Pravda* editorial was the opening argument in a trial of strength designed to intimidate and drown out Ligachev supporters and to assure backers of greater radicalism and a "socialist pluralism of opinions" that they had protectors at the top who were strong enough to prevail against the conservative opposition. The April 5 editorial in essence used Ligachev's own insistence on "constructive" criticism against Ligachev. Ten days later *Sovetskaya Rossiya* printed a *mea culpa*.[36]

On April 11, 14, and 18 Gorbachev held what was described as a "conference" with republic and regional party first secretaries at which they conducted a "painstaking analysis" of proposals for political reform to be presented at the upcoming party conference.[37] This was evidently an occasion for some intensive personal lobbying by Gorbachev in the wake of the crisis with Ligachev, as well as a chance for Gorbachev to assess the crisis' resonance within the regional party apparatus. Moscow was soon swept with rumors that on April 19 the Politburo had ordered Ligachev to take a two-month vacation and had stripped him of his ideology portfolio and given it to Yakovlev. Only Chebrikov, it was said, had come to Ligachev's defense, and Ligachev would soon lose his number two ranking in the leadership.[38] Gorbachev and Ligachev, according to Boris Yeltsin months later, had even stopped talking to each other.[39]

Ligachev, however, not only almost immediately reappeared in public at the Lenin Day ceremony on April 22 but also sat in his usual place next to Gorbachev. Gorbachev subsequently was said to have made a conciliatory gesture toward Ligachev when telling a meeting of editors in May, "We all have a great deal to do together yet."[40] Mathematically, it seemed Gorbachev had enough votes in the Politburo to oust Ligachev, as suggested by the insistent leaks to the Western press that Ligachev was on the verge of being retired. But Ligachev's support in the Central Committee and even more so in the party apparatus was presumably stronger than in the Politburo. On balance, therefore, Gorbachev apparently preferred to keep a chastened Ligachev in the Politburo as an inside critic, subject at least to some Politburo discipline, rather than convert him to a less controllable outside martyr. Expelling Ligachev, moreover, would have further estranged the party apparatus from Gorbachev and his supporters, further straining their fragile leverage on it. Finally, though certainly no longer a radical in the evolving political atmosphere, Ligachev was no retrograde when judged in the context of traditional Soviet politics. Gorbachev was probably right in suggesting that Ligachev still had a lot of political mileage left in service to *perestroika*.

THE 19TH PARTY CONFERENCE

Gorbachev's triumph, however, was far from complete. On Lenin Day his ally Razumovskiy spoke on behalf of the leadership and warned, "It is not superficial democratization that the party has in mind as its guiding principle, but democratization affecting the fundamental structures of society and development of its political system." Institutionally, said Razumovskiy, "the key issue here is the need to radically enhance the role of soviets of peoples' deputies and provide them with full power, as a political foundation of our socialist state."[41] By mid-May, however, spokesmen such as Valentin Falin were signaling that Gorbachev had decided not to try to push through major personnel changes in the Central Committee or Politburo at the upcoming party conference.[42] At least in the short run, Ligachev had achieved what may have been one of the most important tactical goals of the Andreyeva offensive.

In terms of programmatic aims, nevertheless, the theses for the party conference, approved by a Central Committee plenum on May 23, clearly marked a further radicalization of the party line. For the first time the theses set out as one of *perestroika*'s goals the creation of a "socialist legal state." Going further than the January 1987 plenum, the theses urged that there be multicandidate elections of party officials and "free nomination" of soviet deputy candidates; that the term of office of both be fixed at five years; and that each official be limited—with rare exception—to two successive terms. "The formal nomenklatura approach toward the selection and placement of cadres," declared the theses, "has outlived its usefulness. . . . The final decision on cadre questions must be determined by election results." Moreover, "The formation of real pluralism of opinions and open comparison of ideas and interests are a characteristic feature of our time."[43]

Institutionally the theses proposed to "fully restore the role and powers of soviets of people's deputies as sovereign organs of popular representation" and to allow the government to play a "greater role . . . as the supreme executive and administrative organ of state power." In continuing to perform the role of political vanguard, the theses called for the party to cease supplanting the soviets and other state organs. And there was already a hint of the radical reform of the Central Committee apparatus, which in September-October would greatly undermine Ligachev's power base. The party conference, declared the theses, "will have to examine possible proposals for new forms of collegial work by Central Committee members in the period between plenums."[44]

On one symbolic and profoundly significant point, moreover, the 1988 Andreyeva episode coincided with the end of efforts by Gorbachev not to offend or gratuitously repel support from the right by denigrating the memory of Mikhail Suslov. Up to now, despite all the Brezhnev-bashing, few if any critical references to Suslov had been allowed to appear in the Soviet media. In December 1987 in an introduction to an expanded, posthumous version of Anastas Mikoyan's memoirs in *Ogonek*, Sergo Mikoyan had related his father's indignation at the cavalier way editors felt they could treat the original manuscript while Suslov was "in charge of our ideology."[45] However, the mid-January 1988 article in *Komsomolskaya Pravda* on the Leningrad affair and the persecution of former Gosplan chairman and Politburo member N. A. Voznesenskiy, executed in 1950 and administered a political *coup de grace* by Suslov in 1952, had omitted any reference to Suslov.

Nevertheless, it was clear the tide was turning against Suslov when the Politburo commission on Stalin's repressions announced in late March 1988 that on February 26 the Party Control Committee had confirmed the party membership of, among others, Voznesenskiy.[46] On May 3 *Sovetskaya Kultura* printed economist V. Sheynis's reference to "the old Brezhnev-Suslov nucleus," and on June 7 *Pravda*, as we shall see, would have an even more pointed barb. Of course, the earlier reticence on Suslov may have reflected Gorbachev's lingering gratefulness for Suslov's role in sponsoring his early career in Stavropol and even his move to Moscow. But whatever the reason, after the Andreyeva episode it definitely became permissible not only to mention Suslov in public but to do so disparagingly.

The Andreyeva letter had signaled Ligachev's willingness to cast his net to the extreme right. It had been meant to frustrate a shift toward the left by Gorbachev, but instead it seemed to have nudged Gorbachev further and more determinedly in that direction—as suggested symbolically by the undermining of Suslov's reputation. Sheynis suggested, implicitly in this connection, that a more radical platform of reform would set "new social forces in motion" which would "more than compensate for the loss of the dubious support of the disciples of conservatively balanced changes."[47]

Nevertheless, it was a mixed picture for Gorbachev and his supporters as they headed in June toward the 19th Party Conference. The summit in Moscow in late May–early June 1988, at which Gorbachev and Reagan exchanged the ratification instruments for the INF Treaty, reinforced Gorbachev's stature on the world stage and in turn boosted his prestige at home. He and his supporters, however, encountered great difficulty even in Moscow in ensuring the election of supporters of radical restructuring as delegates to the conference.[48] Gorbachev was not totally bereft of grass-roots support, but the delegate selection process exposed his greatest weakness. With the top leadership divided, local party committees were often able to repulse pressure from below by manipulating the election procedures. Gorbachev's only recourse lay in responding in kind by manipulating the delegate selection process in friendlier, more malleable districts. Meantime, while publicly bowing to Gorbachev as leader of the Politburo, Ligachev continued to insist that "the guarantee of the irreversibility of restructuring is the Communist Party and its own healthy democratic development."[49] A report on the Politburo session of June 6 noted, "Communists and working people are putting forward many proposals aimed at enhancing the role of the CPSU." Only after this did it mention other proposals directed "at making party and public life more democratic, and at expanding glasnost."

The same Politburo session, however, presumably also cleared or at least discussed another review of readers' letters by T. Samolis, which appeared the following day in *Pravda*: "Purifying by Means of the Truth." This turned out to be even more radical than Samolis' "Purification" article in February 1986, which had sparked such controversy at the 27th Party Congress and drawn Ligachev's ire. In line with the lifting of the stricture against criticism of Suslov, furthermore, Samolis now cited the letter from one party member who wrote, "The party's ideological work, as far as I can judge, was extremely poor under Suslov and efforts were directed not at improving it but at glorifying the figure of Brezhnev."[50]

Other moves no doubt elated the liberal wing of the party but were not necessarily opposed by Ligachev. Several days after the Samolis article, *Izvestiya* dramatically announced the cancellation of history and social science examinations in the country's schools until the preparation of textbooks that "can be used to teach and to learn without going against one's conscience."[51] Then, although it would not be revealed until after the conclusion of the party conference, the Party Control Committee on June 21 posthumously restored Bukharin's party membership, completing the process of his juridical and political rehabilitation 40 years after his execution by firing squad under Stalin.[52]

The party conference itself featured a dramatic confrontation between Ligachev and Yeltsin; a call—prompted by Gorbachev—for the resignations of Gromyko, Solomentsev, *Pravda* editor Afanasyev, and USA Institute Director Arbatov; and Ligachev's none-too-subtle reminder of the support which he, Chebrikov, Solomentsev, Gromyko, and "a large group of obkom first secretaries" had rendered Gorbachev in March 1985 after Chernenko's death. Ligachev's defense of Gromyko underscored his evolving estrangement from Gorbachev and the changed relations among all three since Ligachev had joined Gorbachev in 1985–86 in undermining Gromyko's reputation. As to Yeltsin, Ligachev somewhat contradictorily said that he had recommended him for membership in the Politburo and Secretariat, yet then accused Yeltsin of not having been able to feed Sverdlovsk oblast without resorting to rationing coupons when he was party boss there—begging the question as to what had prompted Ligachev to sponsor Yeltsin's move to Moscow in the first place.

At the Party Conference Ligachev also revealingly said that he "fully supported" the contrasting speeches by writers Boris Oleynik—notable for its anti-Stalinism—and Yuriy Bondarev—who had delivered perhaps the most critical outburst against radical reform at the conference.[53] "Could our restructuring be compared to an aircraft that has taken off without knowing if there is a landing strip at its destination?" Bondarev had asked. And in a bitter slam at Aleksandr Yakovlev, who in December had declared that "diversity may include weeds and barren flowers," Bondarev complained of the wave of "extremist criticism" that had as its "main postulate: Let all weeds bloom and all evil forces contend" and threatened to "bring ideology to the brink of crisis."[54]

Tactically the Ligachev-Yeltsin exchange was a mixed blessing for Gorbachev. Ligachev's speech in its entirety, and particularly his defense of party workers against charges of unmerited privileges, no doubt found deep resonance in the party apparatus and solidified his support among it. Nevertheless, the duel put Ligachev on the same level as Yeltsin. Moreover, by allowing Yeltsin once again, however imperfectly, to push the political spectrum to the left, the debate created greater room for Gorbachev to maneuver and to monopolize the center even while pushing his program further away from previously accepted convention. But Gorbachev's centrist position also demanded compromise. Thus at the conference Gorbachev asserted that "Glasnost means pluralism of opinion on any issues of domestic and foreign policy, free collation of different points of view, debates." But in the same speech he vigorously denounced the creation of opposition parties as one of several "abuses of democratization" running "fundamentally counter to the tasks of restructuring and . . . contrary to the people's interests."

Institutionally, Gorbachev proposed the creation of a semi-permanently standing two-chamber Supreme Soviet consisting of a total of some 450 deputies (the actual number would wind up being 542), and he moved that regional soviets be strengthened by granting them steady financing from taxation of local enterprises and populations. Deputies to the Supreme Soviet would not, however, be elected directly by the public but rather by a much larger Congress of Peoples Deputies. The more than 2,000 deputies to the congress, later fixed at 2,250 representatives, would in turn be nominated and elected according to complicated rules that would guarantee party domination. Finally, Gorbachev recommended that first secretaries of party committees simultaneously serve as chairmen of the presidiums of their corresponding soviets.

Among his liberal supporters, this last measure proved to be Gorbachev's most controversial proposal, but for contradictory reasons.

Some argued that at the top it would open the way to an excessive accumulation of personal power, perhaps acceptable in the hands of a Gorbachev but dangerous in the hands of someone else. Others argued that the president's indirect election by the Congress of People's Deputies would still leave a Gorbachev too vulnerable to the sentiments of those many deputies who would owe their seats to entrenched party bosses.

The silence from conservatives, meanwhile, suggested their approval. The measure had all the marks of a compromise forced on Gorbachev by party apparatus conservatives led by Ligachev. But it may just as well have been a sweetener proposed by Gorbachev in order to make his parliamentary proposals less unpalatable to these same conservatives. Gorbachev's proposal, in any event, could work in a number of ways not necessarily to the advantage of entrenched party interests. Over time, having to stand for election both in the party and the soviet system could, depending on the level of competitiveness tolerated, lead to a more "political" as opposed to "bureaucratic" governing class in the country, one more willing and able to stand up in public and present and defend a political position, instead of one preferring to maneuver behind closed doors, shielded from external pressure.

Indeed, for both liberals and conservatives, the results of the first elections in March 1989 would come as a stunning surprise. The rules governing the elections contained several remarkably effective sleeper clauses: the right of citizens to vote no and the requirement that winning candidates garner at least 50 percent of the yes votes. It was true that the Congress of People's Deputies was potentially an easily manipulable filter to keep radicals out of the Supreme Soviet. But the composition of that congress filter, to a much greater extent than imagined in summer 1988, would have to be acceptable to the public.

For now Gorbachev argued at the party conference that his dual-leadership proposal would ensure the party's leading role in the parliamentary system while perhaps also—depending on ultimate practice—increasing the authority of the soviets. But this was merely another way of saying that the party would dominate the Supreme Soviet. On an individual level, however, Gorbachev emphasized that it would mean that party first secretaries would have to stand successfully for election as soviet deputies. To some extent, at least, this would have the effect—if soviet elections ceased to be a complete charade—of forcing them to take more than just the sentiments of party members and higher level party authorities into account in fulfilling their duties. Once having done that, however, it would also theoretically give him or her a power base of sorts outside the party. At the very top, an active Supreme Soviet led by a president *cum* general secretary would reduce the chances of a Politburo or Central Committee conspiracy toppling a party leader from power.[55]

On the party itself, Gorbachev made his intentions clear well before the major reorganization of the Secretariat which would take place in the fall, and he secured support for them—at least in principle—in the main resolution of the 19th Party Conference. Gorbachev's speech at the beginning of the conference and the resolution adopted at the end both called for a reorganization of Central Committee and lower-level departments and for a reduction of the apparatus. In more concrete terms than the theses, both Gorbachev and the resolution called for broadening the participation of the Central Committee in Politburo work and for setting up Central Committee commissions to deal with areas of major importance in foreign and domestic policy.[56]

On the sensitive issue of apparatchiks' privileges, despite Ligachev's defense of them at the Party Conference, Aleksandr Yakovlev reportedly told a meeting of media representatives on July 14 of the leadership's intention to close down special stores for the nomenklatura. Two weeks later, at the Central Committee plenum on July 29 Gorbachev was said to have announced that all special stores for regional party and ministerial officials, both in Moscow and republic capitals, would be closed as of September 1. His statement, not included among the published plenum materials, reportedly was met by a "long, stony silence."[57] In a related development, it was at long last announced soon after the plenum that the trial of Brezhnev's son-in-law Yuriy Churbanov would open on September 5.[58]

On the main item on its agenda, the July 29 plenum approved the timetable Gorbachev suggested for discussing and adopting concrete measures for reorganizing the party apparatus and the soviet structure. In October draft amendments to the Constitution and a draft new elections law would be released for public discussion. The whole package would then be considered by the "next session" of the Supreme Soviet, which Gorbachev in his opening speech to the plenum, envisioned as taking place during the second half of November, with the usual party plenum preceding it. Elections would be held in March 1989, and the new Congress of People's Deputies would convene for the first time in April 1989. The party apparatus, meanwhile, both locally and centrally, would be reorganized by the end of 1988.[59]

SEPTEMBER CRISIS, AND ADVANCE

On foreign affairs, Gorbachev at the party conference had taken stock of "new thinking" and affirmed the "priority of values common to all mankind in our age."[60] After the conference, Shevardnadze convened a remarkable conference of his own at the Foreign Ministry and pushed new thinking even further ahead. As had Gorbachev in *Perestroika*, in commenting on the Party Program approved at the 27th Party Congress, Shevardnadze reiterated, "We are fully justified in refusing to see in . . . [peaceful coexistence] a special form of class struggle." But now the foreign minister underscored in even more direct terms that "the struggle between two opposing systems is no longer a determining tendency of the present-day era."[61]

Less than two weeks later, with Gorbachev having gone on vacation after meeting on July 30 with West German Foreign Minister Genscher, Ligachev again took issue with this thesis in much sharper language than at the February 1988 plenum. Speaking in Gorkiy on August 5, Ligachev asserted, "We proceed from the class nature of international relations. Any other formulation of the issue only introduces confusion into the thinking of Soviet people and our friends abroad." Furthermore, "Active involvement in the solution of general human problems by no means signifies any artificial 'braking' of the social and national liberation struggle." On this issue Ligachev was beginning to sound more and more like Chernenko after Brezhnev's death.

Otherwise, however, Ligachev's remarks in Gorkiy showed how far the center of gravity in the debate over the economy and politics had moved since the time of Brezhnev. Ligachev warned against replicating capitalist market relations, which "inevitably are accompanied . . . by deep social stratification, a deepening of inequality, and a concentration of wealth in the hands of a small section of society." But in what appeared to be a response to a challenge at the Party Conference from delegate G. I. Zagaynov to define his attitude to the "market" more precisely,[62] Ligachev declared that a "developed socialist market" with "powerful regulators of economic growth," such as "prices" and "supply and demand," was "undoubtedly necessary." He also called "socialist pluralism" an "indispensable condition for elaborating comprehensively substantiated" policies. But he rejected, as had Gorbachev at the party conference, the notions of a multiparty system and of a political opposition.[63]

Nevertheless, differences not only over deideologizing foreign policy but also over reorganizing the party apparatus were coming to a head in late summer 1988. Even on vacation Gorbachev continued working. In a memorandum to the Politburo dated August 24, 1988—not made public until the end of the year—Gorbachev outlined his thoughts on reorganizing the Central Committee apparatus and bluntly discussed differences within the leadership on the subject. Although the memorandum as published named no names, presumably Ligachev was among those arguing for a slower approach than that favored by Gorbachev. But the Politburo's decision of September 8 approving Gorbachev's proposals again underscored the fact that Ligachev—if he indeed opposed Gorbachev—was in a minority. The Politburo also

decreed that Gorbachev's memorandum be circulated to all republic and regional party secretaries, thereby giving wide circulation to
Gorbachev's discussion of differences within the leadership.

In his memorandum Gorbachev wrote that the Central Committee
staff should be substantially reduced and its economic functions, with
few exceptions, turned over to state organs. He recommended that
the Central Committee's 20 departments be reduced and consolidated
into eight: party organization and cadre work; ideology, socioeconomic
policy, agriculture, defense, state and legal questions, international
affairs, and the traditional "general" and "administration of affairs"
departments. The general secretary argued that it was necessary to
carry through this reorganization without delay, before the fall round
of regional and local party conferences and the election of new party
committees. The Politburo had been mulling this over since April 1985,
he asserted, and its "single point of view" had recently been presented
in the theses for the Party Conference. Yet now, when it came to
putting these ideas into practice, Gorbachev complained that a "certain
difference in approach to the reorganization of the party apparatus"
was cropping up. Referring to memoranda from his colleagues on the
issue, Gorbachev charged that "some comrades" seemed to prefer only
"half steps" and "palliatives." This would only make things worse,
wrote Gorbachev. "Cardinal" measures needed to be adopted and the
Secretariat instructed to work up concrete proposals for consideration
by the Politburo.[64]

After returning from vacation in mid-September, Gorbachev toured
the vast Krasnoyarsk region and allowed Soviet television to show local
citizens haranguing him over deplorable local living conditions. It was
later speculated that these encounters shocked Gorbachev into pushing
for a faster pace of reform. This could not be totally discounted. But a
rereading of Gorbachev's speech to the Central Committee plenum on
July 29, 1988, suggested that his Siberian chats did not come as much
of a surprise. He had, he told the Central Committee in July, recently
had a talk with the venerable author Viktor Astafyev about conditions in
Krasnoyarsk. "The number of problems that have accumulated there!"
Gorbachev exclaimed.[65] In retrospect Gorbachev probably went to Krasnoyarsk looking for exactly what he got. His televised exchanges were
just what he wanted to create the proper atmospherics for another push
on economic reform and against party privilege—although on the latter
issue Gorbachev had written in his August 24 memorandum that the
salaries of party workers should be increased after the party apparatus
was reduced.

In any event, Gorbachev also used his Krasnoyarsk trip implicitly
to rebut Ligachev's remarks in Gorkiy on the class nature of international relations. Outside a Lenin exhibition in the former village

of Shushenskoye on September 15, Gorbachev declared that "Lenin expressed the idea . . . of the priority of the interests of social development over the class interests of the proletariat." Gorbachev defended "the formula of the priority of general human values." The preservation of civilization was a priority that all its constituent parts "must take into account, each one of them, even on the basis of common sense, without referring to the ideological aspect for the time being."[66]

What happened next was far from clear but finally precipitated the personnel changes—first in late September 1988 and then in April 1989—which Gorbachev was denied at the party conference. Possibly some disgruntled Central Committee members sought to take advantage of the leadership disagreements advertised in Gorbachev's August 24 memorandum to launch a desperate last-ditch effort to foil Gorbachev's plan for restructuring the party apparatus. If so, they presumably counted on the support of Ligachev and a few others in the Politburo, even though Ligachev was apparently out of town on vacation, as he made no public appearances during the entire month of September. Perhaps getting wind of this effort, Gorbachev in turn took advantage of it to move the political calendar forward and used it to erode Ligachev's authority even further.

Whatever the case, the crisis did not seem to erupt until the weekend of September 24–25. On September 20 Shevardnadze left Moscow on a trip scheduled to take him, after a brief stopover in Denmark, to a ministerial in Washington and then to the UN General Assembly in New York. On September 23, a Friday, Gorbachev told a meeting of media, ideological, and cultural representatives that "on the basis of the principles formulated at the 19th party conference we are now engaged in reforming the party apparatus. And we want to do it as quickly as possible." Presumably referring to the Politburo's decision of September 8, Gorbachev said, "There has already been discussion of this, and the Politburo has adopted a decision. In connection with the change in the party's functions, the structure of the apparatus of the CPSU Central Committee, republic Communist Party central committees, kraykoms, and obkoms will change, with the emphasis on political and organizational work. The apparatus will also be reduced in size."[67] Despite Gorbachev's comment about proceeding with political reform "as quickly as possible," Shevardnadze's departure for the United States several days before suggested there was no extreme urgency about the matter.

On September 24, nevertheless, a regular session of the Supreme Soviet was announced for October 27.[68] This was the first indication that the schedule for political reform proposed by Gorbachev and approved by the July 29 plenum was off track. The announcement stated that the Supreme Soviet session would deal primarily with the 1988 state plan and budget, yet the July 29 plenum had declared that the next regular session of the Supreme Soviet would take up the proposed reform measures. Gorbachev, furthermore, had envisioned the Supreme Soviet meeting in late November after public discussion of the draft reforms, which would be released in early October.

Even though TASS announced on Sunday, September 25, that Gromyko would be visiting North Korea,[69] no leader then known to be in Moscow made any public appearances, adding to the retrospective impression of a brewing crisis.[70] On Monday, September 26 "well-informed sources" in Moscow later told newsmen that the Politburo had met—minus Ligachev, reportedly vacationing in Pitsunda on the Black Sea—and decided the personnel changes, which were announced later in the week.[71] By Wednesday, September 28 Gerasimov announced in New York that Shevardnadze would be returning to Moscow ahead of schedule to attend a Central Committee plenum on Friday, September 30, which would deal with reorganizing the Central Committee and the party apparatus—conclusive evidence that something unusual was going on in the Soviet capital.[72] The same day an "extraordinary session" of the Supreme Soviet was announced for Saturday, October 1; it would deal, said Foreign Ministry Deputy Spokesman Vadim Perfilyev, with "realizing the decisions" of the 19th Party Conference.[73]

On September 23 Gorbachev had told the group of media, ideological, and cultural representatives with whom he met that they were living in a "transitional period in which all methods, all means of work—old and new—will coexist. We can see," he said, "that some problems are not going to be solved until we intervene in the old way, as before. But what can you do?" he asked. "That's life."[74] Within a week, at the plenum on September 30 and the Supreme Soviet session on October 1, Gorbachev did just that, using the disciplined midwife of the authoritarian old order to bring in a potentially more democratic one.

Before the January 1987 plenum, as well as before the 19th Party Conference in 1988, Gorbachev had lobbied groups of regional party secretaries, and the subsequent meetings had been occasions for lively debate. Now the Central Committee plenum on September 30 and the Supreme Soviet session on October 1 were strictly scripted affairs, the first lasting only an hour and the second a mere forty-five minutes.[75] The personnel changes at the plenum were momentous. Gromyko's retirement marked the clear passing of an era. Solomentsev, Dolgikh, Demichev, and Dobrynin also went on pensions, though Dobrynin would soon reappear as an adviser to Gorbachev on the staff of the Presidium of the Supreme Soviet. Medvedev, already a Central Committee secretary, was named a full member of the Politburo. Chebrikov, a full member of the Politburo, was appointed a Central Committee secretary—an indication that he was about to leave the KGB. MVD

Chairman Aleksandr Vlasov meanwhile was elected a Politburo candidate. Aleksandr Biryukova and Anatoliy Lukyanov were as well, and were simultaneously relieved of their responsibilities as Central Committee secretaries.

In 1962 Khrushchev had tried to dilute the influence of Suslov in the Secretariat by creating a Central Committee Ideological Commission headed by Suslov's rival, L. F. Ilichev.[76] In late 1988 Gorbachev appeared intent on using the same tactic on a massive scale against Ligachev. Organizationally, the changes first vaguely sketched out at the party conference finally began to take shape. Six commissions of the Central Committee were announced: on party building and cadre policy, to be chaired by Razumovskiy; on ideology, to be chaired by Medvedev; on socioeconomic policy, to be chaired by Slyunkov; on agrarian policy, to be chaired by Ligachev; on international policy, to be chaired by Yakovlev; and on legal policy, to be chaired by Chebrikov. The Politburo was furthermore "instructed" to restructure the Central Committee apparatus, as well as that of local party committees.[77] In his memorandum of August 24 Gorbachev had still referred to the Central Committee Secretariat as a working entity. But it soon became apparent that the mandated changes amounted to no less than the end of the Secretariat as a locus of decision making just slightly less important than the Politburo, and the end of Ligachev's status as senior secretary second only to Gorbachev.

Medvedev told a press conference the same day as the plenum that some Central Committee departments would be "enlarged and merged," while departments dealing with specific economic sectors would be abolished." Medvedev also confirmed that Ligachev would "concentrate" on agriculture rather than just dabble in it, and that in Gorbachev's absence the Politburo would be chaired on a rotating basis.[78] There would soon be reports that the Secretariat was no longer meeting regularly.[79] Indeed, *Pravda's* photograph of the leadership lineup on November 7 was cropped to show only full members of the Politburo—no doubt intended to reinforce the message that the Secretariat had fallen on hard days.[80] Then a follow-up Central Committee plenum on November 29 announced, in a resolution listing the members of the new Central Committee commissions, that they would report directly to the Politburo or to a plenum, making no mention whatsoever of the Secretariat.[81]

On October 1 the Supreme Soviet accepted Gromyko's resignation and unanimously elected Gorbachev the new chairman of its Presidium—in line with Gorbachev's own suggestion in principle at the party conference. Gromyko would not live another year, and his death in July 1989 was marked with what would seem to be conclusive demonstrations of the bitterness and black humor with which Gorbachev had come to regard him: Gorbachev did not return from Paris for the funeral; Gromyko did not receive a Red Square funeral; and at Novodevichiy Cemetery he was buried right next to Suslov's wife (surely a more suitable plot was available!). In any event, further indicating Ligachev's decline in status was the identity of the person who nominated Gorbachev for president—not Ligachev, who it should have been by precedent had he still been the undisputed number two, but none other than Lev Zaykov. Despite all the changes at the plenum, Zaykov was still both a Central Committee secretary and a full member of the Politburo, though by custom he would have been expected to give up his secretaryship sometime after replacing Yeltsin as Moscow party leader in November 1987. Zaykov's selection to deliver the opening remarks at the seventieth anniversary of the armed forces in February 1988, nevertheless, had suggested he was still involved in overseeing the military-industrial sector.[82] In April Zaykov had portrayed himself as number three among the senior Central Committee secretaries—behind Gorbachev and Ligachev.[83] Now he was the apparent new number two.

There were other personnel shifts at the Supreme Soviet session. Demichev retired, and Lukyanov was elected first deputy chairman of the Presidium of the Supreme Soviet. Lukyanov would now in effect serve as Gorbachev's alter ego and overseer of the upcoming parliamentary reforms, a new stage in Lukyanov's relationship with his fellow law student at Moscow State University in the early 1950s. In addition, Talyzin replaced the pensioned-off Aleksey Antonov as permanent representative to CEMA, and was downgraded from first deputy premier to deputy premier. Biryukova in turn took over Talyzin's vacant position as chairman of the Bureau for Social Development, and was appointed a deputy premier. Finally, Chebrikov was formally released as chairman of the KGB, and KGB Deputy Chairman Vladimir Kryuchkov was elected in his place.[84] Kryuchkov had worked for Andropov since the 1950s: first in Hungary, then in the Central Committee's Bloc Relations Department, and then in the KGB as well. More recently he had accompanied Gorbachev to the Washington summit in December 1987.

Other major moves soon followed at the session of the Supreme Soviet of the Russian Republic, held on October 3. Vorotnikov was transferred from premier to president of the republic. This would have been a demotion in days gone by but was now a question mark until the new parliamentary reforms sorted themselves out and Vorotnikov's status in his new position became clearer. At the same time, Gorbachev protégé Vlasov was elected new republic premier, a definite promotion. On October 20, Vadim Bakatin would be named new chairman of the MVD.[85]

Only after this massive shuffling of personnel were the draft amendments to the Constitution and to the election law put out for public "discussion" on October 22–23, 1988.[86] There were objections from some of the Baltic republics that the amendments further centralized rather than relaxed Moscow's control, and warnings from some supporters of Gorbachev that the leadership of party and parliament, from Moscow to the peripheries, should not be concentrated in one person at each level. Nevertheless, the amendments were adopted with few changes at the Supreme Soviet session held November 29–December 1, which set elections to the new Congress of People's Deputies for March 26, 1989.[87]

BALLOTING INTO THE FUTURE

In the runups to the elections, publication of the tallies from the voting at the Central Committee plenum on March 15, 1989, for 100 guaranteed CPSU deputies to the Congress of Peoples Deputies revealed some fascinating outcomes. The results seemed to demonstrate Gorbachev's centrist position—smack in the middle between the opposite poles of Ligachev and Yakovlev. Of the 641 participants in the plenum casting ballots, 629 voted for Gorbachev and only 12 against him. In contrast, 563 voted for Ligachev but 78 against—the largest negative count reported. However, while Yakovlev received 582 yes votes, 59 participants voted no—the second largest reported negative tally.[88]

The general elections two weeks later to the 2,250-seat Congress of Peoples Deputies proved full of surprises. According to a 1988 opinion poll cited by sociologist Tatyana Zaslavskaya, by far the second most popular political personality in the country was Boris Yeltsin—"way behind" Gorbachev but "well ahead" of Ryzhkov.[89] Yeltsin demonstrated the immense popularity of his antiprivileges platform when he won election as deputy in a Moscow citywide district by a margin of 5,118,745 to 392,633 votes against a party-backed rival. Even more impressive, however, was the defeat of 34 regional party secretaries, including Politburo candidate member and Leningrad regional party First Secretary Yuriy Solovyov, who lost by a vote of 130,000 to 110,000.[90]

The results of the March 26 elections were a triumph for Gorbachev, yet almost too much of a good thing. There was a danger that the embittered party regulars who had gone down to defeat might revolt against Gorbachev and finally bring him down. However, the personnel changes in the Politburo and Secretariat that Gorbachev had engineered in September-October 1988 deprived disgruntled Central Committee members of the necessary support at the top. As a result, rather than backing away, Gorbachev was able to push forward with a dramatic house cleaning of the Central Committee at a plenum held on April 25, 1989. No fewer than 110 "dead souls" and potential opponents of Gorbachev and reform, including 74 of the 301 full members of the Central Committee, submitted their resignations, and 24 candidate members were promoted to full membership to replace those departing. In many instances—such as former Premier Tikhonov, former Defense Minister Sokolov, and former Chief of the General Staff Ogarkov—it was surprising to be reminded that they were still in the Central Committee.[91] Thus Gorbachev at last was able to achieve at least in part the turnover he had been denied at the party conference the previous summer, and to engineer a "unanimous" vote in favor of the move from the very Central Committee he was purging.[92] A month later, on May 25, 1989, the Congress of Peoples Deputies opened on schedule, and with it a novel experiment in indirect and very much guided democratization.

Nevertheless, immense problems remained at home even without the consequences of the disastrous Armenian earthquake and ethnic strife and regional assertiveness in the Caucasus and the Baltic republics. The economy had yet to take off despite four years of reformist prodding, and economists were predicting consumer hardships for years to come.[93] Gorbachev could not go on forever arguing that the past was far worse than the present, when the widespread belief was that the standard of living was going down rather than up.[94] In the absence of thoroughgoing reform, the initial hopes that improved labor discipline and industrial efficiency would quickly benefit the consumer without additional state allocations to consumption had also long ago proved unrealistic. Reacting to widespread grumbling, the Gorbachev leadership had finally shifted to directly favoring consumption. Economists increasingly gave signs of recognizing that massive investment in civilian industrial modernization without implementation of profound reforms would produce neither a modernized economy nor a more satisfied consumer, but simply waste enormous resources in producing an ever more quickly growing heap of useless goods.[95]

Gorbachev and his supporters, however, often appeared to be prisoners of the economic system they sought to change, fated to be unable to break its grip on the country. The system was rotten to the core, but many of its millions of officials were dependent on its very rottenness for their status and livelihood and resisted changing it. The more the Gorbachev leadership struggled against the bureaucracy, it seemed at times, the tighter became the bureaucracy's noose around the leadership's neck. Moreover, the results of the elections to the Congress of Peoples Deputies had been a misleading reflection of public support for perestroika. Most workers likely continued to prefer, on balance, the security of the inefficient old economic system to the perils of a more productive but competitive new one, even while supporting Gorbachev's drive against the bureaucracy.[96]

The economic situation cried out for radical reform, yet the more radical the reform, the greater the short-term chaos. Gorbachev and his supporters seemed damned if they did and damned if they didn't. More than half measures ran the risk of completely unbalancing the complex Soviet system with no assurance of how soon it could function again or in what fashion. Staying with the system that had ossified under Brezhnev, on the other hand, meant the predictability of slow and sure national decline. Yet half measures often only seemed to make the situation more desperate, introducing the confusion of change while permitting the bureaucracy to stay in place and make matters even worse by sabotaging any elements of progressiveness. Worse yet, even Gorbachev and his advisers seemed to have little intuitive feel for what real economic reform on a national scale would look like. Soviet citizens remained great capitalists and connoisseurs of supply-and-demand relationships at the individual level, with constant deficits honing their instincts for survival. But among economists and ordinary citizens alike, the appreciation for the self-regulating aspects of market forces seemed to go little further than comprehension—and apprehension—of the economics of the bazaar and black market.

It was much too early, however, to write Gorbachev off as a tragic figure when it came to economic reform. Results would take decades, historical judgments even longer; and in any event history has never dealt kindly with the politically suicidal. For now Gorbachev had to be given the benefit of the doubt in his judgment as to how fast and far he could push without risk of being ousted. Gorbachev had proved time and time again to be the master rather than the prisoner of consensus, always manipulating and shifting prevailing opinion toward reform. Yet it often appeared that the requirements for Gorbachev's political survival and national economic recovery were in contradiction. He could not survive without trimming his reformist sails. At the same time, he could not maintain—much less expand—support for perestroika without producing results. But he could not produce results without radical reform, for which there was no consensus at the top, and even then the results might not be apparent for years.

On balance, however, in four decades of political life Gorbachev had shown not only great flair for the sudden and dramatic but also great discipline for the long haul. With startling diplomatic moves having stabilized the external front, Gorbachev and his supporters by 1989 seemed to have settled down to the less dramatic but many times more difficult task of grinding down the Soviet bureaucracy and reshaping the population's approach to economics. Given how much had been achieved so far, to be sure, it was appropriate in many instances to ask whether a conservative backlash could ever put the genie of reform back in the bottle. But when it came to the economy, the more haunting question—and daunting task—was whether or not the Gorbachev regime would ever be able to force the genie of entrepreneurship and competitiveness out of the bottle in the first place on a massive scale. For all its distrust of the party and dislike of its privileges, the bulk of the population was at heart suspicious and fearful of living under conditions of higher prices brought about by price reform; of unemployment, however marginal, even if a stimulus for greater societal welfare; and of widening income disparities even if due to the rewarding of individual enterprise.

It was, of course, a paradox—but one not necessarily condemned to be a contradiction—that in the conditions inherited by Gorbachev the more civil society he and his supporters envisioned could not come about by itself but would be dependent on the judicious application of an iron fist. During his first four years in power Gorbachev repeatedly managed to draw back from old-fashioned dictatorial methods—after using all the powers of his office to strike down the foes of his brand of democratization. But would it always be so? The alternatives seemed bounded by the twin fears that if Gorbachev survived he was bound to develop into a dictator and that if he disappeared, democratization would fall apart.

No one could know the outcome of this grand experiment, in which an authoritarian regime tacked back and forth toward a more open society out of an instinct for national survival. Still, the wonder of it all—and the best witness to the bankruptcy of the Brezhnev era—was that the process of revolutionary reform had even gotten started at all, and that it had been launched by leaders developed and nourished by the same system they now sought to change. The Kremlin was at last in profound transition, and whatever the final destination, neither the country nor its leaders would ever be the same again.

NOTES

1. See the remarkable essay by Igor Arievich, "The Lessons We Never Learned," *New Times*, no. 39 (1988), 24–25.

2. *New York Times*, April 10, 1989.

3. *Washington Post*, December 29, 30, and 31, 1988, and January 6, 1989. Sakharov's U.S. trip coincided with former Czechoslovak leader Alexander Dubcek's first visit abroad in 18 years, to Italy (*Washington Post*, November 13, 1988). Dubcek had earlier told an interviewer that he stopped being aware

of surveillance since Gorbachev's visit to Czechoslovakia in April 1987 (*The Guardian*, January 11, 1988).

4. *Pravda*, December 3, 1987 (FBIS-SOV, December 4, 1987, 48).

5. *Le Monde*, December 4, 1987 (FBIS-SOV, December 4, 1987, 42–45).

6. *Komsomolskaya Pravda*, January 15, 1988 (FBIS-SOV, January 27, 1988, 59–66). This did not, however, mention Suslov's role.

7. *Literary Gazette*, January 27, 1988 (FBIS-SOV, February 9, 1988, 48–55).

8. Moscow Television Service, February 3, 1988 (FBIS-SOV, February 4, 1988, Editorial Report, 51–52).

9. TASS, February 5, 1988 (FBIS-SOV, February 8, 1988, 36).

10. *Red Star*, March 18–20, 1988 (FBIS-SOV, March 24, 1988, 57–63). See also *Nedelya*, no. 8, February 22–28, 1988, signed to press February 24, 1988 (FBIS-SOV, March 2, 1988, 58–61).

11. TASS, January 6, 1988 (FBIS-SOV, January 6, 1988, 47).

12. *Izvestiya*, January 16, 1988 (FBIS-SOV, January 20, 1988, 54–58).

13. Moscow Television Service, January 29, 1988 (FBIS-SOV, February 3, 1988, 41).

14. *Literary Gazette*, February 24, 1988 (FBIS-SOV, February 25, 1988, 55–62).

15. TANJUG, April 30, 1988 report on interview in *Vijesnik* (FBIS-SOV, May 3, 1988, 39–40).

16. *Pravda*, January 13, 1988 (FBIS-SOV, January 13, 1988, 41).

17. *Pravda*, February 19, 1988 (FBIS-SOV, February 19, 1988, 42–59).

18. *Pravda*, February 18, 1988 (FBIS-SOV, February 18, 1988, 57 and 71).

19. *Pravda*, February 19, 1988 (FBIS-SOV, February 19, 1988, 42–59).

20. Moscow Domestic Service, February 18, 1988 (FBIS-SOV, February 18, 1988, 56). On Maslyukov vice Talyzin, see TASS, February 6, 1988 (FBIS-SOV, February 8, 1988, 36). Talyzin remained a first deputy premier and took over the chairmanship of the Bureau of Social Development until he was replaced by Biryukova in October 1988.

21. Speech in Khabarovsk, Moscow Domestic Service, July 31, 1986 (FBIS-SOV, August 4, 1986, R 3).

22. *Komsomolskaya Pravda*, April 21, 1988 (FBIS-SOV, April 22, 1988, 44–47).

23. *Sovetskaya Rossiya*, March 13, 1988 (FBIS-SOV, March 16, 1988, 48–53).

24. Ibid.

25. See Michel Tatu, "19th Party Conference," *Problems of Communism* (May-August 1988): 3, for the career ties of those involved in producing the letter and their links to Ligachev.

26. *L'Unita*, May 23, 1988 (FBIS-SOV, May 31, 1988, 56).

27. Gregg Embree and Anne Crocker, "Summary" of a July 22, 1988, Washington, D.C. conference on the 19th CPSU Conference (Washington, DC: CIA Directorate of Intelligence, August 3, 1988).

28. *Sovetskaya Kultura*, May 3, 1988 (FBIS-SOV, May 4, 1988, 23).

29. See Moscow Domestic Service, March 15, 1988 (FBIS-SOV, March 18, 1988, 48–49); idem, March 18, 1988 (FBIS-SOV, March 21, 1988, 53); and idem, March 18, 1988 (FBIS-SOV, March 22, 1988, 66).

30. *Pravda*, March 23, 1988 (FBIS-SOV, March 23, 1988, 51).

31. Moscow Television Service, March 28, 1988 (FBIS-SOV, March 29, 1988, p. 52).

32. On the highjacking, see TASS, March 10, 1988 (FBIS-SOV, March 10, 1988, p. 35). On Sitnikov's removal, see TASS, April 2, 1988 (FBIS-SOV, April 7, 1988, 37).

33. Moscow Domestic Service, February 17, 1988 (FBIS-SOV, February 18, 1988, 78).

34. *New York Times*, April 6, 1988.

35. *Pravda*, April 5, 1988 (FBIS-SOV, April 5, 1988, 37–43).

36. *Sovetskaya Rossiya*, April 15, 1988 (FBIS-SOV, April 15, 1988, 56–59).

37. Moscow Domestic Service, April 20, 1988 (FBIS-SOV, April 20, 1988, 50).

38. *New York Times* and *Washington Post*, April 22, 1988.

39. *La Repubblica*, January 7, 1989 (FBIS-SOV, January 12, 1989, 59).

40. *Washington Post*, April 23 and May 11, 1988.

41. *Pravda*, April 23, 1988 (FBIS-SOV, April 25, 1988, 64).

42. *Washington Post*, May 17, 1988.

43. *Pravda*, May 27, 1988 (FBIS-SOV, May 27, 1988, 39–50).

44. Ibid.

45. *Ogonek*, no. 50 (December 1987), signed to press December 9, 1987. Mikoyan died in 1978.

46. According to the press release, Voznesenskiy had never been expelled from the party, but his party documents had been "cancelled" after his arrest and conviction (TASS, March 26, 1988 [FBIS-SOV, March 28, 1988, 46]).

47. *Sovetskaya Kultura*, May 3, 1988 (FBIS-SOV, May 4, 1988, 24 and 26). In addition, before long Andrey Kirilenko—Ryzhkov's Sverdlovsk patron and Suslov's nemesis—would also be criticized for his son's alleged habit of wasting "precious foreign currency on organizing stunning safaris — his hobby was shooting African wildlife" (*Nedelya*, no. 29, July 18–24, 1988, signed to press July 20, 1988 [FBIS-SOV, July 29, 1988, 58]).

48. See, for example, *Pravda*, June 4, 1988 (FBIS-SOV, June 6, 1988, 54–57).

49. *Pravda*, June 5, 1988 (FBIS-SOV, June 6, 1988, 58–62).

50. *Pravda*, June 7, 1988 (FBIS-SOV, June 13, 1988, 81).

51. *Izvestiya*, June 10, 1988 (FBIS-SOV, June 13, 1988, 82–83).

52. TASS, July 9, 1988 (FBIS-SOV, July 11, 1988, 70–71).

53. Moscow Domestic Service, July 1, 1988 (FBIS-SOV, July 5, 1988, Supplement, 101–4).

54. *Pravda*, July 1, 1988 (FBIS-SOV, July 5, 1988, Supplement, 6–9).

55. In fact, after the Andreyeva affair one nervous letter writer had called for restricting the Central Committee's power to replacing an incumbent general secretary solely to raising the question, which would then be decided by a nationwide referendum. See *Sovetskaya Kultura*, April 30, 1988 (FBIS-SOV, May 3, 1988, 29–30).

56. For Gorbachev's opening report at the Conference, see *Pravda*, June 29, 1988 (FBIS-SOV, July 1, 1988, Supplement, 1–44); for the resolution on political reform, see *Pravda*, July 5, 1988 (FBIS-SOV, July 5, 1988, Supplement, 130–34).

57. See Giulietto Chiesa's report in *L'Unita*, September 8, 1988 (FBIS-SOV, September 14, 1988, 60).

58. TASS, August 3, 1988 (FBIS-SOV, August 3, 1988, 38).

59. *Pravda*, July 30 and 31, 1988 (FBIS-SOV, August 1, 1988, 35–54).

60. *Pravda*, June 29, 1988 (FBIS-SOV, July 1, 1988, Supplement, 11).

61. *Pravda*, July 26, 1988 (FBIS-SOV, July 26, 1988, 30).

62. *Pravda*, July 2, 1988.

63. *Pravda*, August 6, 1988 (FBIS-SOV, August 8, 1988, 36–40).

64. *Izvestiya TsK KPSS*, no. 1 (1989): 81–86, signed to press January 6, 1989.

65. *Pravda*, July 30, 1988 (FBIS-SOV, August 1, 1988, 46).

66. Moscow Television Service, September 15, 1988 (FBIS-SOV, September 16, 1988, 40).

67. *Pravda*, September 25, 1988 (FBIS-SOV, September 26, 1988, 52).

68. Moscow Domestic Service, September 24, 1988 (FBIS-SOV, September 27, 1988, 44).

69. TASS, September 25, 1988 (FBIS-SOV, September 26, 1988, 30).

70. I am indebted to Jack Sontag for pointing this out.

71. *Washington Post*, October 2, 1988.

72. *New York Times*, September 29, 1988.

73. Moscow Domestic Service and TASS, September 29, 1988 (FBIS-SOV, September 29, 1988, 51).

74. *Pravda*, September 25, 1988 (FBIS-SOV, September 26, 1988, 49).

75. *Washington Post*, October 1 and 2, 1988.

76. Carl A. Linden, *Khrushchev and the Soviet Leadership 1957–1964* (Baltimore: Johns Hopkins University Press, 1966), 151–52.

77. *Pravda*, October 1, 1988 (FBIS-SOV, October 3, 1988, 40–41).

78. TASS, September 30, 1988 (FBIS-SOV, October 3, 1988, 42–43).

79. See Yegor Yakovlev's comments in *L'Unita*, October 12, 1988 (FBIS-SOV, October 20, 1988, 45); and Georgiy Shakhnazarov, in *Yomiuri Shimbun*, October 17, 1988.

80. *Pravda*, November 8, 1988. Curiously, the photograph left out Politburo voting member Vadim Medvedev.

81. *Pravda*, November 29, 1988 (FBIS-SOV, November 29, 1988, 52–57).

82. Moscow Television Service, February 22, 1988 (FBIS-SOV, February 23, 1988, 64–65). A year later Zaykov was still the senior leadership representative present at Armed Forces Day ceremonies.

83. *Newsweek*, April 4, 1988, 37.

84. Moscow Domestic Service, October 1, 1988 (FBIS-SOV, October 3, 1988, 43–49).

85. Moscow Television Service, October 3 and 20, 1988 (FBIS-SOV, October 4 and 21, 1988, 40 and 52, respectively).

86. *Pravda*, October 22–23, 1988 (FBIS-SOV, October 24, 1988, 26–50).

87. Moscow Domestic Service, December 1, 1988 (FBIS-SOV, December 2, 1988, 40).

88. *Pravda*, March 19, 1989 (FBIS-SOV, March 20, 1989, 51–54).

89. *Le Nouvel Observateur*, March 1, 1989.

90. *Washington Post*, March 28 and 30, 1989.

91. *Washington Post*, April 26, 1989.

92. See Central Committee member Vladimir Karpov's rueful recollection of the vote in *Pravda*, January 27, 1990.

93. For the views of Abalkin at the beginning of 1989, for example, see *Moscow News*, no. 6, February 5, 1989 (FBIS-SOV, February 8, 1989, 71–74); for those of Aganbegyan, see *Pravda*, February 6, 1989 (FBIS-SOV, February 8, 1989, 74–77).

94. *Washington Post*, December 24, 1988; and *New York Times*, January 1, 1989.

95. See, for example, Vasiliy Selyunin's critique of Aganbegyan's investment policy and of the "self-consuming economy" which "is increasingly working not for people but for itself" in *Sotsialisticheskaya Industriya*, January 5, 1988 (FBIS-SOV, January 12, 1988, 63–66). For a response by Aganbegyan, see *Komsomolskaya Pravda*, April 23, 1988 (FBIS-SOV, May 2, 1988, 80).

96. See, for example, Elizabeth Teague, "*Perestroika*: Who Stands to Gain, Who Stands to Lose?" paper presented at the Institute for Defense Analyses, March 9, 1989, esp. p. 20.

Bibliography

ADN (East Berlin, news agency).

AFP (Paris, news agency).

Aftenposten (Oslo, daily).

Aganbegyan, Abel, "The Real State of the Soviet Economy," In Stephen F. Cohen, ed., *An End to Silence* (New York: Norton, 1982), 223–27.

AGERPRESS (Bucharest, news agency).

Akhromeyev, S. F., chairman of the Main Editorial Commission, Institute of Military History, USSR Ministry of Defense, *Voyenniy Entsiklopedicheskiy Slovar* [Military encyclopedic dictionary], 2nd ed. (Moscow: Voyenizdat, 1986, signed to press April 21, 1986).

Anonymous, "Trevozhnoye Odinochestvo," *Novoye Russkoye Slovo*, August 11, 1987.

ANSA (Rome, news agency).

AP (New York, news agency).

APN (Moscow, news agency).

Arbeiter-Zeitung (Vienna, daily).

Argumenty i Fakty (Moscow, weekly).

Armacost, Michael, "Reflections on U.S.-Soviet Relations." Speech delivered at the United States Air Force Academy, Colorado Springs, Colorado, May 1, 1985 (Washington, DC: United States Department of State, Bureau of Public Affairs, Current Policy No. 700, May 1985).

Asahi Shimbun (Tokyo, daily).

Aslund, Anders, "Gorbachev's Economic Advisors." *Soviet Economy* 3, no. 3 (1987), 246–69.

Asmus, Ronald D., "East Germany Publicizes Protests." In Vojtech Mastny, ed., *Soviet/East European Survey, 1983–1984* (Durham, NC: Duke University Press, 1985), 68–70.

———"The Policy of Damage Limitation." In Vojtech Mastny, ed., *Soviet/East European Survey, 1983–1984* (Durham, NC: Duke University Press, 1985), 244–48.

Asmus, Ronald D., Kusin, Vladimir V., Wise, Sallie, and Stankovic, Slobodan, "Discord with Moscow." in Vojtech Mastny, ed., *Soviet/East European Survey, 1983–1984* (Durham, NC: Duke University Press, 1985), 248–57.

Avrora (Leningrad, monthly).

Azrael, Jeremy R., "The Soviet Civilian Leadership and the Military High Command, 1976–1986." RAND/R-3521-AF (Santa Monica, CA: RAND

Corporation, June 1987).

BAKHTAR (Kabul, news agency).

Bakinskiy Rabochiy (Baku, daily).

Barbieri, France, "USSR: Plan Proceeding Badly, Party Mobilized," *La Stampa*, February 9, 1978.

Barry, John, "Revealed: The Truth about Labour and Cruise." *The Sunday Times*, February 6, 1983.

Becker, Abraham S., *Ogarkov's Complaint and Gorbachev's Dilemma*, RAND/R-3541-AF (Santa Monica, CA: RAND Corporation, December 1987).

Beijing Review (Beijing, monthly).

Berlingske Tidende (Copenhagen, daily).

Binns, Christopher A. P., "The Development of the Soviet Policy Response to the EEC." *Co-Existence* 14, no. 2 (October 1977): 240–65.

Bjorkman, Thomas N., and Zamostny, Thomas J., "Soviet Politics and Strategy toward the West: Three Cases." *World Politics* 36, no. 2 (January 1984): 189–214.

Bond, Daniel, and Levine, Herbert, "The 11th Five-Year Plan, 1981–85." In Seweryn Bialer and Thane Gustafson, eds., *Russia at the Crossroads* (London: Unwin Hyman, 1982), 87–107.

Bornstein, Morris, "Soviet Economic Growth and Foreign Policy." In Seweryn Bialer, ed., *The Domestic Context of Soviet Foreign Policy* (Boulder, CO: Westview, 1981), 227–55.

Boston Globe (Boston, daily).

Bradsher, Henry S., *Afghanistan and the Soviet Union*, new and expanded ed. (Durham, NC: Duke University Press, 1985).

Breslauer, George W., *Khrushchev and Brezhnev as Leaders: Building Authority in Soviet Politics* (London: Unwin Hyman, 1982).

Brooks, E. Willis, "Russian Precedents of Soviet Successions." Paper presented at Symposium on Soviet Succession in Historical Perspective, American Association for the Advancement of Slavic Studies—Washington, D.C. Chapter, October 2, 1984.

Brown, Archie, "Gorbachev: New Man in the Kremlin." *Problems of Communism* (May-June): 1985, 1–23.

Brzezinski, Zbigniew, *Power and Principle* (New York: Farrar, Straus, Giroux, 1985).

BTA (Sofia, news agency).

Cambio 16 (Madrid, weekly).

Central Committee of the Communist Party of the Soviet Union, *History of the Communist Party of the Soviet Union (Bolsheviks). Short Course* (Moscow: Foreign Languages Publishing House, 1939).

Chernenko, K. U., *Voprosy raboty partiynogo i gosudarstvennogo apparata*, 2d ed., rev. and expanded (Moscow: Politizdat, 1982).

Christian Science Monitor (Boston, daily).

Cockburn, Andrew, *The Threat: Inside the Soviet Military Machine* (New York: Vintage Books, 1984).

Cohn, Stanley H., "Declining Soviet Capital Productivity and the Soviet Military-Industrial Complex." In U.S. Arms Control and Disarmament Agency, *World Military Expenditures and Arms Transfers, 1972–1982* (Washington, DC:

U.S. Government Printing Office, April 1984), 111–16.

Colton, Timothy J., *Commissars, Commanders, and Civilian Authority* (Cambridge, MA: Harvard University Press, 1979).

————"Moscow Politics and the El'tsin Affair." The Harriman Institute *Forum*, 1, no. 6, (June 1988).

Conquest, Robert, *The Great Terror*, rev. ed. (New York: Collier, 1973).

Cooper, Julian, "The Civilian Production of the Soviet Defence Industry." Paper prepared for the Symposium on Soviet Science and Technology organized by the Centre for Russian and East European Studies and the Department of Extramural Studies, University of Birmingham, September 24–25, 1984.

Corriere della Sera (Milan, daily).

Cronin, Richard P., *Afghanistan Peace Talks: An Annotated Chronology and Analysis of the United Nations-sponsored Negotiations.* Congressional Research Service Report for Congress, 88–149 F, February 19, 1988.

Dagens Nyheter (Stockholm, daily).

Daily Telegraph (London, daily).

Davis, Christopher, "'Perestroika' in the Soviet Defense Sector, 1985–87: National Security Elite Participation and Turnover." Paper prepared for Conference on Elites and Political Power in the USSR, Centre for Russian and East European Studies, University of Birmingham, July 1–2, 1987.

Detente (Leeds, quarterly).

Diehl, Jackson, "Eastern Europe. The High-Stakes Quest for High Tech." *Washington Post*, October 19, 20, and 21, 1986.

Doder, Dusko, *Shadows and Whispers* (New York: Random House, 1986).

Dornberg, John. *Brezhnev. The Masks of Power* (New York: Basic Books, 1974).

DPA (Hamburg, news agency).

Druzhba Narodov (Moscow, monthly).

Ekonomicheskaya Gazeta (Moscow, weekly).

Embree, Gregg, and Crocker, Anne, "Summary" of July 22, 1988, Washington, D.C. Conference on the 19th CPSU Conference, United States Central Intelligence Agency, Directorate of Intelligence, August 3, 1988.

Feifer, George, "Russian Disorders." *Harper's*, (February 1981): 41–55.

Financial Times (London, daily).

Fisher, Alan W., *The Crimean Tatars* (Stanford, CA: Hoover Institution Press, 1978).

Foreign Broadcast Information Service, *Daily Report for China* [FBIS-CH]; *for East Asia* [FBIS-EA]; *for Eastern Europe* [FBIS-EE]; *for the Soviet Union* [FBIS-SOV]; *for Western Europe* [FBIS-WE] (Springfield, VA: National Technical Information Service, various years).

Frankfurter Allgemeine Zeitung (Frankfurt, daily).

Frontline (Madras, every other week).

Fukuyama, Francis, "Moscow's Post-Brezhnev Reassessment of the Third World." RAND/R-3337-USDP (Santa Monica, CA: RAND Corporation, February 1986).

————."Soviet Civil-Military Relations and the Power Projection Mission." RAND/R-3504-AF (Santa Monica, CA: RAND Corporation, April 1987).

Gareyev, M. A., *M. V. Frunze—Voyenniy Teoretik* (Moscow: Voyenizdat, 1985, signed to press October 17, 1984).

Garthoff, Raymond L., "New Thinking in Soviet Military Doctrine." *Washington Quarterly* 11, no. 3 (Summer 1988) 131-58.

———."The Making of the ABM Uproar." *Washington Post*, September 20, 1987.

———."History Confirms the Traditional Meaning." *Arms Control Today*, 17, no. 7 (September 1987): 15-19.

———.*Détente and Confrontation* (Washington, DC: Brookings Institution, 1985).

Gelman, Harry, *The Brezhnev Politburo and the Decline of Détente* (Ithaca, NY: Cornell University Press, 1984).

General-Anzeiger (Bonn, daily).

Gidwitz, Betsy, "Labor Unrest in the Soviet Union." *Problems of Communism*, (November-December) 1982, 25–42.

Goble, Paul A., "The Nationality Problem." in *Soviet Society Under Gorbachev*, Maurice Friedberg and Heyward Isham, editors, M. E. Sharpe, Inc. (New York: Armonk, 1987), 76–100.

Gorbachev, Mikhail, *Perestroika*, new, updated ed. (New York: Perennial Library, 1988).

———. *Izbrannye rechi i stati*, Volumes 1 and 2 (Moscow: Politizdat, 1987).

———. *Nastoichivo Dvigatsya Vpered [To move forward persistently]*. Speech delivered at May 17, 1985 Leningrad Party Organization Aktiv Meeting (Moscow: Politizdat, 1985, signed to press May 24, 1985).

———. *Zhivoye Tvorchestvo Naroda*. Report at the December 10, 1984, session of the Moscow All-Union Scientific and Practical Conference "On the Perfection of Developed Socialism and Ideological Work of the Party in Light of the Decisions of the June 1983 CPSU Central Committee Plenum" (Moscow: Politizdat, 1984, signed to press December 13, 1984).

Griffith, William E., "The Soviets and Western Europe: An Overview." in Herbert J. Ellison, ed., *Soviet Policy toward Western Europe* (Seattle: University of Washington Press, 1983), 3–30.

Gromyko, A. A., and Ponomarev, B. N., eds, *Istoriya Vneshney Politiki SSSR, 1945–1975*, Vol. 2 (Moscow: Nauka, 1976).

The Guardian (London, daily).

Ha'Aretz (Tel Aviv, daily).

Hahn, Werner, "Electoral Choice in the Soviet Bloc." *Problems of Communism* (March-April 1987): 29–39.

Haig, Alexander M., Jr., *Caveat* (New York: Macmillan, 1984).

Helsinki Watch, "News from the USSR." *News from Helsinki Watch* no. 3, September 15, 1987.

Herken, Gregg, "The Earthly Origins of Star Wars." *Bulletin of the Atomic Scientists* (October 1987): 20–28.

Herspring, Dale R., "On Perestroyka: Gorbachev, Yazov, and the Military." *Problems of Communism* (July-August 1987): 99- 107.

———.*The Soviet High Command, 1967–1989* (Princeton, NJ: Princeton University Press, 1990).

Hoagland, Jim, "An Inside View of Power." *Washington Post*, February

27, 1988.

Hoffman, David, "Iceland Talks: One Word Chills Hope." *Washington Post*, October 19, 1986.

Holloway, David, *The Soviet Union and the Arms Race* (New Haven, CT: Yale University Press, 1984).

Horizont (East Berlin, monthly).

Hufvudstadsbladet (Helsinki, daily).

Hunt, Kenneth, Murphy, Bill, Asmus, Ronald D., and Kusin, Vladimir V., "New Soviet Missiles for Eastern Europe." In Vojtech Mastny, ed., *Soviet/East European Survey, 1983–1984* (Durham, NC: Duke University Press, 1985), 93–97.

Institute of Marxism-Leninism, Central Committee of the Communist Party of the Soviet Union, *Leonid Ilyich Brezhnev. Kratkiy biograficheskiy ocherk* (Moscow: Politizdat, 1982).

International Affairs (Moscow, monthly).

International Herald Tribune (Paris, daily).

Izvestiya (Moscow, daily).

Izvestiya TsK KPSS (Moscow, monthly).

Jane's Defence Weekly (Horley, England, weekly).

Johnson, A. Ross, *The Impact of Eastern Europe on Soviet Policy toward Western Europe*. RAND/R-3332-AF (Santa Monica, CA: RAND Corporation, March 1986).

Jones, Ellen, "The Defense Council in Soviet Leadership Decision-Making." Paper presented at Seminar on Soviet National Security Decision-Making, cosponsored by the Network of Women in Slavic Studies and the Kennan Institute for Advanced Russian Studies, Washington, D.C., May 3, 1984.

Karp, Craig, *Afghanistan: Seven Years of Soviet Occupation* (Washington, DC: United States Department of State, Bureau of Public Affairs, Special Report No. 155, December 1986).

———. *Afghan Resistance and Soviet Occupation* (Washington, DC: United States Department of State, Bureau of Public Affairs, Special Report No. 118, December 1984).

Kaufman, Richard F., "Causes of the Slowdown in Soviet Defense." *Soviet Economy* 1, no. 1 (January-March 1985): 9–31.

Kazakhstanskaya Pravda (Alma Ata, daily).

Kharavyi (Nicosia, daily).

Khrushchev, Nikita S., *The Crimes of the Stalin Era*, annotated by Boris I. Nicolaevsky, *The New Leader*, Supplement, 1962.

Kissinger, Henry A., "Kissinger: How to Deal with Gorbachev." *Newsweek*, March 2, 1987, 39–47.

———. *White House Years* (Boston: Little, Brown, 1979).

Knabe, Bernd, "The New Leadership and the 'Enemies of the People.'" In German Federal Institute for East European and International Studies, Cologne, *The Soviet Union 1982–1983* (New York: Holmes & Meier, 1985), 83–93.

Kommunist (Moscow, 18 times yearly).

Kommunist Tadzhikistana (Dushanbe, daily).

Kommunist Vooruzhennykh Sil (Moscow, twice monthly).

Komsomolskaya Pravda (Moscow, daily).

Kraft, Joseph, "Letter from Moscow." *The New Yorker*, January 31, 1983, 104–19.

Kuklinski, Ryszard J., "The War against the Nation as Seen from Inside." *Kultura* (Paris), no. 4/475 (April 1987): 3–57.

Kurier (Vienna, daily).

Kyodo (Tokyo, news agency).

Lee, Gary, and Diehl, Jackson, "Moscow and the East Bloc." *Washington Post*, October 12–13, 1987.

Leonhard, Wolfgang, "Kremlin Reported to Prepare Leadership Reshuffle." *Die Zeit*, January 24, 1975.

Levine, Art, "The Devil in Gorbachev." *Washington Post*, June 5, 1988.

Limberg, Wayne, "Moscow and Regional Conflicts: Linkage Revisited." Paper presented at the National Conference of the American Political Science Association, Washington, D.C., September 2, 1988.

Linden, Carl A., *Khrushchev and the Soviet Leadership 1957–1964* (Baltimore: Johns Hopkins University Press, 1966).

Literary Gazette [Literaturnaya Gazeta] (Moscow, weekly).

Los Angeles Times (Los Angeles, daily).

Magyar Hirlap (Budapest, daily).

Mainichi Shimbun (Tokyo, daily).

Marsh, Peter, "The Development of Relations between the EEC and COMECON." In Peter Jones, ed., *International Year Book of Foreign Policy Analysis*, Vol. 2 (New York: Crane, Russak, 1975), 74–103.

Materialy Vneocherednogo Plenuma Tsentralnogo Komiteta KPSS, 11 marta 1985 (Moscow: Politizdat, 1985, signed to press March 14, 1985).

Materialy Vneocherednogo Plenuma Tsentralnogo Komiteta KPSS (Moscow: Politizdat, 1984, signed to press February 13, 1984).

Le Matin (Lausanne, daily).

Le Monde (Paris, daily).

McCauley, Martin, "Gorbachev as Leader." In Martin McCauley, ed., *The Soviet Union under Gorbachev* (New York: St. Martin's, 1987), 9–37.

Meditsinskaya Gazeta (Moscow, weekly).

Medvedev, Roy A., *Nikolai Bukharin* (New York: W .W. Norton, 1980).

———. *On Socialist Democracy* (New York: Alfred A. Knopf, 1975).

Medvedev, Zhores A., *Andropov* (New York: Penguin, 1984).

———. *Gorbachev* (New York: W. W. Norton, 1986).

Il Messaggero (Rome, daily).

Meyer, Stephen M., "The Sources and Prospects of Gorbachev's New Political Thinking on Security." *International Security* 13, no. 2 (Fall 1988): 124–63.

Mirovaya Ekonomika i Mezhdunarodnyye Otnosheniya (Moscow, monthly).

Mlynar, Zdenek, "My School Companion Mikhail Gorbachev." *L'Unita*, April 9, 1985.

MONTSAME (Ulan Bator, news agency).

Moscow Magazine (Moscow, monthly).

Moscow News (Moscow, weekly).

Moskovskaya Pravda (Moscow, daily).

Nagorski, Andrew, *Reluctant Farewell* (New York: Holt, Rinehart and Winston, 1985).

Nedelya (Moscow, weekly).

Nepszava (Budapest, daily).

Neue Zurcher Zeitung (Zurich, daily).

Neues Deutschland (East Berlin, daily).

New Times (Moscow, weekly).

New York Times (New York, daily).

Newhouse, John, "The Diplomatic Round (Arms Control)." *New Yorker,* December 31, 1984, 40–52.

Newsweek (New York, weekly).

Nin (Belgrade, weekly).

Nitze, Paul H., "Negotiating with the Soviets." *Department of State Bulletin* 84, no. 2089 (August 1984): 34–37.

————."The Nuclear and Space Negotiations: Translating Promise to Progress." Speech delivered at the World Affairs Council, Boston, Massachusetts, January 14, 1987 (Washington, DC: United States Department of State, Bureau of Public Affairs, Current Policy No. 910, February 1987).

North Atlantic Treaty Organization, Special Consultative Group (NATO SCG), *INF: Progress Report to Ministers.* (Brussels: NATO Press Service, December 8, 1983).

Le Nouvel Observateur (Paris, weekly).

Novoye Russkoye Slovo (New York, daily).

Novoye Vremya [New Times] (Moscow, weekly).

Novyy Mir (Moscow, monthly).

NRC Handelsblad (Rotterdam, daily).

Oberdorfer, Don, "4th Summit Reflects a New Era." *Washington Post,* May 29, 1988.

————."Afghanistan: The Soviet Decision to Pull Out." *Washington Post,* April 17, 1988.

————."At Reykjavik, Soviets Were Prepared and U.S. Improvised." *Washington Post,* February 17, 1987.

The Observer (London, weekly).

Ogarkov, N. V., *Istoriya uchit bditel'nosti* (Moscow: Voyenizdat, 1985, signed to press April 8, 1985).

————."Strategiya Voyennaya [Military strategy]." In N. V. Ogarkov, chairman, Main Editorial Commission, *Sovetskaya Voyennaya Entsiklopediya [Soviet military encyclopedia],* Vol. 7 (Moscow: Voyenizdat, 1979, signed to press September 7, 1979), 555–65.

————. Chairman of the Main Editorial Commission, Institute of Military History, USSR Ministry of Defense, *Voyenniy Entsiklopedicheskiy Slovar [Military encyclopedic dictionary]* (Moscow: Voyenizdat, 1983, signed to press January 14, 1983).

————. *Vsegda v gotovnosti k zashchite Otechestva* (Moscow: Voyenizdat, 1982, signed to press January 26, 1982).

Ogonek (Moscow, weekly).

Olcott, Anthony, "Glasnost' and Soviet Culture." In Maurice Friedberg and Heyward Isham, eds., *Soviet Society under Gorbachev* (Armonk, NY: M. E. Sharpe, 1987), 101–30.

Otechestven Front (Sofia, daily).

Ottaway, David B., 'What Is 'Afghan Lesson' for Superpowers?" *Washington Post*, February 12, 1989.

Paese Sera (Rome, daily).

El Pais (Madrid, daily).

Papp, Daniel S., "The Impact of the Shevardnadze-Dobrynin Apparatus on Soviet Foreign Policy." Paper presented at Conference on Gorbachev's "New Thinking" and Soviet Foreign Policy, Airlie House, Virginia, May 10–11, 1988.

Parrott, Bruce, "Soviet National Security under Gorbachev." *Problems of Communism* (November-December 1988): 1–36.

Party Life [Partiinaya Zhizn] (Moscow, twice monthly).

Peel, Quentin, "The Foreign Face of Perestroika." *Financial Times*, July 29, 1988.

Penkovskiy, Oleg, *The Penkovskiy Papers* (New York: Avon, 1965).

Planovoye Khozyaistvo (Moscow, monthly).

Ploss, Sidney I., *Moscow and the Polish Crisis* (Boulder, CO: Westview, 1986).

———. "Signs of Struggle." *Problems of Communism* (September-October 1982): 41–52.

Politicheskoye Samoobrazovaniye (Moscow, monthly).

Pond, Elizabeth, "Europe Questions America's Promise." *Christian Science Monitor*, July 28, 1987.

Pravda (Bratislava, daily).

Pravda Ukrainy (Kiev, daily).

Presidium Verkhovnogo Soveta SSSR, *Deputaty Verkhovnogo Soveta SSSR Odinnadtsatogo Sozyva* (Moscow: Izvestiya, 1984).

Press Association (London, news agency).

Die Presse (Vienna, daily).

Problemy Mira i Sotsializma (Prague, monthly).

Puschel, Karen, "Gorbachev and Arms Control: Learning to Live with SDI." *Survival* 31, no. 1, (January–February): 34–51.

Quick (Hamburg, weekly).

Rabotnichesko Delo (Sofia, daily).

Radio Free Europe/Radio Liberty Research, Ronald D. Asmus, compiler, *East Berlin and Moscow: The Documentation of a Dispute*. RAD Background Report,/158, Munich, August 25, 1984.

Radio Liberty Research, Alexander G. Rahr, compiler, *A Biographic Directory of 100 Leading Soviet Officials*, 4th ed., rev. with some additions (Munich: RFE/RL, January 1989).

———. Alexander G. Rahr, compiler, *A Biographic Directory of 100 Leading Soviet Officials*, 4th ed., (Munich: RFE/RL, October 1988).

———. Gavin Helf, compiler, *A Biographic Directory of Soviet Regional Party Leaders. Part I. RSFSR Oblasts, Krais, and ASSRs*, 2nd ed.(Munich: RFE/RL, August 1988).

———. Gavin Helf, compiler, *A Biographic Directory of Soviet Regional Party Leaders. Part II. Union Republic Oblasts and ASSRs* 2nd ed. (Munich: RFE/RL, August 1988).

———. Gavin Helf, compiler, *A Biographic Directory of Soviet Regional Party Leaders. Part I. RSFSR Oblasts, Krais, and ASSRs* (Munich: RFE/RL, August 1987).

————. Alexander G. Rahr, compiler, *A Biographic Directory of 100 Leading Soviet Officials*, 3rd ed. (Munich: RFE/RL, March 1986).

————. Alexander G. Rahr, compiler, *A Biographic Directory of 100 Leading Soviet Officials* 2nd ed. (Munich: RFE/RL, August 1984).

————. Alexander G. Rahr, compiler, *A Biographic Directory of 100 Leading Soviet Officials* (Munich: RFE/RL, February 1981).

Rahr, Alexander, "Further Changes in the Military." Radio Liberty Research, RL 276/87, July 15, 1987.

————. "Gorbachev's Fellow Student Gets Top Post." Radio Liberty Research, RL 97/87, February 27, 1987.

————. "A New Man in Power." In Vojtech Mastny, ed., *Soviet/East European Survey, 1983–1984* (Durham, NC: Duke University Press, 1985) 111–16.

————. "Gorbachev as the Heir Apparent." In Vojtech Mastny, ed., *Soviet/East European Survey, 1983–1984* (Durham, NC: Duke University Press, 1985), 122–27.

————. "A New Chief Ideologist in the Kremlin." Radio Liberty Research, RL 183/85, June 5, 1985.

————. "Biographies of the Chief Soviet Negotiators at the Geneva Arms Talks." Radio Liberty Research, RL 67/85, March 5, 1985.

Reagan, Ronald, "Prospects for World Peace." Address to the UN General Assembly, New York City, September 22, 1986 (Washington, DC: United States Department of State, Bureau of Public Affairs, Current Policy No. 867, September 1986).

————. "A Foundation for Enduring Peace." Address to the UN General Assembly, October 24, 1985 (Washington, DC: United States Department of State, Bureau of Public Affairs, Current Policy No. 756, October 1985).

————. "Reducing World Tensions." Address before the UN General Assembly, New York, September 24, 1984 (Washington, DC: United States Department of State, Bureau of Public Affairs, Current Policy No. 615, September 1984).

Red Star [Krasnaya Zvezda] (Moscow, daily).

Reddaway, Peter, *Soviet Policies on Dissent and Emigration: The Radical Change of Course Since 1979*. Kennan Institute for Advanced Russian Studies, Colloquium Paper No. 192, Washington DC, August 28, 1984.

Renmin Ribao (Beijing, daily).

La Repubblica (Rome, daily).

Respublika (Tallin, twice monthly).

Reuters (London, news agency).

Rizospastis (Athens, daily).

Rude Pravo (Prague, daily).

Rumer, Boris Z., *Investment and Reindustrialization in the Soviet Economy* (Boulder, CO: Westview, 1984).

Russkaya Mysl (Paris, weekly).

Rybakov, Anatoli, *Children of the Arbat*, Harold Shukman, trans. (Boston: Little, Brown, 1988).

San Francisco Examiner (San Francisco, daily).

Schmidt-Hauer, Christian, *Gorbachev: The Path to Power* (Topsfield, MA.: Salem House, 1986).

Schwartz, Morton, *Soviet Perceptions of the United States* (Berkeley: University of California Press, 1978).

Scott, Harriet Fast, "Soviet Defense Minister Sokolov." *International Defense Review*, 12/1985, 1902.

Scott, Harriet Fast, and Scott, William F., *The Armed Forces of the USSR*, 3rd ed., rev. and updated (Boulder, CO: Westview, 1984).

Segal, Gerald, *Sino-Soviet Relations after Mao*. Adelphi Paper No. 202 (London: International Institute for Strategic Studies, 1985).

Sestanovich, Stephen, "Do the Soviets Feel Pinched by Third World Adventures?" *Washington Post*, May 20, 1984.

Shevchenko, Arkady N., *Breaking with Moscow* (New York: Alfred A.Knopf, 1985).

Shulman, Marshall D., *Stalin's Foreign Policy Reappraised* (Boulder, CO: Westview Press, 1985).

Shultz, George, "Vienna Meeting: Commitment, Cooperation, and the Challenge of Compliance." Address at the closing session of the Conference on Security and Cooperation in Europe (CSCE), Vienna, Austria, January 17, 1989 (Washington, DC: United States Department of State, Bureau of Public Affairs, Current Policy No. 1145, January 1989).

———. "The INF Treaty: Strengthening U.S. Security." Statement before the Senate Foreign Relations Committee, January 25, 1988 (Washington, DC: United States Department of State, Bureau of Public Affairs, Current Policy No. 1038, February 1988).

———. "Nuclear Weapons, Arms Control, and the Future of Deterrence." Speech at the University of Chicago, November 17, 1986. In *Department of State Bulletin* 87, No. 2118 (January 1987): 31–35.

———."Arms Control, Strategic Stability, and Global Security." Address before the North Atlantic Assembly, San Fransisco, California, October 14, 1985 (Washington, DC: United States Department of State, Bureau of Public Affairs, Current Policy No. 750, October 1985.)

Sidey, Hugh, "Taking Gromyko's Measure." *Time*, October 15, 1984, 35.

Smith, Gerard, *Doubletalk. The Story of SALT I* (New York: Doubleday, 1980).

Smith, Paul A., Jr., "Brezhnev: Ascent to Power." *Orbis*, 15, no. 2 (Summer 1971), 576–608.

Smith, R. Jeffrey, "Missile Deployments Roil Europe." *Science* 223, (January 27, 1984): 371–76.

Sobraniye Postanovlenii Pravitel'stva SSSR (Moscow, weekly).

Sotsialisticheskaya Industriya (Moscow, daily).

Sovershenno Sekretno (Moscow, monthly).

Sovetskaya Kultura (Moscow, three times weekly).

Sovetskaya Moldavia (Kishinev, daily).

Sovetskaya Rossiya (Moscow, daily).

Der Spiegel (Hamburg, weekly).

Spielmann, Karl F., "Defense Industrialists in the USSR." *Problems of Communism* (September-October 1976): 52–69.

SPK (Phnom Penh, news agency).

La Stampa (Turin, daily).

Steele, Jonathan, and Abraham, Eric, *Andropov in Power* (Garden City, NY: Anchor/Doubleday, 1984).

Stern (Hamburg, weekly).

Sueddeutsche Zeitung (Munich, daily).

Sunday Telegraph (London, weekly).

Sunday Times (London, weekly).

Svenska Dagbladet (Stockholm, daily).

Ta Nea (Athens, daily).

Talbott, Strobe, "The Road to Zero." *Time*, December 14, 1987, 18–30.

———. *Deadly Gambits* (New York: Alfred A. Knopf, 1984).

———. *Endgame* (New York: Harper & Row, 1980).

TANJUG (Belgrade, news agency).

Tarsadalmi Szemle (Budapest, monthly).

TASS (Moscow, news agency).

Tatu, Michel, "19th Party Conference." *Problems of Communism* (May-August 1988): 1–15.

———. *Power in the Kremlin* (New York: Viking, 1970).

Teague, Elizabeth, "*Perestroika*: Who Stands to Gain, Who Stands to Lose?" Paper presented at the Institute for Defense Analyses, March 9, 1989.

———. "War Scare in the USSR." In Vojtech Mastny, ed., *Soviet/East European Survey, 1983–1984* (Durham, NC: Duke University Press, 1985), 71–76.

———. "Debate over Economic Reform Continues." Radio Liberty Research, RL 188/85, June 7, 1985.

———. "Crackdown on Labor Discipline Proposed." Radio Liberty Research, RL 302/83, August 10, 1983.

———. "Andropov's First Hundred Days: Domestic Policy." Radio Liberty Research, RL 92/83, February 21, 1983.

———. "Change of Leadership in Krasnodar Krai." Radio Liberty Research, RL 305/82, July 28, 1982.

Teatr (Moscow, monthly).

Time (New York, weekly).

The Times (London, daily).

Tokyo Shimbun (Tokyo, daily).

Trainor, Bernard E., "Soviet Arms Doctrine in Flux: An Emphasis on the Defense." *New York Times*, March 7, 1988.

Triska, Jan F., ed., *Soviet Communism: Programs and Rules* (San Francisco: Chandler, 1962).

Trottier, Paul, and Karp, Craig, *Afghanistan: Five Years of Occupation* (Washington, DC: United States Department of State, Bureau of Public Affairs, Special Report No. 120, December 1984).

Trud (Moscow, daily).

Tsentralnoye Statisticheskoye Upravleniye, *Narodnoye Khozyaystvo SSSR v 1980 g.* and *... v 1985 g.* (Moscow: Finansy i Statistika, 1981 and 1986, respectively).

Uchitelskaya Gazeta (Moscow, daily).

Ueberroth, Peter, *Made in America* (New York: William Morrow, 1985).

Ulam, Adam B., *Expansion and Coexistence* (New York: Praeger, 1968).

L'Unita (Milan and Rome, daily).

United States Arms Control and Disarmament Agency, *Arms Control and Disarmament Agreements*, 1982 ed. (Washington, DC: U.S. Government Printing Office, 1982).

————. *Documents on Disarmament—1977* (Washington, DC: U.S. Government Printing Office, 1979).

United States Central Intelligence Agency, *Directory of USSR Ministry of Foreign Affairs Officials*, LDA 87–12484 (Springfield, VA: National Technical Information Service, July 1987).

————. *Directory of Soviet Officials: National Organizations*, LDA 87–12090 (Springfield, VA: National Technical Information Service, June 1987).

————. *Directory of USSR Ministry of Defense and Armed Forces Officials*, LDA 86–11907 (Springfield, VA: National Technical Information Service, October 1986).

————. *Directory of Soviet Officials: National Organizations*, CR 86–11691 (Springfield, VA: National Technical Information Service, June 1986).

————. *Directory of USSR Ministry of Foreign Affairs Officials*, CR 83–12416 (Springfield, VA: National Technical Information Service, June 1983).

————. *Directory of USSR Ministry of Foreign Affairs Officials*, CR 80–13493 (Springfield, VA: National Technical Information Service, August 1980).

————. *Directory of USSR Ministry of Foreign Affairs Officials*, CR 77–11829 (Springfield, VA: National Technical Information Service, April 1977).

————. *Directory of USSR Ministry of Foreign Affairs Officials*, CR 76–11637 (Springfield, VA: National Technical Information Service, April 1976).

————. *Directory of USSR Ministry of Foreign Affairs Officials*, A (CR) 74–26 (Springfield, VA: National Technical Information Service, July 1974).

————. *Directory of Headquarters Personnel — USSR Ministry of Foreign Affairs*, A 72–31 (Springfield, VA: National Technical Information Service, October 1972).

United States Central Intelligence Agency, Office of Soviet Analysis, "USSR: Economic Trends and Policy Developments." Briefing Paper dated September 14, 1983, presented at Hearings on the Allocation of Resources in the Soviet Union and China—1983, before the U.S. Congress, Joint Economic Committee, Subcommittee on International Trade, Finance, and Security Economic, September 20, 1983.

United States Congress, Joint Economic Committee, "The Soviet Economy in 1988: Gorbachev Changes Course." Paper presented by the United States Central Intelligence Agency and the Defense Intelligence Agency to the National Security Economic Subcommittee, April 12, 1989.

————. "Gorbachev's Modernization Program: A Status Report." Paper presented by the United States Central Intelligence Agency and the Defense Intelligence Agency to the National Security Economic Subcommittee, March 19, 1987.

United States Department of Defense, *Soviet Military Power 1986* (Washington, DC: US Government Printing Office, March 1986).

United States Department of State, "New Soviet Legislation Restricts Rights, Strengthens Internal Security." Foreign Affairs Note, July 1984.

————.*Realism, Strength, Negotiation: Key Foreign Policy Statements of the Reagan Administration* (Washington, DC: Bureau of Public Affairs, May 1984).

————.*Documents on Disarmament—1960* (Washington, DC: U.S. Government Printing Office, 1961).

Urban, Mark L., "The Limited Contingent of Soviet Forces in Afghanistan." *Jane's Defence Weekly*, 1985, 3, no. 2 (January 12, 1985): 71–73.

USA: Economics, Politics, and Ideology (Moscow, monthly).

Ustinov, D. F., *Sluzhim Rodine, delu kommunizma* (Moscow: Voyenizdat, 1982, signed to press February 15, 1982).

Valenta, Jiri, "Soviet Decisionmaking on Afghanistan, 1979." In Jiri Valenta and William Potter, eds., *Soviet Decisionmaking for National Security* (Boston: Unwin Hyman, 1984).

Van Hollen, Eliza, "Afghanistan: Three Years of Occupation" (Washington, DC: United States Department of State, Bureau of Public Affairs, Special Report No. 106, December 1982).

————. "Afghanistan: 2 Years of Occupation" (Washington, DC: United States Department of State, Bureau of Public Affairs, Special Report No. 91, December 1981).

Vechernyaya Moskva (Moscow, daily).

Vedemosti Verkhovnogo Soveta RSFSR (Moscow, weekly).

Vedemosti Verkhovnogo Soveta SSSR (Moscow, weekly).

Vestnik Akademii Nauk SSSR (Moscow, monthly).

Vestnik Ministerstva Inostrannykh Del SSR [Herald of the USSR Foreign Ministry] (Moscow, every two weeks).

De Volkskrant (Amsterdam, daily).

Volksstimme (Vienna, daily).

Voprosy Filosofii (Moscow, monthly).

Voprosy Istorii (Moscow, monthly).

Voprosy Istorii KPSS (Moscow, monthly).

Voyenniy Vestnik (Moscow, monthly).

Wall Street Journal (New York, daily).

Warner, Edward L., III, Bonan, Josephine J., and Packman, Erma F., "Key Personnel and Organizations of the Soviet Military High Command." RAND N-2567-AF (Santa Monica, CA: RAND Corporation, April 1987).

Washington Post (Washington, D.C., daily).

Weidenfeld, Werner, "The European Community and Eastern Europe." *Aussen Politik* 38, no. 2 (1987): 134–43.

Die Welt (Hamburg, daily).

Wessell, Nils H., "Soviet Views of Multipolarity and the Emerging Balance of Power." *Orbis* 22, no. 4 (Winter 1979): 785–813.

Wettig, Gerhard, "Sufficiency in Defense—A New Guideline for the Soviet Military Posture?" Radio Liberty Research, RL 372/87, September 23, 1987.

————. "The Present Soviet View on Trends in Germany." In Harry Gelman, ed. *The Future of Soviet Policy toward Western Europe*,(Santa Monica, CA: RAND Corporation, September 1985), 66–97.

————. "How the INF Negotiations in Geneva Failed." *Aussen Politik*, Vol. 35 no. 2 (1984): 123–39.

————. "Germany, Europe, and the Soviets." In Herbert J. Ellison, ed., *Soviet Policy toward Western Europe* (Seattle: University of Washington Press, 1983), 31–60.

Wolfe, Thomas W., "Soviet Military Policy at the Fifty-Year Mark." In Kurt London, ed., *The Soviet Union. A Half-Century of Communism* (Baltimore: Johns Hopkins University Press, 1968), 247–74.

————. *Soviet Power in Europe 1945–1970* (Baltimore: Johns Hopkins University Press, 1970).

World Marxist Review (Prague, monthly).

Xinhua (Beijing, news agency).

Yomiuri Shimbun (Tokyo, daily).

Zarya Vostoka (Tbilisi, daily).

Zhurnalist (Moscow, monthly).

Zlotnik, Marc, "Chernenko Succeeds." *Problems of Communism*, March–April 1984): 17–31.

Znamya (Moscow, monthly).

Index

About the Author —————————————————————————————————

John W. Parker has been an analyst of Soviet politics and national security issues for the United States Department of State since 1974. He has a B.A. from Indiana University and a Ph.D. from Yale University. He first visited the Soviet Union in 1965 as a student; accompanied a United States Information Agency cultural exchange exhibit on a tour of six Soviet cities in 1972; escorted Roy Clark and the Oakridge Boys on their tour of the USSR in 1976; worked in the Political Section of the American Embassy in Moscow from 1978 to 1980; and since August 1989 has been head of that embassy's Political Internal unit. The author's research interests center on contemporary Soviet politics. This is his first book.